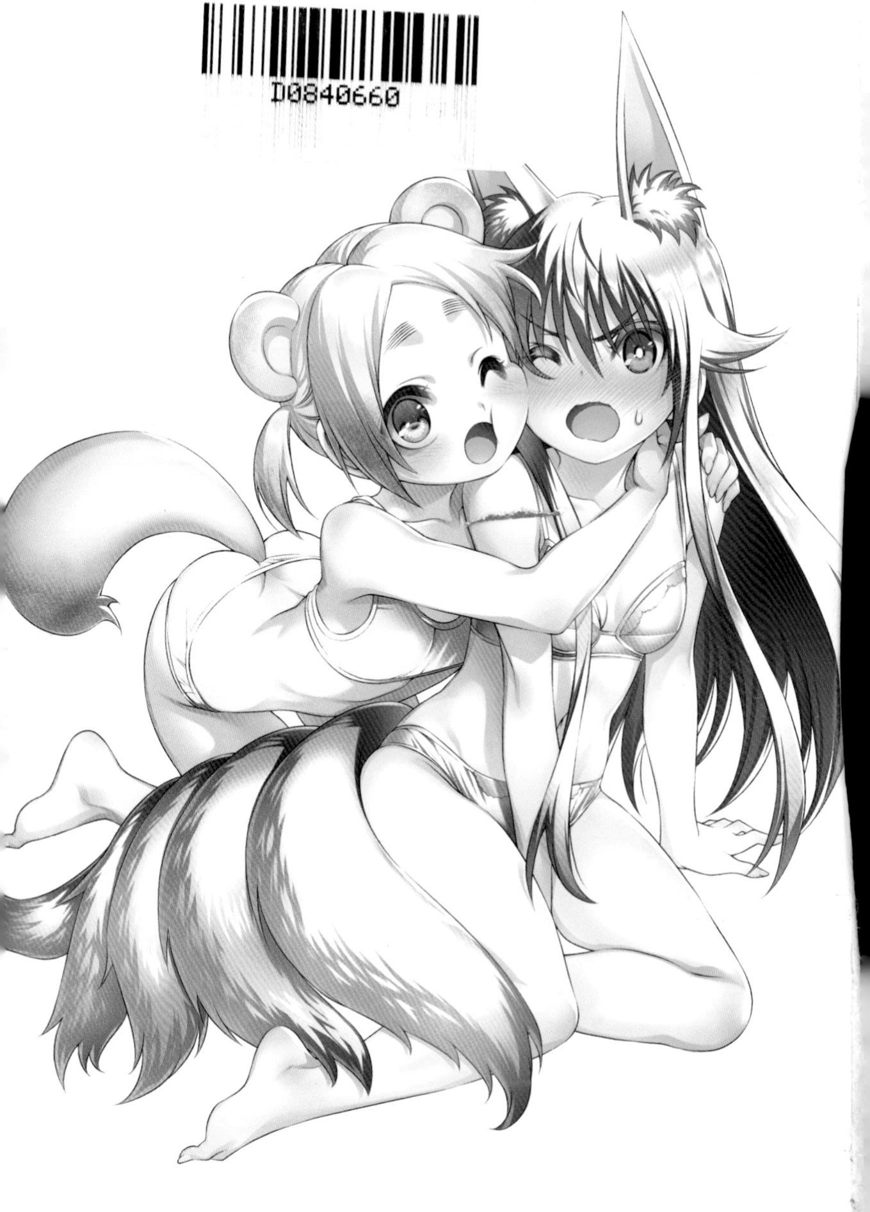

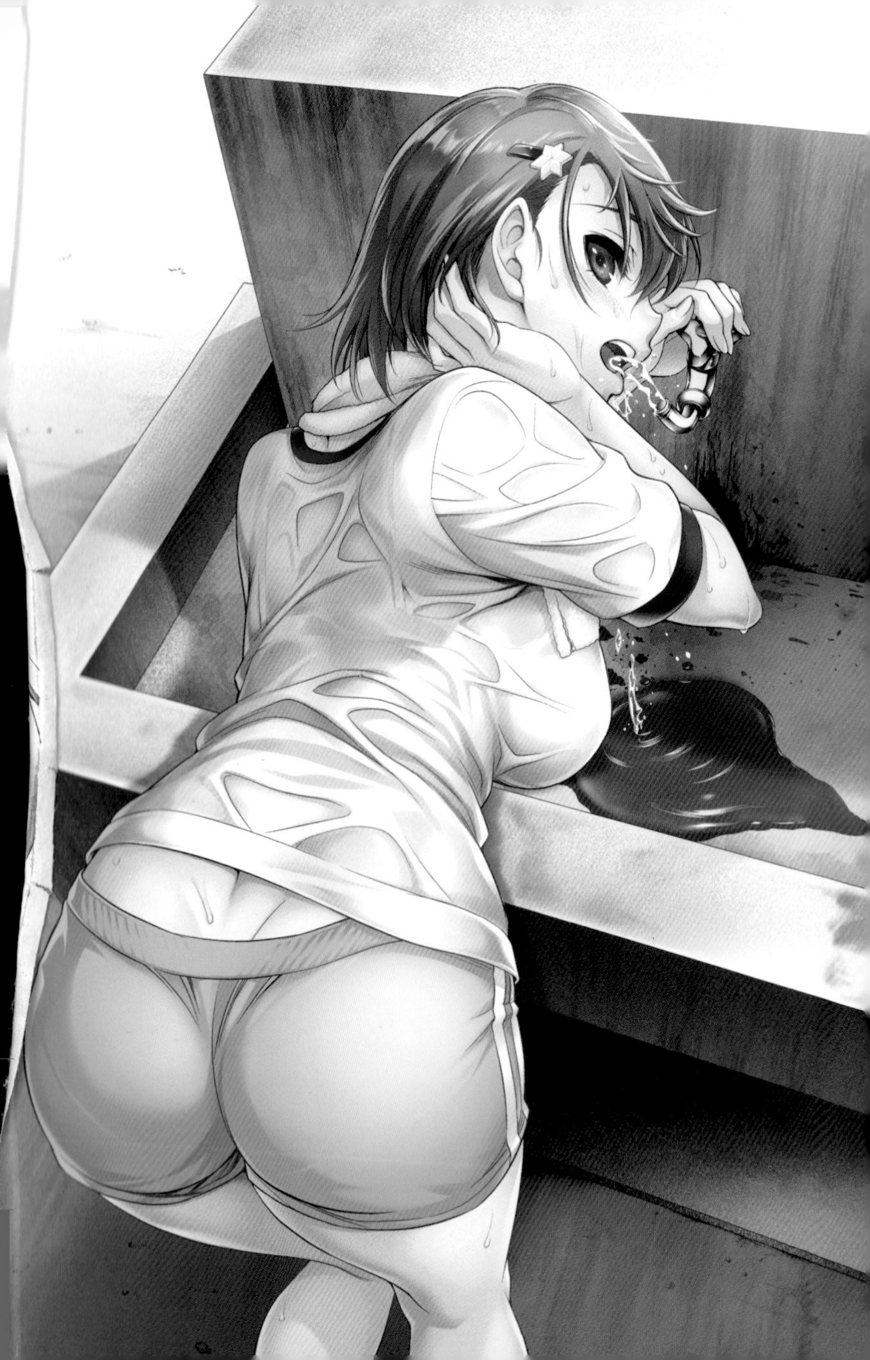

Yuuna and the Haunted Hot Springs

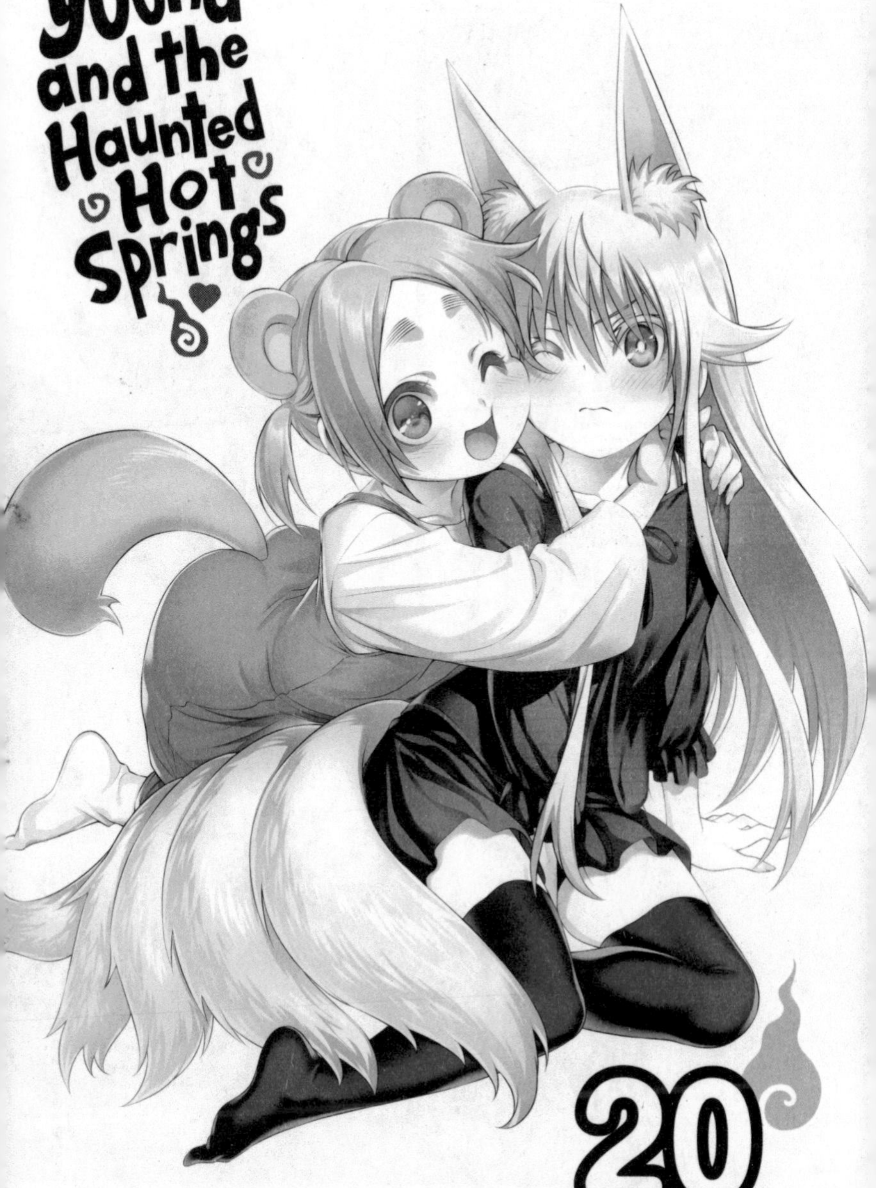

20

Character Introductions

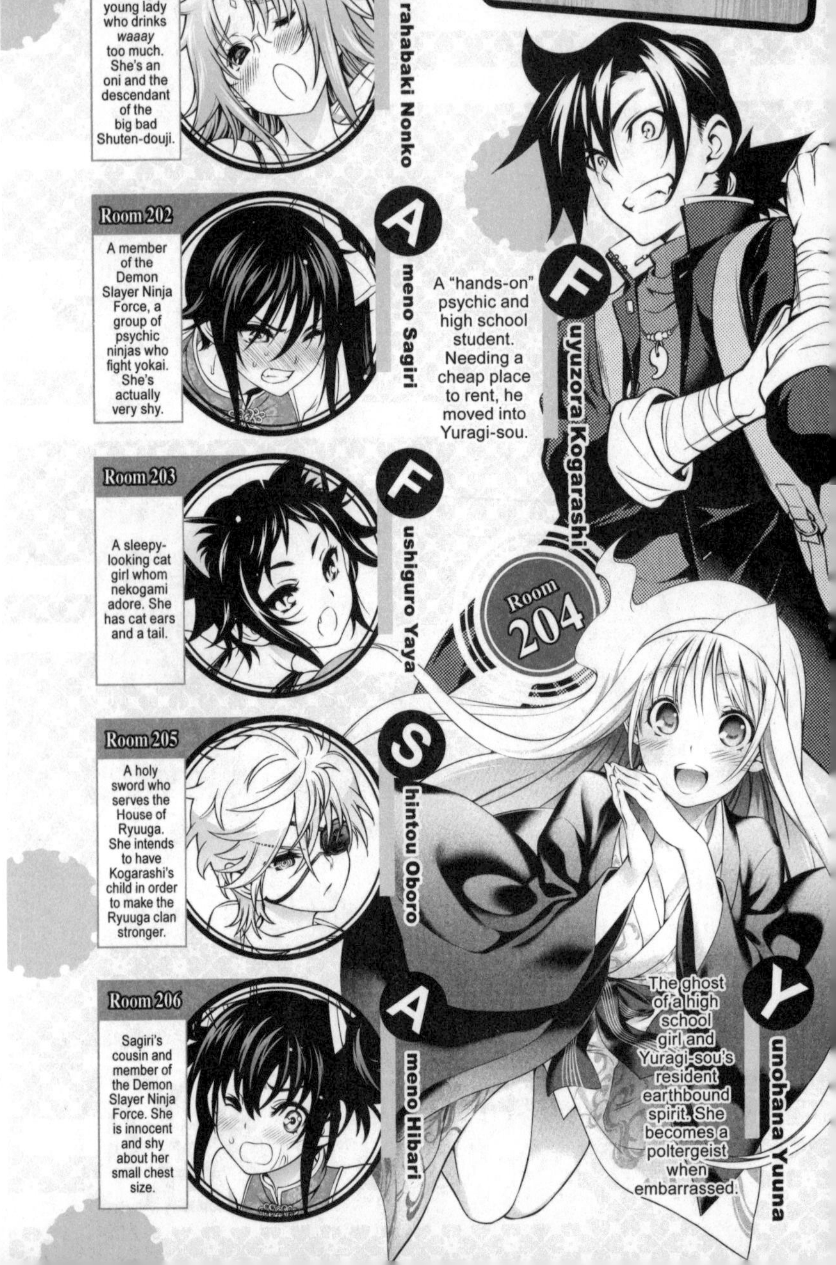
Room 204
Fuyuzora Kogarashi
A "hands-on" psychic and high school student. Needing a cheap place to rent, he moved into Yuragi-sou.
Yunohana Yuuna
The ghost of a high school girl and Yuragi-sou's resident earthbound spirit. She becomes a poltergeist when embarrassed.
Room 201
Arahabaki Nonko
A sexy young lady who drinks *waaay* too much. She's an oni and the descendant of the big bad Shuten-douji.
Room 202
Amenono Sagiri
A member of the Demon Slayer Ninja Force, a group of psychic ninjas who fight yokai. She's actually very shy.
Room 203
Fushiguro Yaya
A sleepy-looking cat girl whom nekogami adore. She has cat ears and a tail.
Room 205
Shintou Oboro
A holy sword who serves the House of Ryuuga. She intends to have Kogarashi's child in order to make the Ryuuga clan stronger.
Room 206
Amenono Hibari
Sagiri's cousin and member of the Demon Slayer Ninja Force. She is innocent and shy about her small chest size.

Caretaker's Room

Nakai Chitose

Despite her youthful appearance, she's a zashiki-warashi and Yuragi-sou's oldest resident. She can manipulate people's luck.

Hiougi Karura

Daughter of the Dai-tengu, who governs Kyoto. Praised as a genius, she studies various techniques, reviving them in the modern era.

Caretaker's Room

Shigaraki Koyuzu

A young bake-danuki girl. She looks up to Chisaki and is studying her boobs.

Mikogami Matora

An extremely powerful yokai known as a Nue. Her hobby is fighting and she's always seeking out stronger opponents.

Miyazaki Chisaki

The most beautiful and popular girl in Kogarashi's class. She has a naughty imagination.

Kiishi Asaka

A vassal of Tenko Nadare, the current head of the Tenko Family. A beautiful muscle-bound girl who is devoted to swimming.

Katsuragi Miria

A Youko Girl. As a member of the Katsuragi family she has long desired to be among the top of the Tenko clan and will get close to Yuuna to accomplish it.

Summary

While living in Yuragi-sou, a hot spring inn-turned-boardinghouse with an unusual history, "hands-on" psychic Fuyuzora Kogarashi promised Yuuna, the earthbound spirit of a high school girl, that he would make her happy and help her pass on. Kogarashi came out victorious in the parallel realm despite having been turned into a child by Tenko Nadare. In an effort to move toward a mutually satisfying future, the Tenko family recognized the benefits to their cooperation. Later, Hyoudou gets a camera that shows people nude, one of the seven wonders of Yukemuri High School. This can't be good...

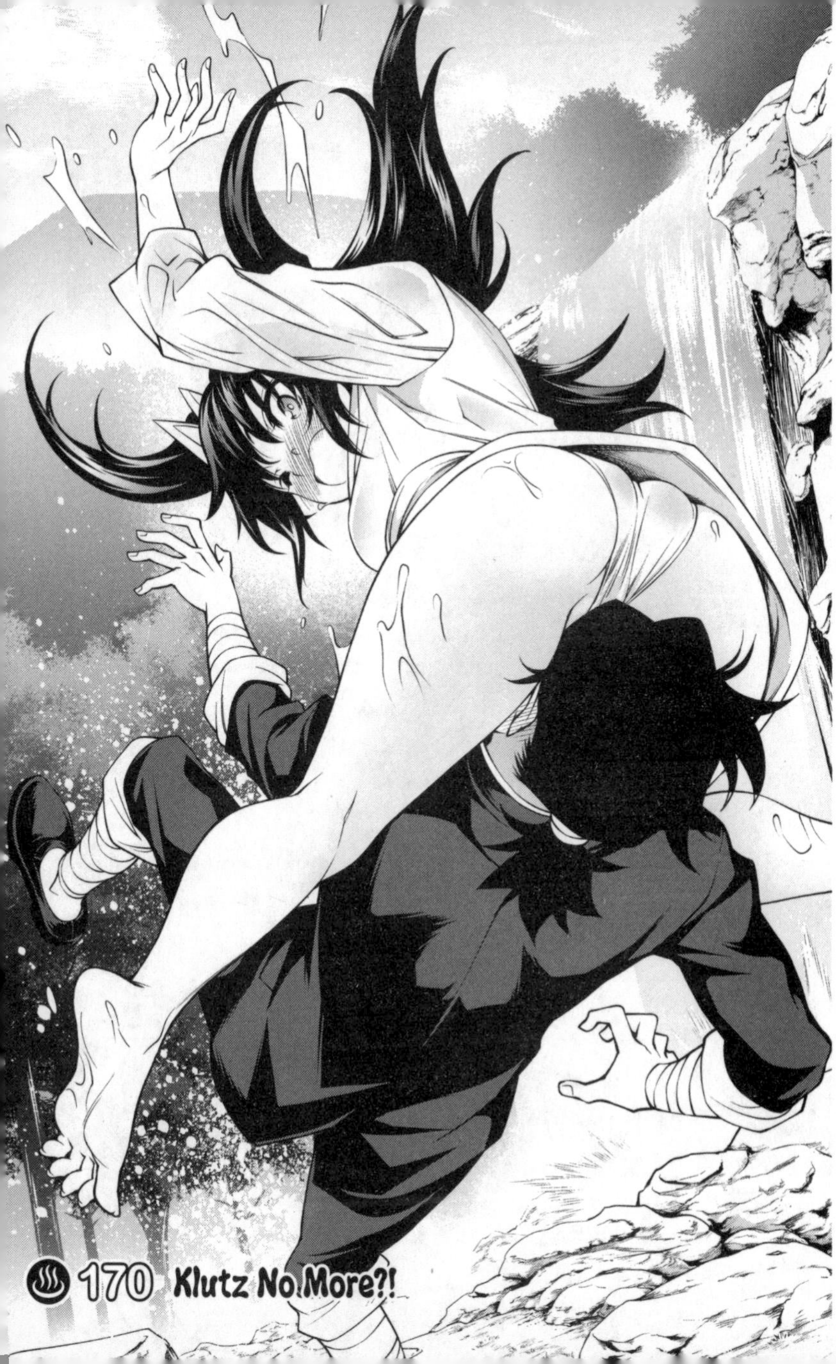

170 Klutz No More?!

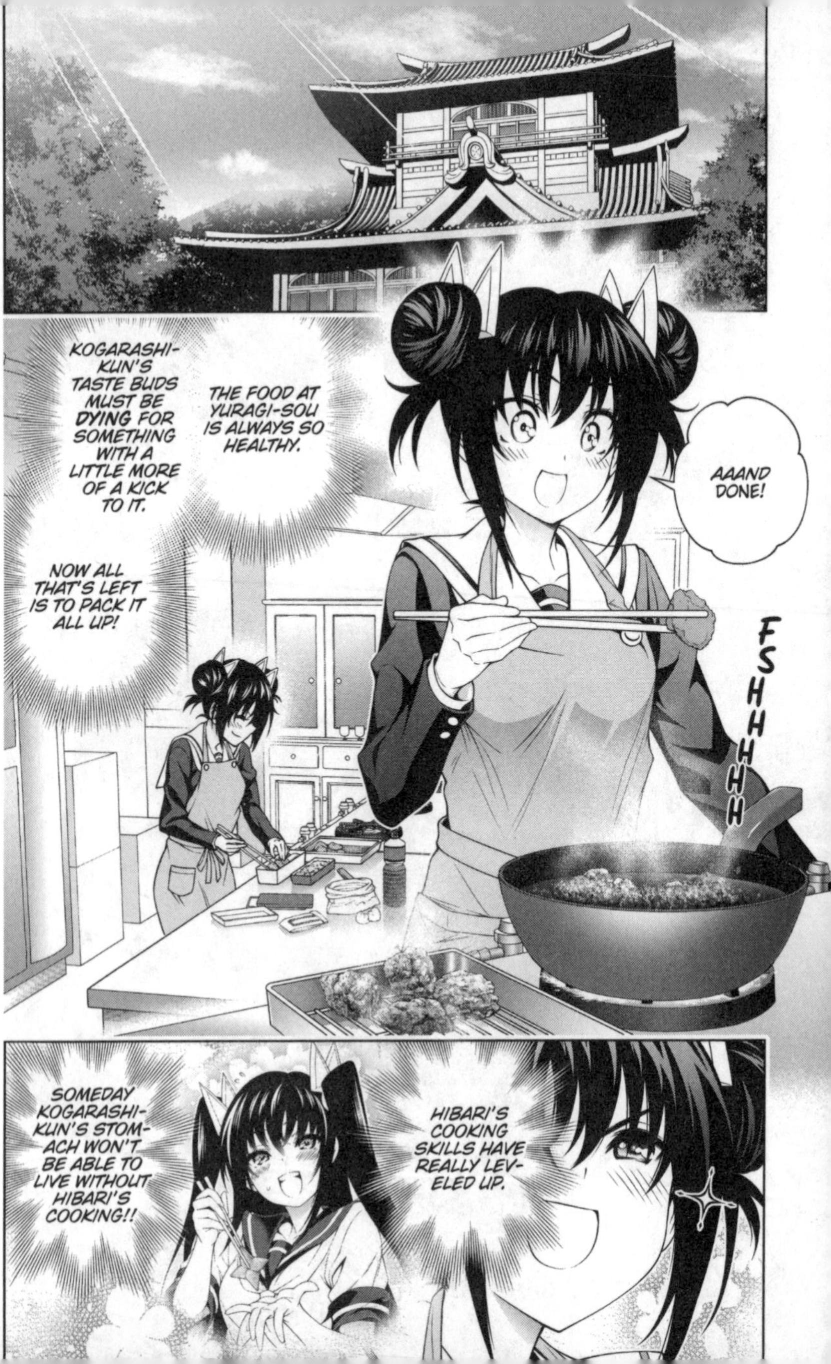
AAAND DONE!
FSHHHHHH
THE FOOD AT YURAGI-SOU IS ALWAYS SO HEALTHY.
KOGARASHI-KUN'S TASTE BUDS MUST BE **DYING** FOR SOMETHING WITH A LITTLE MORE OF A KICK TO IT.
NOW ALL THAT'S LEFT IS TO PACK IT ALL UP!
HIBARI'S COOKING SKILLS HAVE REALLY LEVELED UP.
SOMEDAY KOGARASHI-KUN'S STOMACH WON'T BE ABLE TO LIVE WITHOUT HIBARI'S COOKING!!

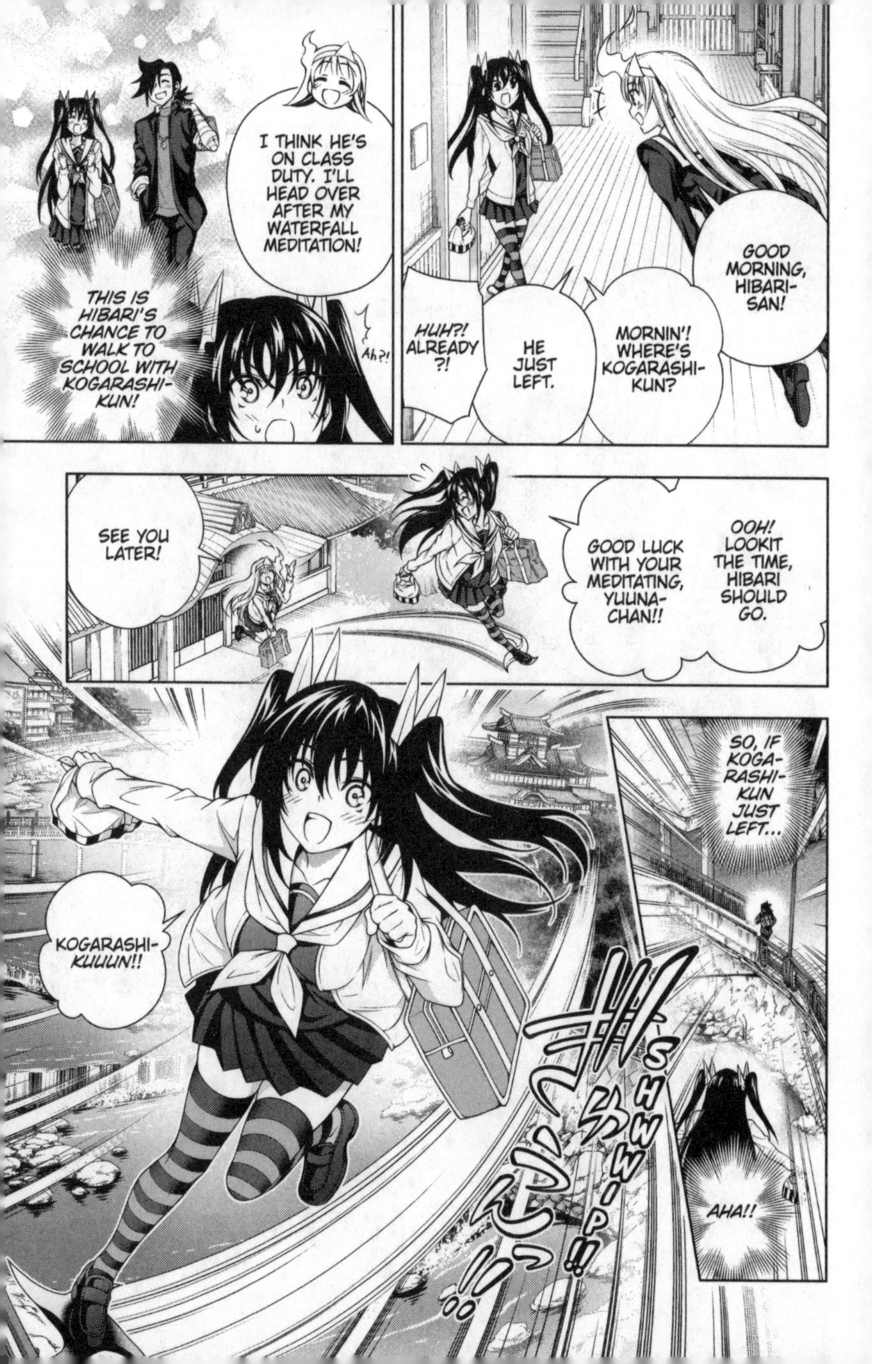

GOOD MORNING, HIBARI-SAN!
MORNIN'! WHERE'S KOGARASHI-KUN?
HE JUST LEFT.
HUH?! ALREADY ?!
I THINK HE'S ON CLASS DUTY. I'LL HEAD OVER AFTER MY WATERFALL MEDITATION!
Ah?!
THIS IS HIBARI'S CHANCE TO WALK TO SCHOOL WITH KOGARASHI-KUN!
OOH! LOOKIT THE TIME, HIBARI SHOULD GO.
GOOD LUCK WITH YOUR MEDITATING, YUUNA-CHAN!!
SEE YOU LATER!
SO, IF KOGARASHI-KUN JUST LEFT...
AHA!!
SHWWWIP!!
KOGARASHI-KUUUN!!

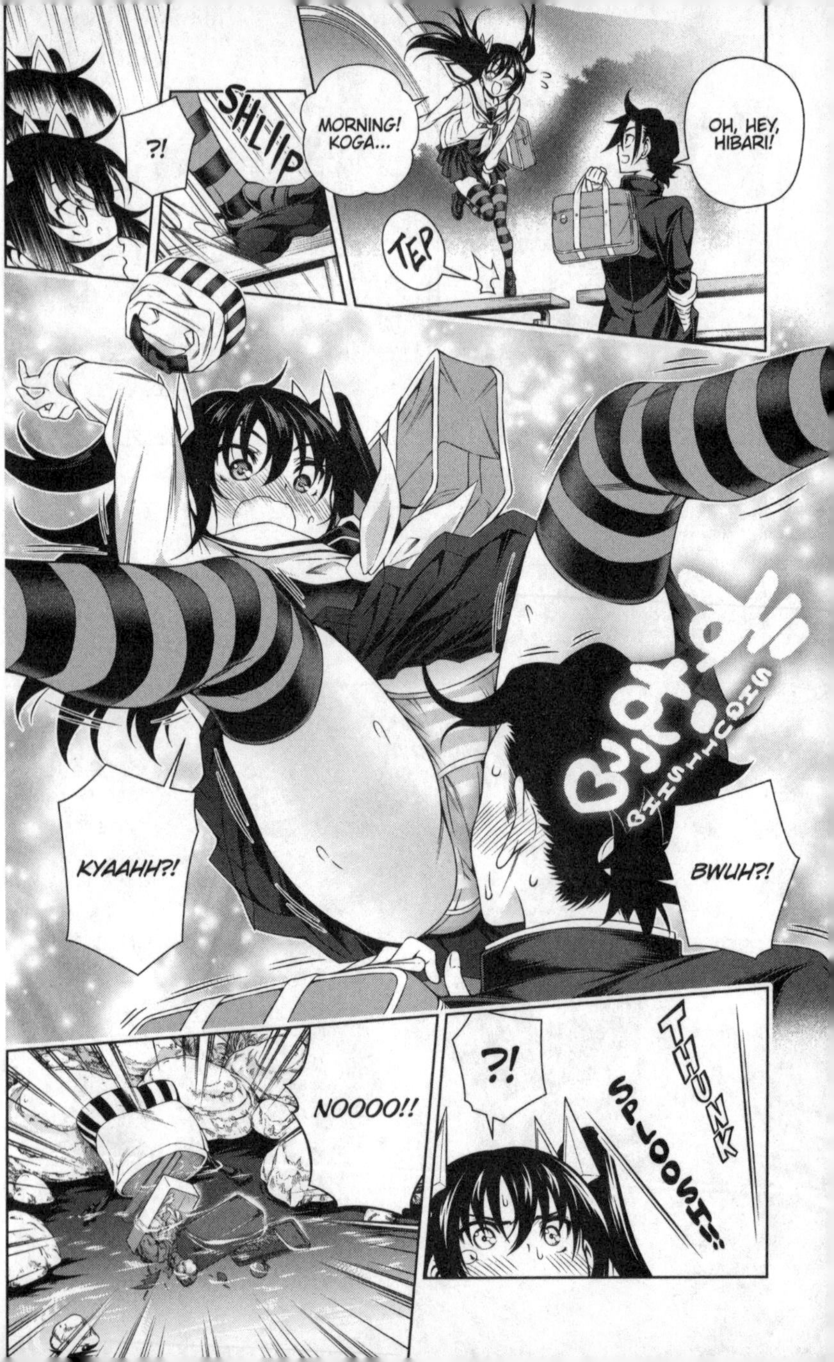
OH, HEY, HIBARI!
MORNING! KOGA...
TEP
SHLIIP
?!
BWUH?!
KYAAHH?!
THUNK
SPLOOSH!!
?!
NOOOO!!

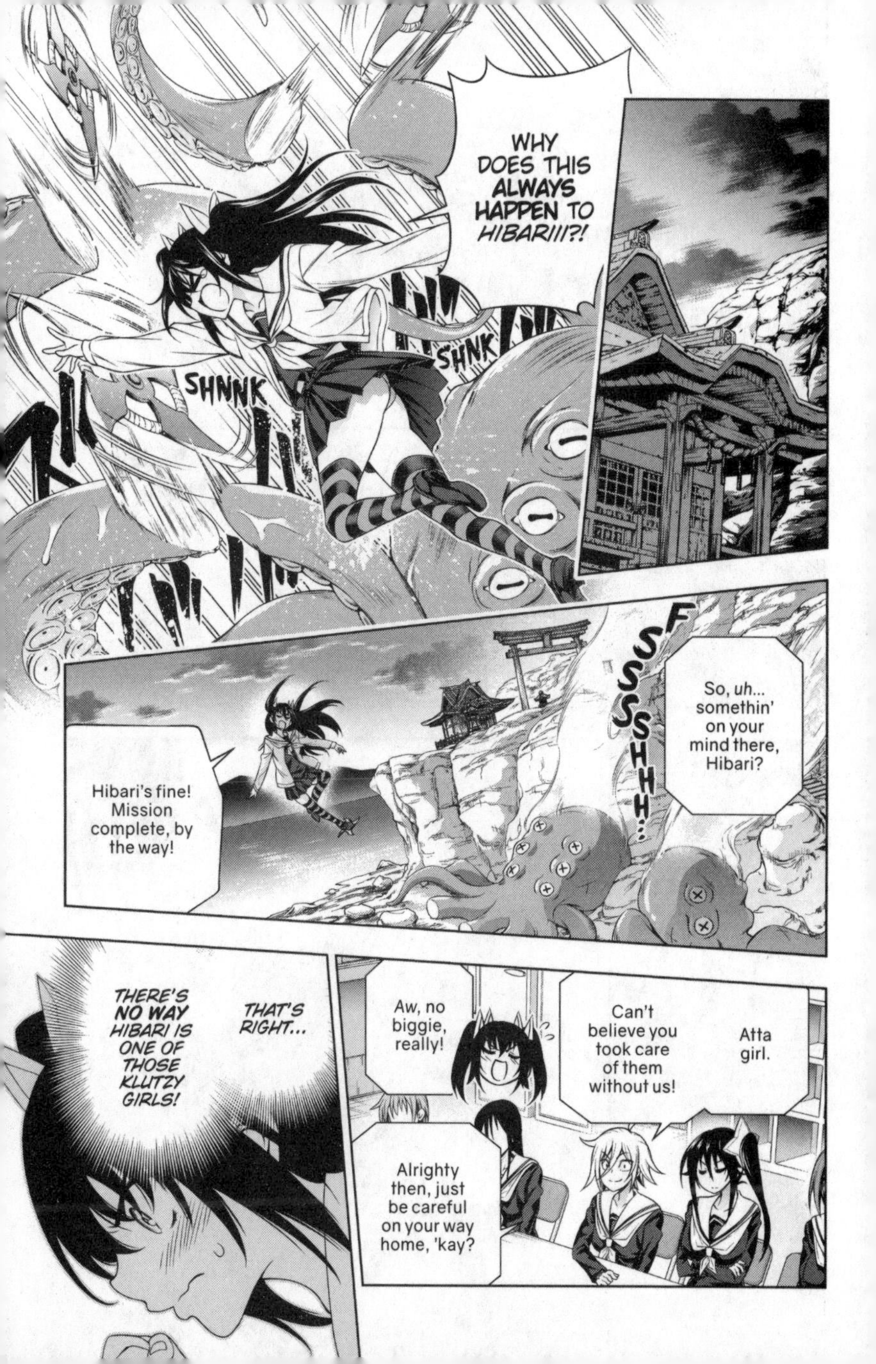
WHY DOES THIS ALWAYS HAPPEN TO HIBARIII?!
SHNK
SHNNK
FSSSSHHH...
So, uh... somethin' on your mind there, Hibari?
Hibari's fine! Mission complete, by the way!
Atta girl.
Can't believe you took care of them without us!
Aw, no biggie, really!
Alrighty then, just be careful on your way home, 'kay?
THAT'S RIGHT...
THERE'S NO WAY HIBARI IS ONE OF THOSE KLUTZY GIRLS!

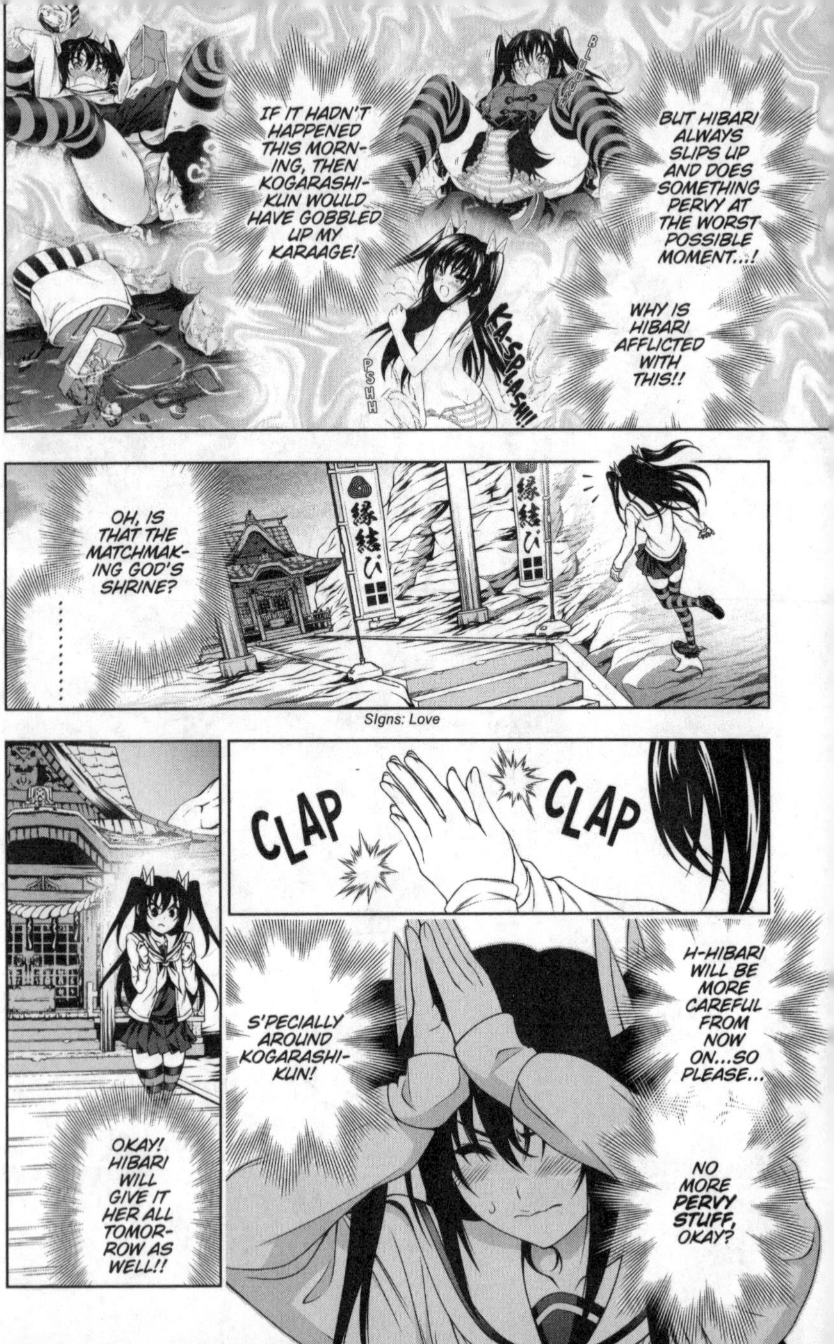
BUT HIBARI ALWAYS SLIPS UP AND DOES SOMETHING PERVY AT THE WORST POSSIBLE MOMENT...!
BLUUSH
IF IT HADN'T HAPPENED THIS MORNING, THEN KOGARASHI-KUN WOULD HAVE GOBBLED UP MY KARAAGE!
WHY IS HIBARI AFFLICTED WITH THIS!!
KA-SPLASH!!
PSHH
縁結び
縁結び
OH, IS THAT THE MATCHMAKING GOD'S SHRINE?
......
SIgns: Love
CLAP
CLAP
H-HIBARI WILL BE MORE CAREFUL FROM NOW ON...SO PLEASE...
S'PECIALLY AROUND KOGARASHI-KUN!
NO MORE PERVY STUFF, OKAY?
OKAY! HIBARI WILL GIVE IT HER ALL TOMORROW AS WELL!!

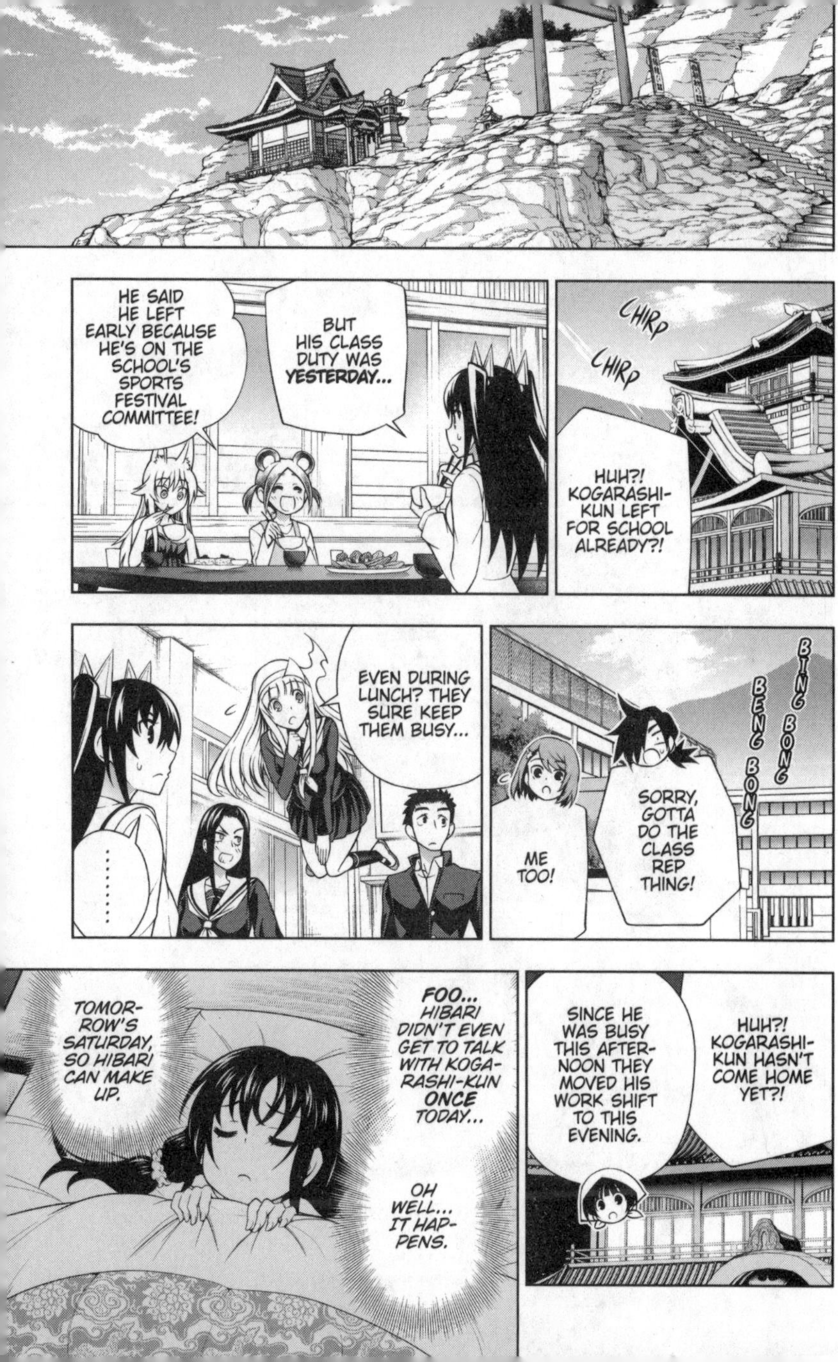
CHIRP
CHIRP
HUH?! KOGARASHI-KUN LEFT FOR SCHOOL ALREADY?!
HE SAID HE LEFT EARLY BECAUSE HE'S ON THE SCHOOL'S SPORTS FESTIVAL COMMITTEE!
BUT HIS CLASS DUTY WAS YESTERDAY...
BING BONG
BENG BONG
SORRY, GOTTA DO THE CLASS REP THING!
ME TOO!
EVEN DURING LUNCH? THEY SURE KEEP THEM BUSY...
......
HUH?! KOGARASHI-KUN HASN'T COME HOME YET?!
SINCE HE WAS BUSY THIS AFTER-NOON THEY MOVED HIS WORK SHIFT TO THIS EVENING.
FOO... HIBARI DIDN'T EVEN GET TO TALK WITH KOGA-RASHI-KUN ONCE TODAY...
OH WELL... IT HAP-PENS.
TOMOR-ROW'S SATURDAY, SO HIBARI CAN MAKE UP.

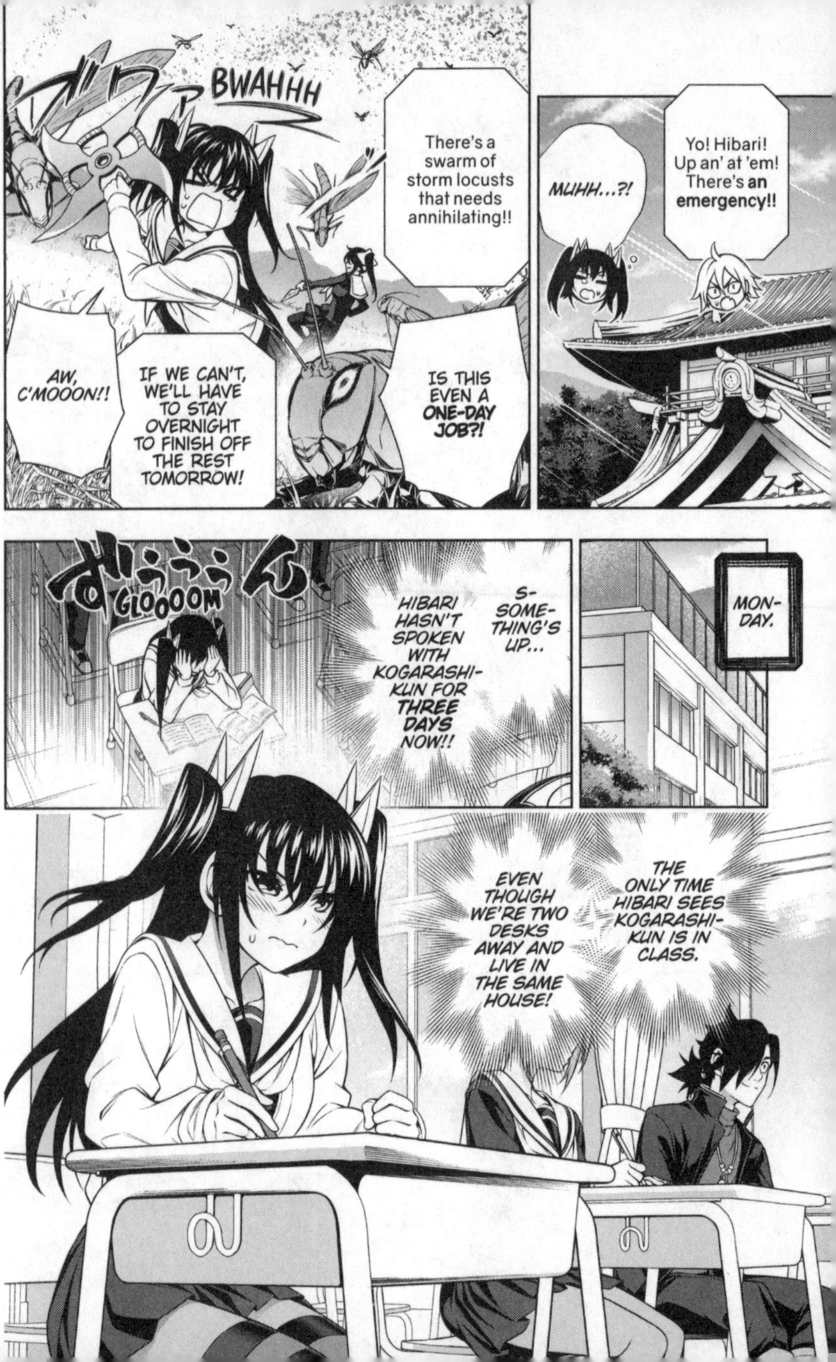
Yo! Hibari! Up an' at 'em! There's an emergency!!
MUHH...?!
There's a swarm of storm locusts that needs annihilating!!
BWAHHH
IS THIS EVEN A ONE-DAY JOB?!
IF WE CAN'T, WE'LL HAVE TO STAY OVERNIGHT TO FINISH OFF THE REST TOMORROW!
AW, C'MOOON!!
MON-DAY.
GLOOOOM
S-SOMETHING'S UP...
HIBARI HASN'T SPOKEN WITH KOGARASHI-KUN FOR THREE DAYS NOW!!
THE ONLY TIME HIBARI SEES KOGARASHI-KUN IS IN CLASS.
EVEN THOUGH WE'RE TWO DESKS AWAY AND LIVE IN THE SAME HOUSE!

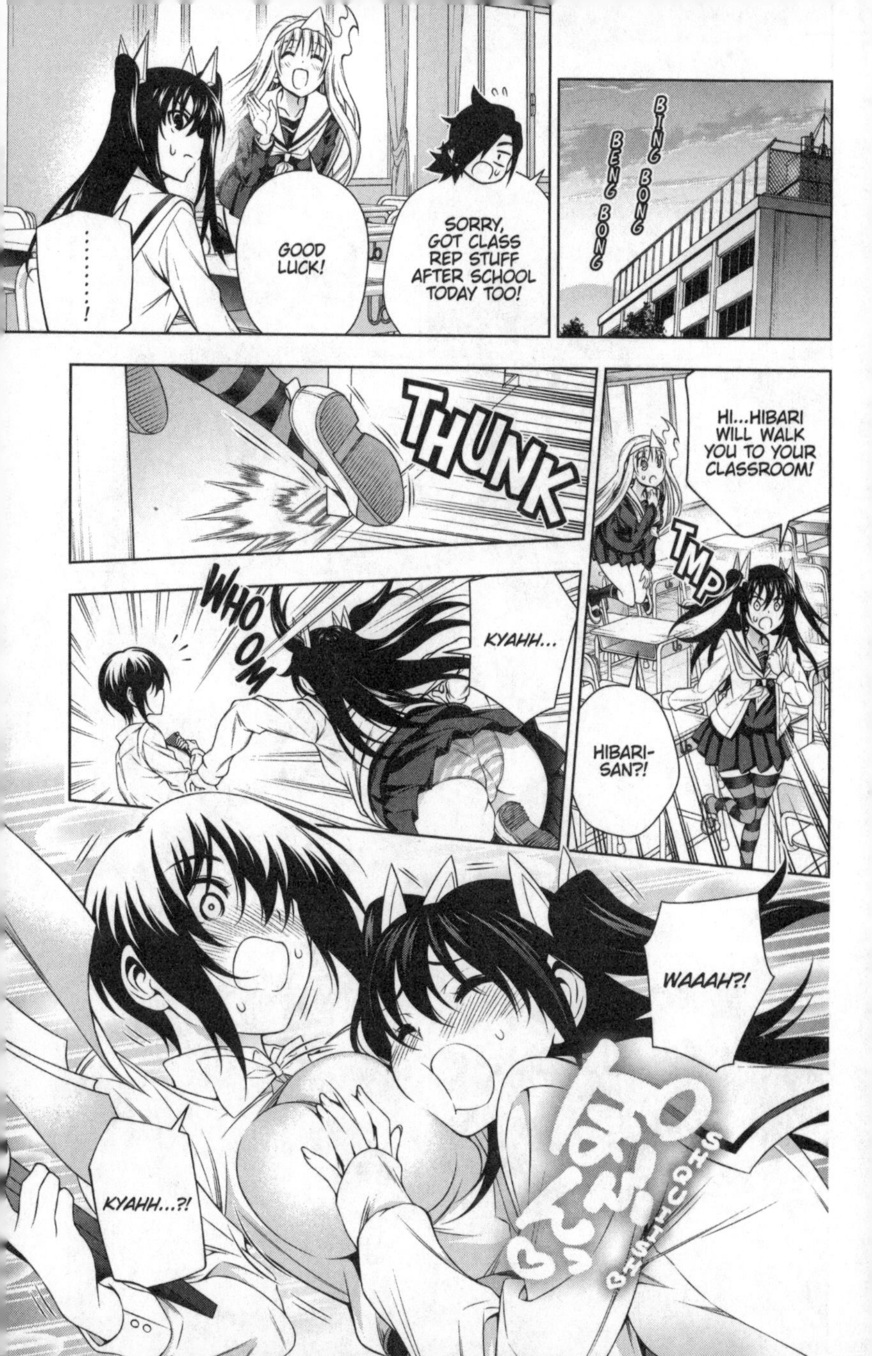
BING BONG
BENG BONG
SORRY, GOT CLASS REP STUFF AFTER SCHOOL TODAY TOO!
GOOD LUCK!
......!
HI...HIBARI WILL WALK YOU TO YOUR CLASSROOM!
TMP
HIBARI-SAN?!
THUNK
WHOOM
KYAHH...
WAAAH?!
SHQUISH
KYAHH...?!

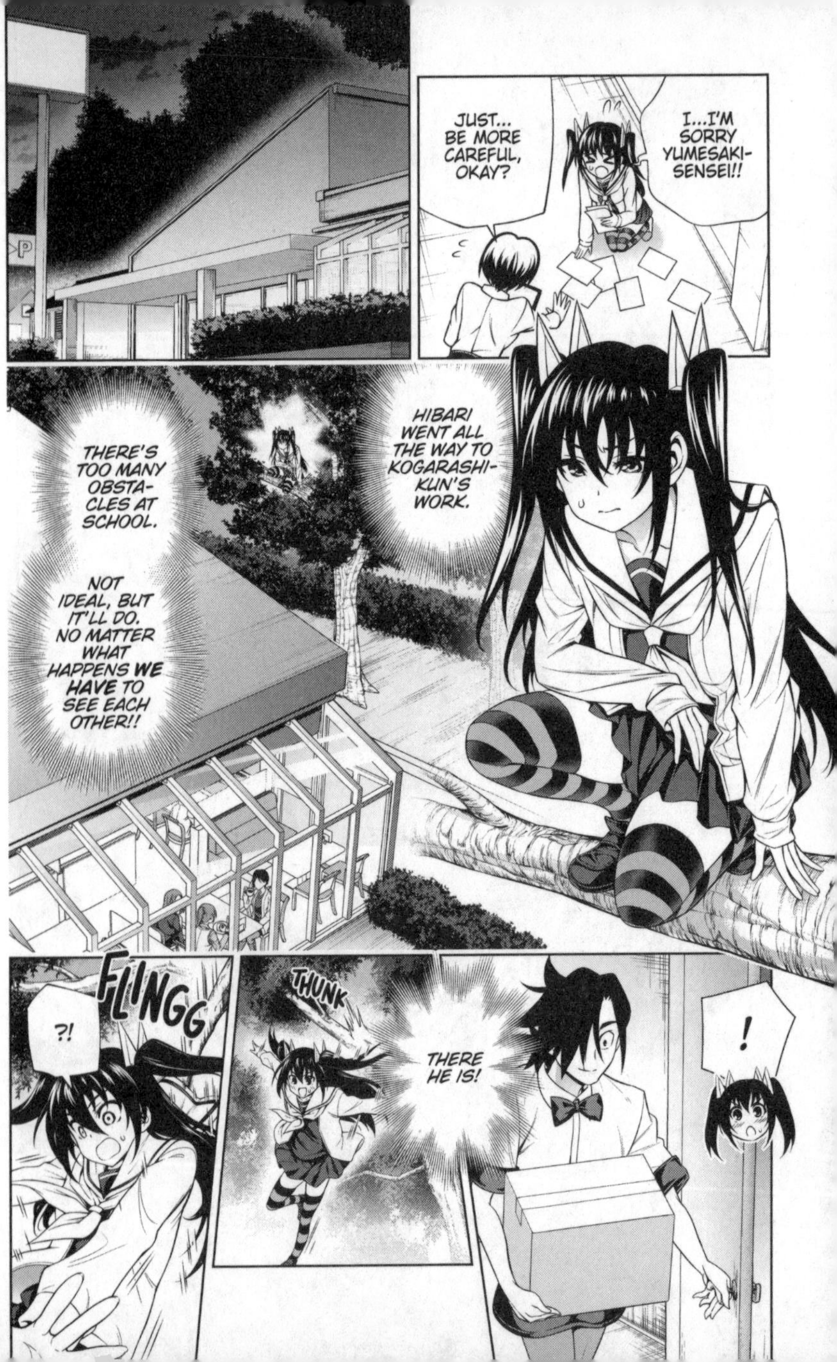
I...I'M SORRY YUMESAKI-SENSEI!!
JUST... BE MORE CAREFUL, OKAY?
HIBARI WENT ALL THE WAY TO KOGARASHI-KUN'S WORK.
THERE'S TOO MANY OBSTACLES AT SCHOOL.
NOT IDEAL, BUT IT'LL DO. NO MATTER WHAT HAPPENS **WE HAVE** TO SEE EACH OTHER!!
!
THUNK
THERE HE IS!
FLINGG
?!

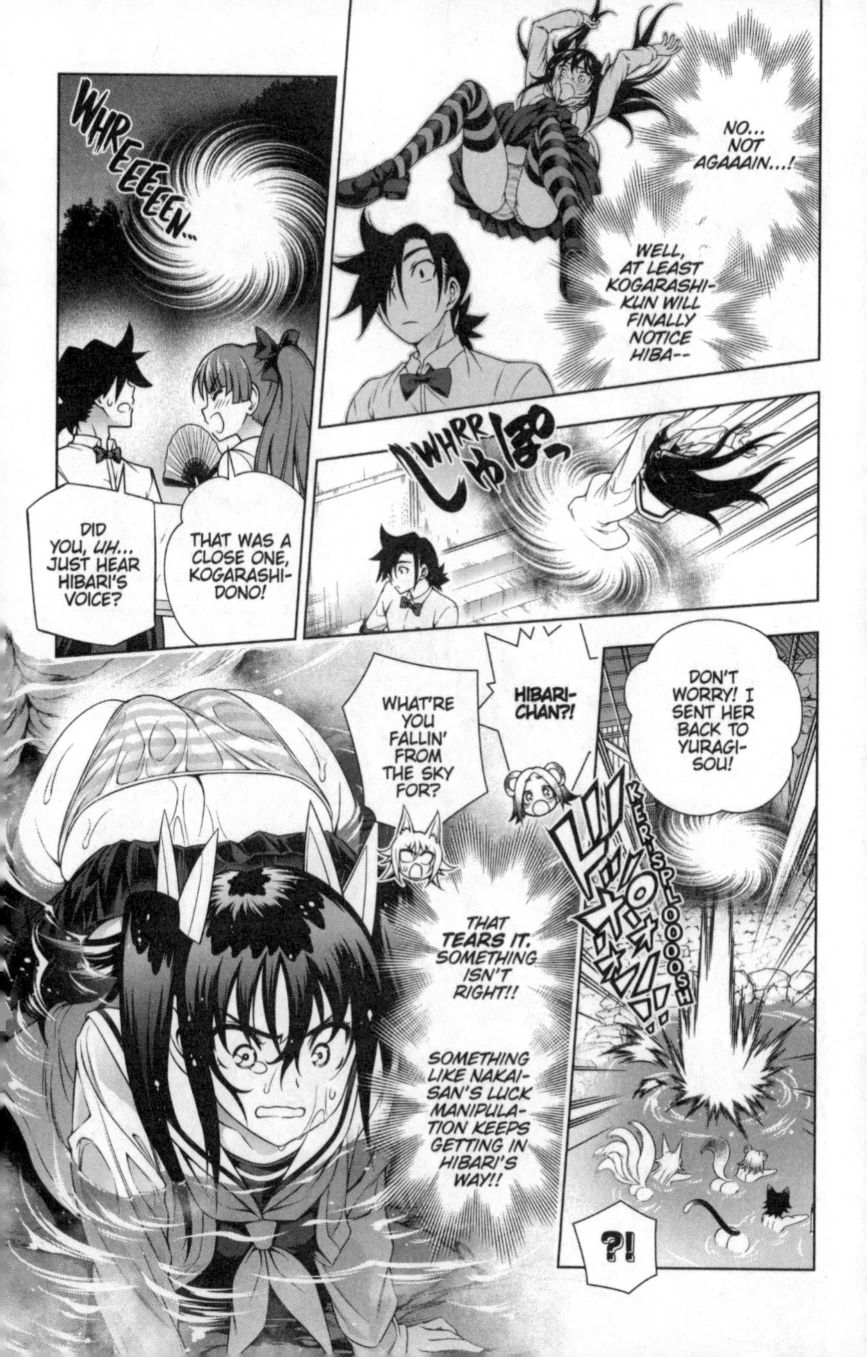
NO... NOT AGAAAIN...!
WELL, AT LEAST KOGARASHI-KUN WILL FINALLY NOTICE HIBA--
WHRR
しゅぽっ
WHREEEEEN...
THAT WAS A CLOSE ONE, KOGARASHI-DONO!
DID YOU, UH... JUST HEAR HIBARI'S VOICE?
DON'T WORRY! I SENT HER BACK TO YURAGI-SOU!
KERSPLOOOOSH
?!
HIBARI-CHAN?!
WHAT'RE YOU FALLIN' FROM THE SKY FOR?
THAT TEARS IT. SOMETHING ISN'T RIGHT!!
SOMETHING LIKE NAKAI-SAN'S LUCK MANIPULATION KEEPS GETTING IN HIBARI'S WAY!!

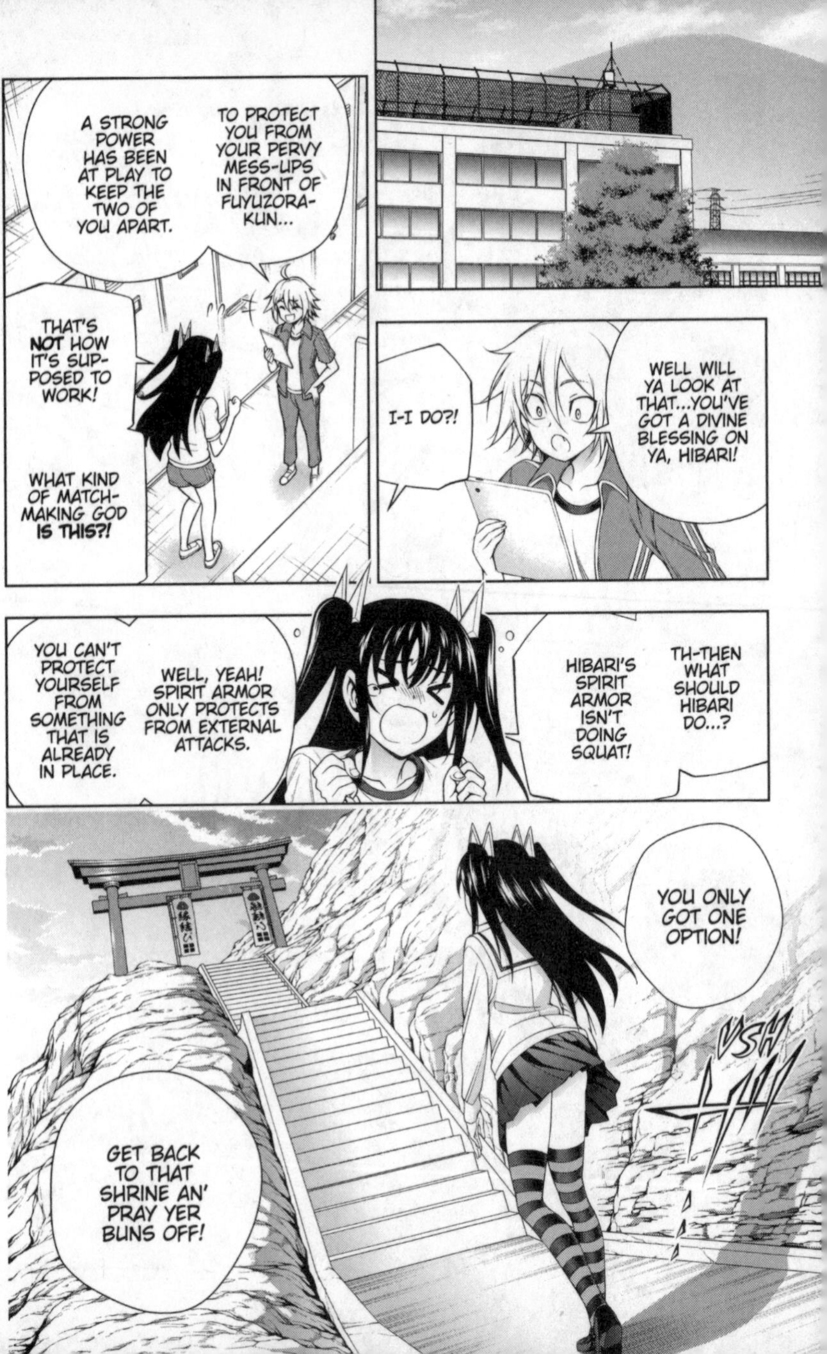
WELL WILL YA LOOK AT THAT...YOU'VE GOT A DIVINE BLESSING ON YA, HIBARI!
I-I DO?!
TO PROTECT YOU FROM YOUR PERVY MESS-UPS IN FRONT OF FUYUZORA-KUN...
A STRONG POWER HAS BEEN AT PLAY TO KEEP THE TWO OF YOU APART.
THAT'S **NOT** HOW IT'S SUPPOSED TO WORK!
WHAT KIND OF MATCHMAKING GOD **IS THIS?!**
TH-THEN WHAT SHOULD HIBARI DO...?
HIBARI'S SPIRIT ARMOR ISN'T DOING SQUAT!
WELL, YEAH! SPIRIT ARMOR ONLY PROTECTS FROM EXTERNAL ATTACKS.
YOU CAN'T PROTECT YOURSELF FROM SOMETHING THAT IS ALREADY IN PLACE.
YOU ONLY GOT ONE OPTION!
VSHH
GET BACK TO THAT SHRINE AN' PRAY YER BUNS OFF!

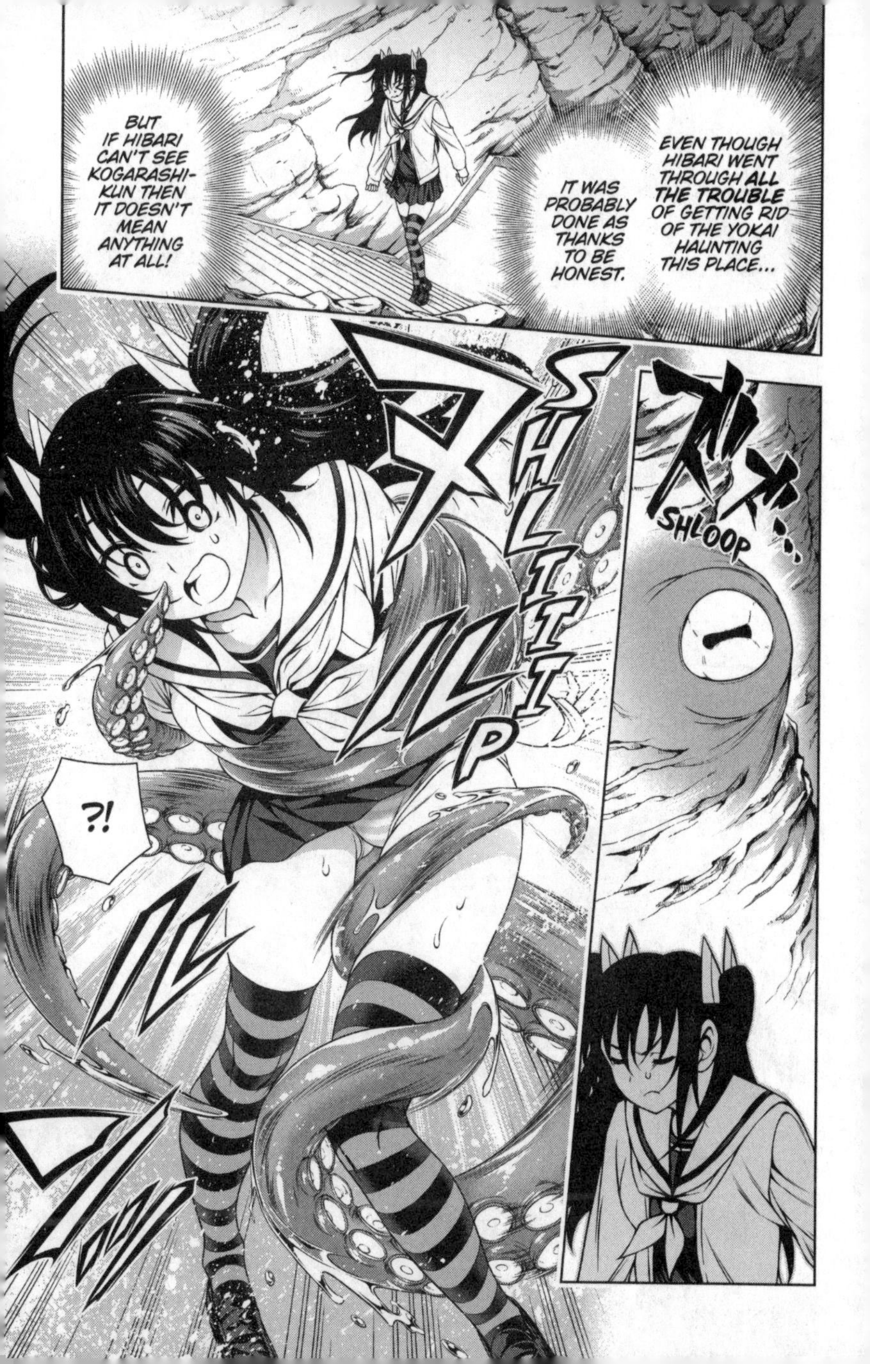
EVEN THOUGH HIBARI WENT THROUGH **ALL THE TROUBLE** OF GETTING RID OF THE YOKAI HAUNTING THIS PLACE...
IT WAS PROBABLY DONE AS THANKS TO BE HONEST.
BUT IF HIBARI CAN'T SEE KOGARASHI-KUN THEN IT DOESN'T MEAN ANYTHING AT ALL!
SHLOOP
SHLIIIP
?!

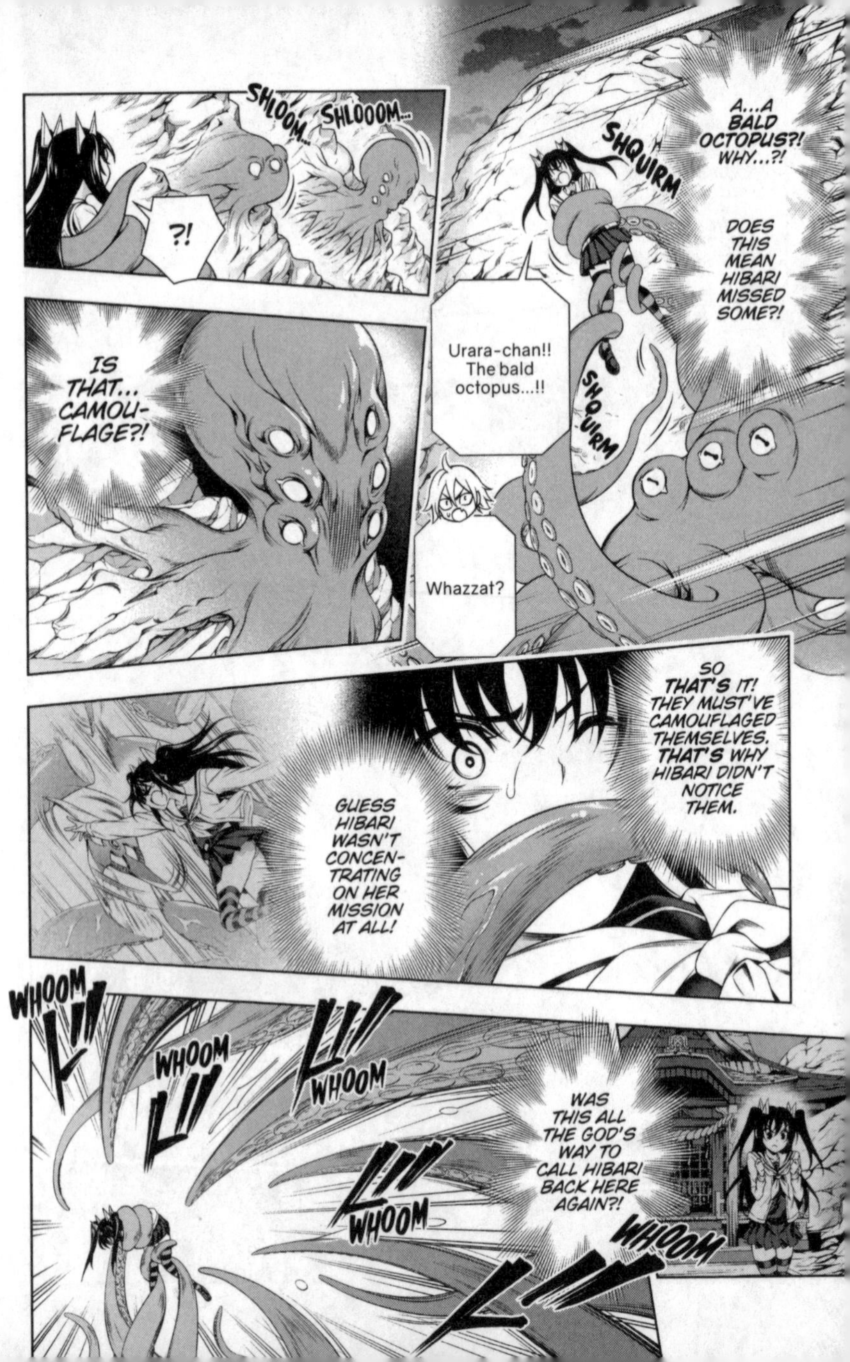
A...A BALD OCTOPUS?! WHY...?!
SHQUIRM
DOES THIS MEAN HIBARI MISSED SOME?!
Urara-chan!! The bald octopus...!!
SHQUIRM
Whazzat?
SHLOOOM...
SHLOOM...
?!
IS THAT... CAMOU-FLAGE?!
SO THAT'S IT! THEY MUST'VE CAMOUFLAGED THEMSELVES. THAT'S WHY HIBARI DIDN'T NOTICE THEM.
GUESS HIBARI WASN'T CONCEN-TRATING ON HER MISSION AT ALL!
WHOOM
WAS THIS ALL THE GOD'S WAY TO CALL HIBARI BACK HERE AGAIN?!
WHOOM
WHOOM
WHOOM
WHOOM

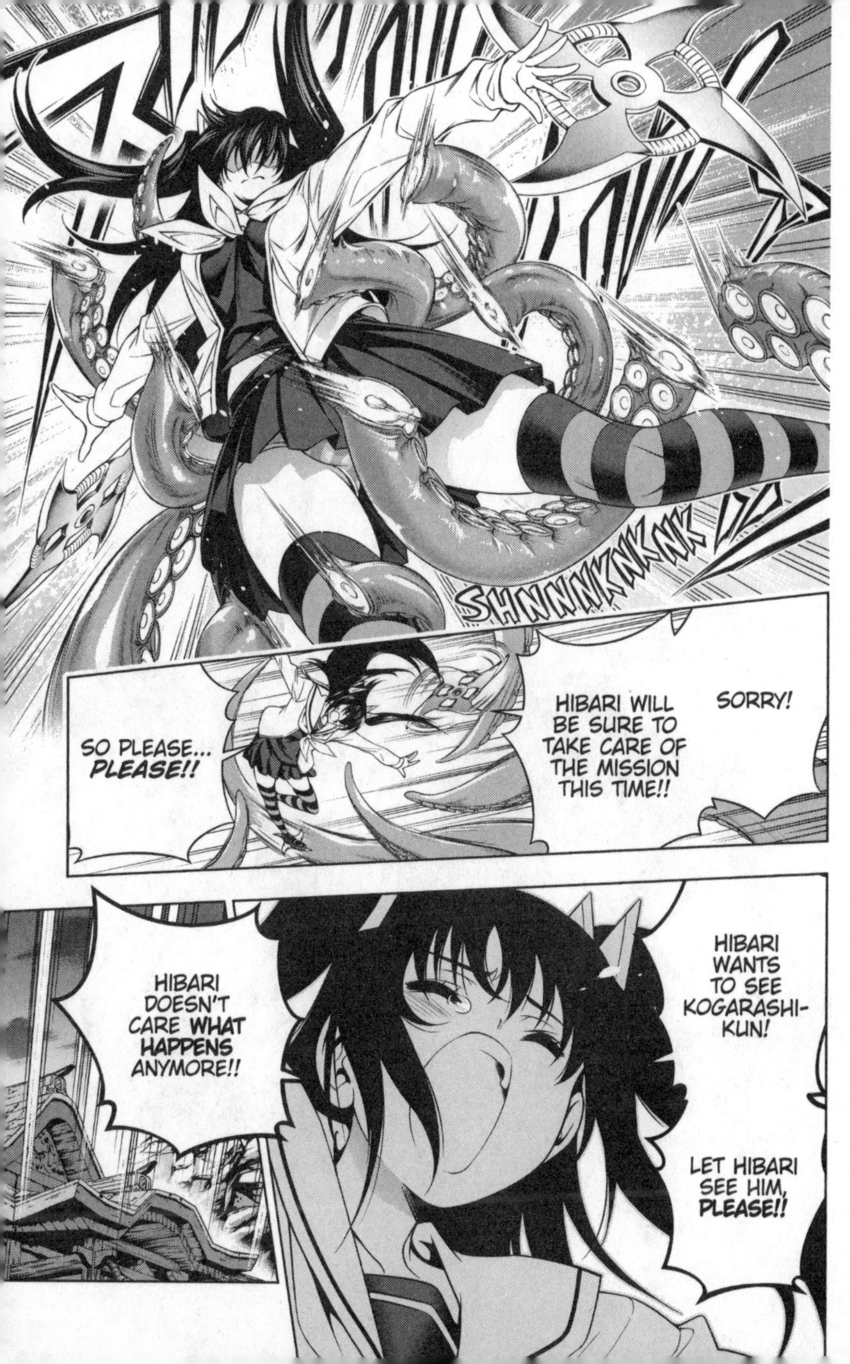
SHNNNKNKNK
SORRY!
HIBARI WILL BE SURE TO TAKE CARE OF THE MISSION THIS TIME!!
SO PLEASE... *PLEASE!!*
HIBARI WANTS TO SEE KOGARASHI-KUN!
LET HIBARI SEE HIM, **PLEASE!!**
HIBARI DOESN'T CARE **WHAT** HAPPENS ANYMORE!!

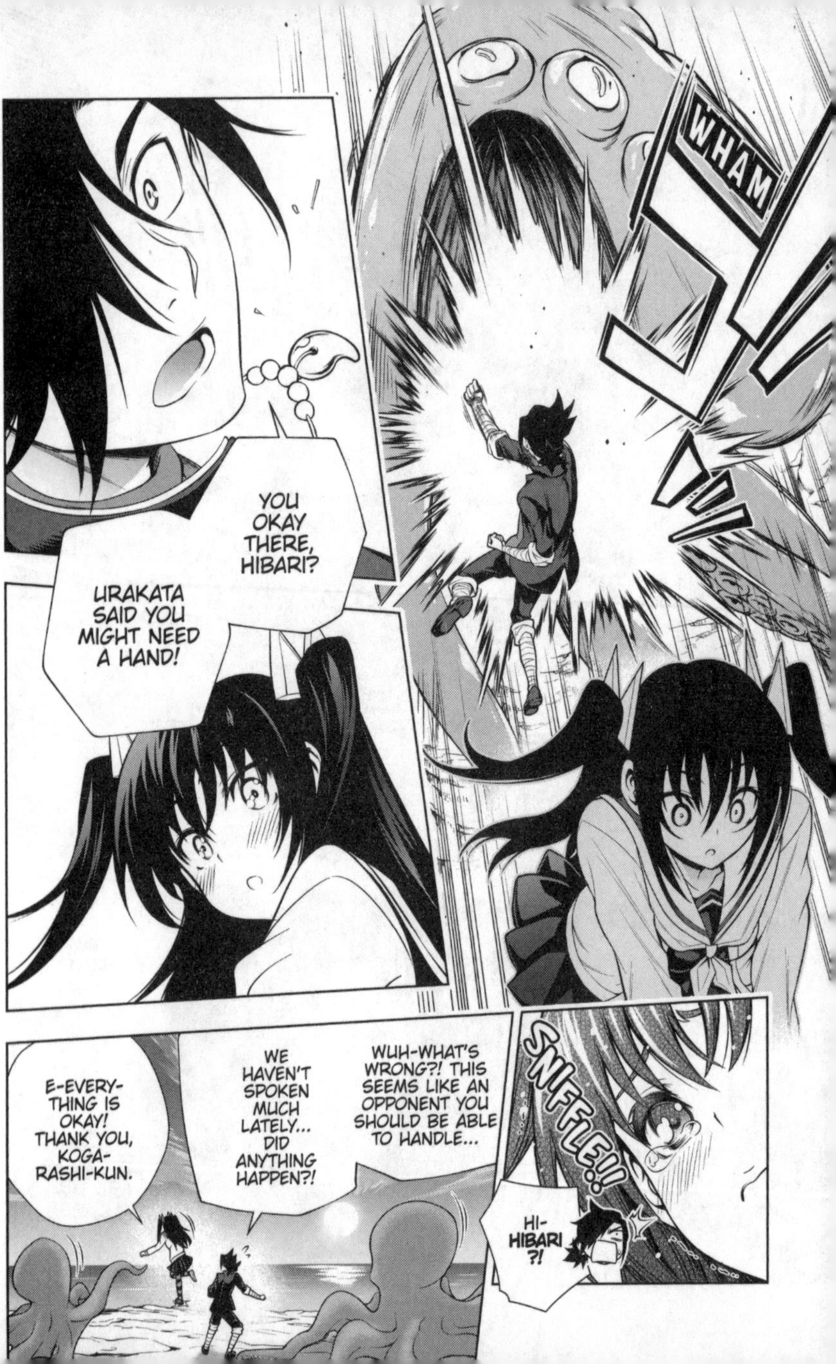
WHAM
YOU OKAY THERE, HIBARI?
URAKATA SAID YOU MIGHT NEED A HAND!
SNIFFLE!!
HI-HIBARI?!
WUH-WHAT'S WRONG?! THIS SEEMS LIKE AN OPPONENT YOU SHOULD BE ABLE TO HANDLE...
WE HAVEN'T SPOKEN MUCH LATELY... DID ANYTHING HAPPEN?!
E-EVERYTHING IS OKAY! THANK YOU, KOGA-RASHI-KUN.

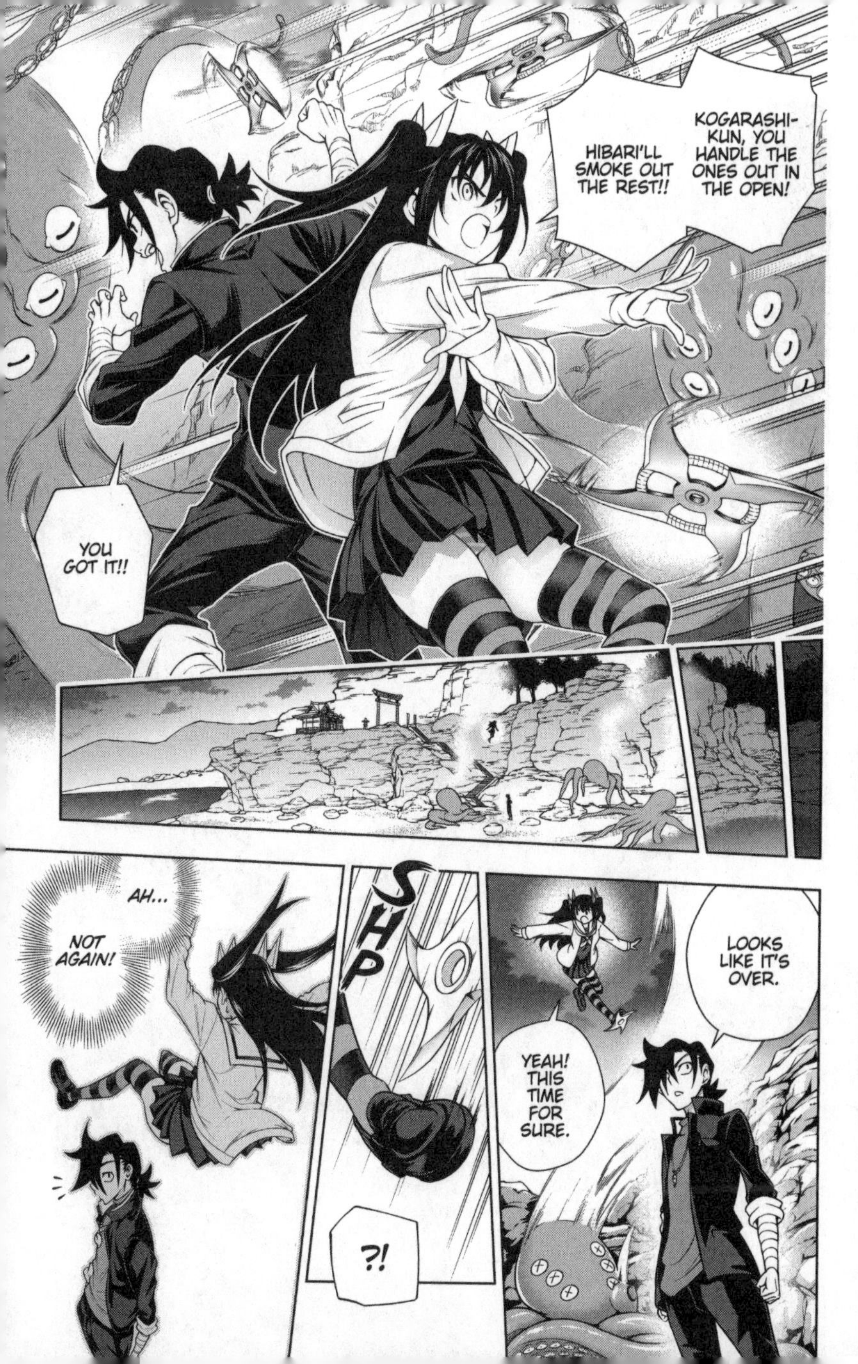
KOGARASHI-KUN, YOU HANDLE THE ONES OUT IN THE OPEN!
HIBARI'LL SMOKE OUT THE REST!!
YOU GOT IT!!
LOOKS LIKE IT'S OVER.
YEAH! THIS TIME FOR SURE.
SHP
?!
AH...
NOT AGAIN!

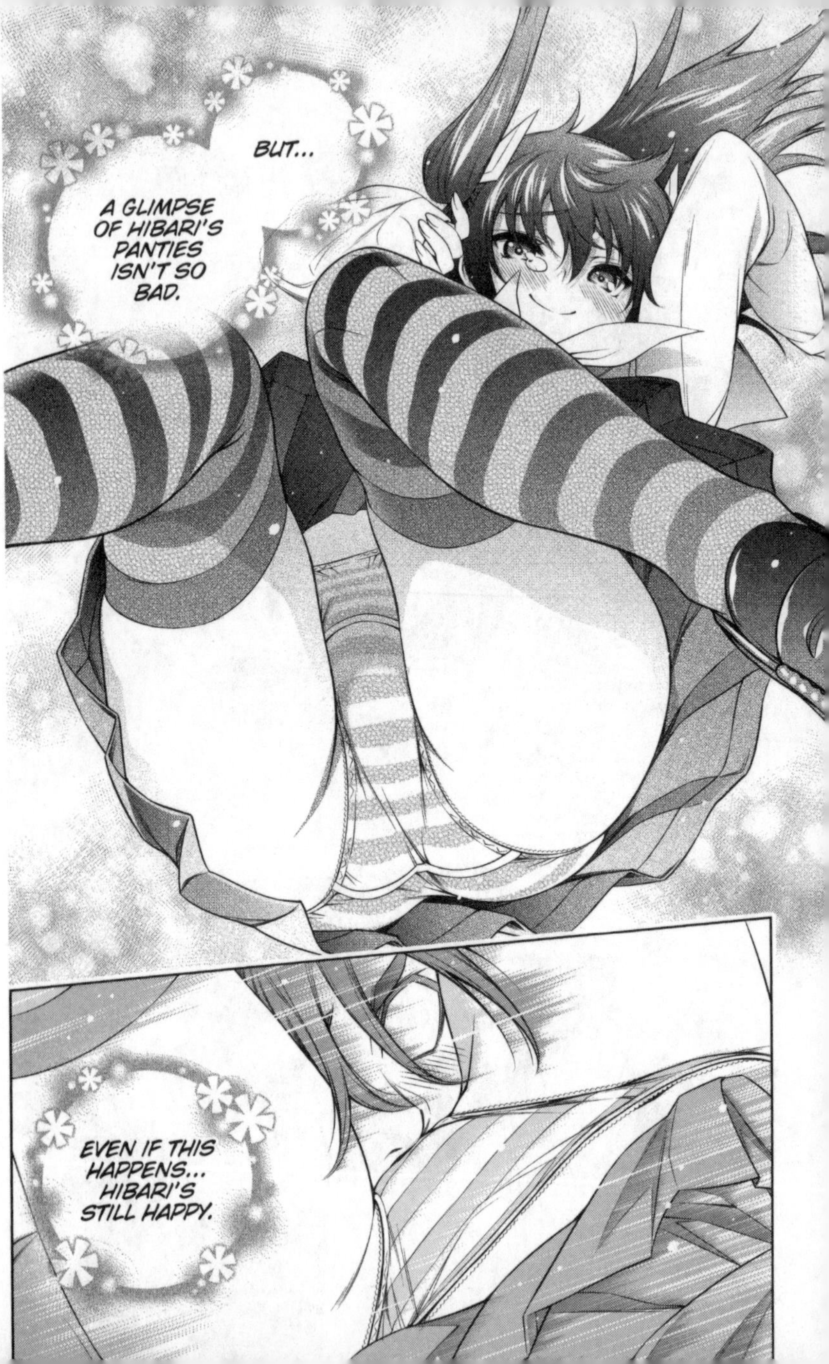
BUT...
A GLIMPSE OF HIBARI'S PANTIES ISN'T SO BAD.
EVEN IF THIS HAPPENS... HIBARI'S STILL HAPPY.

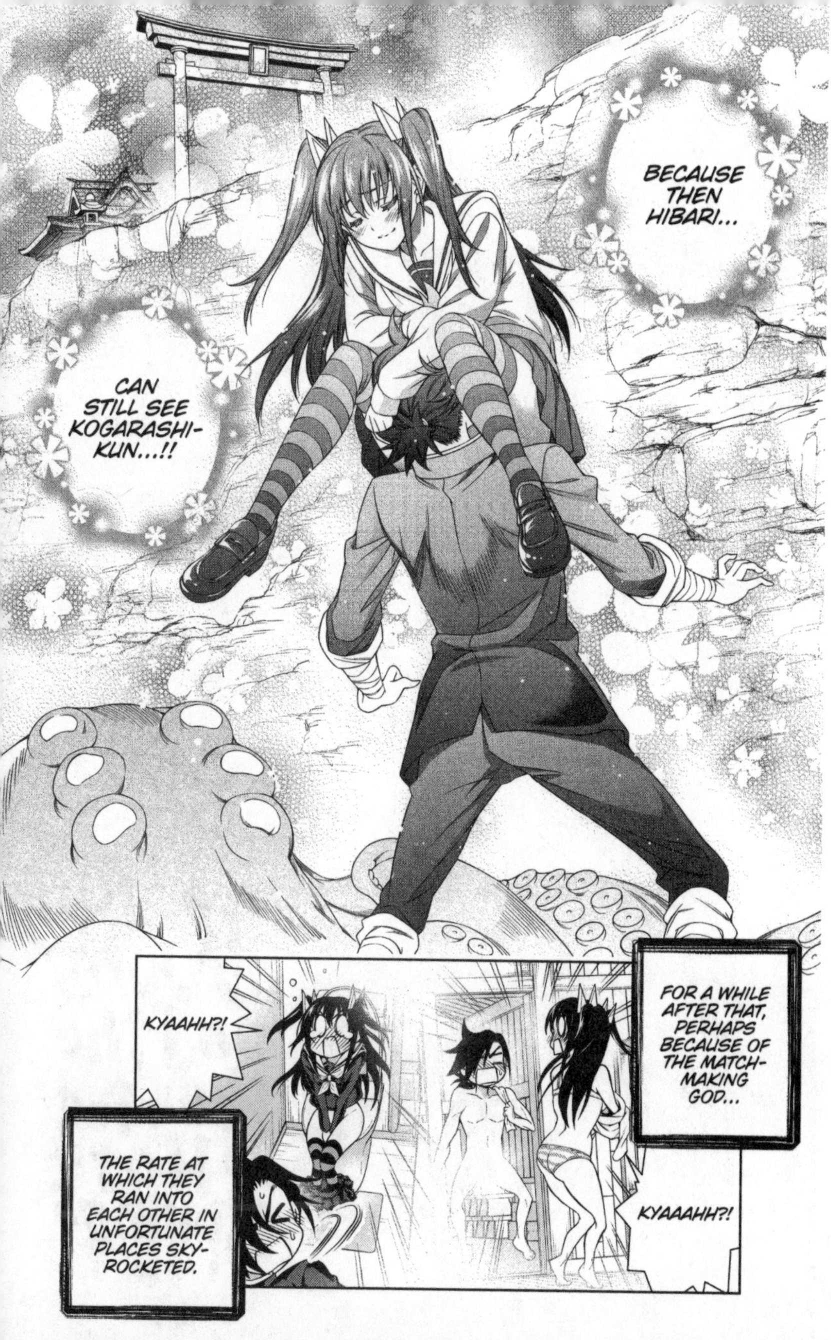
BECAUSE THEN HIBARI...
CAN STILL SEE KOGARASHI-KUN...!!
FOR A WHILE AFTER THAT, PERHAPS BECAUSE OF THE MATCH-MAKING GOD...
KYAAAHH?!
KYAAHH?!
THE RATE AT WHICH THEY RAN INTO EACH OTHER IN UNFORTUNATE PLACES SKY-ROCKETED.

Yuuna and the Haunted Hot Springs

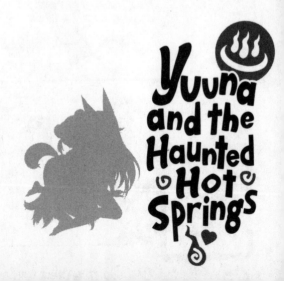

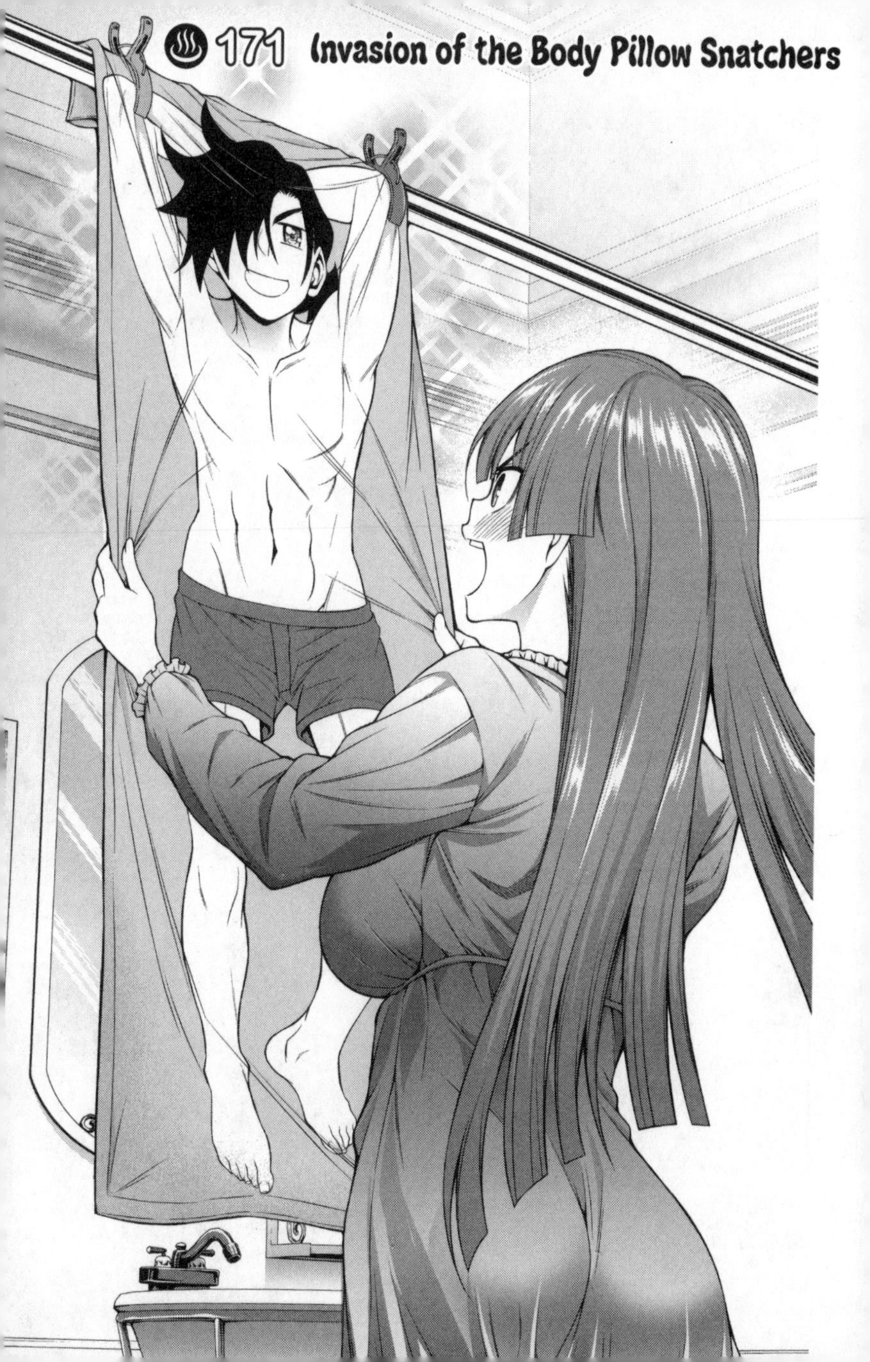
171 Invasion of the Body Pillow Snatchers

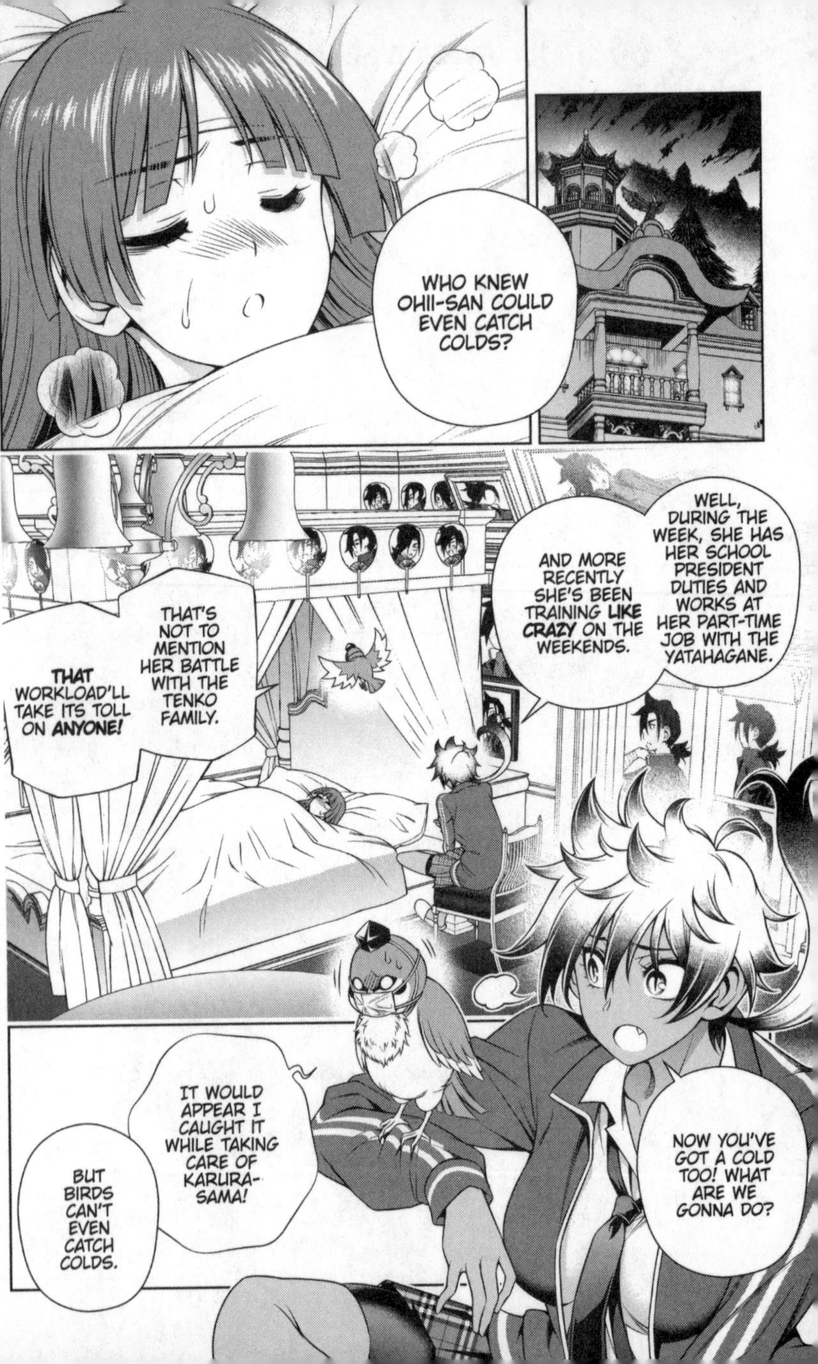
WHO KNEW OHII-SAN COULD EVEN CATCH COLDS?
WELL, DURING THE WEEK, SHE HAS HER SCHOOL PRESIDENT DUTIES AND WORKS AT HER PART-TIME JOB WITH THE YATAHAGANE.
AND MORE RECENTLY SHE'S BEEN TRAINING **LIKE CRAZY** ON THE WEEKENDS.
THAT'S NOT TO MENTION HER BATTLE WITH THE TENKO FAMILY.
THAT WORKLOAD'LL TAKE ITS TOLL ON **ANYONE!**
NOW YOU'VE GOT A COLD TOO! WHAT ARE WE GONNA DO?
IT WOULD APPEAR I CAUGHT IT WHILE TAKING CARE OF KARURA-SAMA!
BUT BIRDS CAN'T EVEN CATCH COLDS.

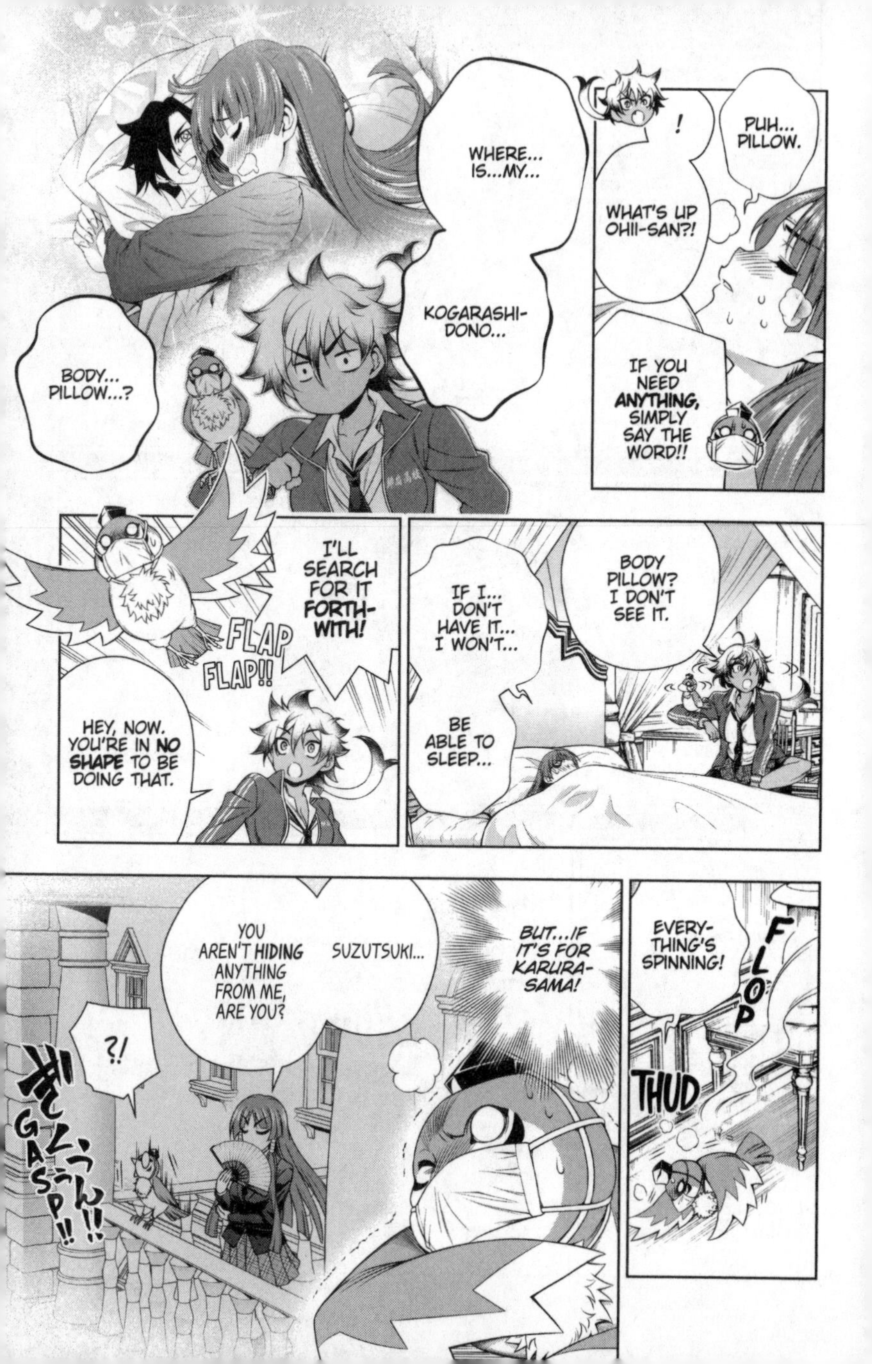
PUH... PILLOW.
!
WHAT'S UP OHII-SAN?!
IF YOU NEED **ANYTHING,** SIMPLY SAY THE WORD!!
WHERE... IS...MY...
KOGARASHI-DONO...
BODY... PILLOW...?
BODY PILLOW? I DON'T SEE IT.
IF I... DON'T HAVE IT... I WON'T...
BE ABLE TO SLEEP...
I'LL SEARCH FOR IT **FORTH-WITH!**
FLAP FLAP!!
HEY, NOW. YOU'RE IN **NO SHAPE** TO BE DOING THAT.
EVERY-THING'S SPINNING!
FLOP
THUD
BUT...IF IT'S FOR KARURA-SAMA!
SUZUTSUKI...
YOU AREN'T **HIDING** ANYTHING FROM ME, ARE YOU?
?!
ぎくぅん!!
GASP!!

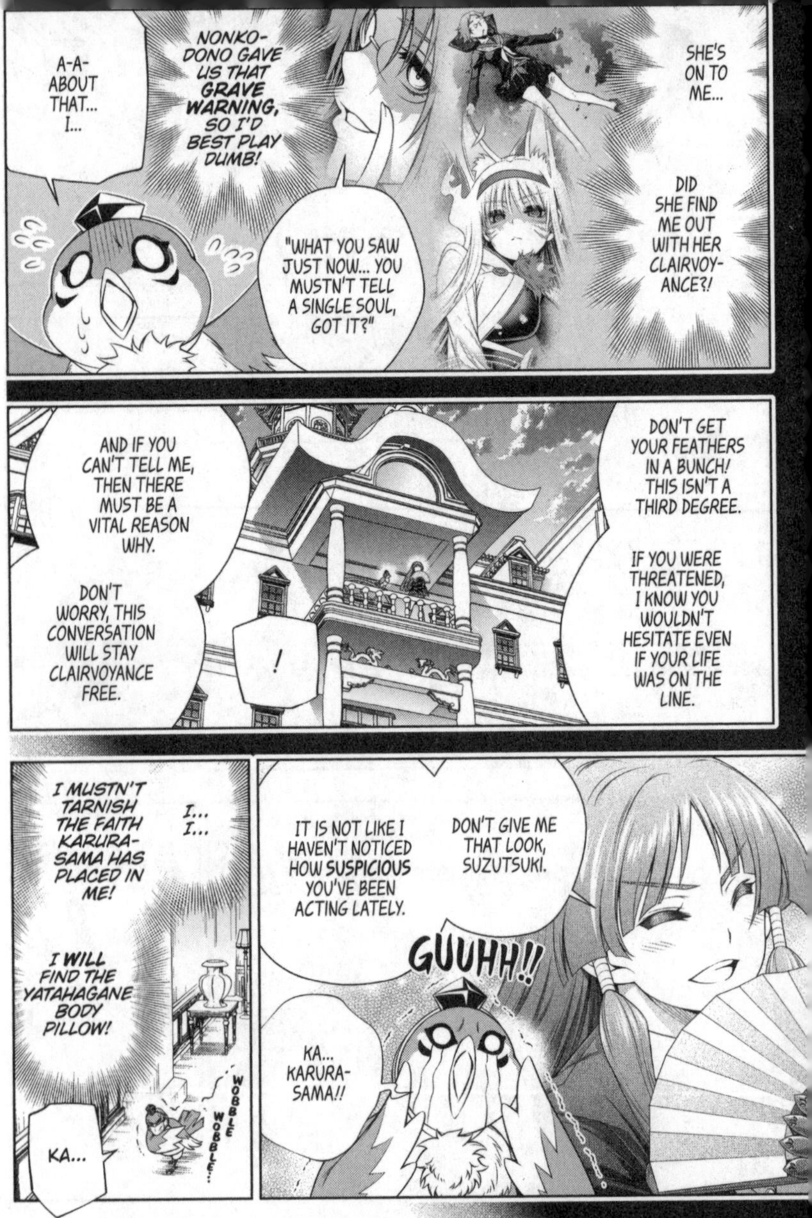
SHE'S ON TO ME...
DID SHE FIND ME OUT WITH HER CLAIRVOYANCE?!
"WHAT YOU SAW JUST NOW... YOU MUSTN'T TELL A SINGLE SOUL, GOT IT?"
NONKO-DONO GAVE US THAT GRAVE WARNING, SO I'D BEST PLAY DUMB!
A-A-ABOUT THAT... I...
DON'T GET YOUR FEATHERS IN A BUNCH! THIS ISN'T A THIRD DEGREE.
IF YOU WERE THREATENED, I KNOW YOU WOULDN'T HESITATE EVEN IF YOUR LIFE WAS ON THE LINE.
!
AND IF YOU CAN'T TELL ME, THEN THERE MUST BE A VITAL REASON WHY.
DON'T WORRY, THIS CONVERSATION WILL STAY CLAIRVOYANCE FREE.
DON'T GIVE ME THAT LOOK, SUZUTSUKI.
IT IS NOT LIKE I HAVEN'T NOTICED HOW SUSPICIOUS YOU'VE BEEN ACTING LATELY.
GUUHH!!
KA... KARURA-SAMA!!
I... I...
I MUSTN'T TARNISH THE FAITH KARURA-SAMA HAS PLACED IN ME!
I WILL FIND THE YATAHAGANE BODY PILLOW!
WOBBLE WOBBLE...
KA...

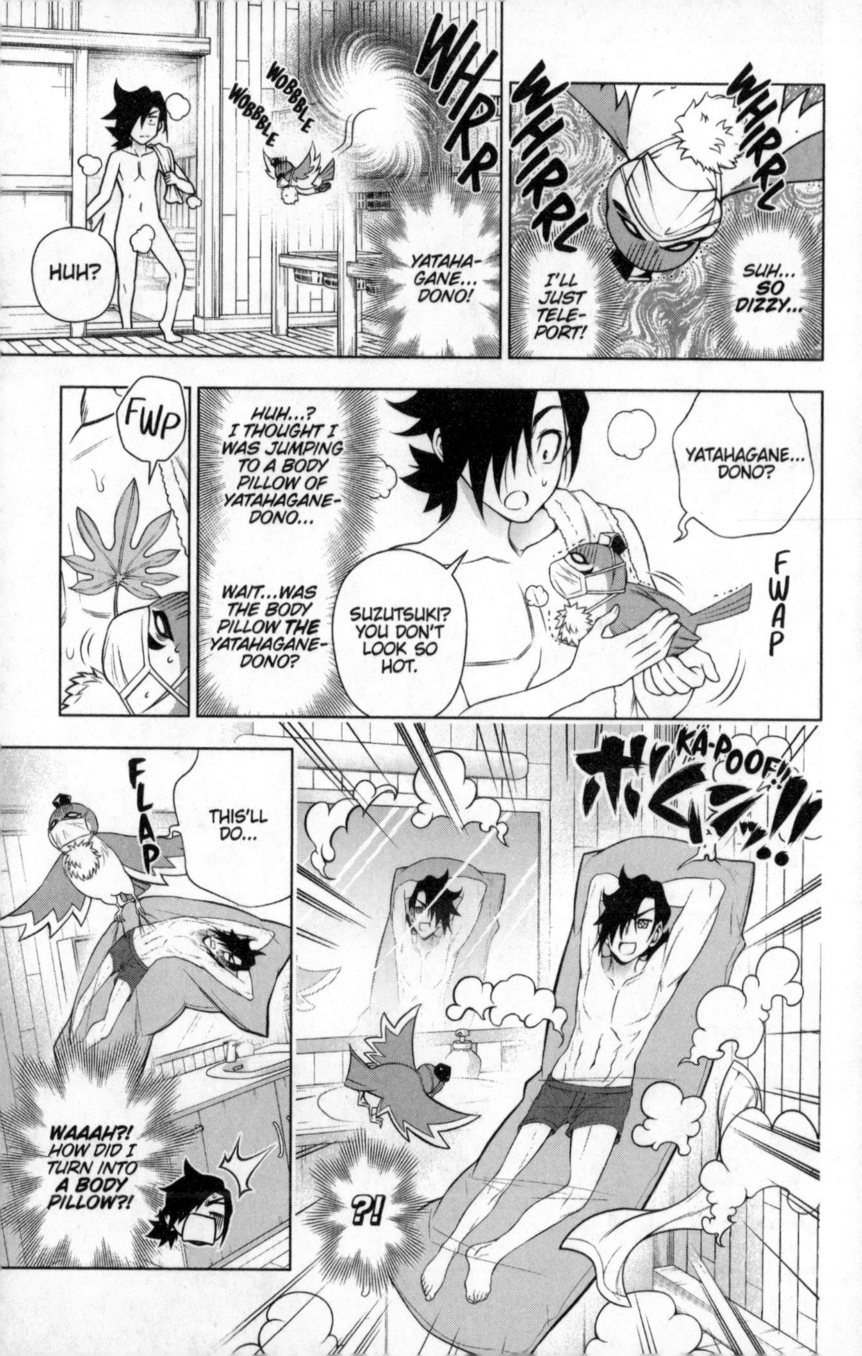
WHIRRL
WHIRRL
SUH... SO DIZZY...
I'LL JUST TELEPORT!
WHIRR
YATAHA-GANE... DONO!
WOBBBLE
WOBBBLE
HUH?
YATAHAGANE... DONO?
FWAP
HUH...? I THOUGHT I WAS JUMPING TO A BODY PILLOW OF YATAHAGANE-DONO...
SUZUTSUKI? YOU DON'T LOOK SO HOT.
WAIT...WAS THE BODY PILLOW THE YATAHAGANE-DONO?
FWP
KA-POOF!!
?!
THIS'LL DO...
FLAP
WAAAH?! HOW DID I TURN INTO A BODY PILLOW?!

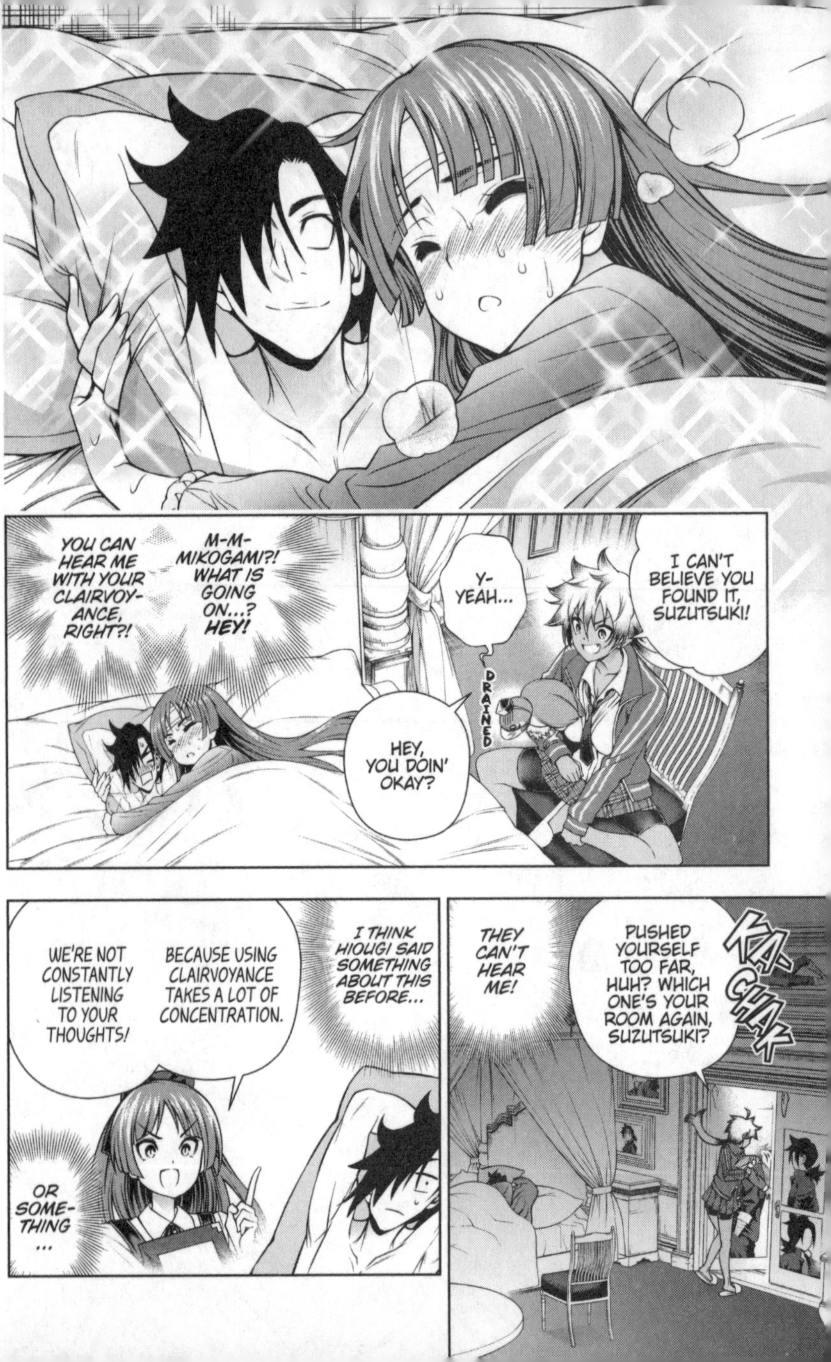
I CAN'T BELIEVE YOU FOUND IT, SUZUTSUKI!
Y-YEAH...
DRAINED
HEY, YOU DOIN' OKAY?
M-M-MIKOGAMI?! WHAT IS GOING ON...? HEY!
YOU CAN HEAR ME WITH YOUR CLAIRVOYANCE, RIGHT?!
KA-CHAK
PUSHED YOURSELF TOO FAR, HUH? WHICH ONE'S YOUR ROOM AGAIN, SUZUTSUKI?
THEY CAN'T HEAR ME!
I THINK HIOUGI SAID SOMETHING ABOUT THIS BEFORE...
BECAUSE USING CLAIRVOYANCE TAKES A LOT OF CONCENTRATION.
WE'RE NOT CONSTANTLY LISTENING TO YOUR THOUGHTS!
OR SOMETHING...

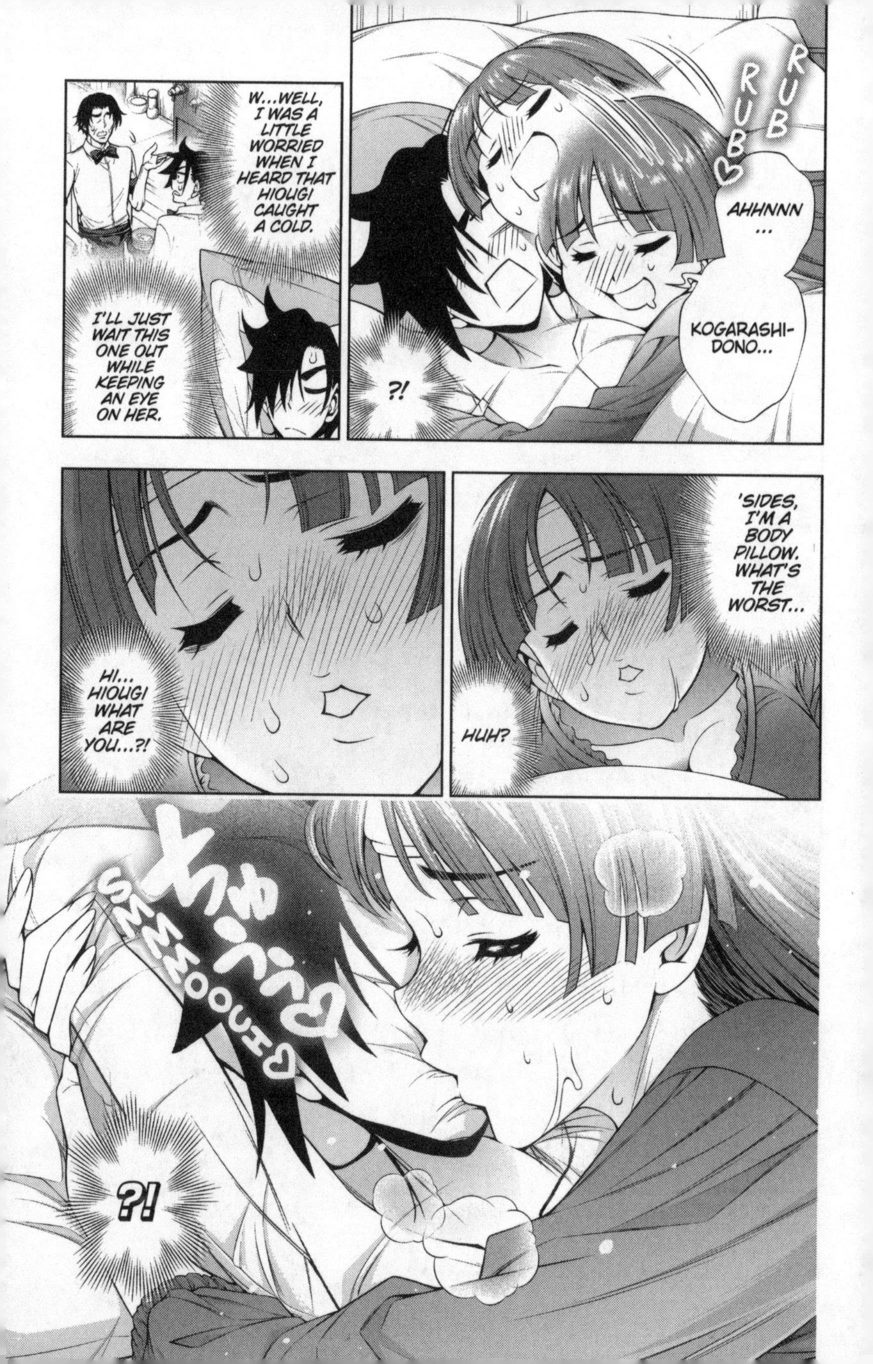
RUB RUB
RUB♡
AHHHNN...
KOGARASHI-DONO...
?!
W...WELL, I WAS A LITTLE WORRIED WHEN I HEARD THAT HIOUGI CAUGHT A COLD.
I'LL JUST WAIT THIS ONE OUT WHILE KEEPING AN EYE ON HER.
'SIDES, I'M A BODY PILLOW. WHAT'S THE WORST...
HUH?
HI... HIOUGI WHAT ARE YOU...?!
SMMMOOCH♡
?!

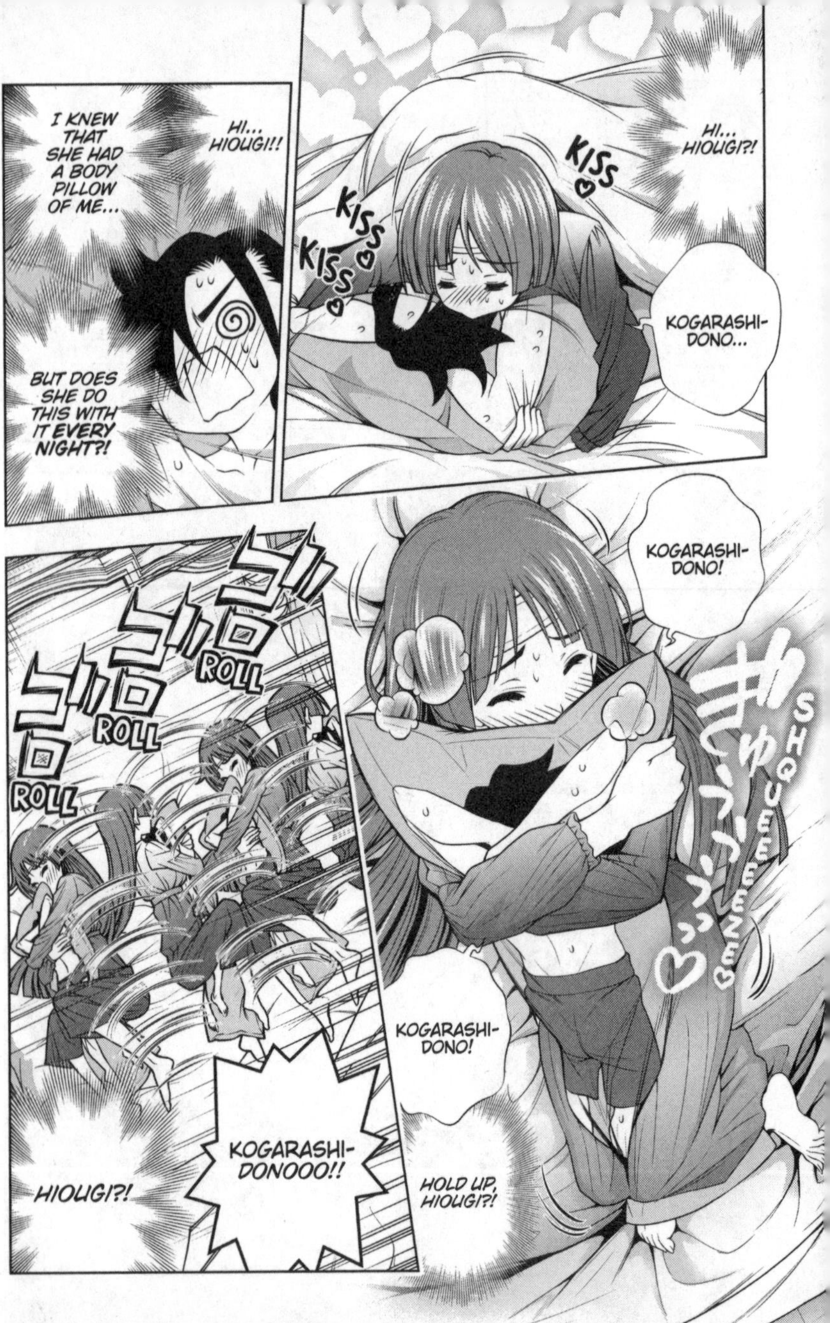
HI... HIOUGI?!
KISS
KISS
KISS
KISS
KOGARASHI-DONO...
HI... HIOUGI!!
I KNEW THAT SHE HAD A BODY PILLOW OF ME...
BUT DOES SHE DO THIS WITH IT EVERY NIGHT?!
KOGARASHI-DONO!
SHQUEEEEEZE
KOGARASHI-DONO!
HOLD UP, HIOUGI?!
ROLL
ROLL
ROLL
KOGARASHI-DONOOO!!
HIOUGI?!

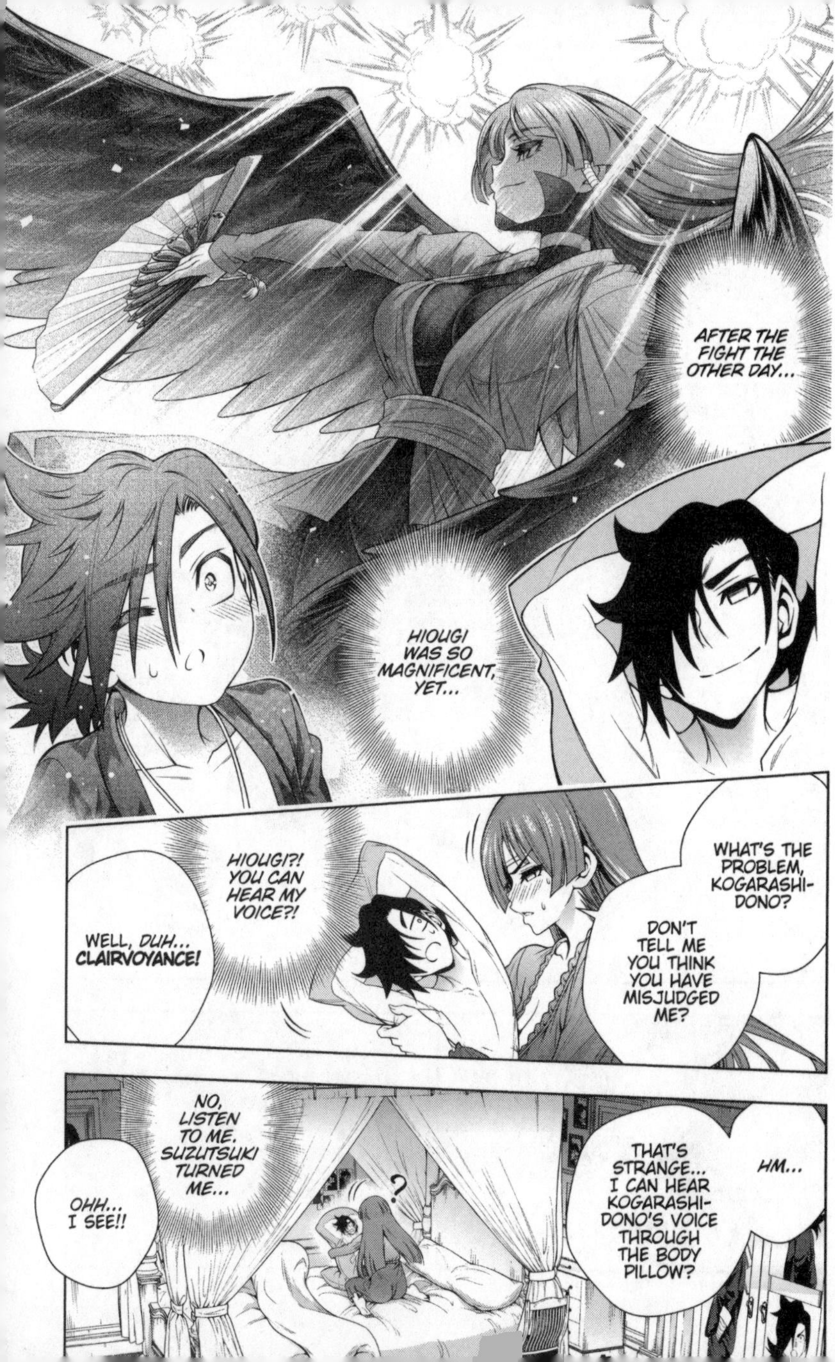
AFTER THE FIGHT THE OTHER DAY...
HIOUGI WAS SO MAGNIFICENT, YET...
WHAT'S THE PROBLEM, KOGARASHI-DONO?
DON'T TELL ME YOU THINK YOU HAVE MISJUDGED ME?
HIOUGI?! YOU CAN HEAR MY VOICE?!
WELL, DUH... CLAIRVOYANCE!
HM...
THAT'S STRANGE... I CAN HEAR KOGARASHI-DONO'S VOICE THROUGH THE BODY PILLOW?
?
NO, LISTEN TO ME. SUZUTSUKI TURNED ME...
OHH... I SEE!!

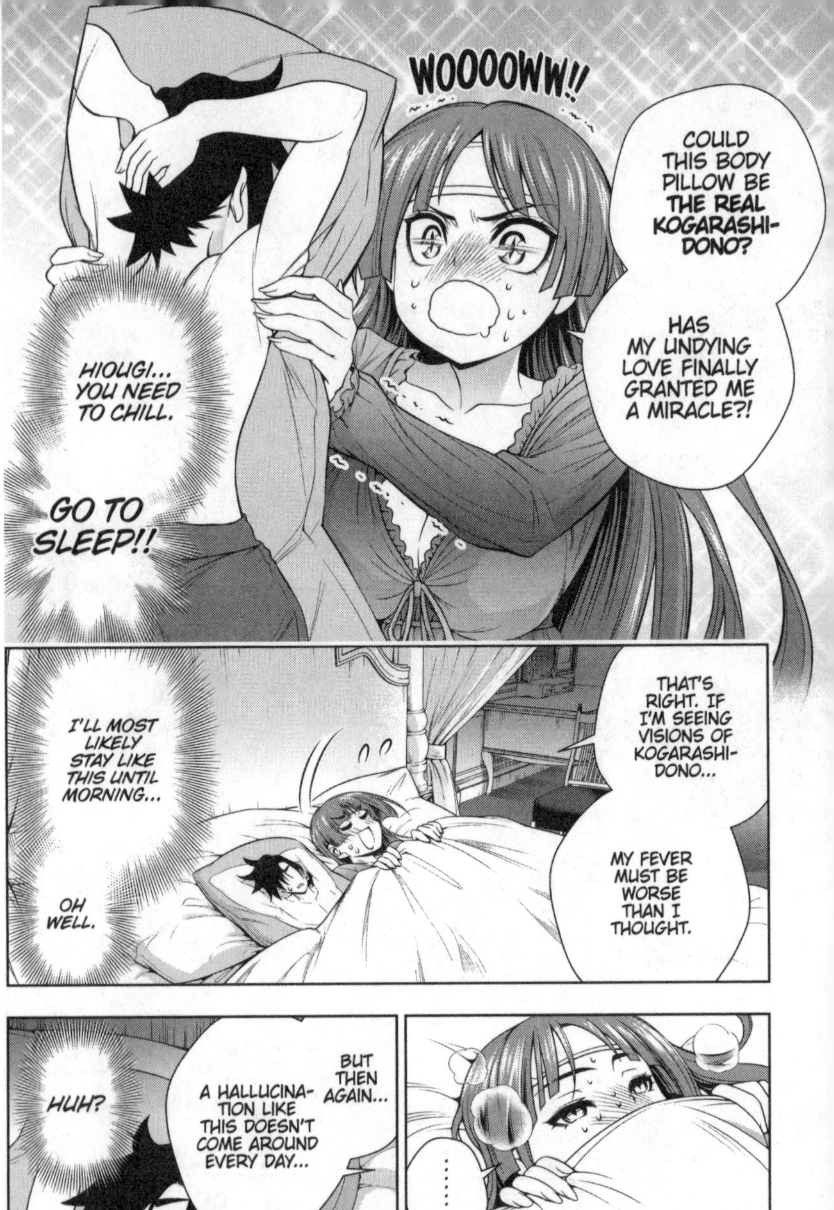
WOOOOWW!!
COULD THIS BODY PILLOW BE THE REAL KOGARASHI-DONO?
HAS MY UNDYING LOVE FINALLY GRANTED ME A MIRACLE?!
HIOUGI... YOU NEED TO CHILL.
GO TO SLEEP!!
THAT'S RIGHT. IF I'M SEEING VISIONS OF KOGARASHI-DONO...
MY FEVER MUST BE WORSE THAN I THOUGHT.
I'LL MOST LIKELY STAY LIKE THIS UNTIL MORNING...
OH WELL.
......
BUT THEN AGAIN...
A HALLUCINATION LIKE THIS DOESN'T COME AROUND EVERY DAY...
HUH?

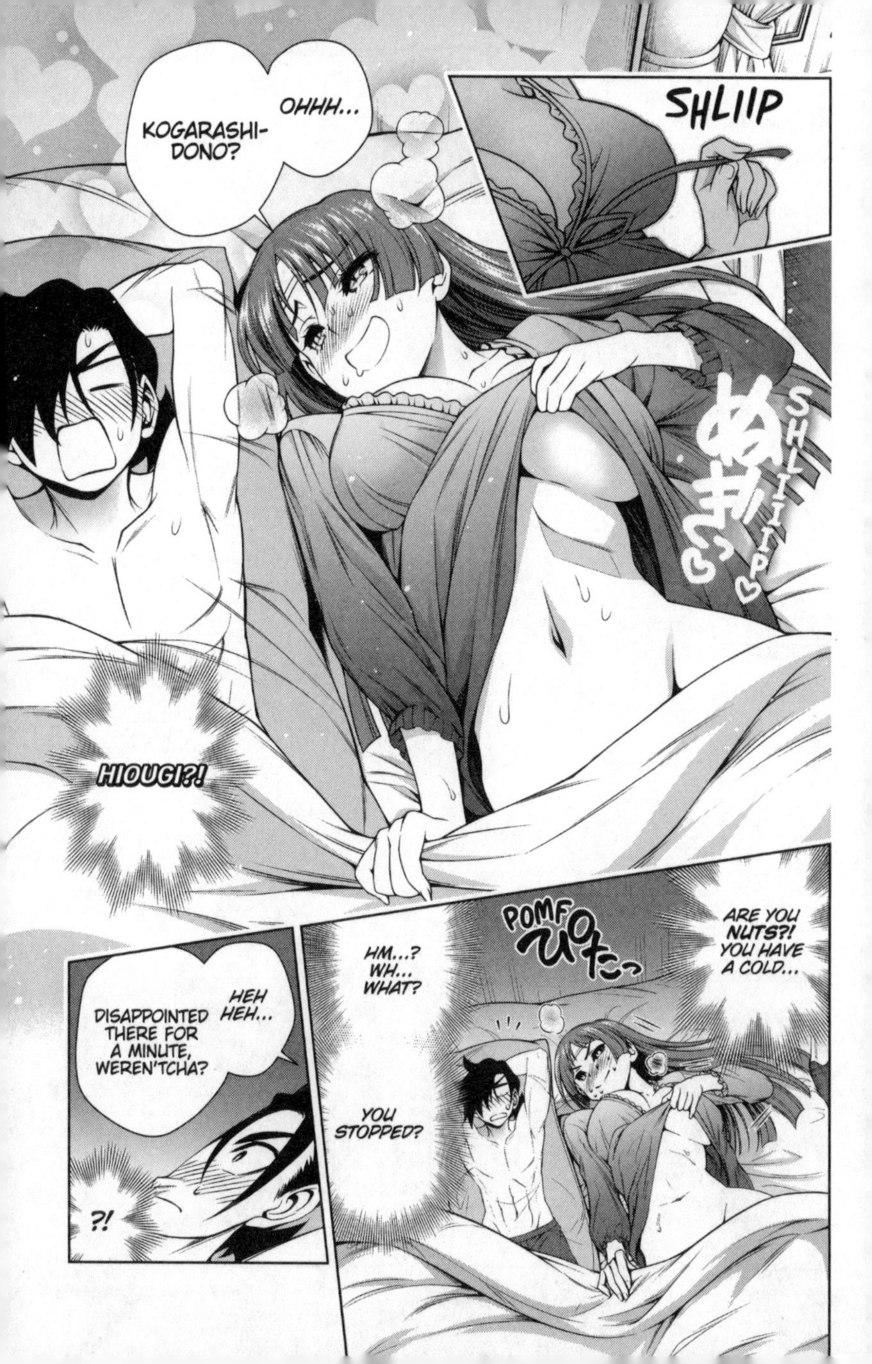
SHLIIP
OHHH... KOGARASHI-DONO?
SHLIIIP
HIOUGI?!
POMF
ぴたっ
ARE YOU NUTS?! YOU HAVE A COLD...
HM...? WH... WHAT?
YOU STOPPED?
HEH HEH... DISAPPOINTED THERE FOR A MINUTE, WEREN'TCHA?
?!

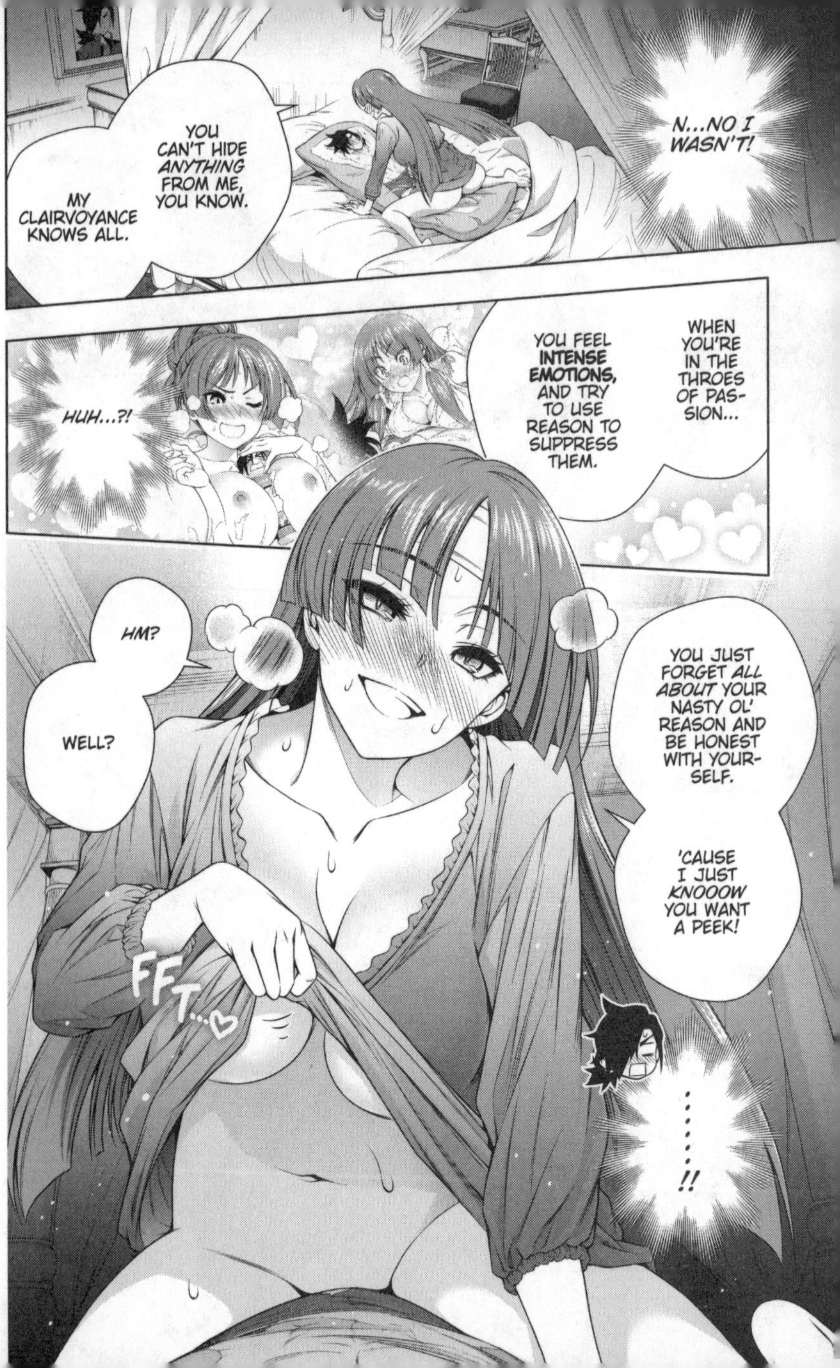
N...NO I WASN'T!
YOU CAN'T HIDE ANYTHING FROM ME, YOU KNOW.
MY CLAIRVOYANCE KNOWS ALL.
WHEN YOU'RE IN THE THROES OF PAS-SION...
YOU FEEL INTENSE EMOTIONS, AND TRY TO USE REASON TO SUPPRESS THEM.
HUH...?!
YOU JUST FORGET ALL ABOUT YOUR NASTY OL' REASON AND BE HONEST WITH YOUR-SELF.
HM?
WELL?
'CAUSE I JUST KNOOOW YOU WANT A PEEK!
FFT...♡
......!!

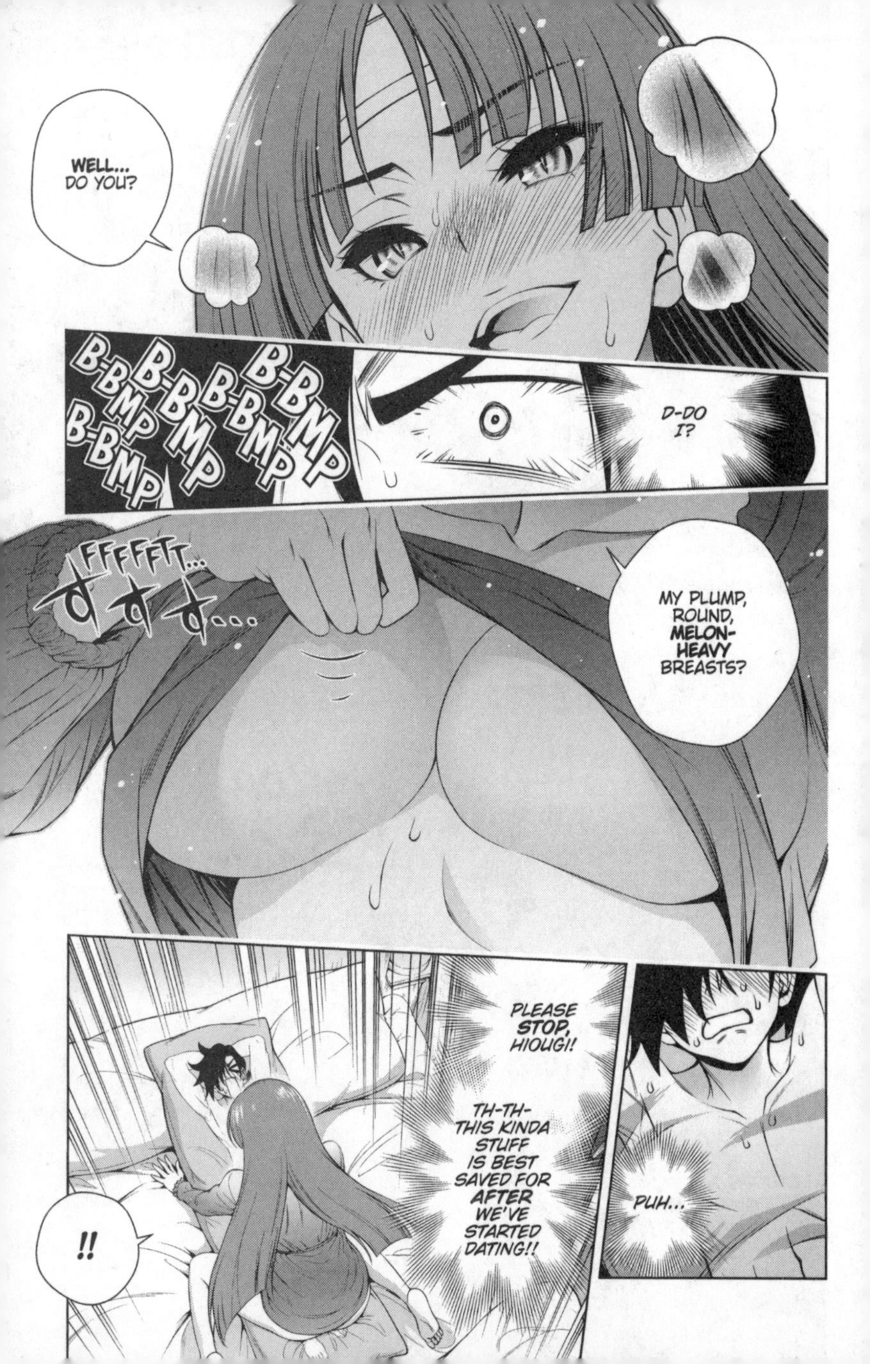
WELL... DO YOU?
D-DO I?
B-BMP B-BMP B-BMP B-BMP
MY PLUMP, ROUND, MELON-HEAVY BREASTS?
FFFFFT...
PUH...
PLEASE STOP, HIOUGI!
TH-TH-THIS KINDA STUFF IS BEST SAVED FOR AFTER WE'VE STARTED DATING!!
!!

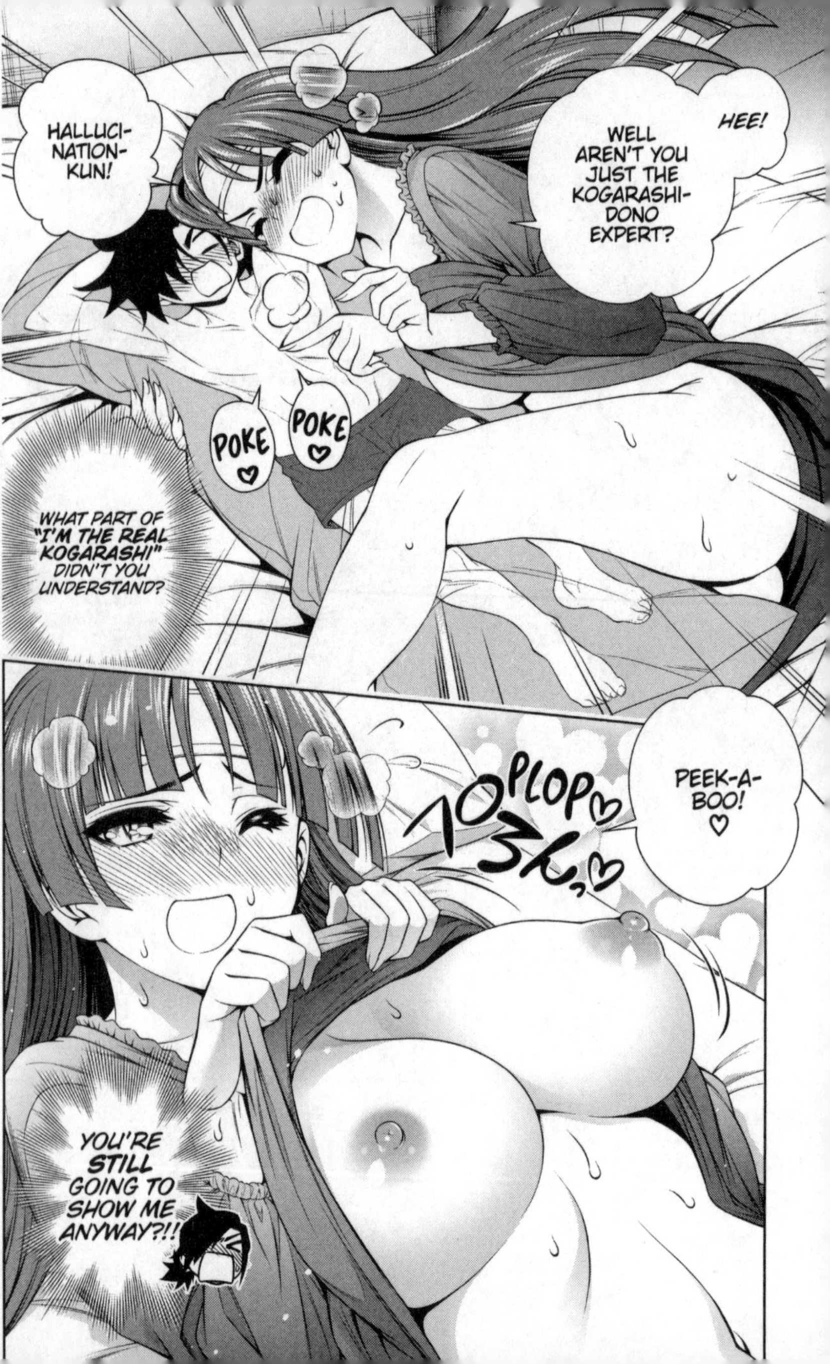
HEE!
WELL AREN'T YOU JUST THE KOGARASHI-DONO EXPERT?
HALLUCI-NATION-KUN!
POKE ♡
POKE ♡
WHAT PART OF "I'M THE REAL KOGARASHI" DIDN'T YOU UNDERSTAND?
PEEK-A-BOO! ♡
PLOP ♡
YOU'RE STILL GOING TO SHOW ME ANYWAY?!!

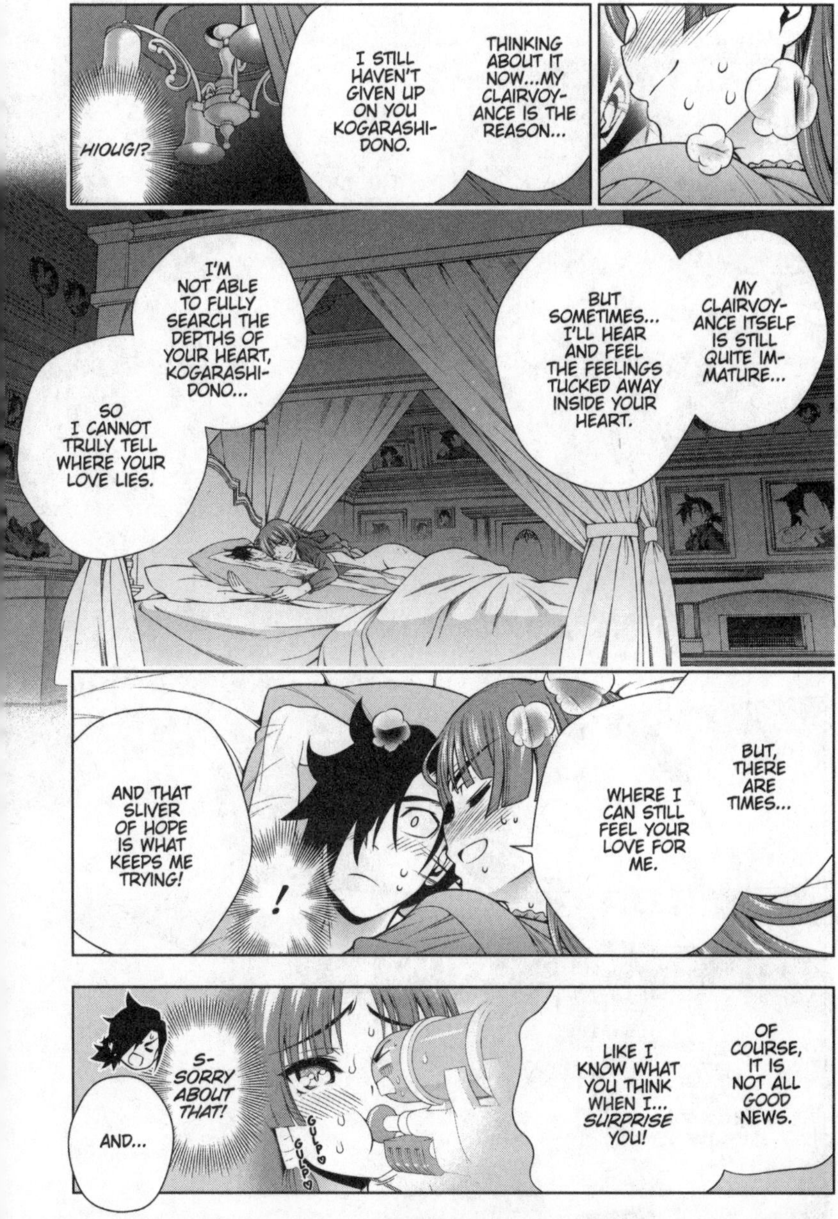
THINKING ABOUT IT NOW...MY CLAIRVOYANCE IS THE REASON...
I STILL HAVEN'T GIVEN UP ON YOU KOGARASHI-DONO.
HIOUGI!?
MY CLAIRVOYANCE ITSELF IS STILL QUITE IMMATURE...
BUT SOMETIMES... I'LL HEAR AND FEEL THE FEELINGS TUCKED AWAY INSIDE YOUR HEART.
I'M NOT ABLE TO FULLY SEARCH THE DEPTHS OF YOUR HEART, KOGARASHI-DONO...
SO I CANNOT TRULY TELL WHERE YOUR LOVE LIES.
BUT, THERE ARE TIMES...
WHERE I CAN STILL FEEL YOUR LOVE FOR ME.
!
AND THAT SLIVER OF HOPE IS WHAT KEEPS ME TRYING!
OF COURSE, IT IS NOT ALL GOOD NEWS.
LIKE I KNOW WHAT YOU THINK WHEN I... *SURPRISE* YOU!
GULP GULP♡
S-SORRY ABOUT THAT!
AND...

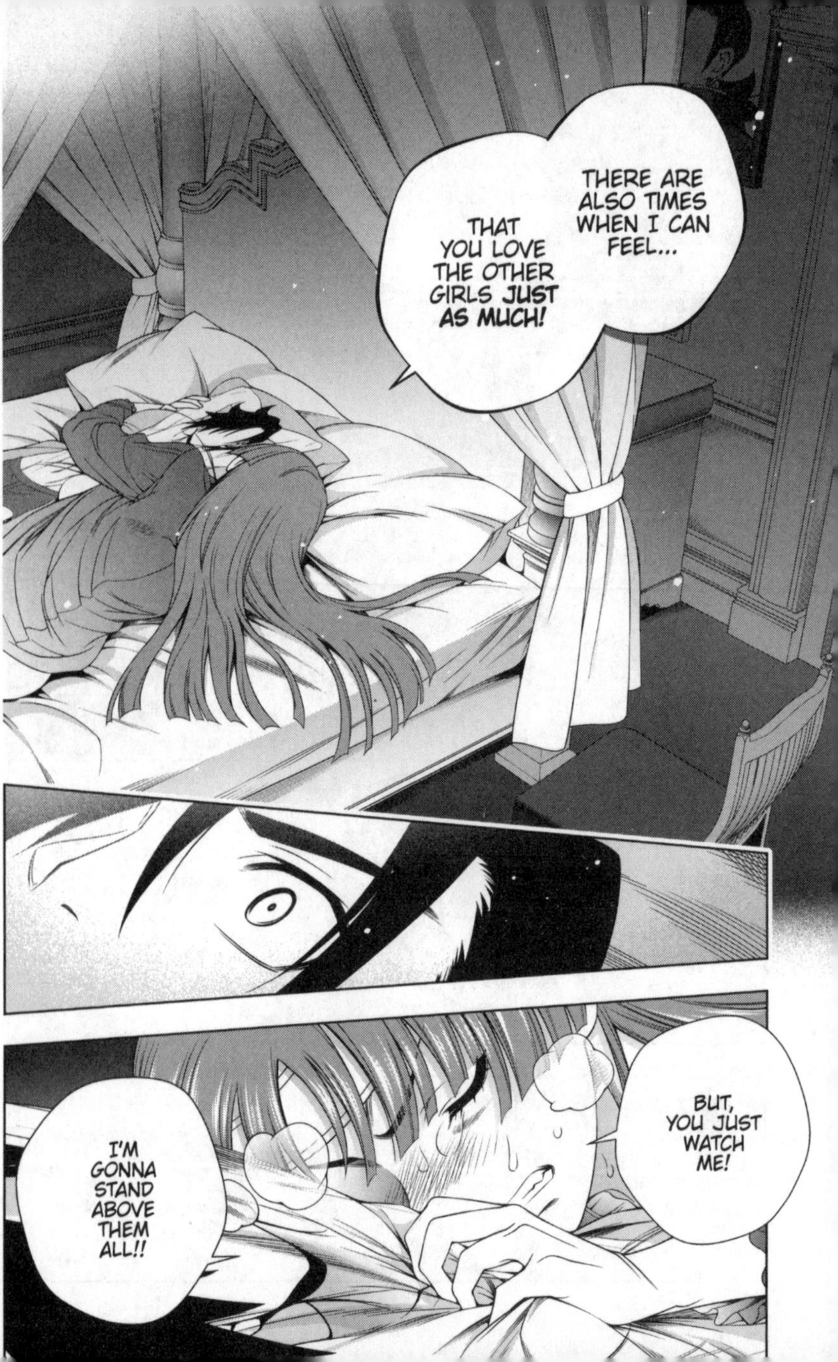
THERE ARE ALSO TIMES WHEN I CAN FEEL...
THAT YOU LOVE THE OTHER GIRLS **JUST AS MUCH!**
BUT, YOU JUST WATCH ME!
I'M GONNA STAND ABOVE THEM ALL!!

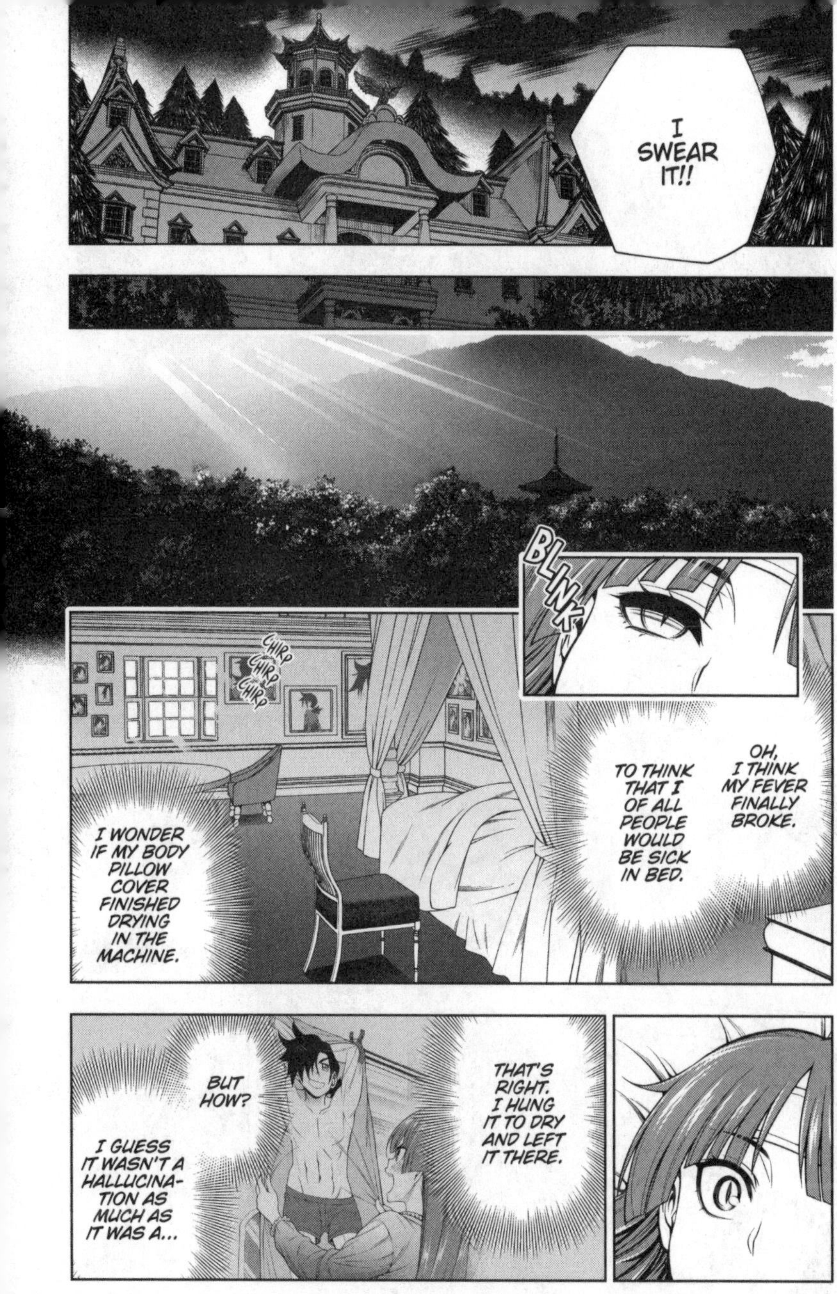
I SWEAR IT!!
BLINK
OH, I THINK MY FEVER FINALLY BROKE.
TO THINK THAT I OF ALL PEOPLE WOULD BE SICK IN BED.
CHIRP CHIRP CHIRP
I WONDER IF MY BODY PILLOW COVER FINISHED DRYING IN THE MACHINE.
THAT'S RIGHT. I HUNG IT TO DRY AND LEFT IT THERE.
BUT HOW?
I GUESS IT WASN'T A HALLUCINATION AS MUCH AS IT WAS A...

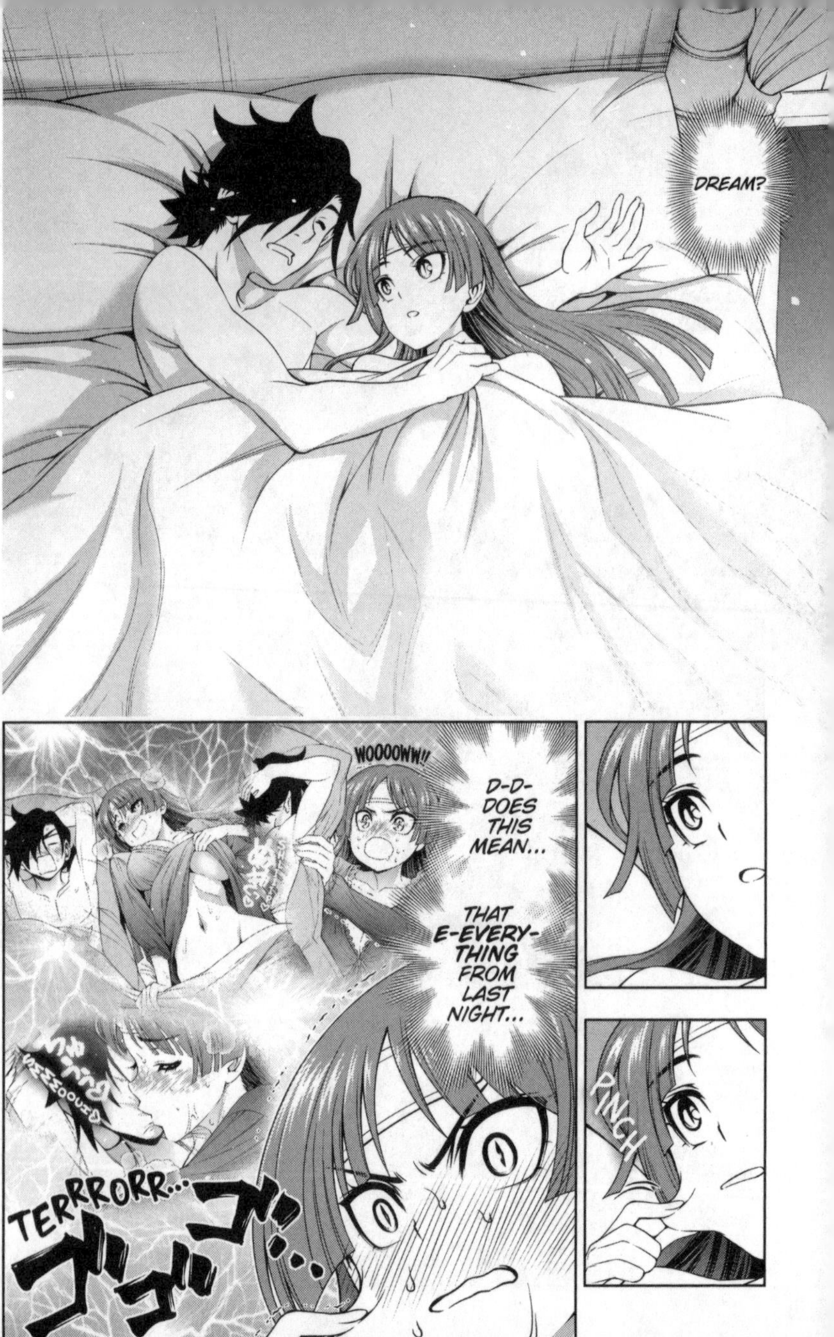
DREAM?
PINCH
WOOOOWW!!
D-D-DOES THIS MEAN...
THAT E-EVERYTHING FROM LAST NIGHT...
TERRRORR...

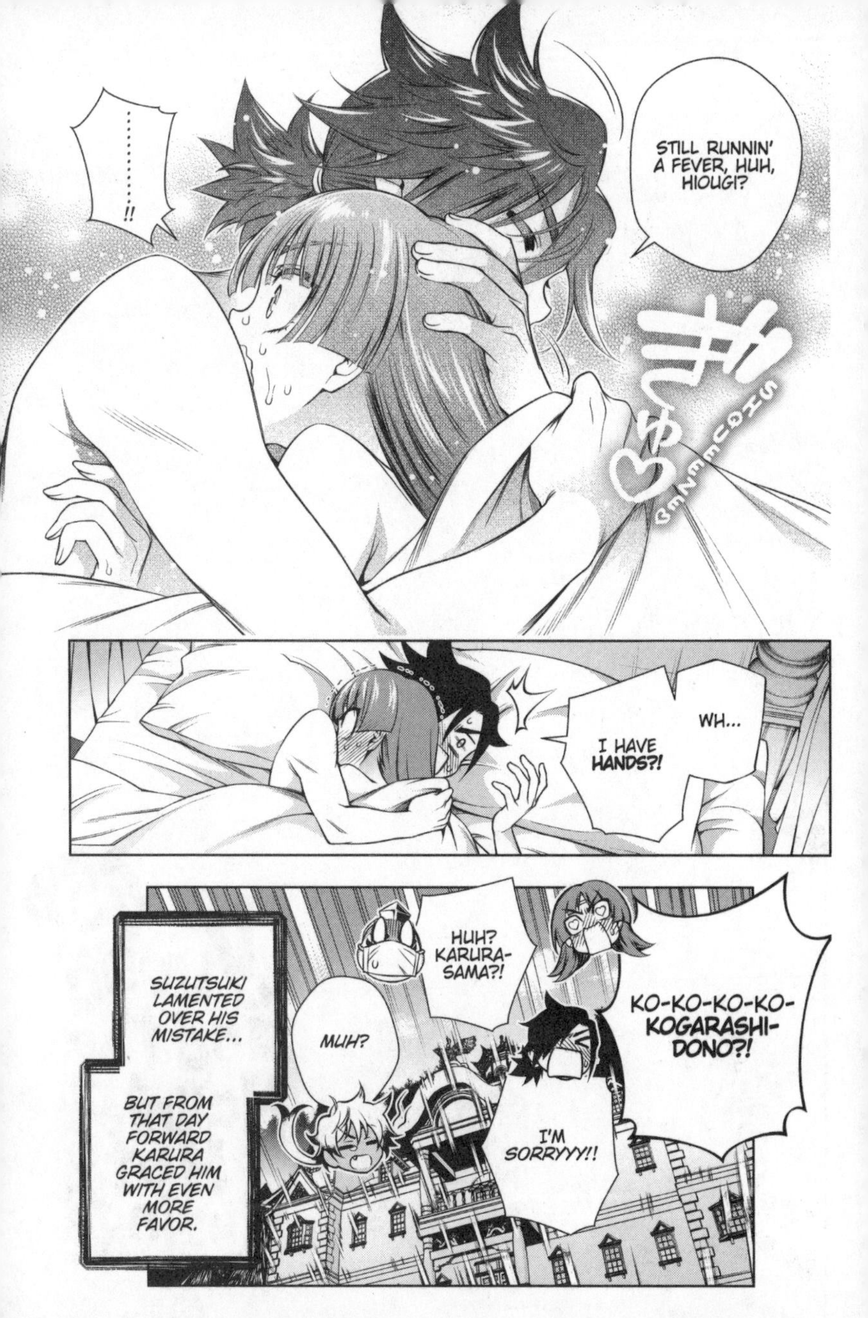
STILL RUNNIN' A FEVER, HUH, HIOUGI?
ぎゅ♡
SQUEEZE
......!!
WH...
I HAVE HANDS?!
KO-KO-KO-KO-KOGARASHI-DONO?!
HUH? KARURA-SAMA?!
I'M SORRYYY!!
MUH?
SUZUTSUKI LAMENTED OVER HIS MISTAKE...
BUT FROM THAT DAY FORWARD KARURA GRACED HIM WITH EVEN MORE FAVOR.

Yuuna and the Haunted Hot Springs

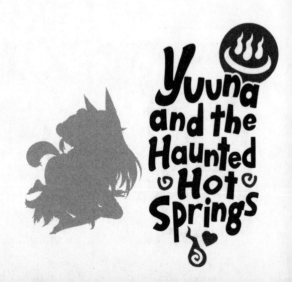

172 Yuuna's Macho Man Transformation

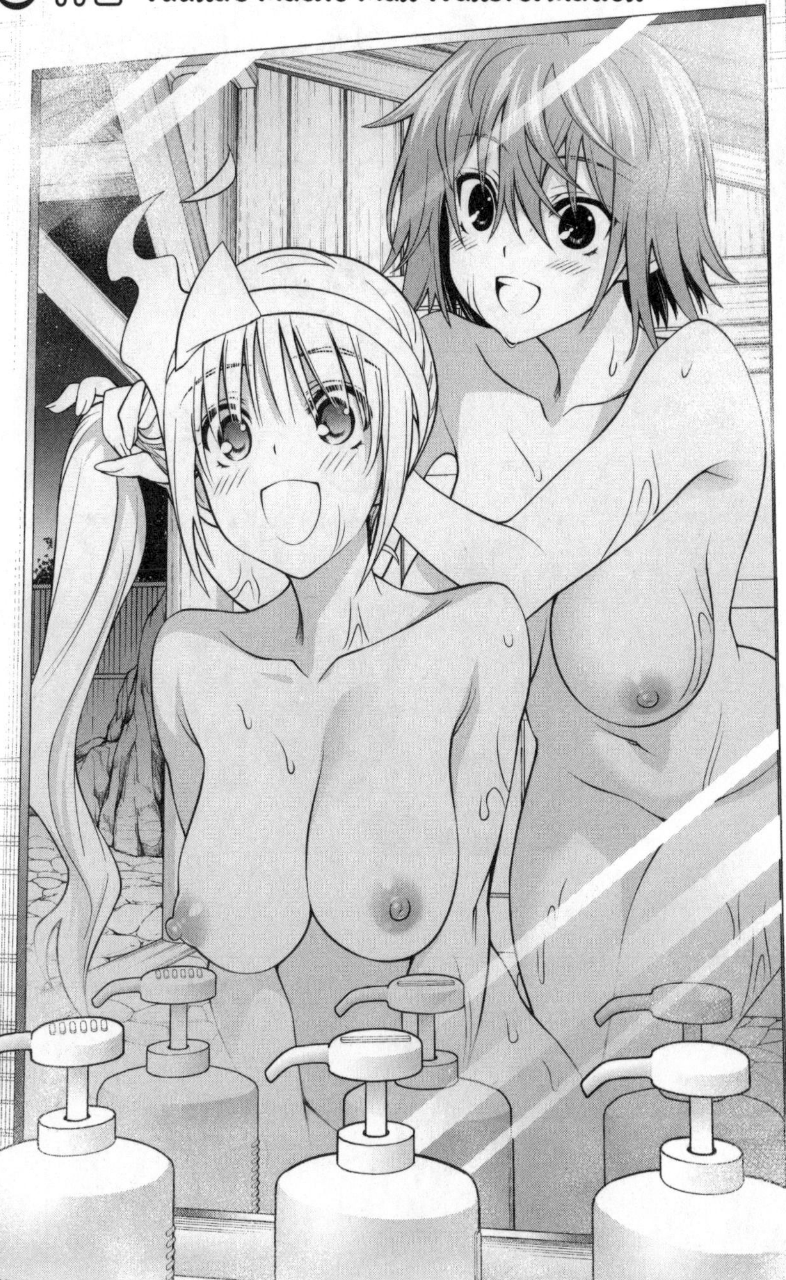

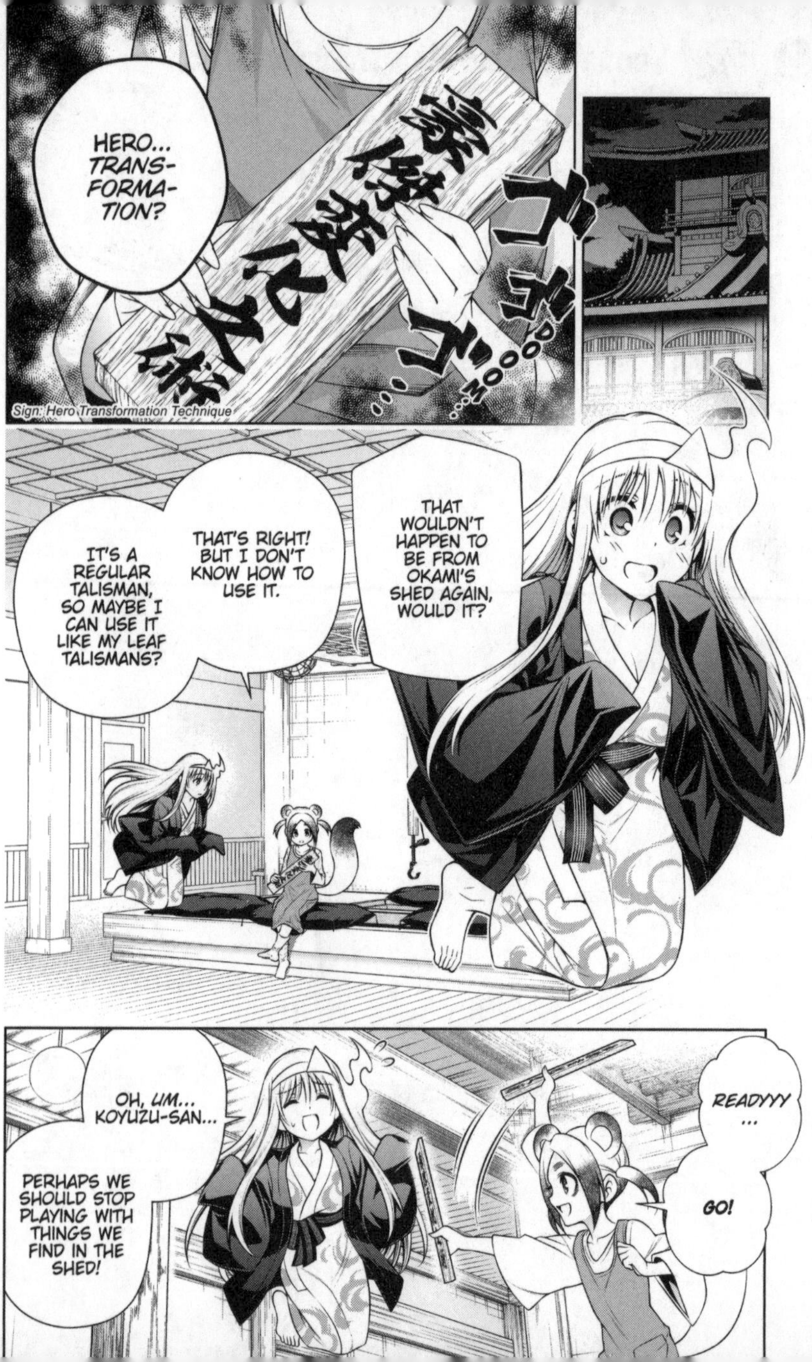

ゴゴゴ
DOOOM...
豪傑変化ノ術
Sign: Hero Transformation Technique
HERO... TRANS- FORMA- TION?
THAT WOULDN'T HAPPEN TO BE FROM OKAMI'S SHED AGAIN, WOULD IT?
THAT'S RIGHT! BUT I DON'T KNOW HOW TO USE IT.
IT'S A REGULAR TALISMAN, SO MAYBE I CAN USE IT LIKE MY LEAF TALISMANS?
READYYY ...
GO!
OH, UM... KOYUZU-SAN...
PERHAPS WE SHOULD STOP PLAYING WITH THINGS WE FIND IN THE SHED!

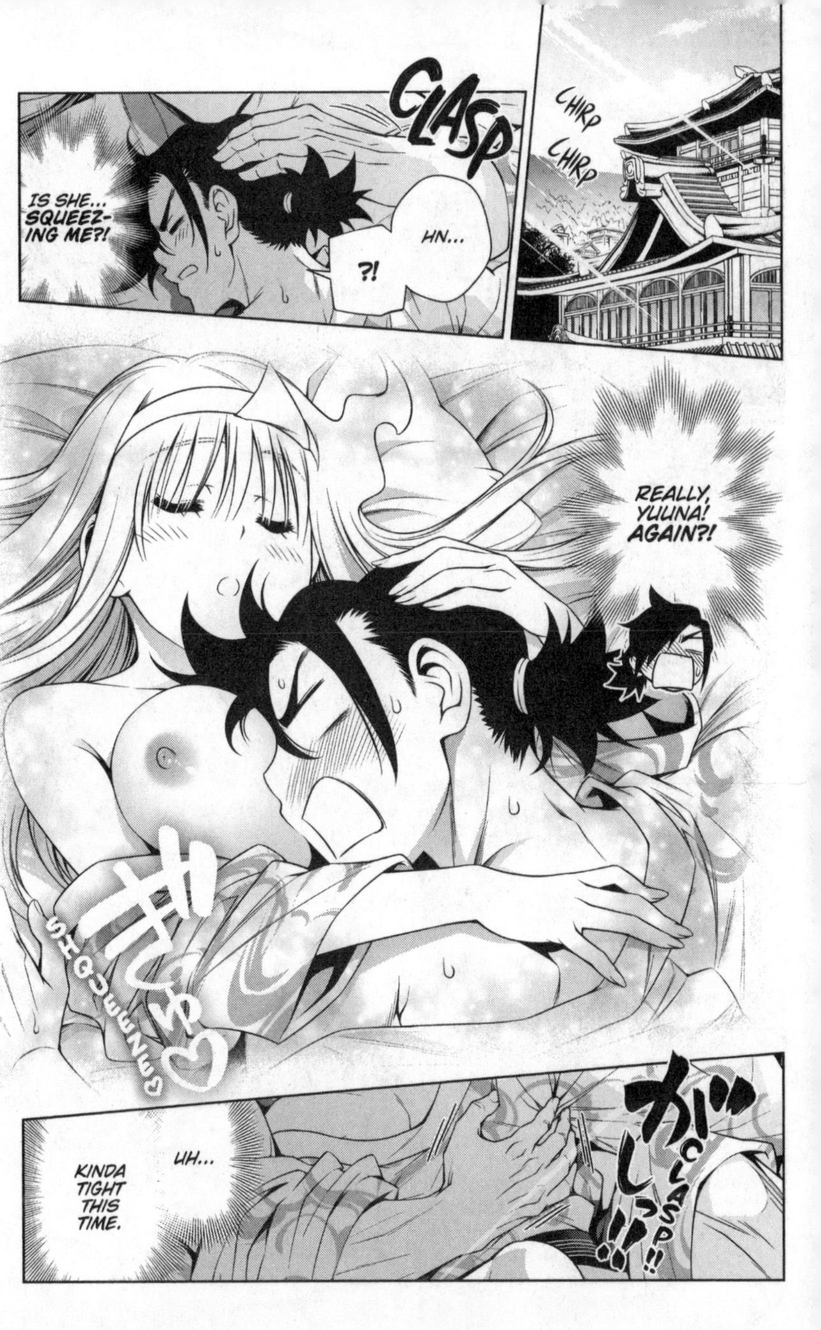
CHIRP
CHIRP
CLASP
HN...
?!
IS SHE... SQUEEZ-ING ME?!
REALLY, YUUNA! AGAIN?!
SQUEEEZE♡
CLASP!!
UH...
KINDA TIGHT THIS TIME.

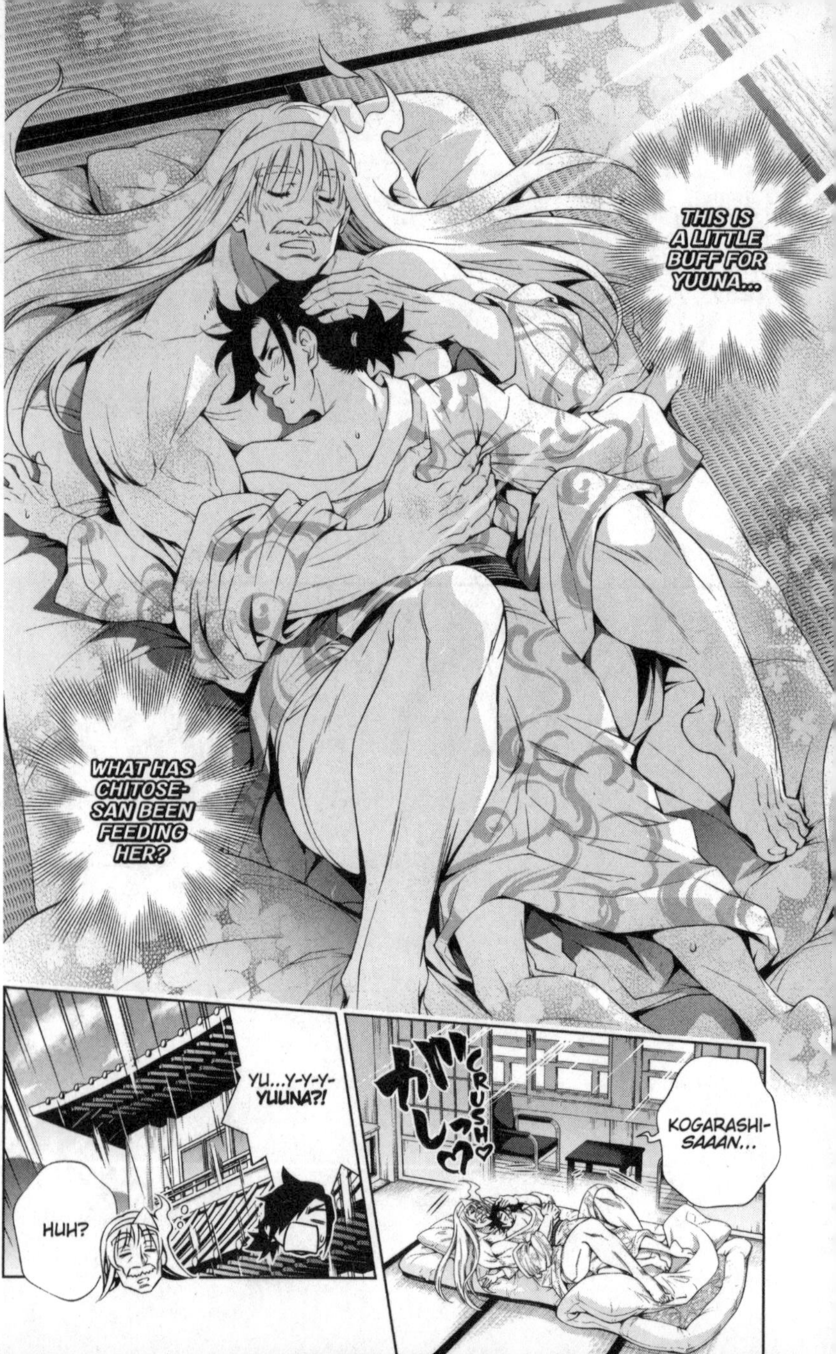
THIS IS A LITTLE BUFF FOR YUUNA...
WHAT HAS CHITOSE-SAN BEEN FEEDING HER?
KOGARASHI-SAAAN...
CRUSH♥
YU...Y-Y-Y-YUUNA?!
HUH?

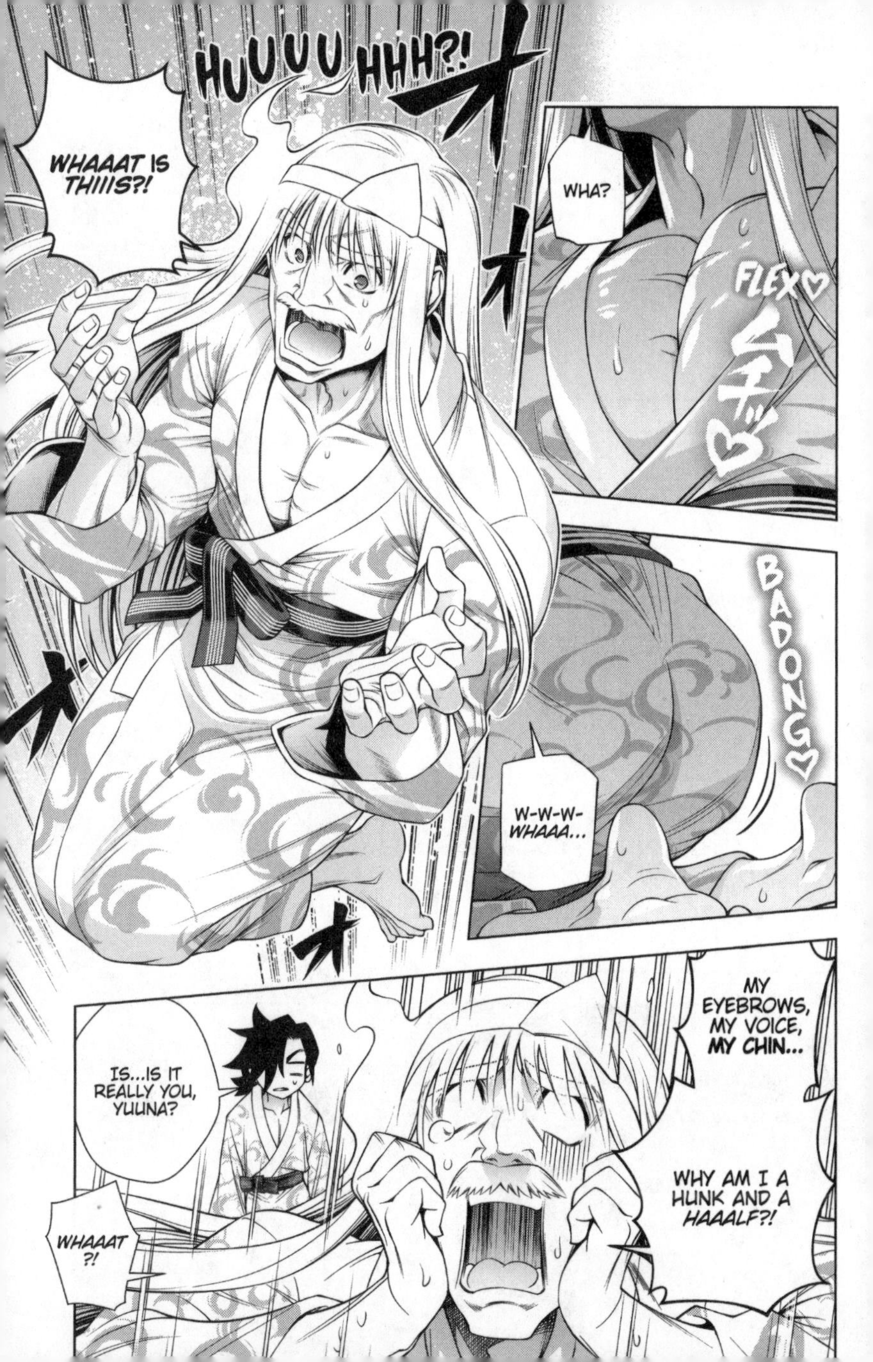
WHA?
FLEX♡
ムチッ♡
BADONG♡
W-W-W-WHAAA...
HUUUUHHH?!
WHAAAT IS THIIIS?!
MY EYEBROWS, MY VOICE, MY CHIN...
WHY AM I A HUNK AND A HAAALF?!
IS...IS IT REALLY YOU, YUUNA?
WHAAAT ?!

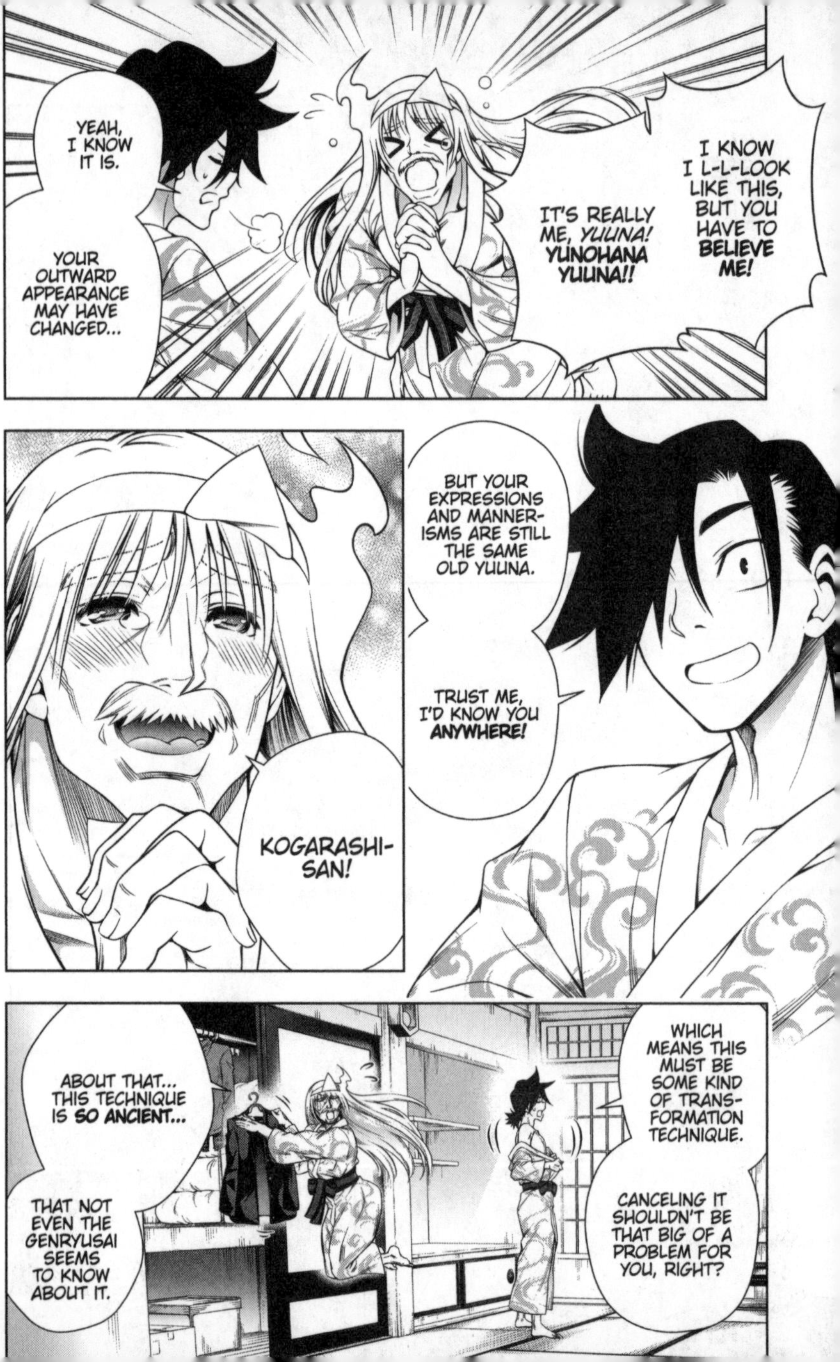
I KNOW I L-L-LOOK LIKE THIS, BUT YOU HAVE TO **BELIEVE ME!**
IT'S REALLY ME, *YUUNA!* **YUNOHANA YUUNA!!**
YEAH, I KNOW IT IS.
YOUR OUTWARD APPEARANCE MAY HAVE CHANGED...
BUT YOUR EXPRESSIONS AND MANNERISMS ARE STILL THE SAME OLD YUUNA.
TRUST ME, I'D KNOW YOU **ANYWHERE!**
KOGARASHI-SAN!
WHICH MEANS THIS MUST BE SOME KIND OF TRANSFORMATION TECHNIQUE.
CANCELING IT SHOULDN'T BE THAT BIG OF A PROBLEM FOR YOU, RIGHT?
ABOUT THAT... THIS TECHNIQUE IS **SO ANCIENT...**
THAT NOT EVEN THE GENRYUSAI SEEMS TO KNOW ABOUT IT.

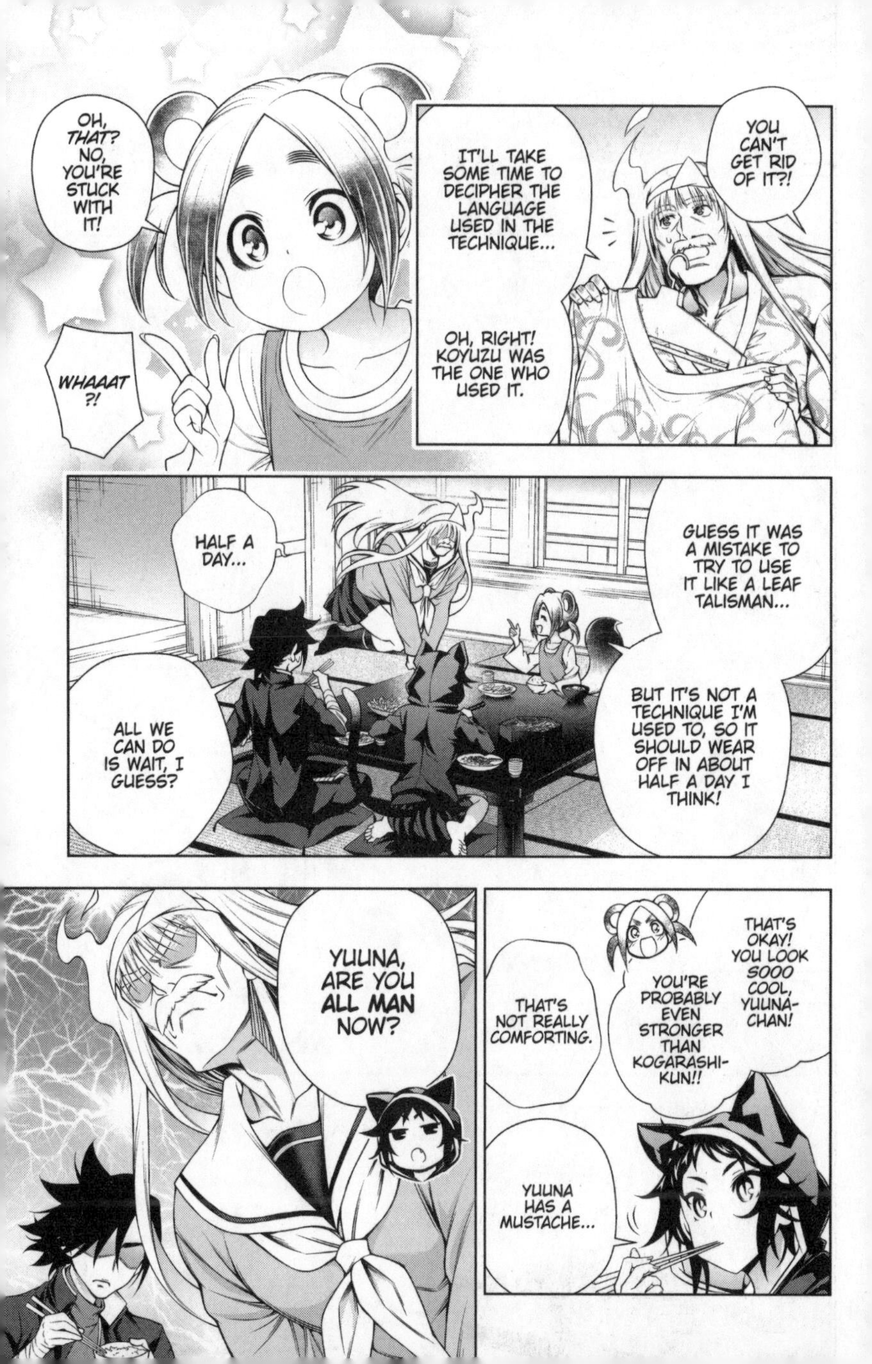
YOU CAN'T GET RID OF IT?!
IT'LL TAKE SOME TIME TO DECIPHER THE LANGUAGE USED IN THE TECHNIQUE...
OH, RIGHT! KOYUZU WAS THE ONE WHO USED IT.
OH, *THAT*? NO, YOU'RE STUCK WITH IT!
WHAAAT ?!
GUESS IT WAS A MISTAKE TO TRY TO USE IT LIKE A LEAF TALISMAN...
BUT IT'S NOT A TECHNIQUE I'M USED TO, SO IT SHOULD WEAR OFF IN ABOUT HALF A DAY I THINK!
HALF A DAY...
ALL WE CAN DO IS WAIT, I GUESS?
THAT'S OKAY! YOU LOOK SOOO COOL, YUUNA-CHAN!
YOU'RE PROBABLY EVEN STRONGER THAN KOGARASHI-KUN!!
THAT'S NOT REALLY COMFORTING.
YUUNA HAS A MUSTACHE...
YUUNA, ARE YOU ALL MAN NOW?

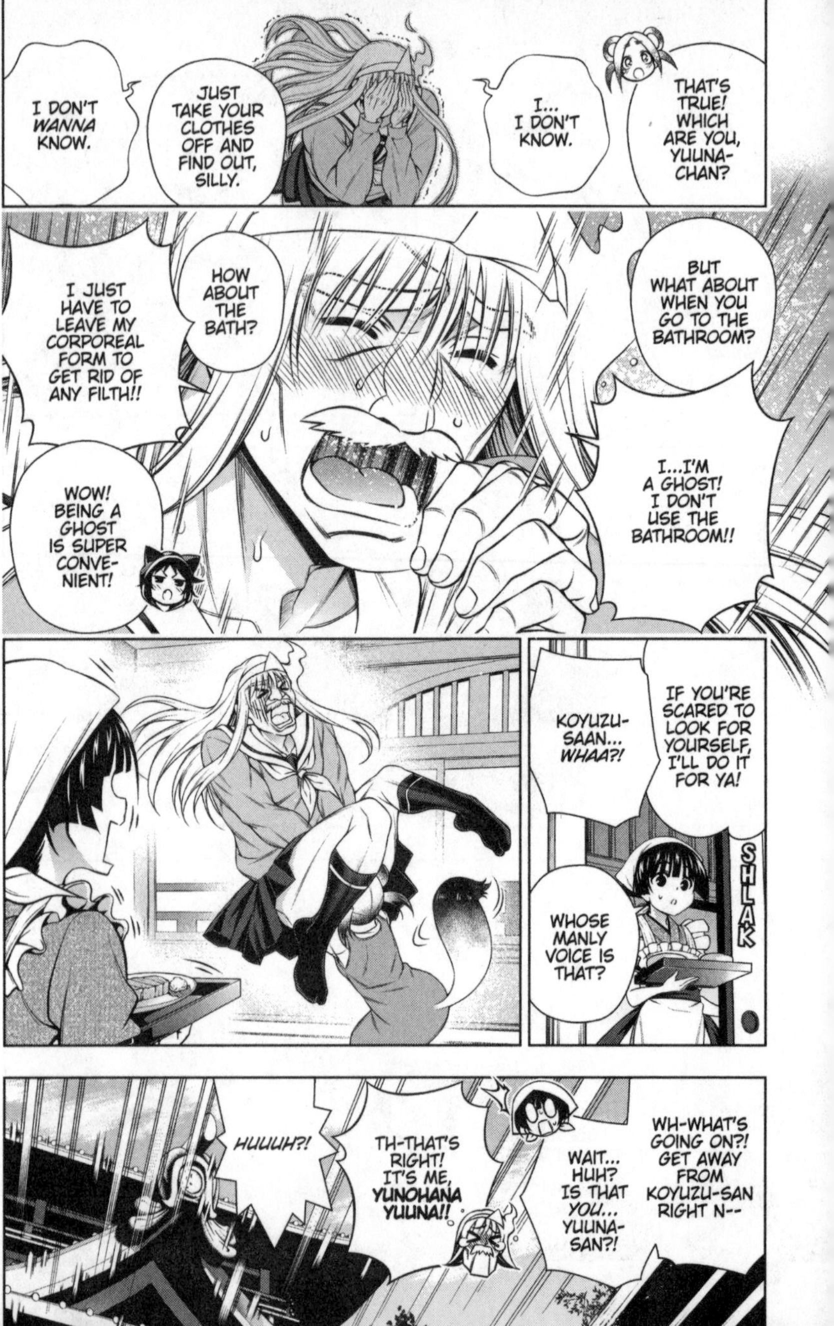
THAT'S TRUE! WHICH ARE YOU, YUUNA-CHAN?
I... I DON'T KNOW.
JUST TAKE YOUR CLOTHES OFF AND FIND OUT, SILLY.
I DON'T *WANNA* KNOW.
BUT WHAT ABOUT WHEN YOU GO TO THE BATHROOM?
I...I'M A GHOST! I DON'T USE THE BATHROOM!!
HOW ABOUT THE BATH?
I JUST HAVE TO LEAVE MY CORPOREAL FORM TO GET RID OF ANY FILTH!!
WOW! BEING A GHOST IS SUPER CONVENIENT!
IF YOU'RE SCARED TO LOOK FOR YOURSELF, I'LL DO IT FOR YA!
KOYUZU-SAAN... *WHAA?!*
SHLAK
WHOSE MANLY VOICE IS THAT?
WH-WHAT'S GOING ON?! GET AWAY FROM KOYUZU-SAN RIGHT N--
WAIT... HUH? IS THAT *YOU*... YUUNA-SAN?!
TH-THAT'S RIGHT! IT'S ME, **YUNOHANA YUUNA!!**
HUUUH?!

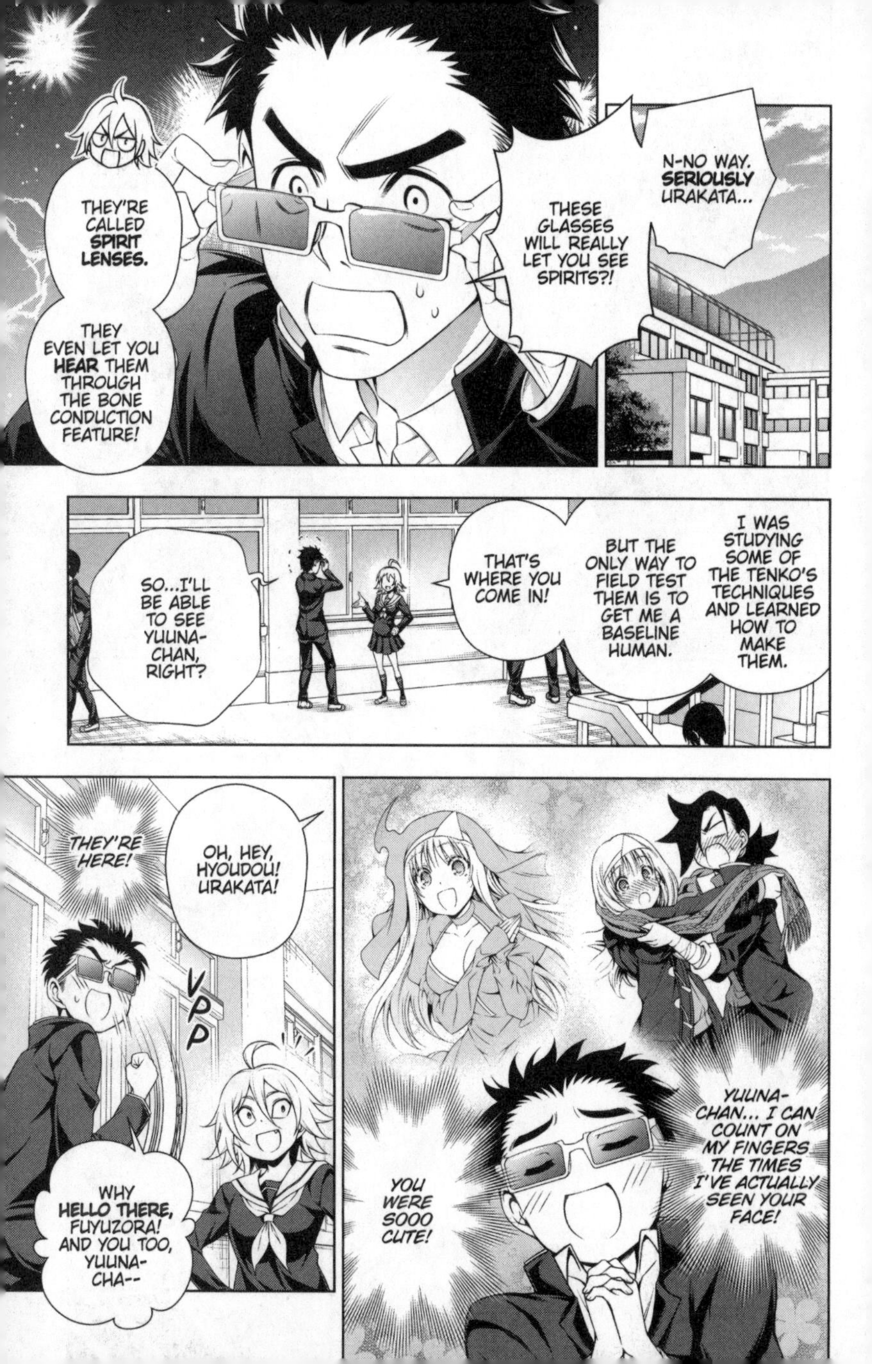
N-NO WAY. SERIOUSLY URAKATA...
THESE GLASSES WILL REALLY LET YOU SEE SPIRITS?!
THEY'RE CALLED SPIRIT LENSES.
THEY EVEN LET YOU HEAR THEM THROUGH THE BONE CONDUCTION FEATURE!
I WAS STUDYING SOME OF THE TENKO'S TECHNIQUES AND LEARNED HOW TO MAKE THEM.
BUT THE ONLY WAY TO FIELD TEST THEM IS TO GET ME A BASELINE HUMAN.
THAT'S WHERE YOU COME IN!
SO...I'LL BE ABLE TO SEE YUUNA-CHAN, RIGHT?
YUUNA-CHAN... I CAN COUNT ON MY FINGERS THE TIMES I'VE ACTUALLY SEEN YOUR FACE!
YOU WERE SOOO CUTE!
OH, HEY, HYOUDOU! URAKATA!
THEY'RE HERE!
VPP
WHY HELLO THERE, FUYUZORA! AND YOU TOO, YUUNA-CHA--

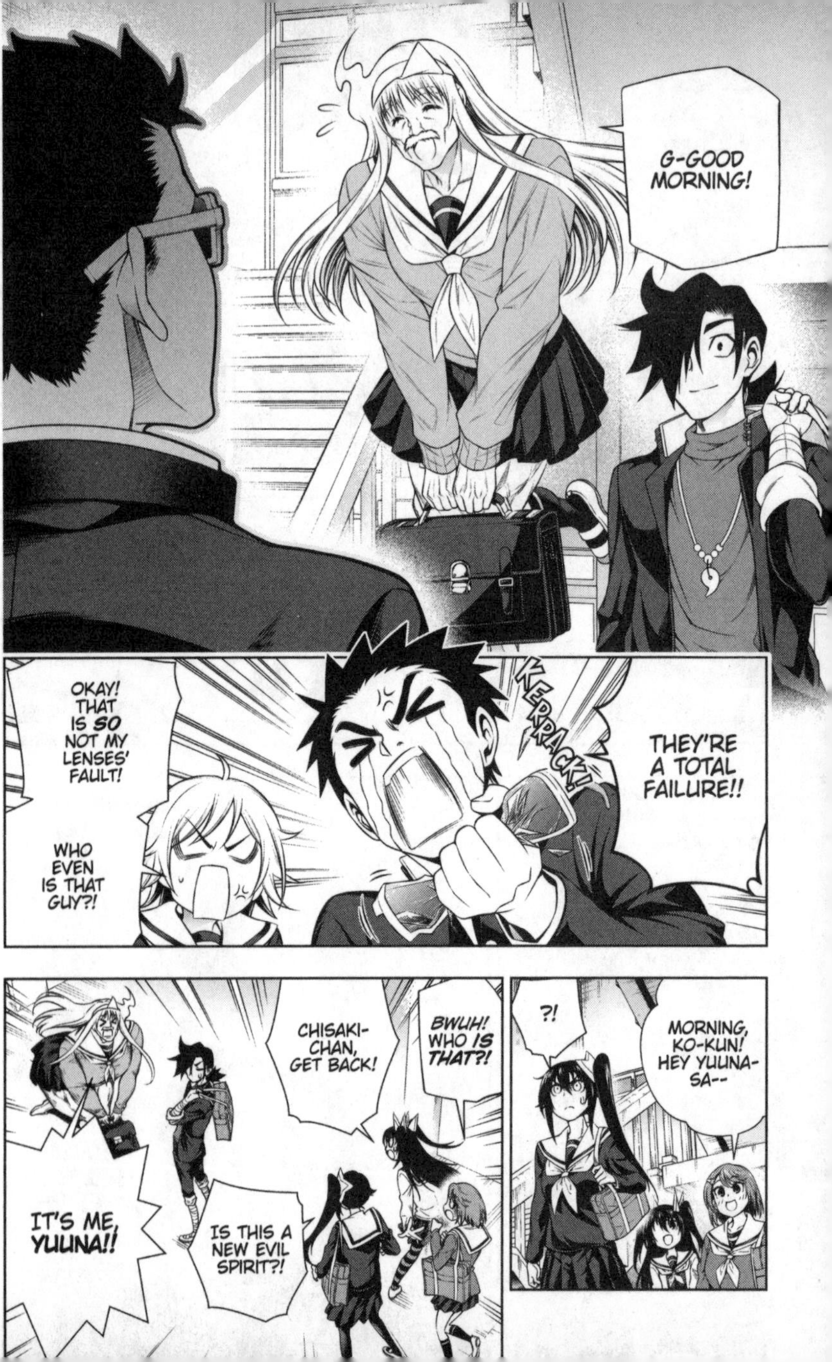
G-GOOD MORNING!
THEY'RE A TOTAL FAILURE!!
KERPACK!
OKAY! THAT IS **SO** NOT MY LENSES' FAULT!
WHO EVEN IS THAT GUY?!
MORNING, KO-KUN! HEY YUUNA-SA--
?!
BWUH! WHO **IS** **THAT?!**
CHISAKI-CHAN, GET BACK!
IS THIS A NEW EVIL SPIRIT?!
IT'S ME, YUUNA!!

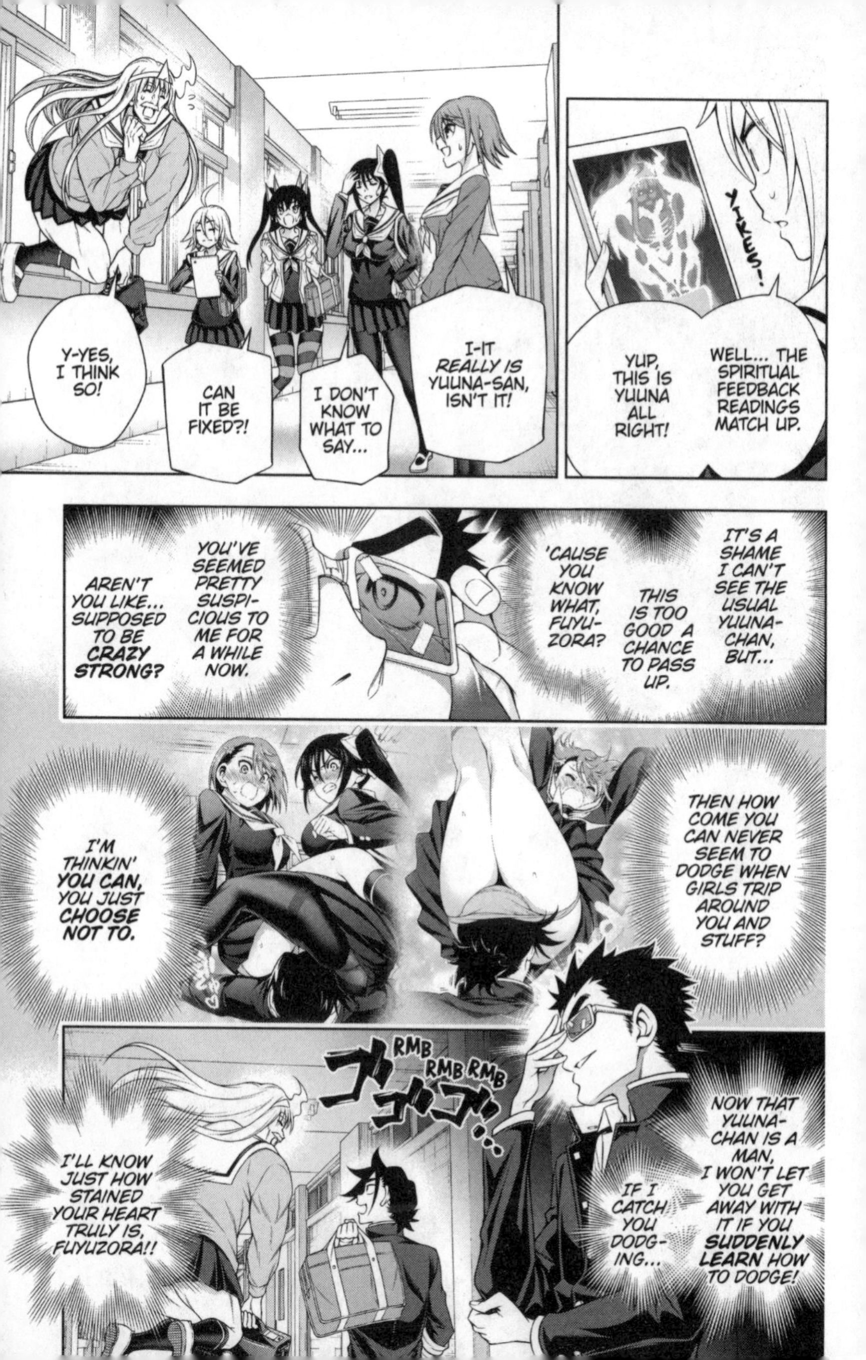
YIKES!
WELL... THE SPIRITUAL FEEDBACK READINGS MATCH UP.
YUP, THIS IS YUUNA ALL RIGHT!
I-IT REALLY IS YUUNA-SAN, ISN'T IT!
I DON'T KNOW WHAT TO SAY...
CAN IT BE FIXED?!
Y-YES, I THINK SO!
IT'S A SHAME I CAN'T SEE THE USUAL YUUNA-CHAN, BUT...
THIS IS TOO GOOD A CHANCE TO PASS UP.
'CAUSE YOU KNOW WHAT, FUYUZORA?
YOU'VE SEEMED PRETTY SUSPICIOUS TO ME FOR A WHILE NOW.
AREN'T YOU LIKE... SUPPOSED TO BE CRAZY STRONG?
THEN HOW COME YOU CAN NEVER SEEM TO DODGE WHEN GIRLS TRIP AROUND YOU AND STUFF?
I'M THINKIN' YOU CAN, YOU JUST CHOOSE NOT TO.
NOW THAT YUUNA-CHAN IS A MAN, I WON'T LET YOU GET AWAY WITH IT IF YOU SUDDENLY LEARN HOW TO DODGE!
RMB RMB RMB
IF I CATCH YOU DODGING...
I'LL KNOW JUST HOW STAINED YOUR HEART TRULY IS, FUYUZORA!!

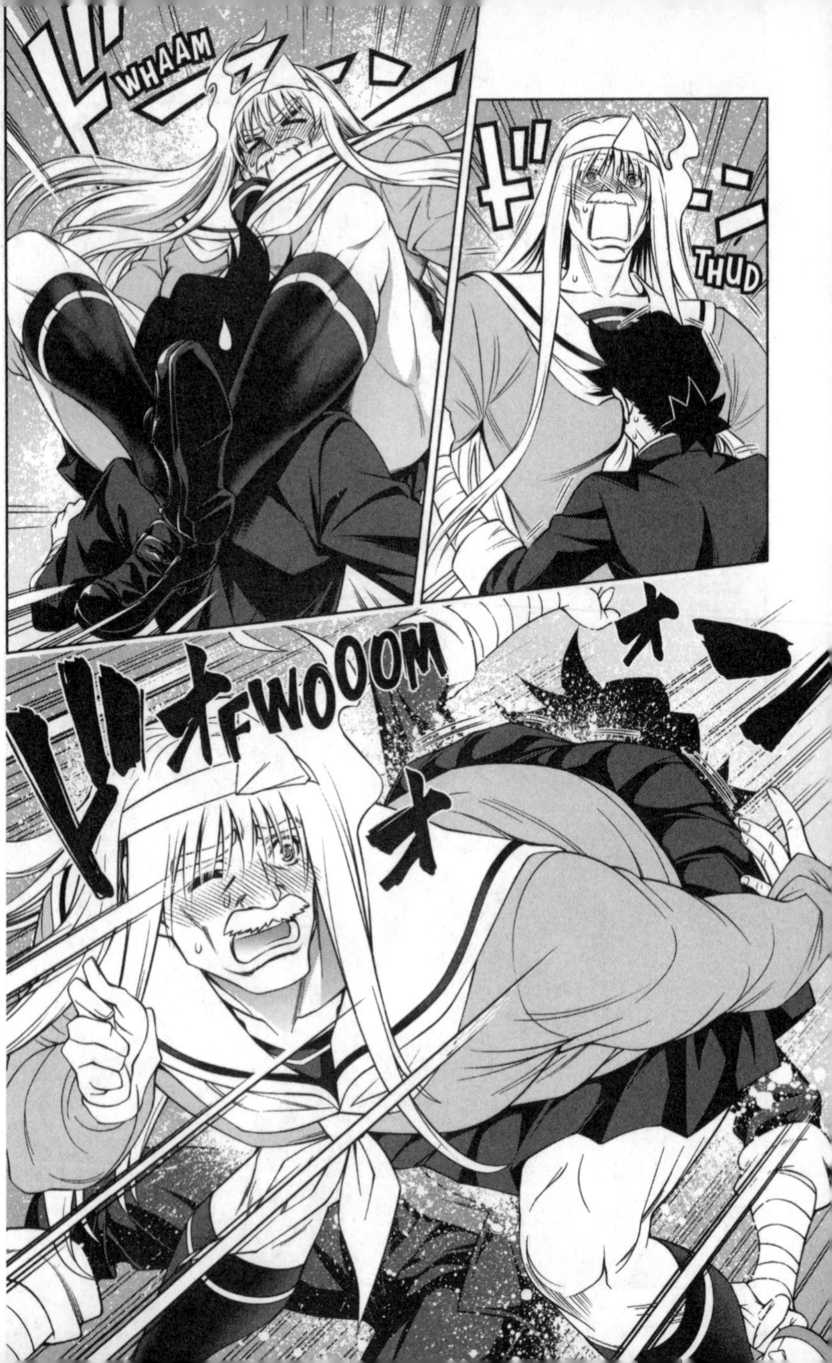
THUD
WHAAM
FWOOOM

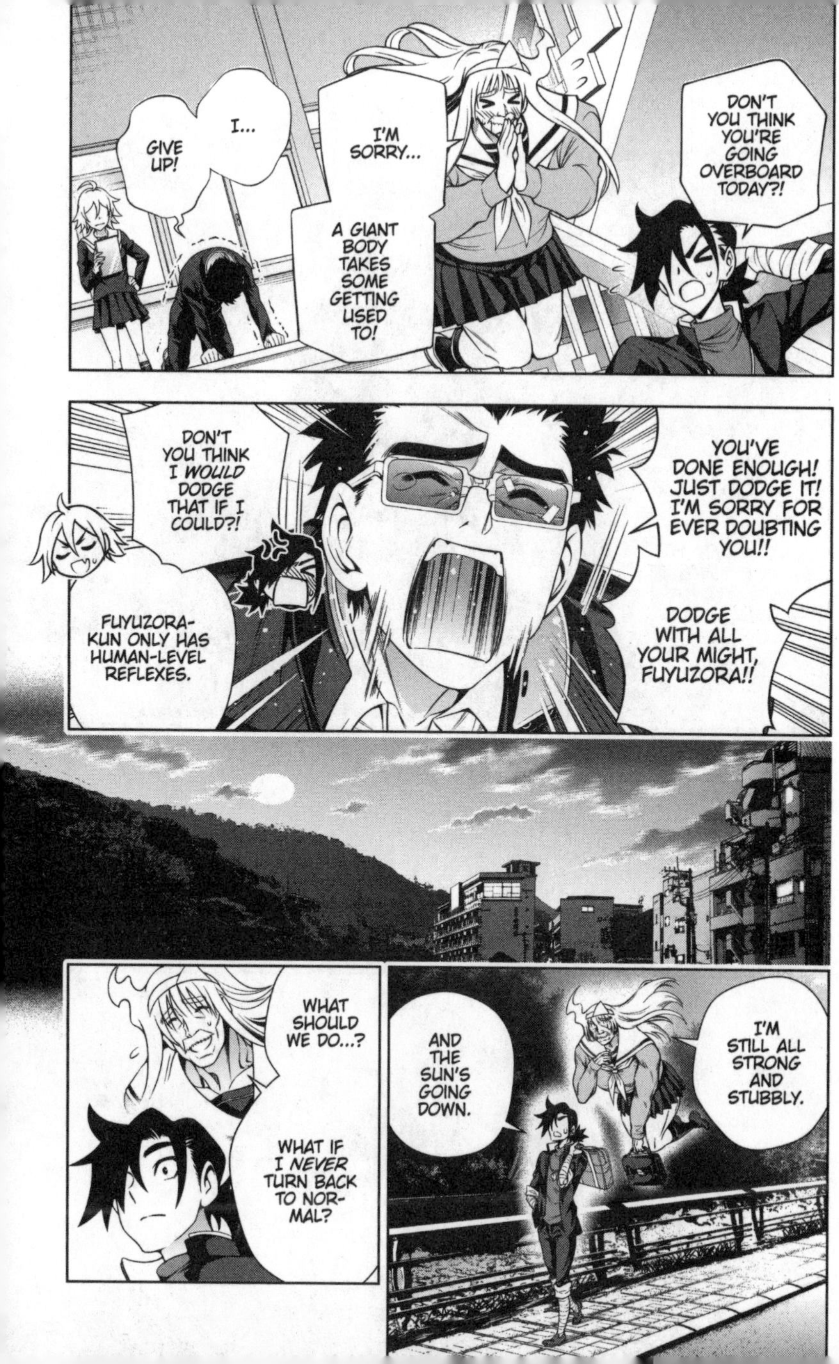
DON'T YOU THINK YOU'RE GOING OVERBOARD TODAY?!
I'M SORRY...
A GIANT BODY TAKES SOME GETTING USED TO!
I...
GIVE UP!
YOU'VE DONE ENOUGH! JUST DODGE IT! I'M SORRY FOR EVER DOUBTING YOU!!
DODGE WITH ALL YOUR MIGHT, FUYUZORA!!
DON'T YOU THINK I *WOULD* DODGE THAT IF I COULD?!
FUYUZORA-KUN ONLY HAS HUMAN-LEVEL REFLEXES.
I'M STILL ALL STRONG AND STUBBLY.
AND THE SUN'S GOING DOWN.
WHAT SHOULD WE DO...?
WHAT IF I *NEVER* TURN BACK TO NOR-MAL?

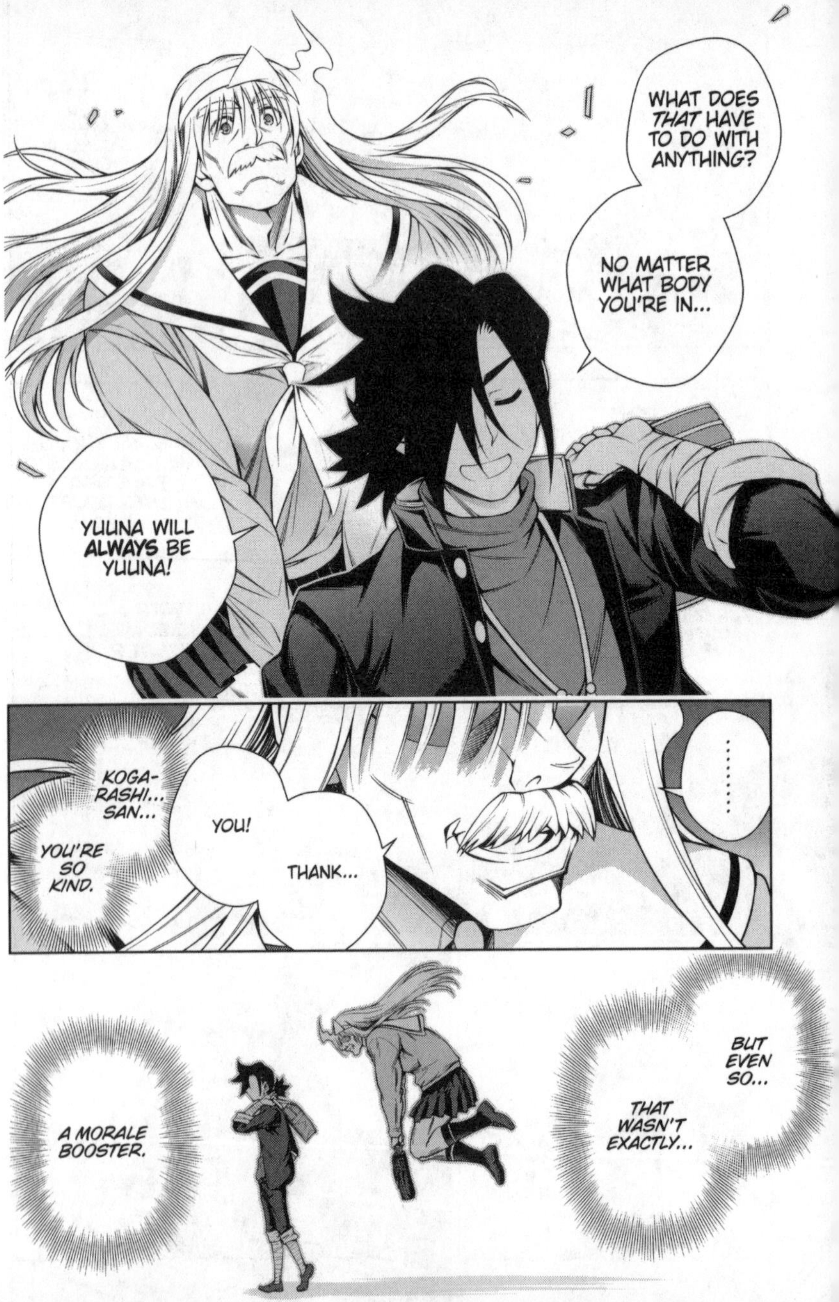
WHAT DOES THAT HAVE TO DO WITH ANYTHING?
NO MATTER WHAT BODY YOU'RE IN...
YUUNA WILL ALWAYS BE YUUNA!
......
THANK... YOU!
KOGA-RASHI... SAN...
YOU'RE SO KIND.
BUT EVEN SO...
THAT WASN'T EXACTLY...
A MORALE BOOSTER.

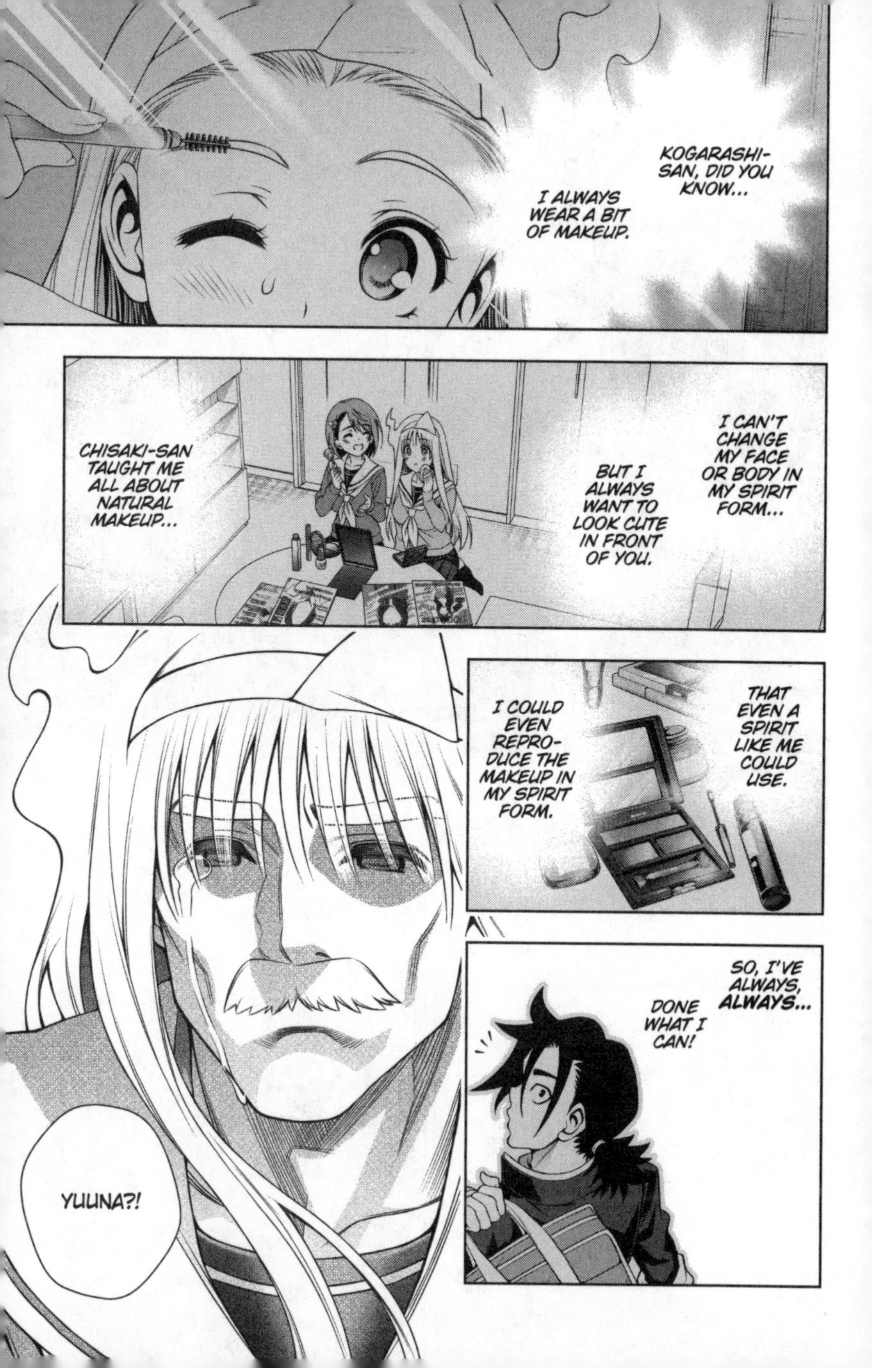
KOGARASHI-SAN, DID YOU KNOW...
I ALWAYS WEAR A BIT OF MAKEUP.
I CAN'T CHANGE MY FACE OR BODY IN MY SPIRIT FORM...
BUT I ALWAYS WANT TO LOOK CUTE IN FRONT OF YOU.
CHISAKI-SAN TAUGHT ME ALL ABOUT NATURAL MAKEUP...
THAT EVEN A SPIRIT LIKE ME COULD USE.
I COULD EVEN REPRODUCE THE MAKEUP IN MY SPIRIT FORM.
SO, I'VE ALWAYS, **ALWAYS**...
DONE WHAT I CAN!
YUUNA?!

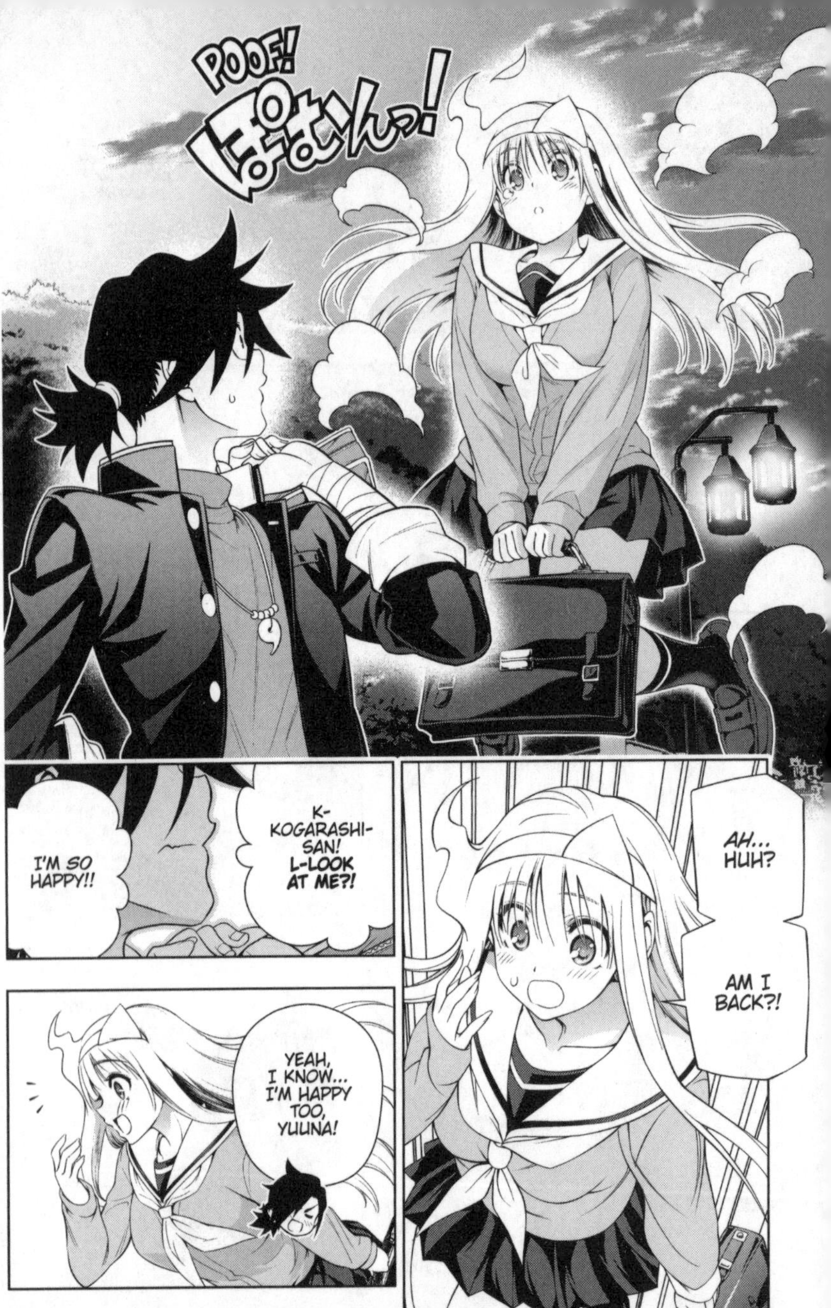
POOF!
ぽぉんっ!
AH... HUH?
AM I BACK?!
K-KOGARASHI-SAN! L-LOOK AT ME?!
I'M SO HAPPY!!
YEAH, I KNOW... I'M HAPPY TOO, YUUNA!

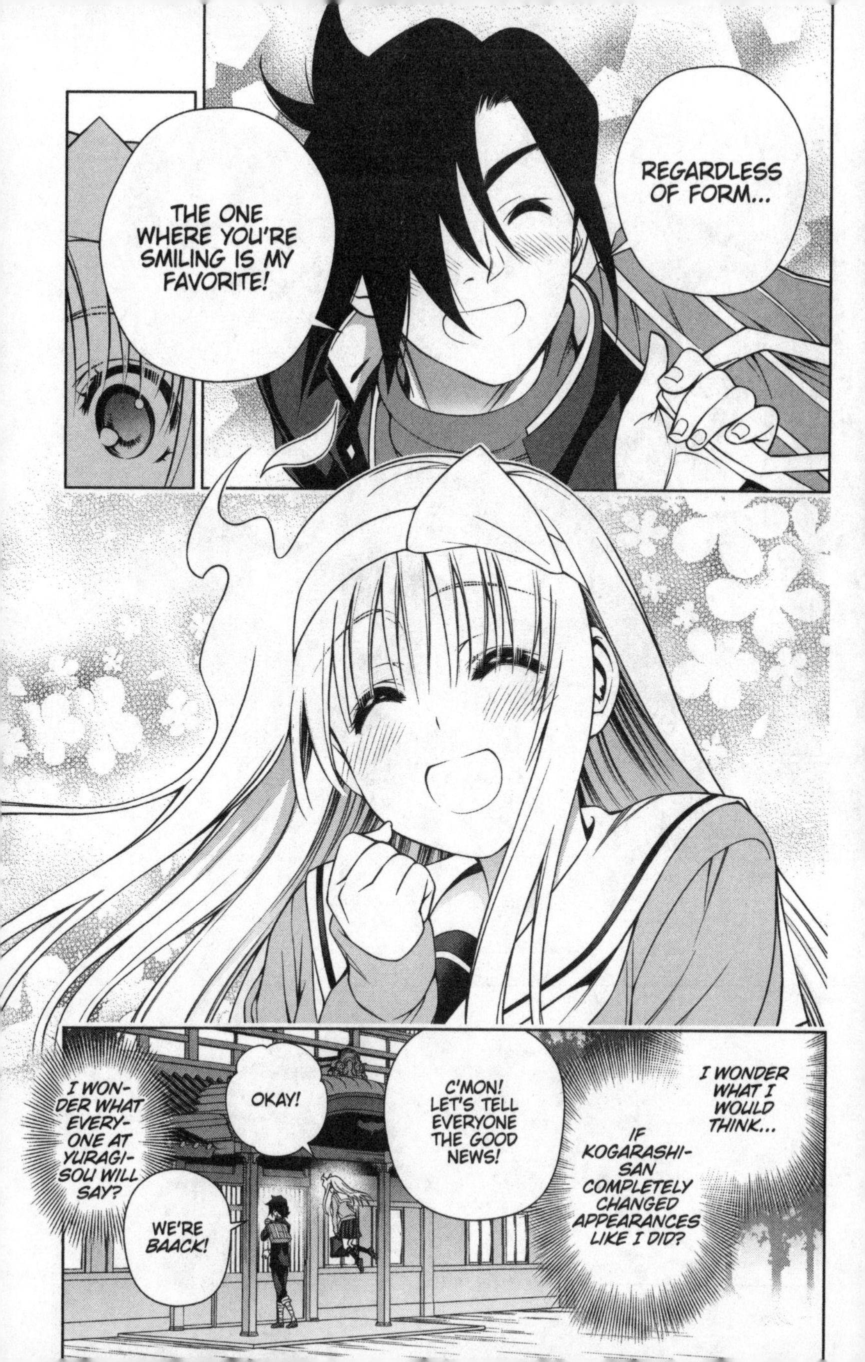
REGARDLESS OF FORM...
THE ONE WHERE YOU'RE SMILING IS MY FAVORITE!
I WONDER WHAT I WOULD THINK...
IF KOGARASHI-SAN COMPLETELY CHANGED APPEARANCES LIKE I DID?
C'MON! LET'S TELL EVERYONE THE GOOD NEWS!
OKAY!
I WON-DER WHAT EVERY-ONE AT YURAGI-SOU WILL SAY?
WE'RE BAACK!

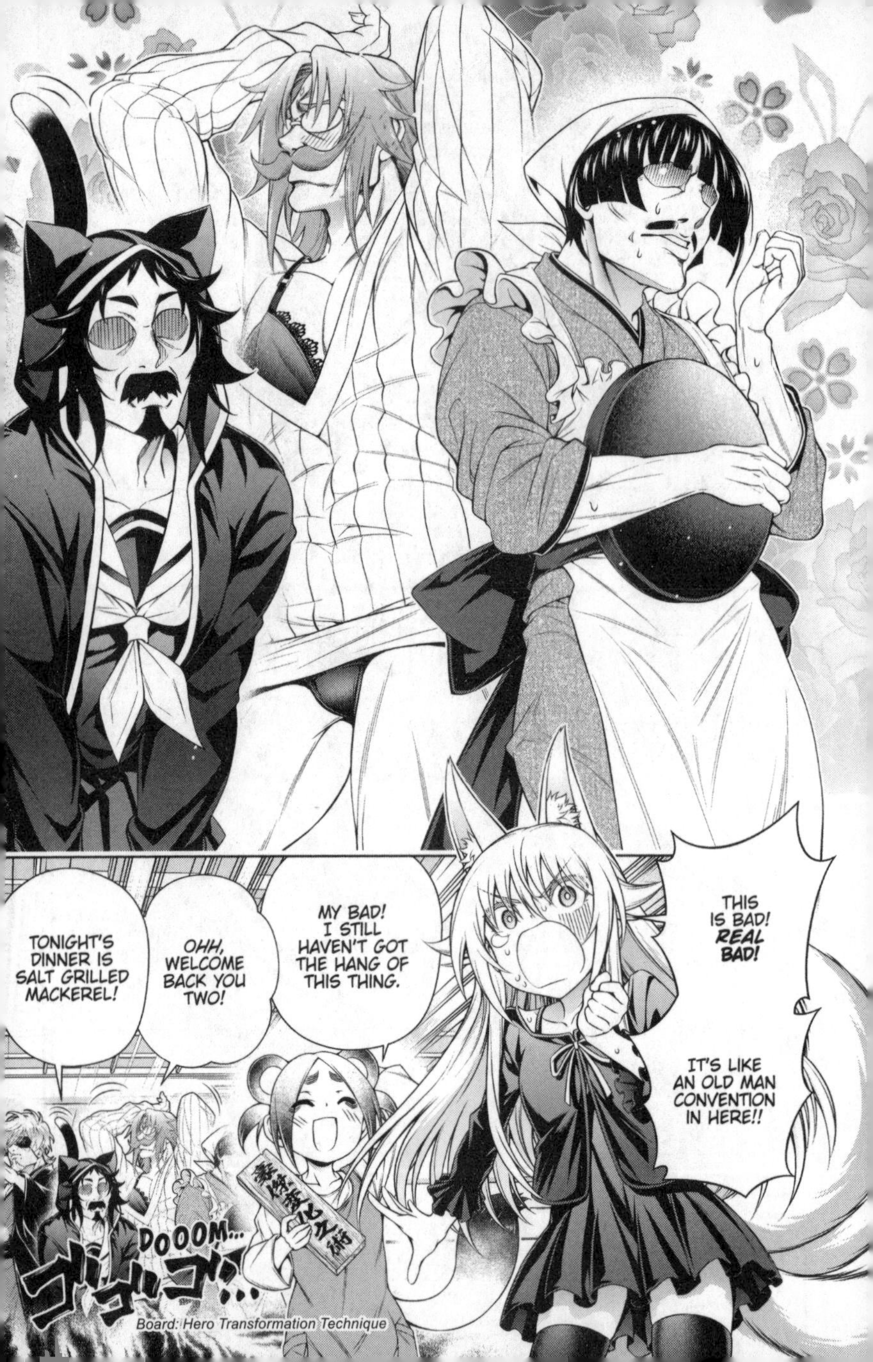
THIS IS BAD! REAL BAD!
IT'S LIKE AN OLD MAN CONVENTION IN HERE!!
MY BAD! I STILL HAVEN'T GOT THE HANG OF THIS THING.
OHH, WELCOME BACK YOU TWO!
TONIGHT'S DINNER IS SALT GRILLED MACKEREL!
DOOOM...
Board: Hero Transformation Technique

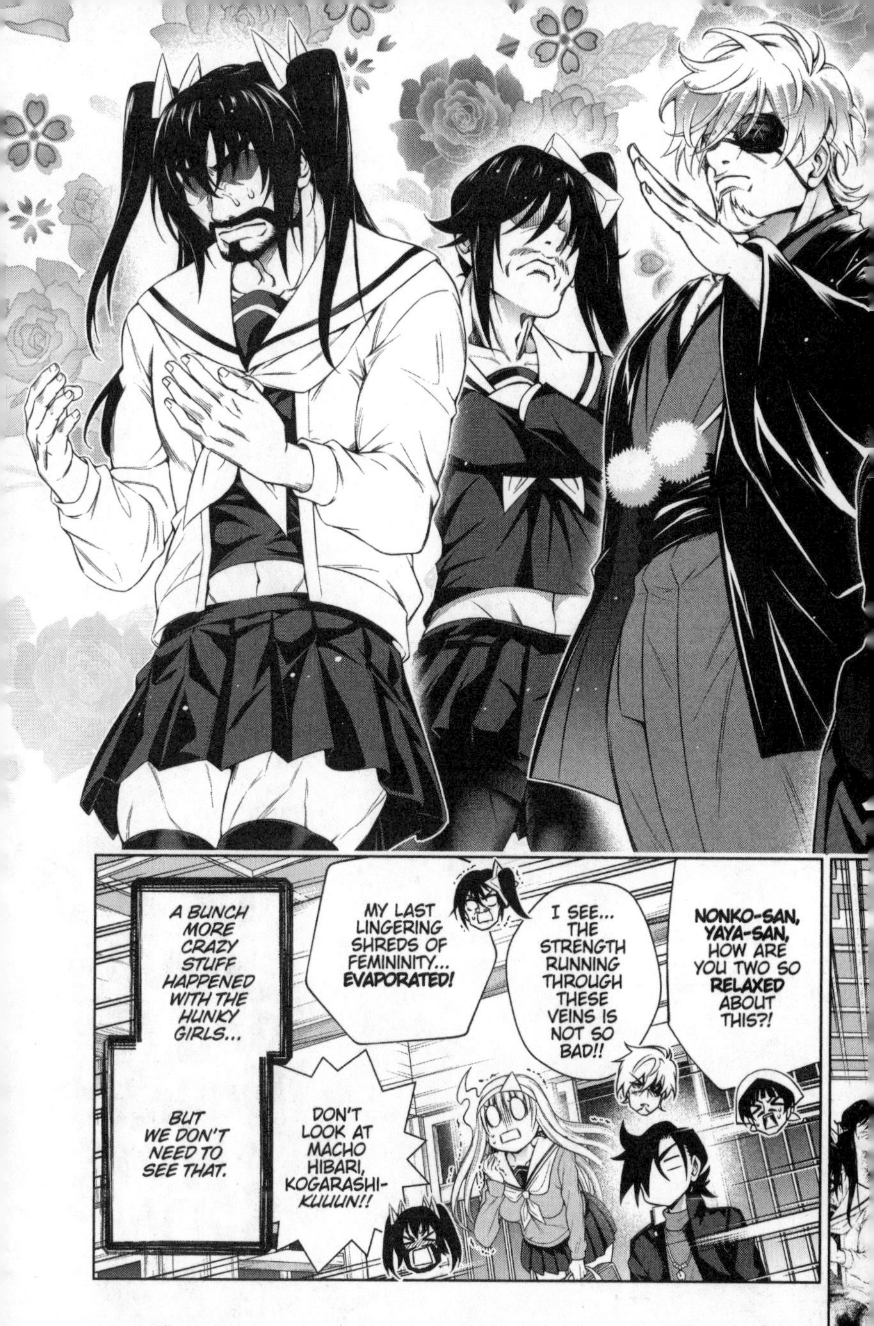
NONKO-SAN, YAYA-SAN, HOW ARE YOU TWO SO RELAXED ABOUT THIS?!
I SEE... THE STRENGTH RUNNING THROUGH THESE VEINS IS NOT SO BAD!!
MY LAST LINGERING SHREDS OF FEMININITY... EVAPORATED!
DON'T LOOK AT MACHO HIBARI, KOGARASHI-KUUUN!!
A BUNCH MORE CRAZY STUFF HAPPENED WITH THE HUNKY GIRLS...
BUT WE DON'T NEED TO SEE THAT.

Yuuna and the Haunted Hot Springs

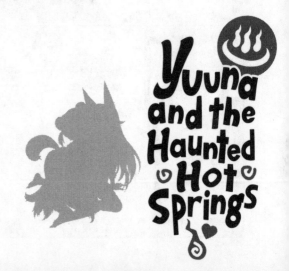

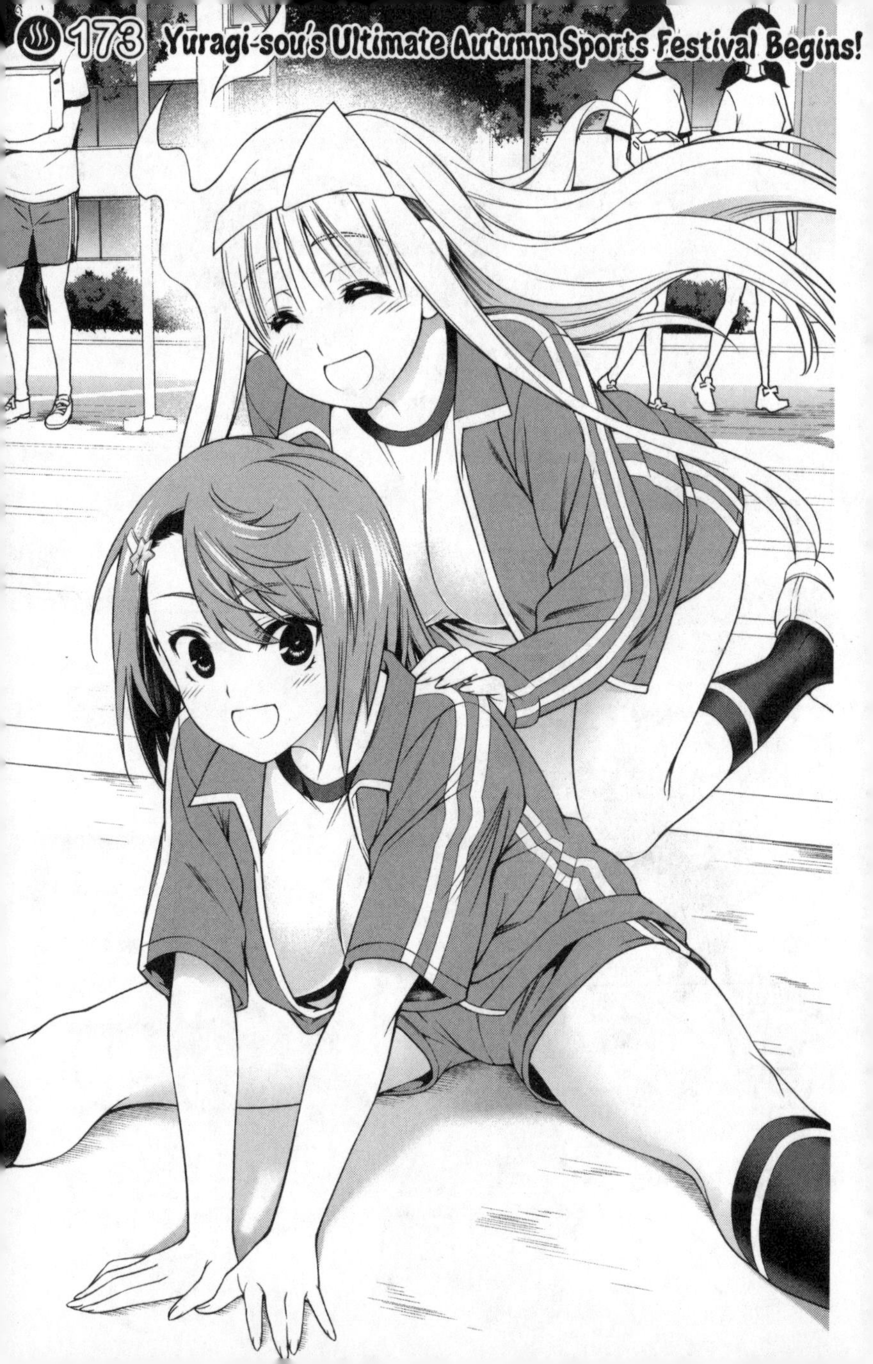
173 Yuragi-sou's Ultimate Autumn Sports Festival Begins!

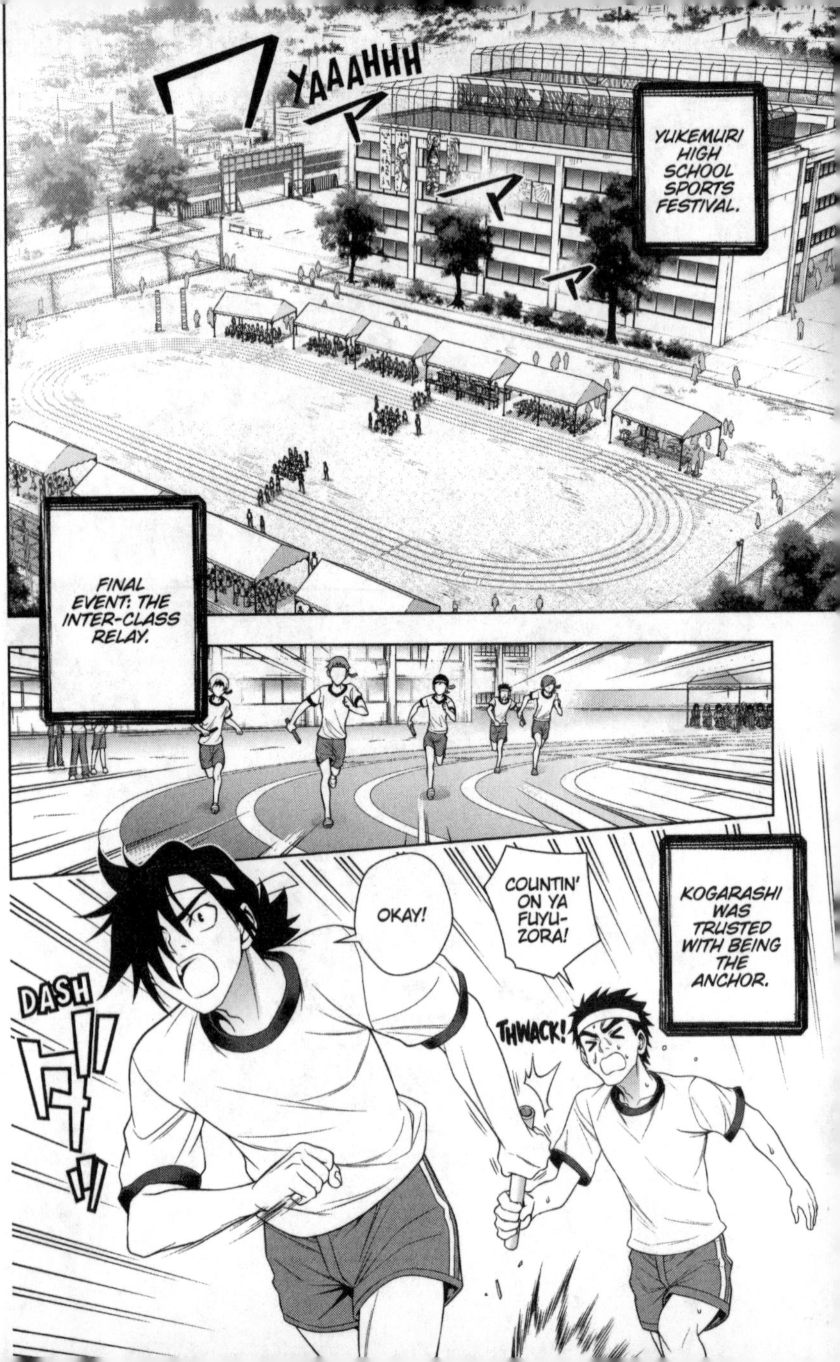
YAAAHHH
YUKEMURI HIGH SCHOOL SPORTS FESTIVAL.
FINAL EVENT: THE INTER-CLASS RELAY.
KOGARASHI WAS TRUSTED WITH BEING THE ANCHOR.
COUNTIN' ON YA FUYU-ZORA!
THWACK!
OKAY!
DASH

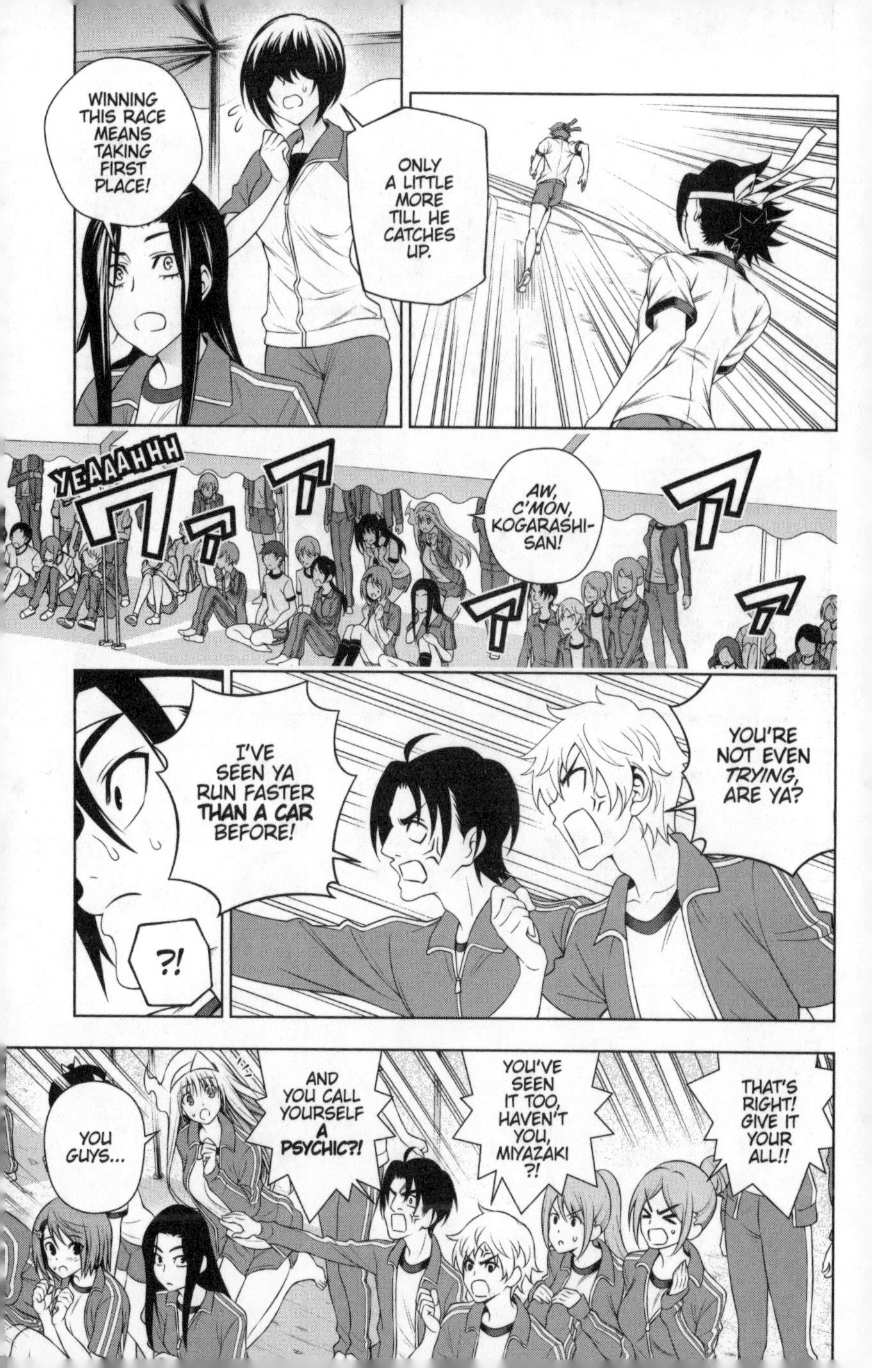
ONLY A LITTLE MORE TILL HE CATCHES UP.
WINNING THIS RACE MEANS TAKING FIRST PLACE!
AW, C'MON, KOGARASHI-SAN!
YEAAAHHH
YOU'RE NOT EVEN *TRYING*, ARE YA?
I'VE SEEN YA RUN FASTER **THAN A CAR** BEFORE!
?!
THAT'S RIGHT! GIVE IT YOUR ALL!!
YOU'VE SEEN IT TOO, HAVEN'T YOU, MIYAZAKI?!
AND YOU CALL YOURSELF A **PSYCHIC?!**
YOU GUYS...

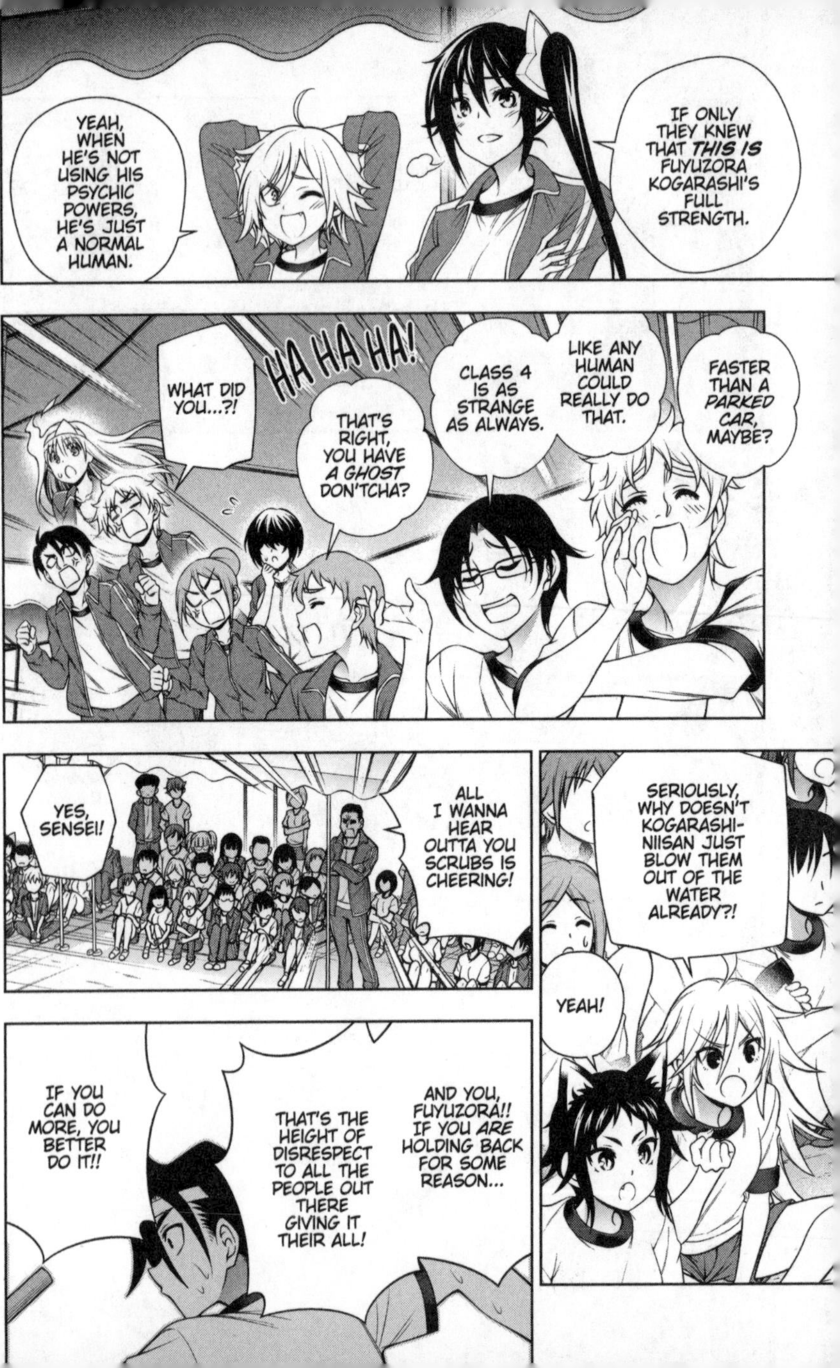
IF ONLY THEY KNEW THAT *THIS IS* FUYUZORA KOGARASHI'S FULL STRENGTH.
YEAH, WHEN HE'S NOT USING HIS PSYCHIC POWERS, HE'S JUST A NORMAL HUMAN.
FASTER THAN A *PARKED* CAR, MAYBE?
LIKE ANY HUMAN COULD REALLY DO THAT.
CLASS 4 IS AS STRANGE AS ALWAYS.
HA HA HA!
THAT'S RIGHT, YOU HAVE A *GHOST* DON'TCHA?
WHAT DID YOU...?!
SERIOUSLY, WHY DOESN'T KOGARASHI-NIISAN JUST BLOW THEM OUT OF THE WATER ALREADY?!
YEAH!
ALL I WANNA HEAR OUTTA YOU SCRUBS IS CHEERING!
YES, SENSEI!
AND YOU, FUYUZORA!! IF YOU *ARE* HOLDING BACK FOR SOME REASON...
THAT'S THE HEIGHT OF DISRESPECT TO ALL THE PEOPLE OUT THERE GIVING IT THEIR ALL!
IF YOU CAN DO MORE, YOU BETTER DO IT!!

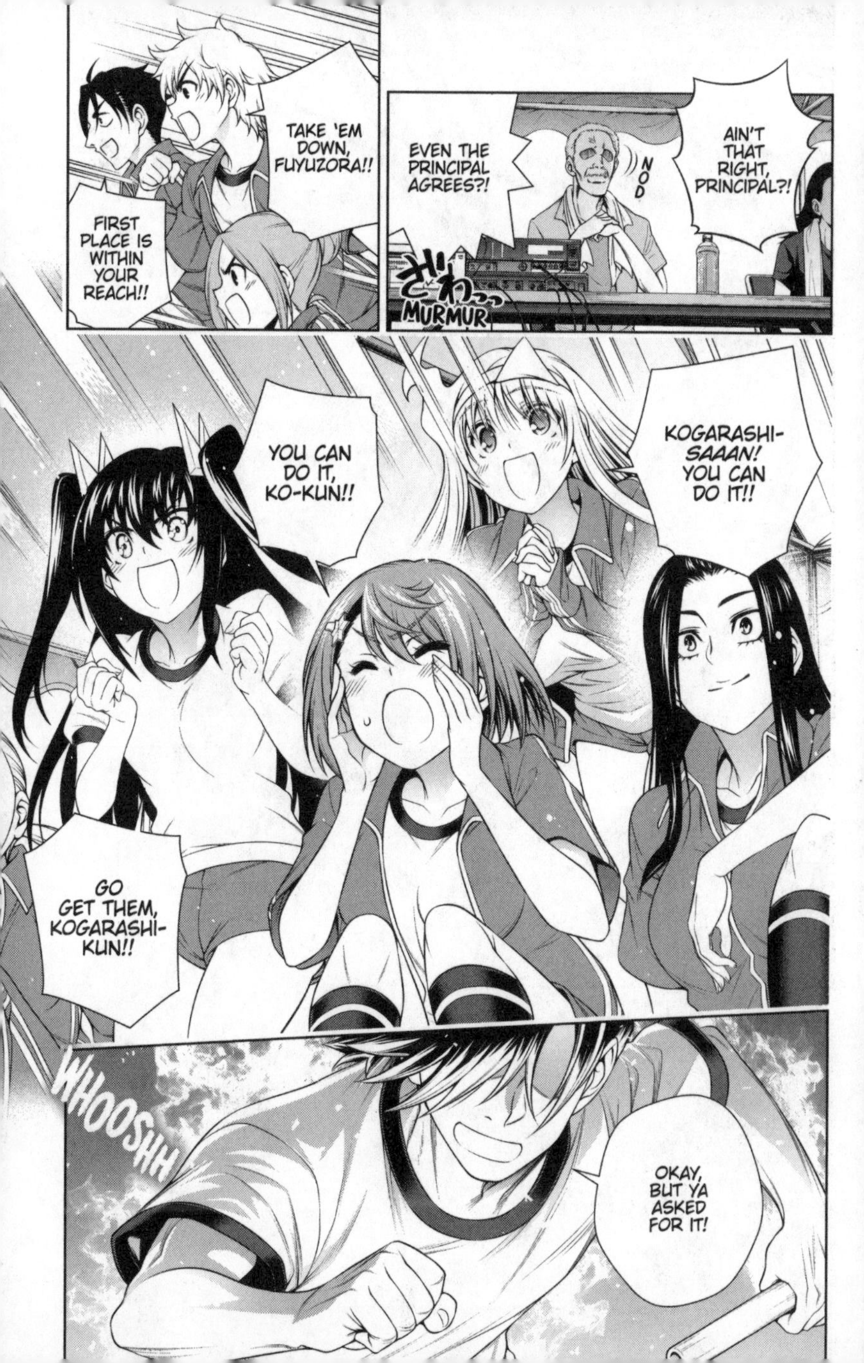
AIN'T THAT RIGHT, PRINCIPAL?!
NOD
EVEN THE PRINCIPAL AGREES?!
ざわ
MURMUR
TAKE 'EM DOWN, FUYUZORA!!
FIRST PLACE IS WITHIN YOUR REACH!!
KOGARASHI-SAAAN! YOU CAN DO IT!!
YOU CAN DO IT, KO-KUN!!
GO GET THEM, KOGARASHI-KUN!!
OKAY, BUT YA ASKED FOR IT!
WHOOSHH

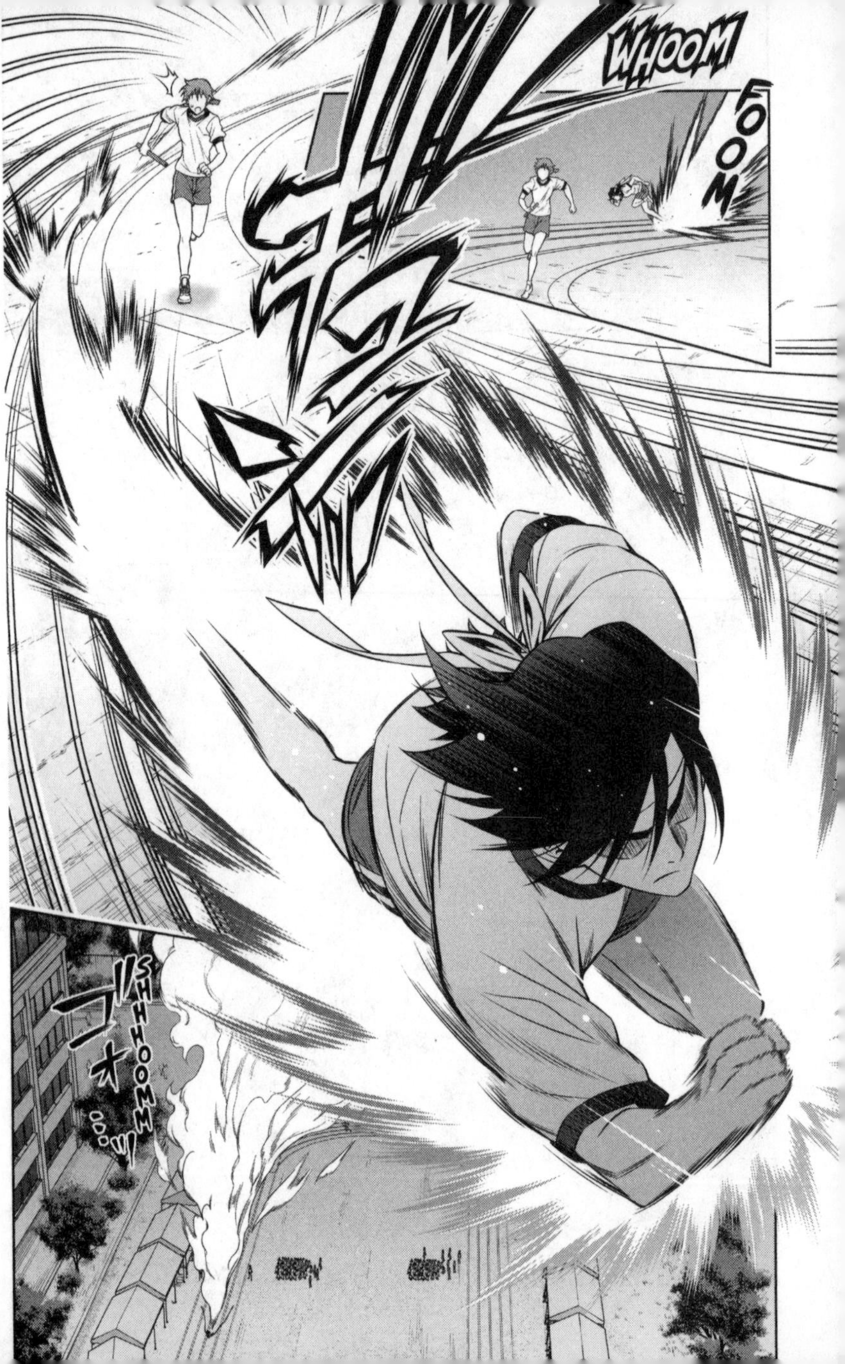
WHOOM
FOOM
ゴオ…!!
SHHHOOMM!

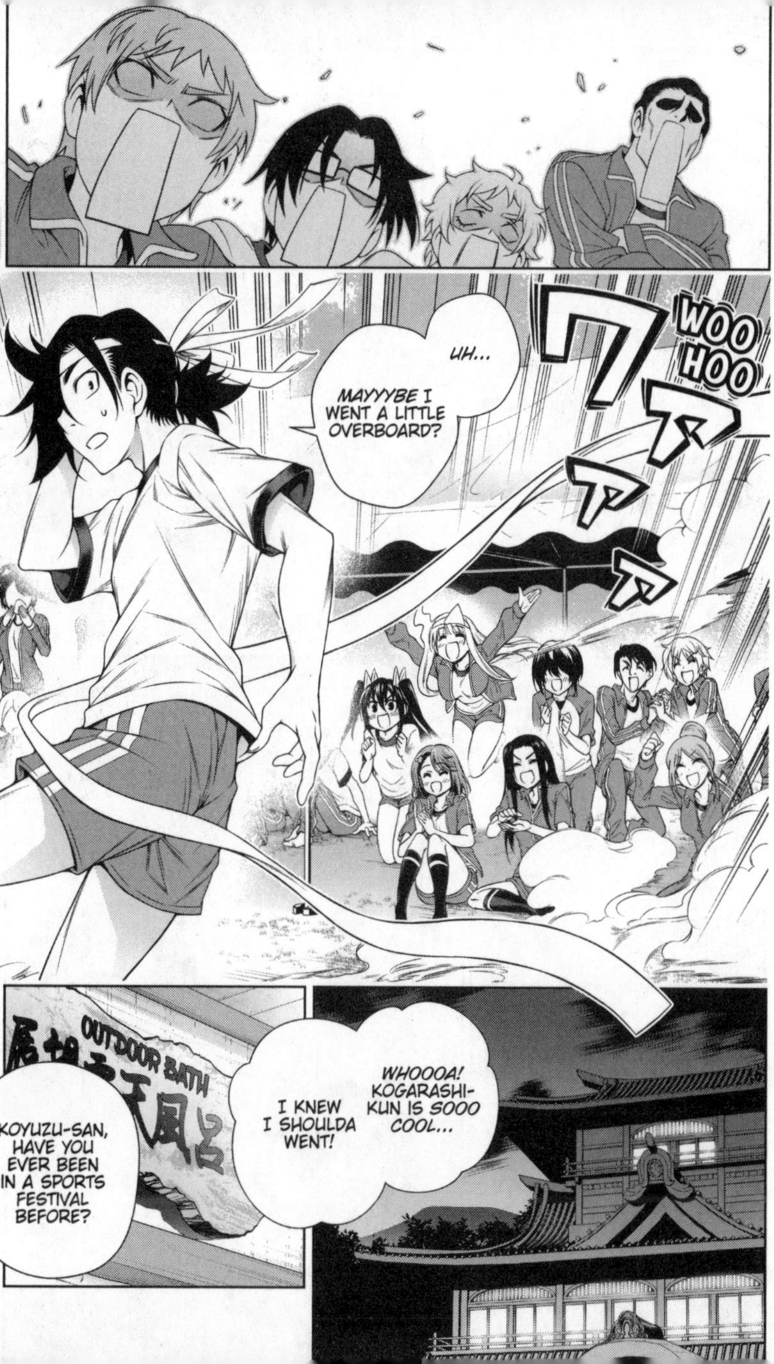
WOO HOO
UH...
MAYYYBE I WENT A LITTLE OVERBOARD?
WHOOOA! KOGARASHI-KUN IS SOOO COOL...
I KNEW I SHOULDA WENT!
OUTDOOR BATH
KOYUZU-SAN, HAVE YOU EVER BEEN IN A SPORTS FESTIVAL BEFORE?

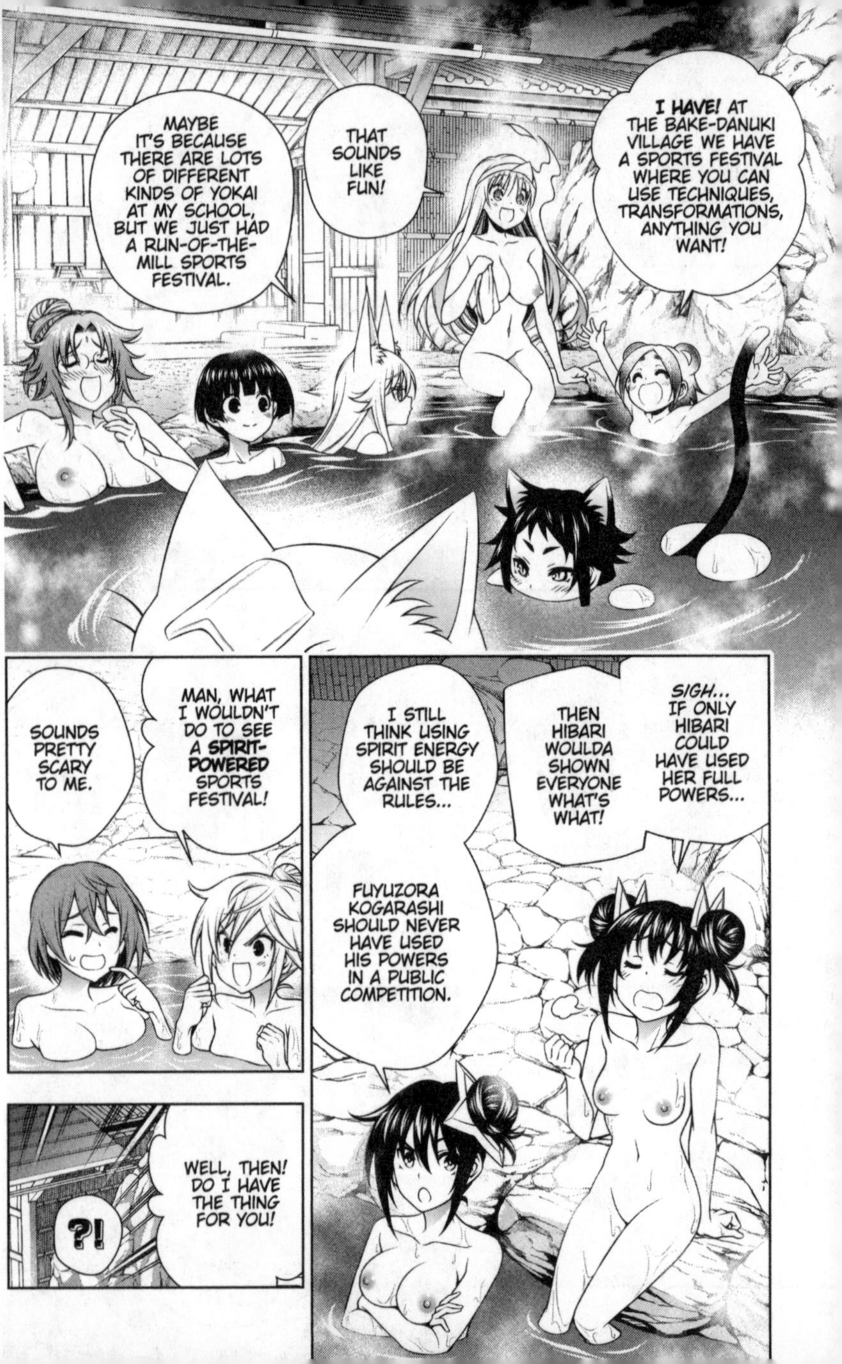
I HAVE! AT THE BAKE-DANUKI VILLAGE WE HAVE A SPORTS FESTIVAL WHERE YOU CAN USE TECHNIQUES, TRANSFORMATIONS, ANYTHING YOU WANT!
THAT SOUNDS LIKE FUN!
MAYBE IT'S BECAUSE THERE ARE LOTS OF DIFFERENT KINDS OF YOKAI AT MY SCHOOL, BUT WE JUST HAD A RUN-OF-THE-MILL SPORTS FESTIVAL.
SIGH... IF ONLY HIBARI COULD HAVE USED HER FULL POWERS...
THEN HIBARI WOULDA SHOWN EVERYONE WHAT'S WHAT!
I STILL THINK USING SPIRIT ENERGY SHOULD BE AGAINST THE RULES...
FUYUZORA KOGARASHI SHOULD NEVER HAVE USED HIS POWERS IN A PUBLIC COMPETITION.
MAN, WHAT I WOULDN'T DO TO SEE A SPIRIT-POWERED SPORTS FESTIVAL!
SOUNDS PRETTY SCARY TO ME.
WELL, THEN! DO I HAVE THE THING FOR YOU!
?!

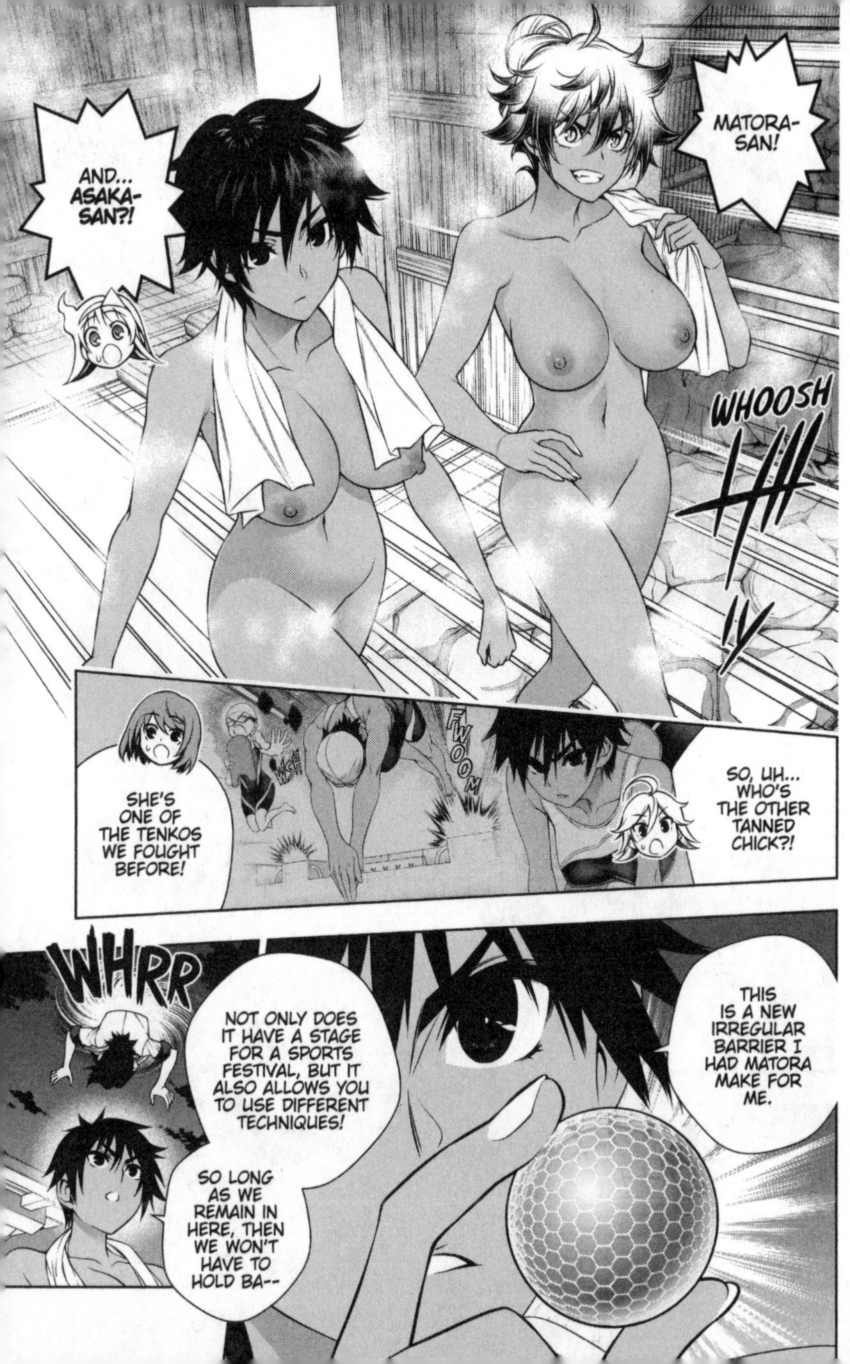
MATORA-SAN!
AND... ASAKA-SAN?!
WHOOSH
SO, UH... WHO'S THE OTHER TANNED CHICK?!
FWOOM
WSH
SHE'S ONE OF THE TENKOS WE FOUGHT BEFORE!
THIS IS A NEW IRREGULAR BARRIER I HAD MATORA MAKE FOR ME.
NOT ONLY DOES IT HAVE A STAGE FOR A SPORTS FESTIVAL, BUT IT ALSO ALLOWS YOU TO USE DIFFERENT TECHNIQUES!
WHRR
SO LONG AS WE REMAIN IN HERE, THEN WE WON'T HAVE TO HOLD BA--

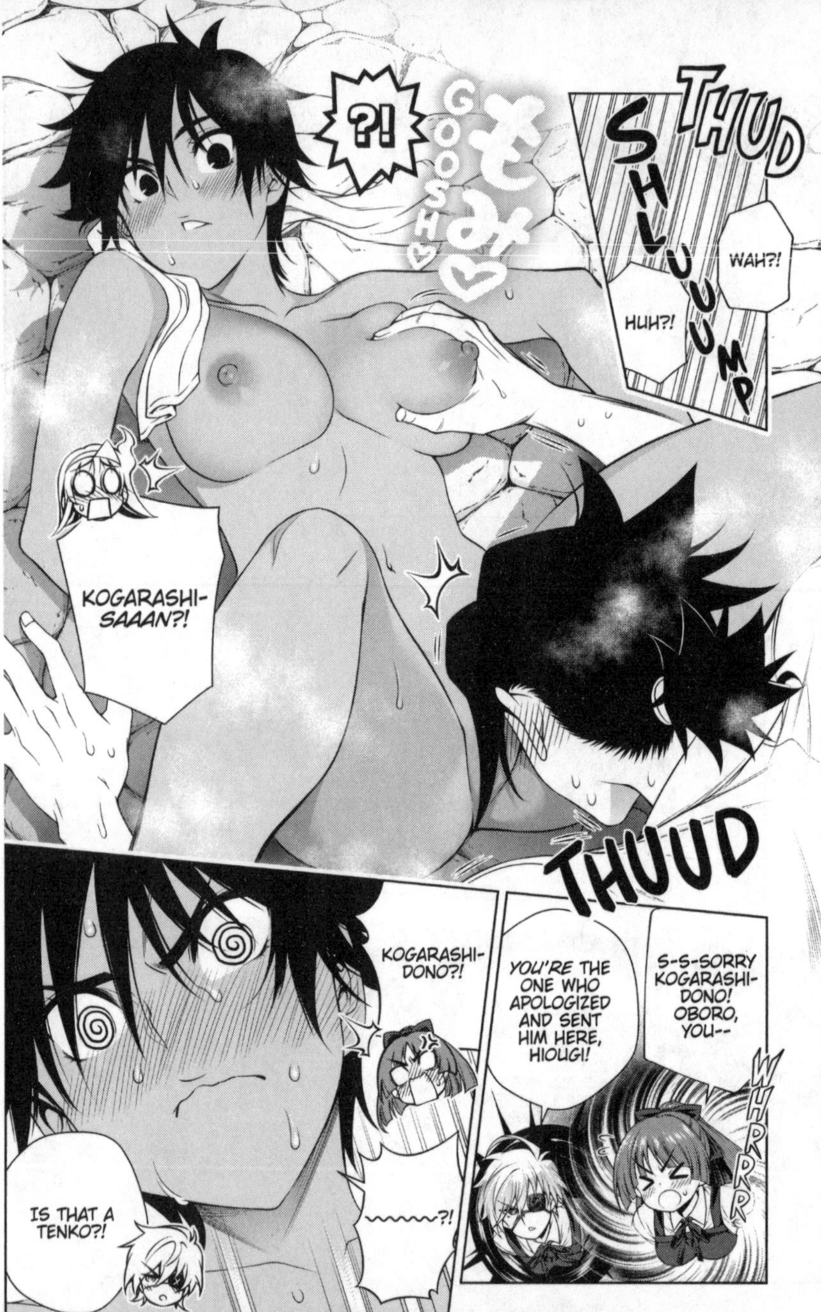
THUD
SHLUUUUMP
WAH?!
HUH?!
もみ♡
GOOSH♡
?!
KOGARASHI-SAAAN?!
THUUD
WHRRRR
S-S-SORRY KOGARASHI-DONO! OBORO, YOU--
YOU'RE THE ONE WHO APOLOGIZED AND SENT HIM HERE, HIOUGI!
KOGARASHI-DONO?!
~~~~~?!
IS THAT A TENKO?!
~~~~~

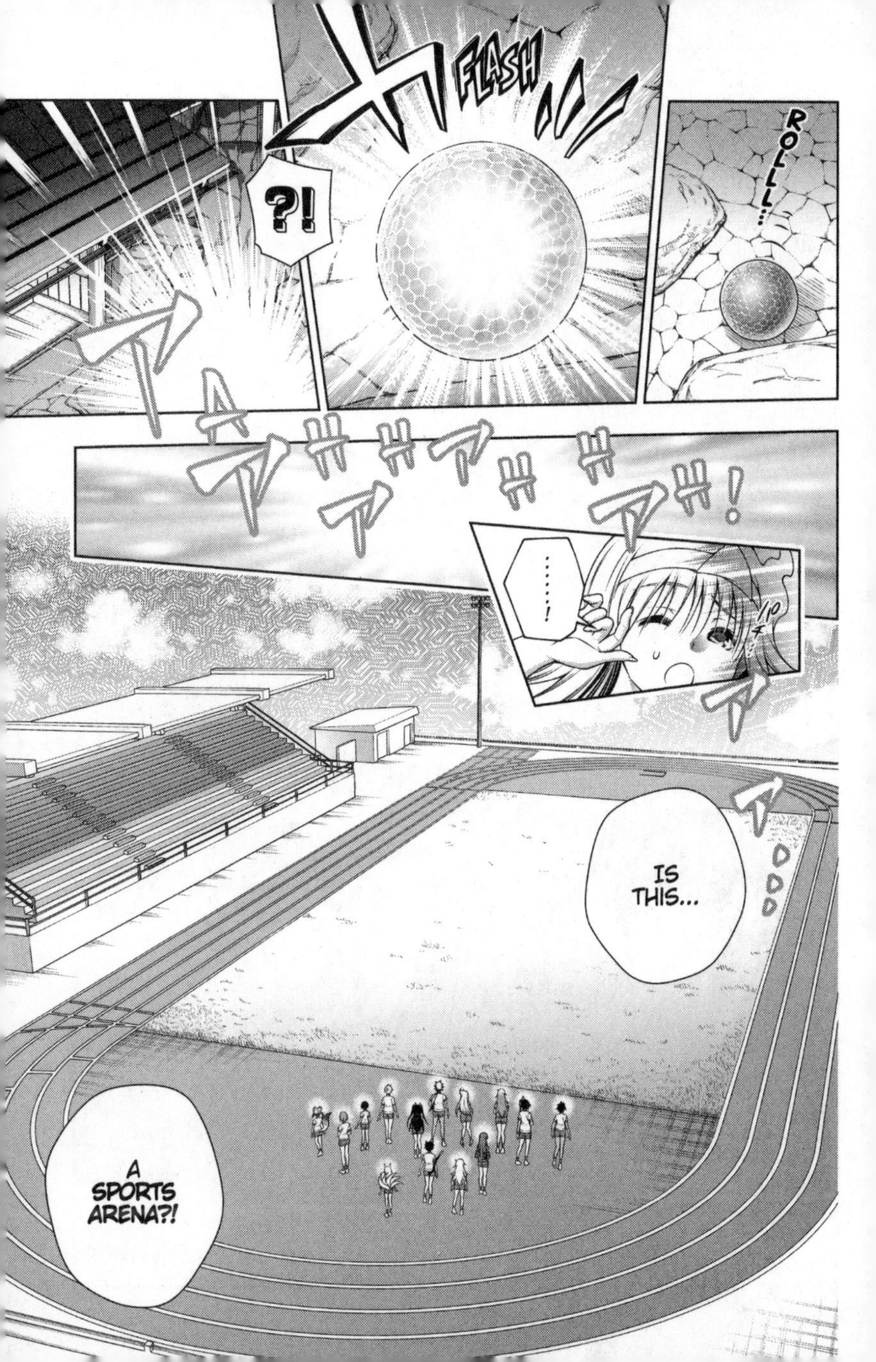
ROLLL...
FLASH
?!
......!
IS THIS...
A SPORTS ARENA?!

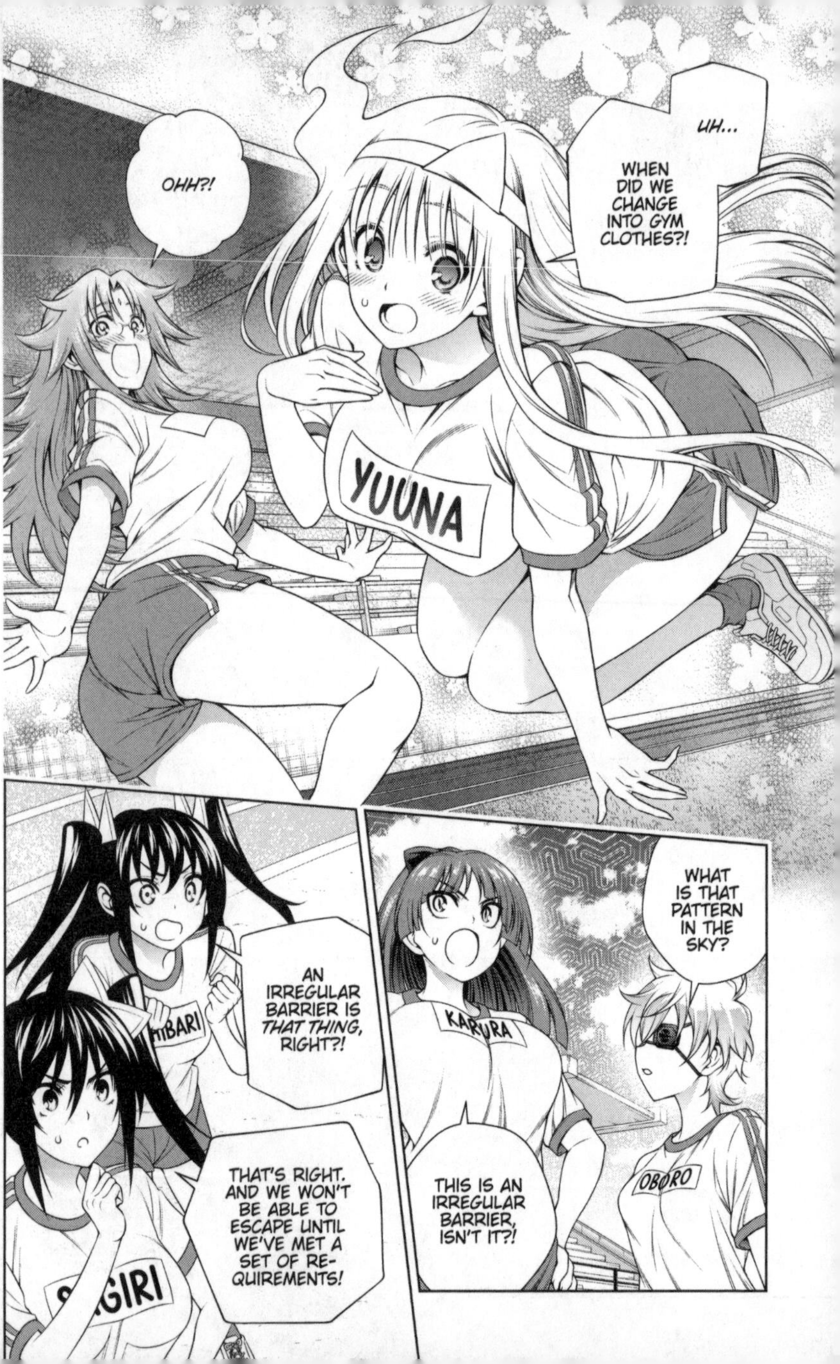
UH... WHEN DID WE CHANGE INTO GYM CLOTHES?!
OHH?!
YUUNA
WHAT IS THAT PATTERN IN THE SKY?
THIS IS AN IRREGULAR BARRIER, ISN'T IT?!
OBORO
AN IRREGULAR BARRIER IS *THAT THING*, RIGHT?!
HIBARI
THAT'S RIGHT. AND WE WON'T BE ABLE TO ESCAPE UNTIL WE'VE MET A SET OF RE-QUIREMENTS!

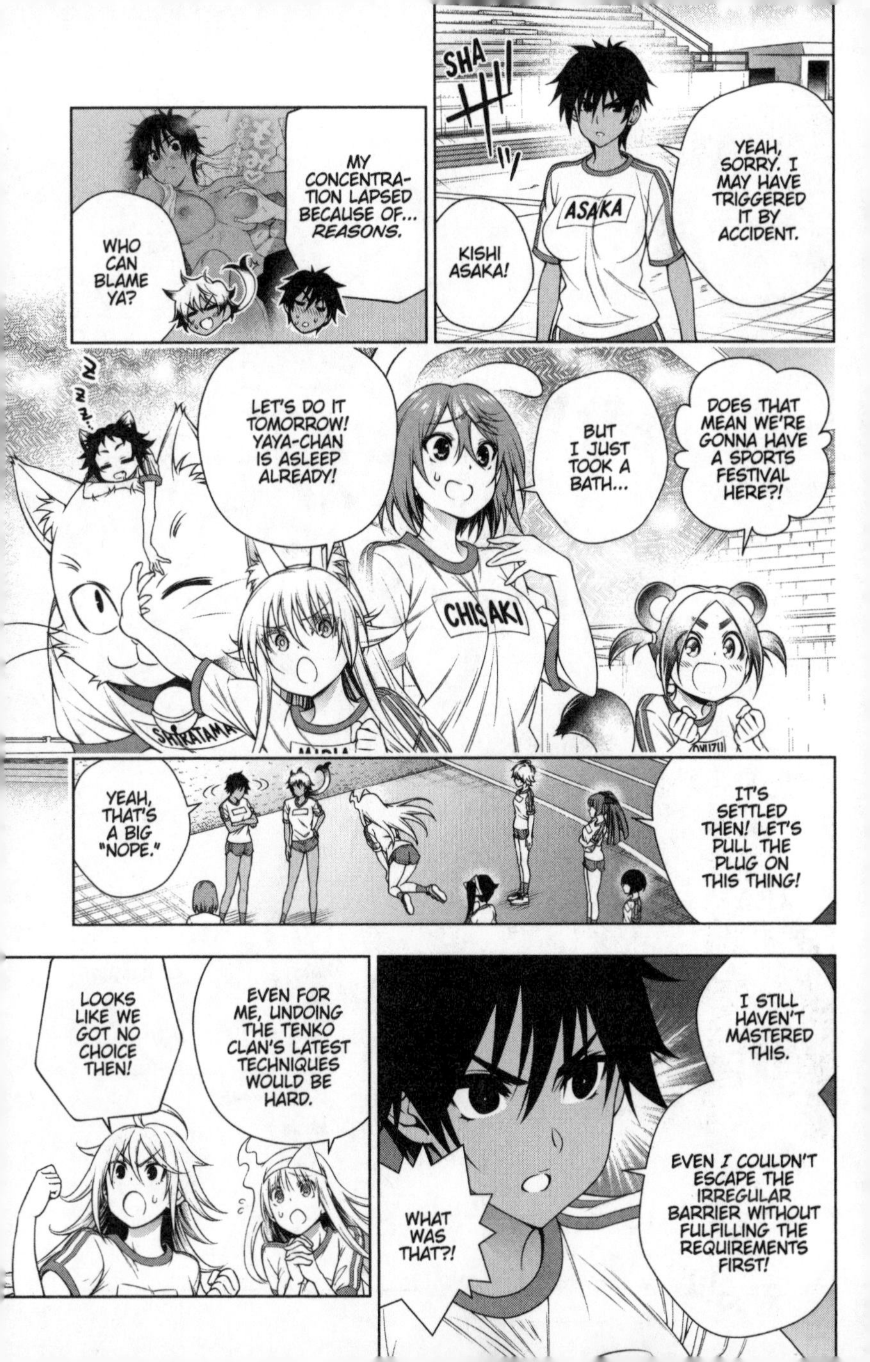
SHA
YEAH, SORRY. I MAY HAVE TRIGGERED IT BY ACCIDENT.
ASAKA
KISHI ASAKA!
MY CONCENTRATION LAPSED BECAUSE OF... *REASONS.*
WHO CAN BLAME YA?
DOES THAT MEAN WE'RE GONNA HAVE A SPORTS FESTIVAL HERE?!
BUT I JUST TOOK A BATH...
CHISAKI
LET'S DO IT TOMORROW! YAYA-CHAN IS ASLEEP ALREADY!
SHIRATAMA
IT'S SETTLED THEN! LET'S PULL THE PLUG ON THIS THING!
YEAH, THAT'S A BIG "NOPE."
I STILL HAVEN'T MASTERED THIS.
EVEN *I* COULDN'T ESCAPE THE IRREGULAR BARRIER WITHOUT FULFILLING THE REQUIREMENTS FIRST!
WHAT WAS THAT?!
EVEN FOR ME, UNDOING THE TENKO CLAN'S LATEST TECHNIQUES WOULD BE HARD.
LOOKS LIKE WE GOT NO CHOICE THEN!

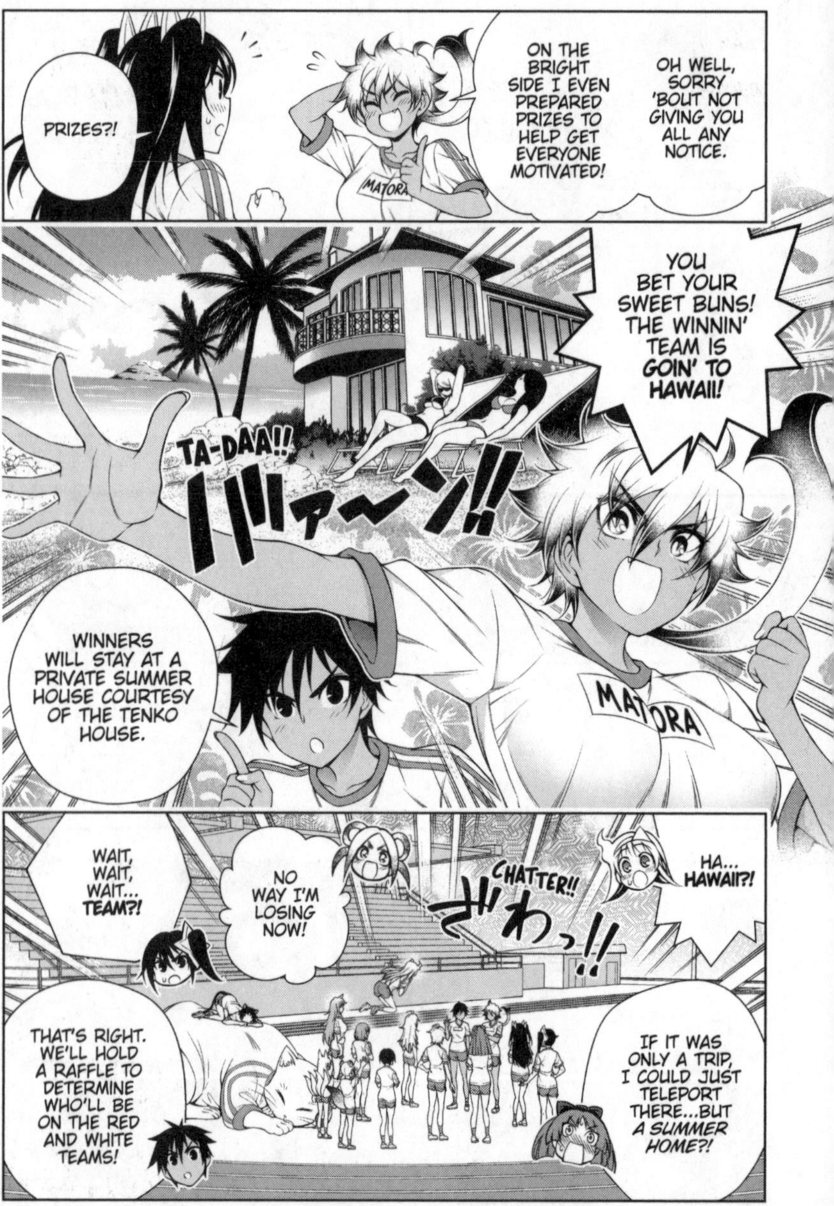
OH WELL, SORRY 'BOUT NOT GIVING YOU ALL ANY NOTICE.
ON THE BRIGHT SIDE I EVEN PREPARED PRIZES TO HELP GET EVERYONE MOTIVATED!
MATORA
PRIZES?!
YOU BET YOUR SWEET BUNS! THE WINNIN' TEAM IS GOIN' TO HAWAII!
TA-DAA!!
MATORA
WINNERS WILL STAY AT A PRIVATE SUMMER HOUSE COURTESY OF THE TENKO HOUSE.
HA... HAWAII?!
CHATTER!!
NO WAY I'M LOSING NOW!
WAIT, WAIT, WAIT... TEAM?!
IF IT WAS ONLY A TRIP, I COULD JUST TELEPORT THERE...BUT A SUMMER HOME?!
THAT'S RIGHT. WE'LL HOLD A RAFFLE TO DETERMINE WHO'LL BE ON THE RED AND WHITE TEAMS!

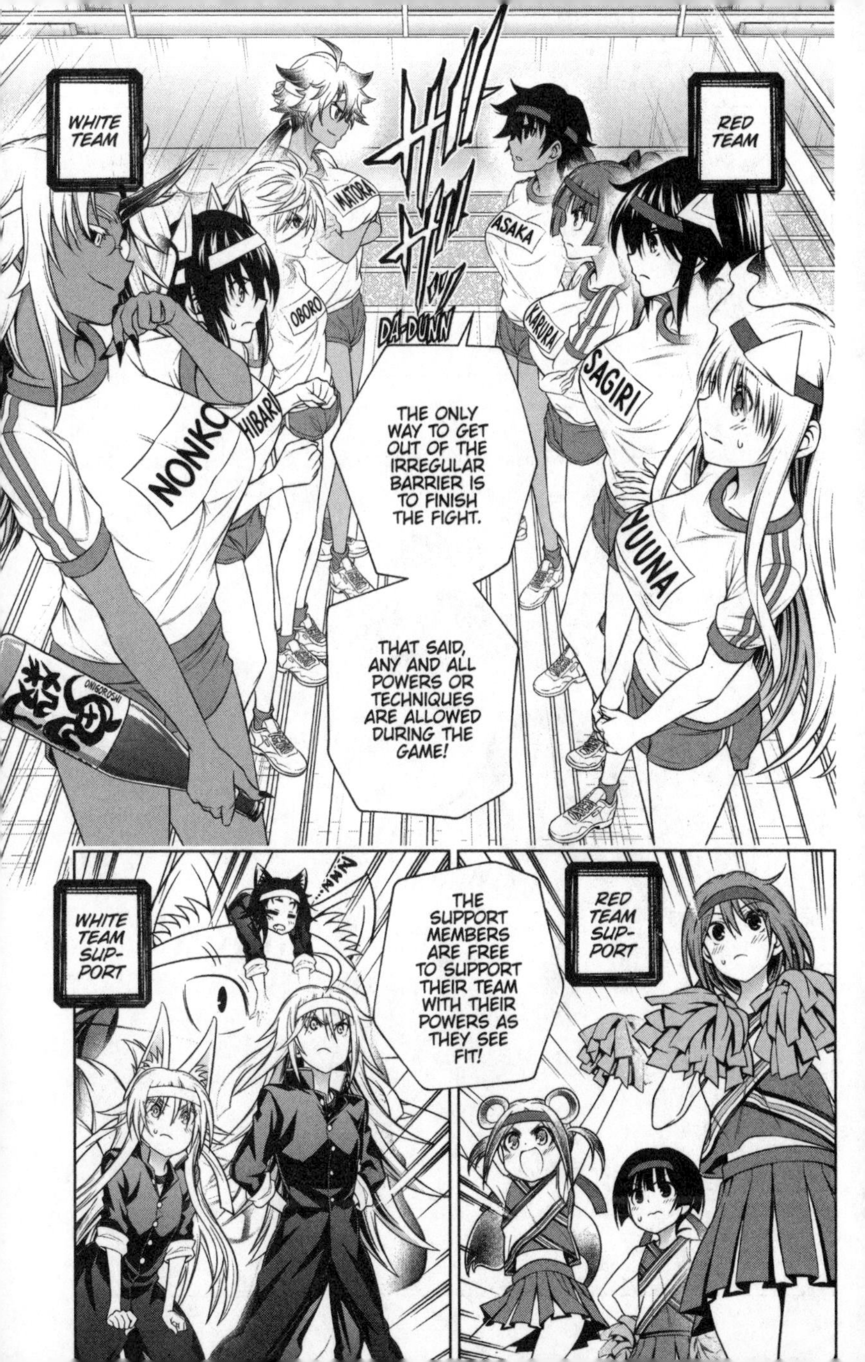
RED TEAM
WHITE TEAM
ASAKA
KARURA
SAGIRI
YUUNA
MATORA
OBORO
HIBARI
NONKO
ONIGOROSHI
DA-DUNN
THE ONLY WAY TO GET OUT OF THE IRREGULAR BARRIER IS TO FINISH THE FIGHT.
THAT SAID, ANY AND ALL POWERS OR TECHNIQUES ARE ALLOWED DURING THE GAME!
RED TEAM SUP-PORT
THE SUPPORT MEMBERS ARE FREE TO SUPPORT THEIR TEAM WITH THEIR POWERS AS THEY SEE FIT!
NNN...
WHITE TEAM SUP-PORT

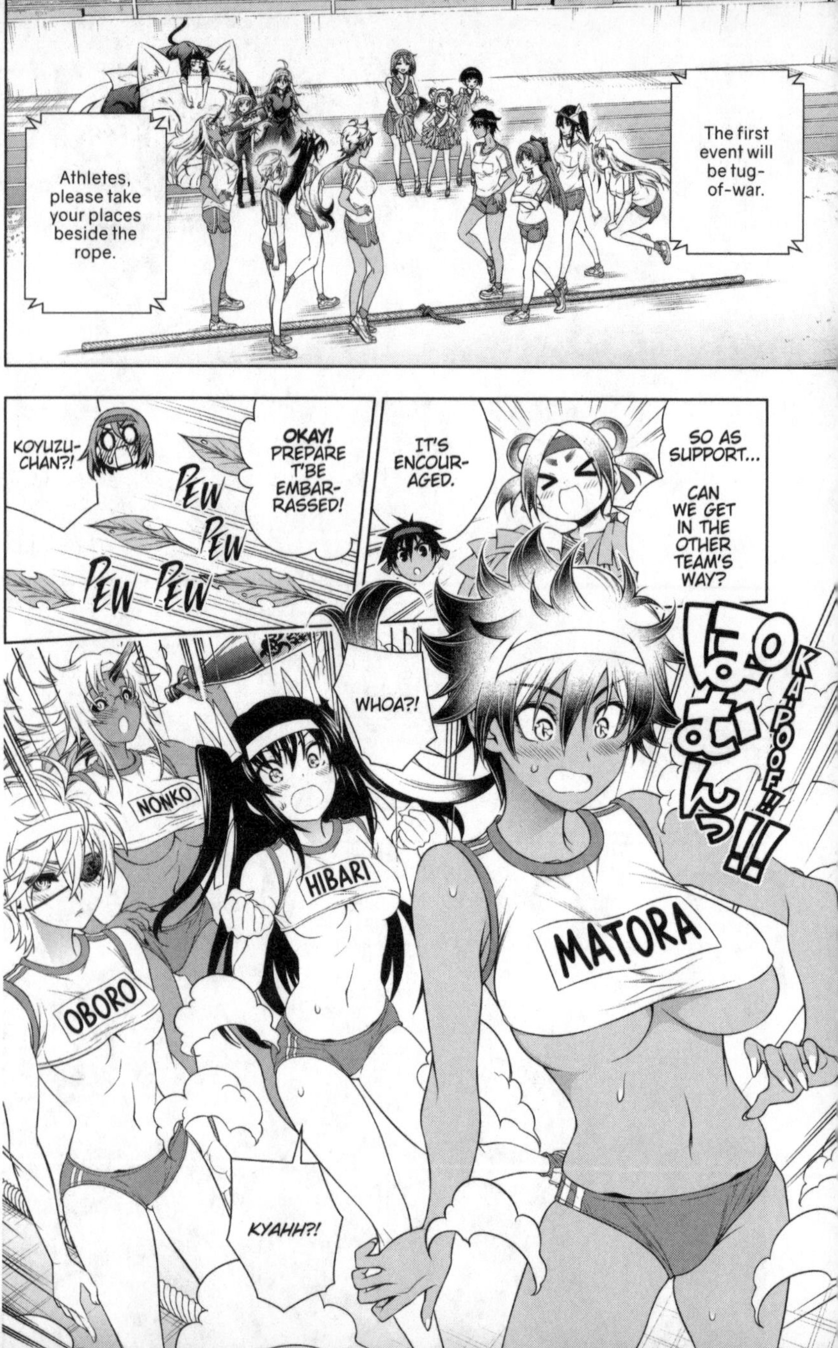
The first event will be tug-of-war.
Athletes, please take your places beside the rope.
SO AS SUPPORT... CAN WE GET IN THE OTHER TEAM'S WAY?
IT'S ENCOURAGED.
OKAY! PREPARE T'BE EMBARRASSED!
KOYUZU-CHAN?!
PEW PEW PEW PEW
ぽむんっ!!
KAPOOF!!
WHOA?!
MATORA
HIBARI
NONKO
OBORO
KYAHH?!

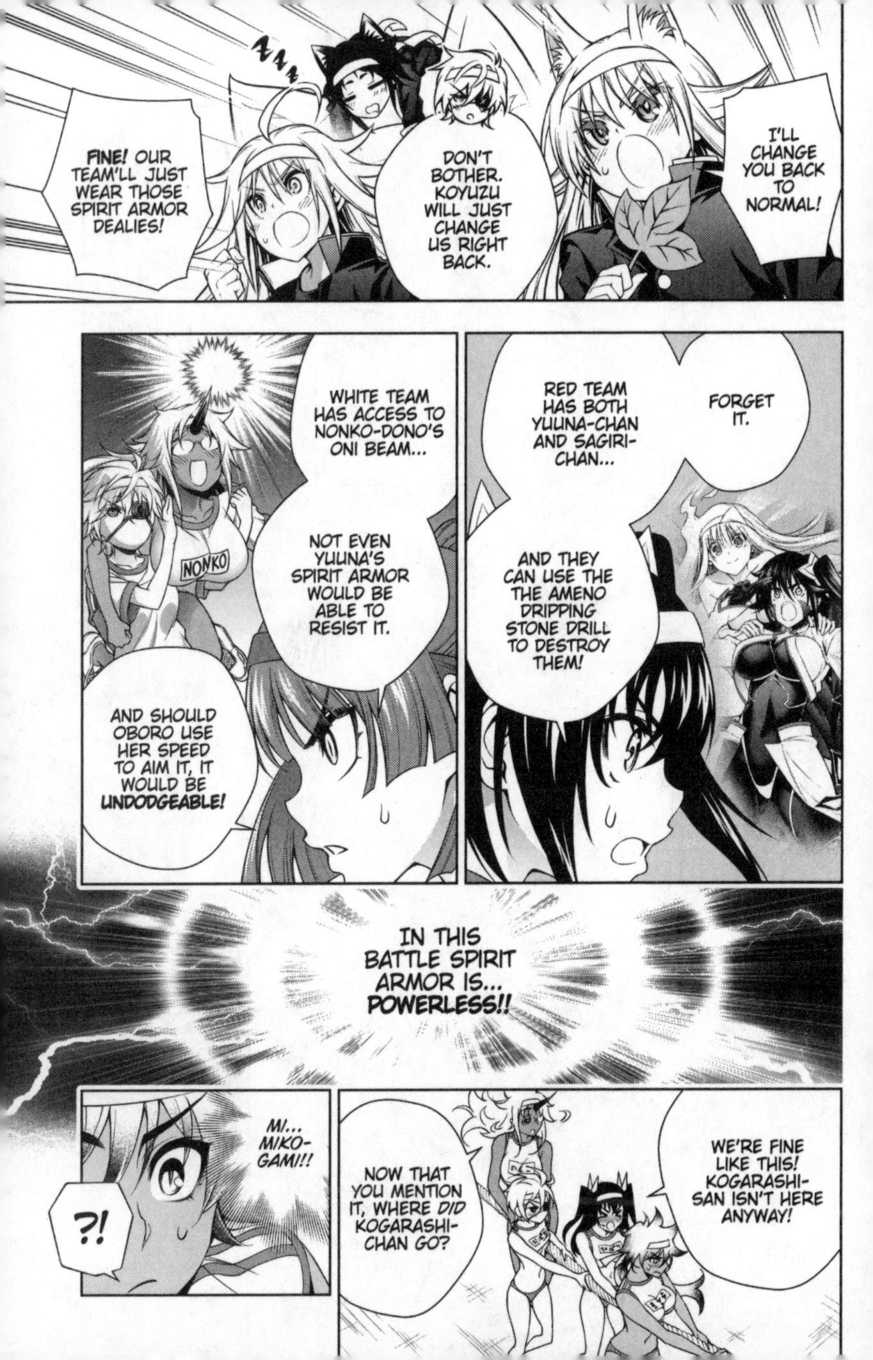
I'LL CHANGE YOU BACK TO NORMAL!
DON'T BOTHER. KOYUZU WILL JUST CHANGE US RIGHT BACK.
ZZZ
FINE! OUR TEAM'LL JUST WEAR THOSE SPIRIT ARMOR DEALIES!
FORGET IT.
RED TEAM HAS BOTH YUUNA-CHAN AND SAGIRI-CHAN...
AND THEY CAN USE THE THE AMENO DRIPPING STONE DRILL TO DESTROY THEM!
WHITE TEAM HAS ACCESS TO NONKO-DONO'S ONI BEAM...
NOT EVEN YUUNA'S SPIRIT ARMOR WOULD BE ABLE TO RESIST IT.
NONKO
AND SHOULD OBORO USE HER SPEED TO AIM IT, IT WOULD BE **UNDODGEABLE!**
IN THIS BATTLE SPIRIT ARMOR IS... **POWERLESS!!**
WE'RE FINE LIKE THIS! KOGARASHI-SAN ISN'T HERE ANYWAY!
NOW THAT YOU MENTION IT, WHERE *DID* KOGARASHI-CHAN GO?
MI... MIKO-GAMI!!
?!

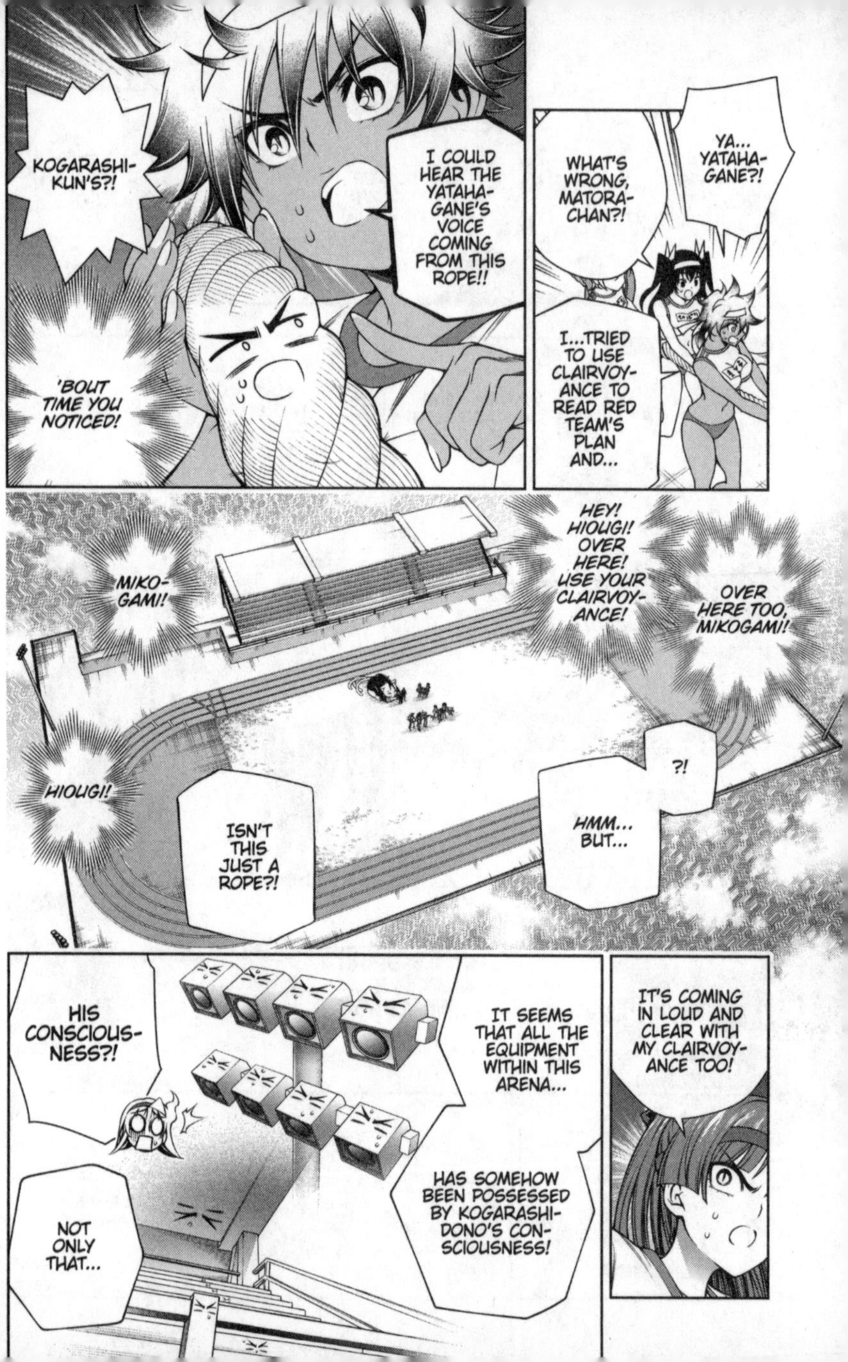
YA... YATAHA-GANE?!
WHAT'S WRONG, MATORA-CHAN?!
I...TRIED TO USE CLAIRVOY-ANCE TO READ RED TEAM'S PLAN AND...
I COULD HEAR THE YATAHA-GANE'S VOICE COMING FROM THIS ROPE!!
KOGARASHI-KUN'S?!
'BOUT TIME YOU NOTICED!
OVER HERE TOO, MIKOGAMI!
HEY! HIOUGI! OVER HERE! USE YOUR CLAIRVOY-ANCE!
MIKO-GAMI!
?!
HMM... BUT...
ISN'T THIS JUST A ROPE?!
HIOUGI!
IT'S COMING IN LOUD AND CLEAR WITH MY CLAIRVOY-ANCE TOO!
IT SEEMS THAT ALL THE EQUIPMENT WITHIN THIS ARENA...
HIS CONSCIOUS-NESS?!
HAS SOMEHOW BEEN POSSESSED BY KOGARASHI-DONO'S CON-SCIOUSNESS!
NOT ONLY THAT...

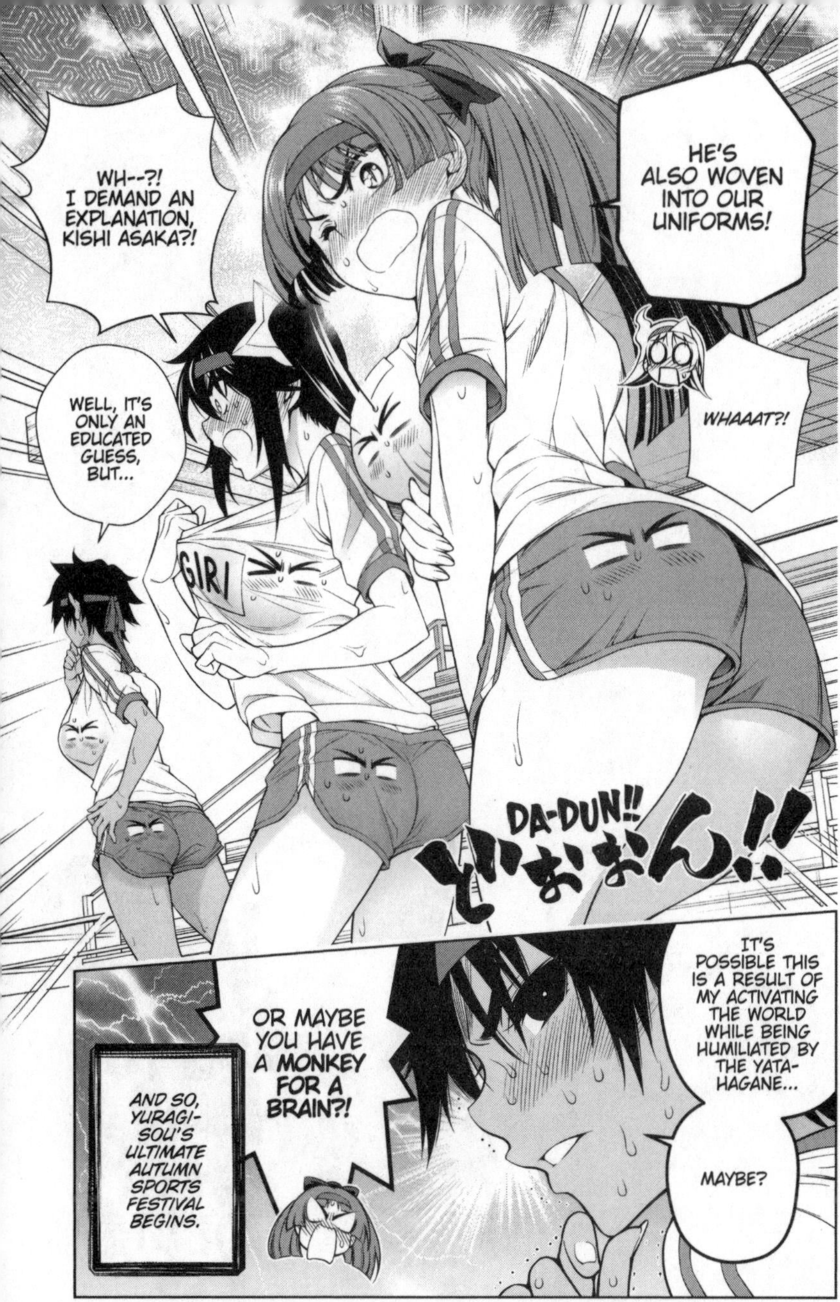
HE'S ALSO WOVEN INTO OUR UNIFORMS!
WH--?! I DEMAND AN EXPLANATION, KISHI ASAKA?!
WHAAAT?!
WELL, IT'S ONLY AN EDUCATED GUESS, BUT...
GIRI
DA-DUN!!
どおおん!!
IT'S POSSIBLE THIS IS A RESULT OF MY ACTIVATING THE WORLD WHILE BEING HUMILIATED BY THE YATA-HAGANE...
MAYBE?
OR MAYBE YOU HAVE A MONKEY FOR A BRAIN?!
AND SO, YURAGI-SOU'S ULTIMATE AUTUMN SPORTS FESTIVAL BEGINS.

Yuuna and the Haunted Hot Springs

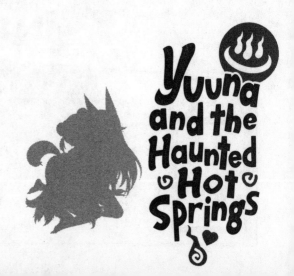

174 An All-Kogarashi Sports Festival?!

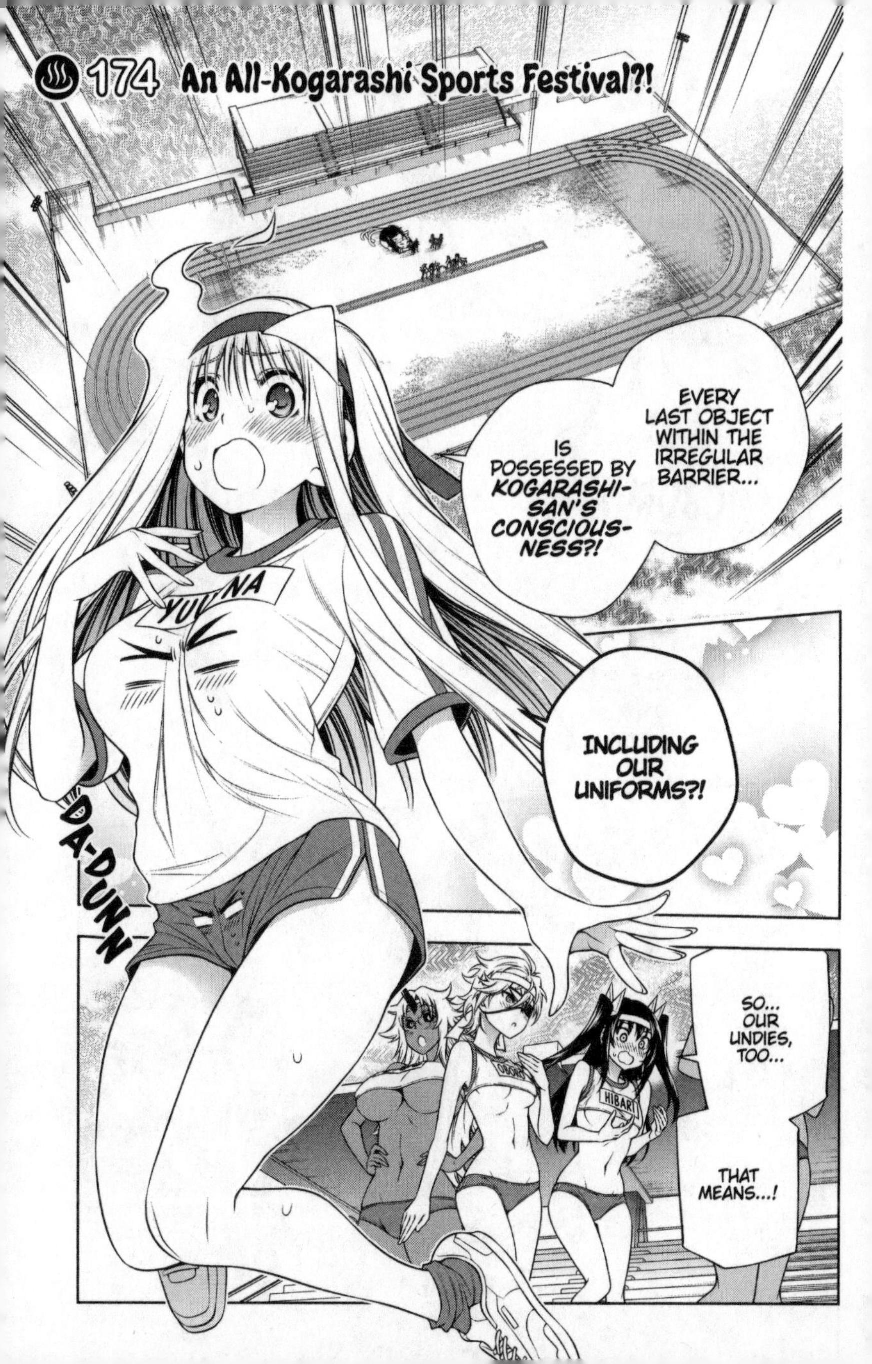
EVERY LAST OBJECT WITHIN THE IRREGULAR BARRIER...
IS POSSESSED BY KOGARASHI-SAN'S CONSCIOUS-NESS?!
INCLUDING OUR UNIFORMS?!
YUUNA
DA-DUNN
SO... OUR UNDIES, TOO...
THAT MEANS...!
HIBARI

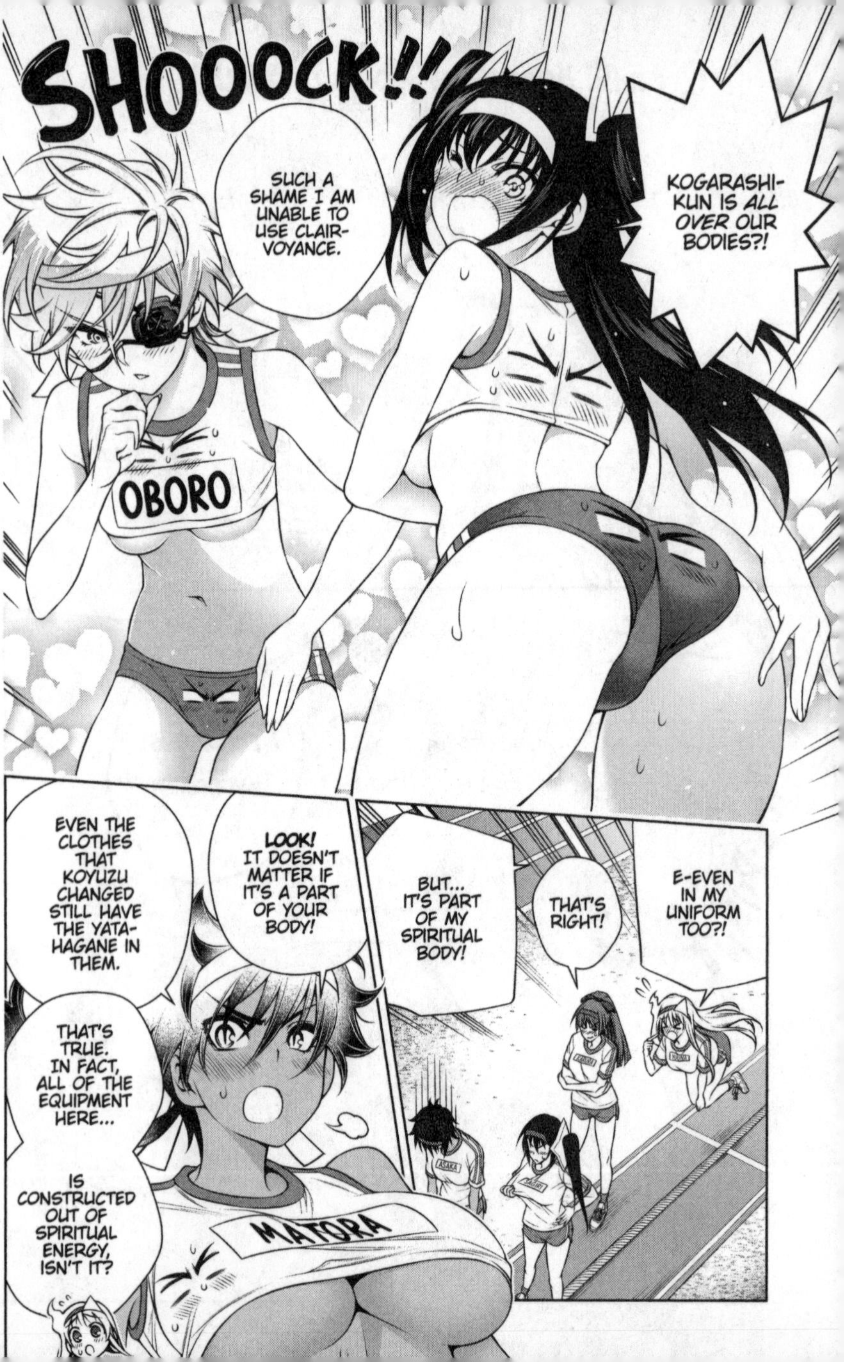
KOGARASHI-KUN IS *ALL OVER* OUR BODIES?!
SHOOOCK!!
SUCH A SHAME I AM UNABLE TO USE CLAIR-VOYANCE.
OBORO
E-EVEN IN MY UNIFORM TOO?!
THAT'S RIGHT!
BUT... IT'S PART OF MY SPIRITUAL BODY!
LOOK! IT DOESN'T MATTER IF IT'S A PART OF YOUR BODY!
EVEN THE CLOTHES THAT KOYUZU CHANGED STILL HAVE THE YATA-HAGANE IN THEM.
THAT'S TRUE. IN FACT, ALL OF THE EQUIPMENT HERE...
IS CONSTRUCTED OUT OF SPIRITUAL ENERGY, ISN'T IT?
MATORA

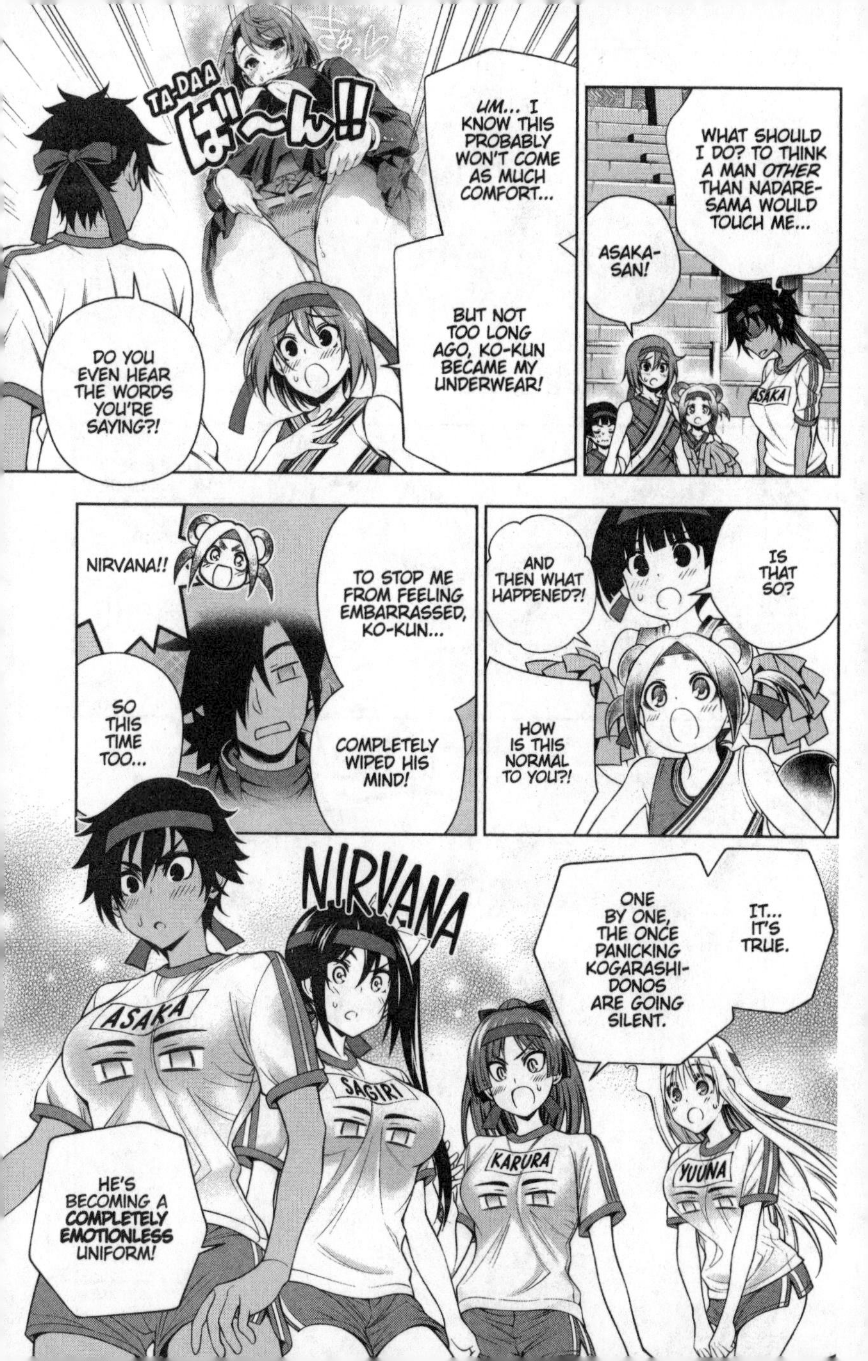
WHAT SHOULD I DO? TO THINK A MAN *OTHER* THAN NADARE-SAMA WOULD TOUCH ME...
ASAKA-SAN!
ASAKA
UM... I KNOW THIS PROBABLY WON'T COME AS MUCH COMFORT...
BUT NOT TOO LONG AGO, KO-KUN BECAME MY UNDERWEAR!
TA-DAA ば〜ん!!
DO YOU EVEN HEAR THE WORDS YOU'RE SAYING?!
IS THAT SO?
AND THEN WHAT HAPPENED?!
HOW IS THIS NORMAL TO YOU?!
TO STOP ME FROM FEELING EMBARRASSED, KO-KUN...
COMPLETELY WIPED HIS MIND!
NIRVANA!!
SO THIS TIME TOO...
IT... IT'S TRUE.
ONE BY ONE, THE ONCE PANICKING KOGARASHI-DONOS ARE GOING SILENT.
NIRVANA
ASAKA
SAGIRI
KARURA
YUUNA
HE'S BECOMING A **COMPLETELY EMOTIONLESS** UNIFORM!

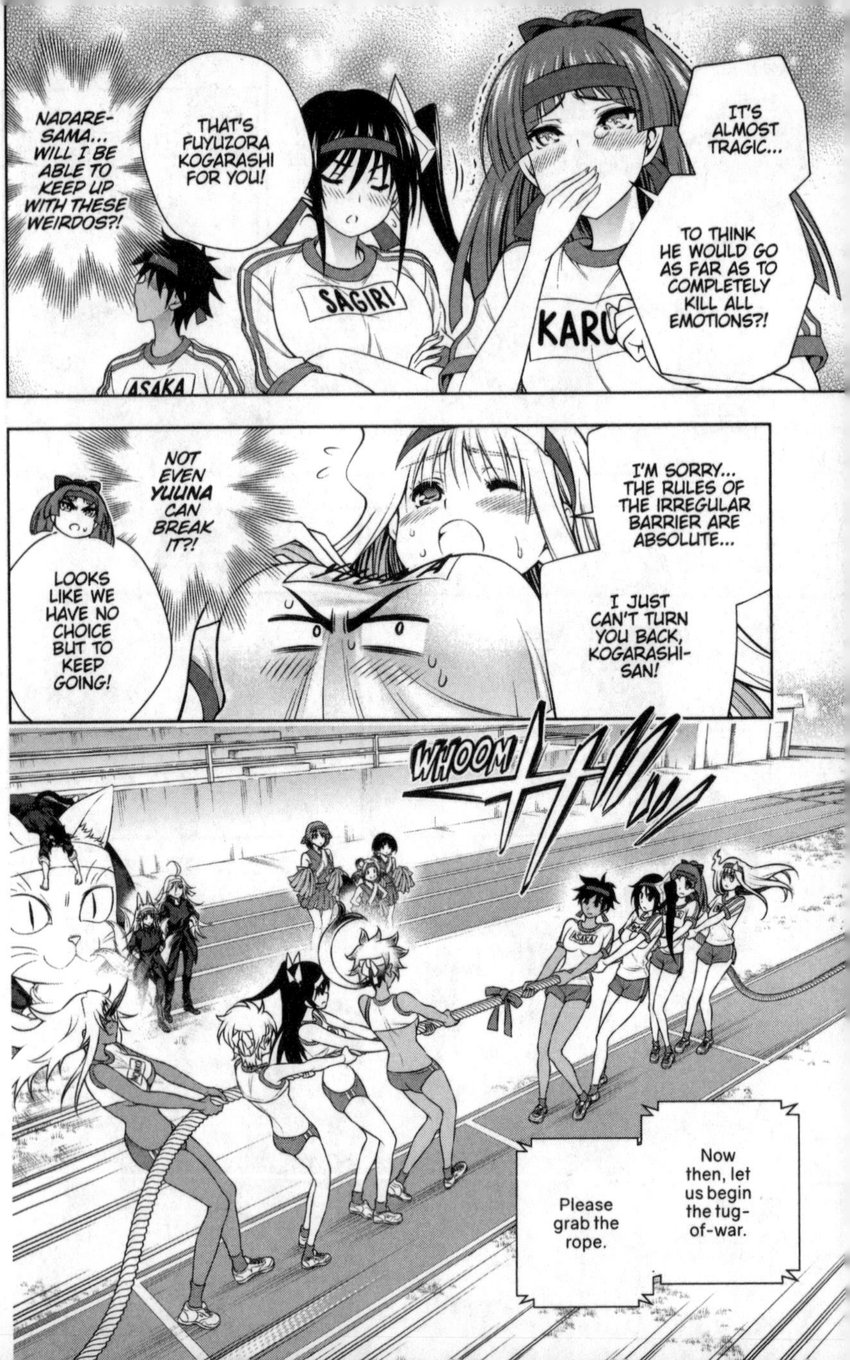
IT'S ALMOST TRAGIC...
TO THINK HE WOULD GO AS FAR AS TO COMPLETELY KILL ALL EMOTIONS?!
KARU
THAT'S FUYUZORA KOGARASHI FOR YOU!
SAGIRI
NADARE-SAMA... WILL I BE ABLE TO KEEP UP WITH THESE WEIRDOS?!
ASAKA
I'M SORRY... THE RULES OF THE IRREGULAR BARRIER ARE ABSOLUTE...
I JUST CAN'T TURN YOU BACK, KOGARASHI-SAN!
NOT EVEN YUUNA CAN BREAK IT?!
LOOKS LIKE WE HAVE NO CHOICE BUT TO KEEP GOING!
WHOOM
ASAKA
Now then, let us begin the tug-of-war.
Please grab the rope.

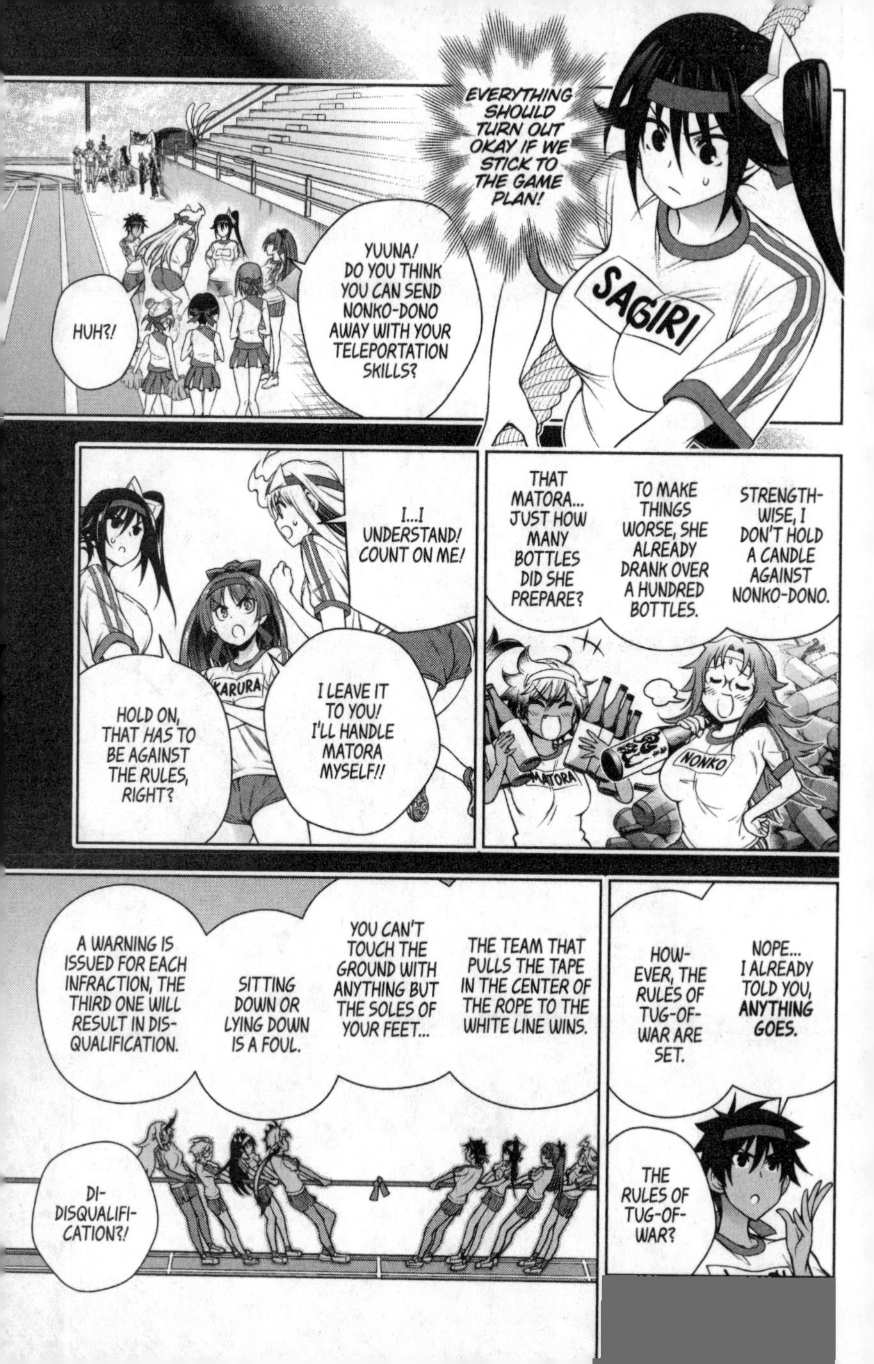
EVERYTHING SHOULD TURN OUT OKAY IF WE STICK TO THE GAME PLAN!
SAGIRI
YUUNA! DO YOU THINK YOU CAN SEND NONKO-DONO AWAY WITH YOUR TELEPORTATION SKILLS?
HUH?!
STRENGTH-WISE, I DON'T HOLD A CANDLE AGAINST NONKO-DONO.
TO MAKE THINGS WORSE, SHE ALREADY DRANK OVER A HUNDRED BOTTLES.
THAT MATORA... JUST HOW MANY BOTTLES DID SHE PREPARE?
NONKO
MATORA
I...I UNDERSTAND! COUNT ON ME!
I LEAVE IT TO YOU! I'LL HANDLE MATORA MYSELF!!
KARURA
HOLD ON, THAT *HAS* TO BE AGAINST THE RULES, RIGHT?
NOPE... I ALREADY TOLD YOU, **ANYTHING GOES.**
HOW-EVER, THE RULES OF TUG-OF-WAR ARE SET.
THE RULES OF TUG-OF-WAR?
THE TEAM THAT PULLS THE TAPE IN THE CENTER OF THE ROPE TO THE WHITE LINE WINS.
YOU CAN'T TOUCH THE GROUND WITH ANYTHING BUT THE SOLES OF YOUR FEET...
SITTING DOWN OR LYING DOWN IS A FOUL.
A WARNING IS ISSUED FOR EACH INFRACTION, THE THIRD ONE WILL RESULT IN DIS-QUALIFICATION.
DI-DISQUALIFI-CATION?!

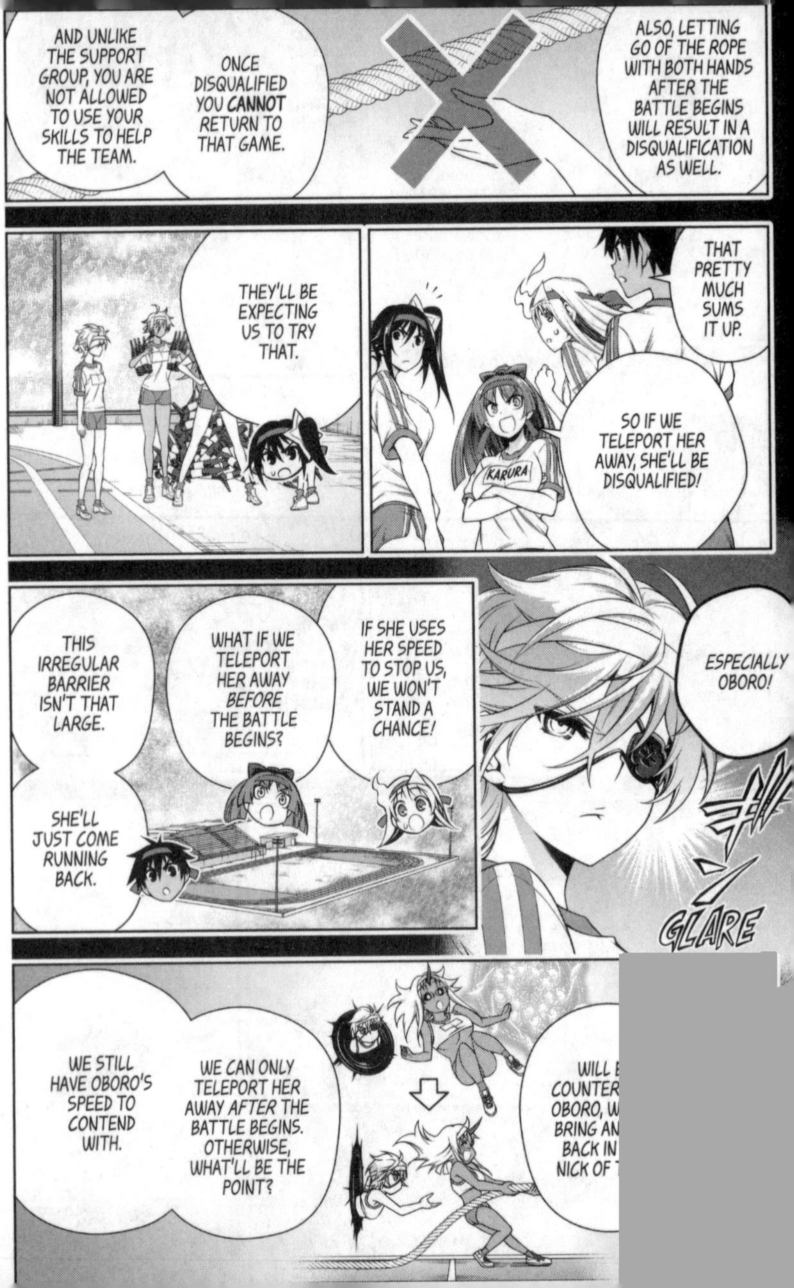

ALSO, LETTING GO OF THE ROPE WITH BOTH HANDS AFTER THE BATTLE BEGINS WILL RESULT IN A DISQUALIFICATION AS WELL.
ONCE DISQUALIFIED YOU CANNOT RETURN TO THAT GAME.
AND UNLIKE THE SUPPORT GROUP, YOU ARE NOT ALLOWED TO USE YOUR SKILLS TO HELP THE TEAM.
THAT PRETTY MUCH SUMS IT UP.
KARURA
SO IF WE TELEPORT HER AWAY, SHE'LL BE DISQUALIFIED!
THEY'LL BE EXPECTING US TO TRY THAT.
ESPECIALLY OBORO!
GLARE
IF SHE USES HER SPEED TO STOP US, WE WON'T STAND A CHANCE!
WHAT IF WE TELEPORT HER AWAY BEFORE THE BATTLE BEGINS?
THIS IRREGULAR BARRIER ISN'T THAT LARGE.
SHE'LL JUST COME RUNNING BACK.
WILL B COUNTER OBORO, W BRING AN BACK IN NICK OF T
WE CAN ONLY TELEPORT HER AWAY AFTER THE BATTLE BEGINS. OTHERWISE, WHAT'LL BE THE POINT?
WE STILL HAVE OBORO'S SPEED TO CONTEND WITH.

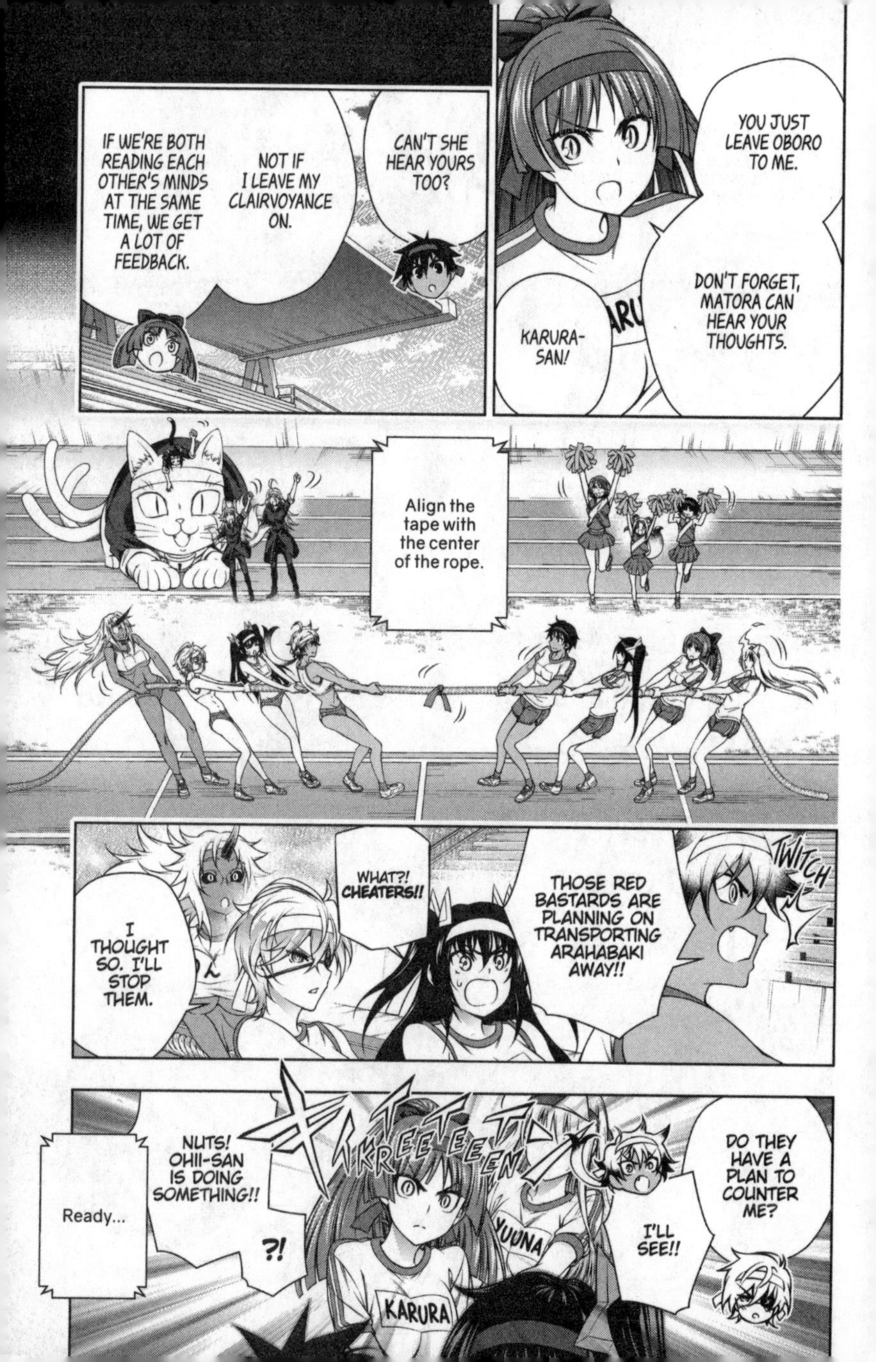
YOU JUST LEAVE OBORO TO ME.
DON'T FORGET, MATORA CAN HEAR YOUR THOUGHTS.
KARURA-SAN!
CAN'T SHE HEAR YOURS TOO?
NOT IF I LEAVE MY CLAIRVOYANCE ON.
IF WE'RE BOTH READING EACH OTHER'S MINDS AT THE SAME TIME, WE GET A LOT OF FEEDBACK.
Align the tape with the center of the rope.
TWITCH
THOSE RED BASTARDS ARE PLANNING ON TRANSPORTING ARAHABAKI AWAY!!
WHAT?! CHEATERS!!
I THOUGHT SO. I'LL STOP THEM.
DO THEY HAVE A PLAN TO COUNTER ME?
KREEEEEEN
I'LL SEE!!
NUTS! OHII-SAN IS DOING SOMETHING!!
?!
Ready...

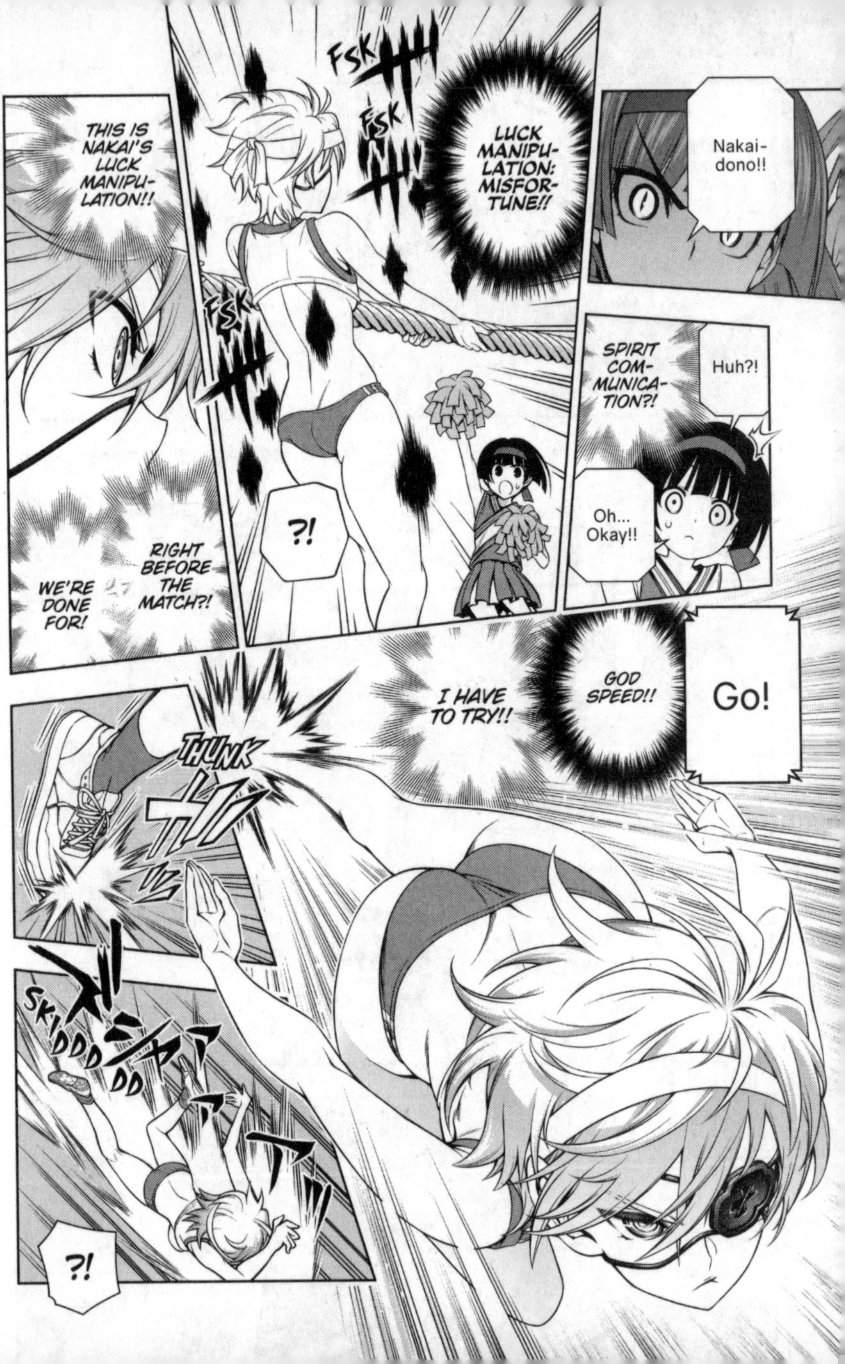

Nakai-dono!!
Huh?!
SPIRIT COMMUNICATION?!
Oh... Okay!!
FSK
FSK
LUCK MANIPULATION: MISFORTUNE!!
FSK
?!
THIS IS NAKAI'S LUCK MANIPULATION!!
RIGHT BEFORE THE MATCH?!
WE'RE DONE FOR!
Go!
GOD SPEED!!
I HAVE TO TRY!!
THUNK
SKIDDDDDD
?!

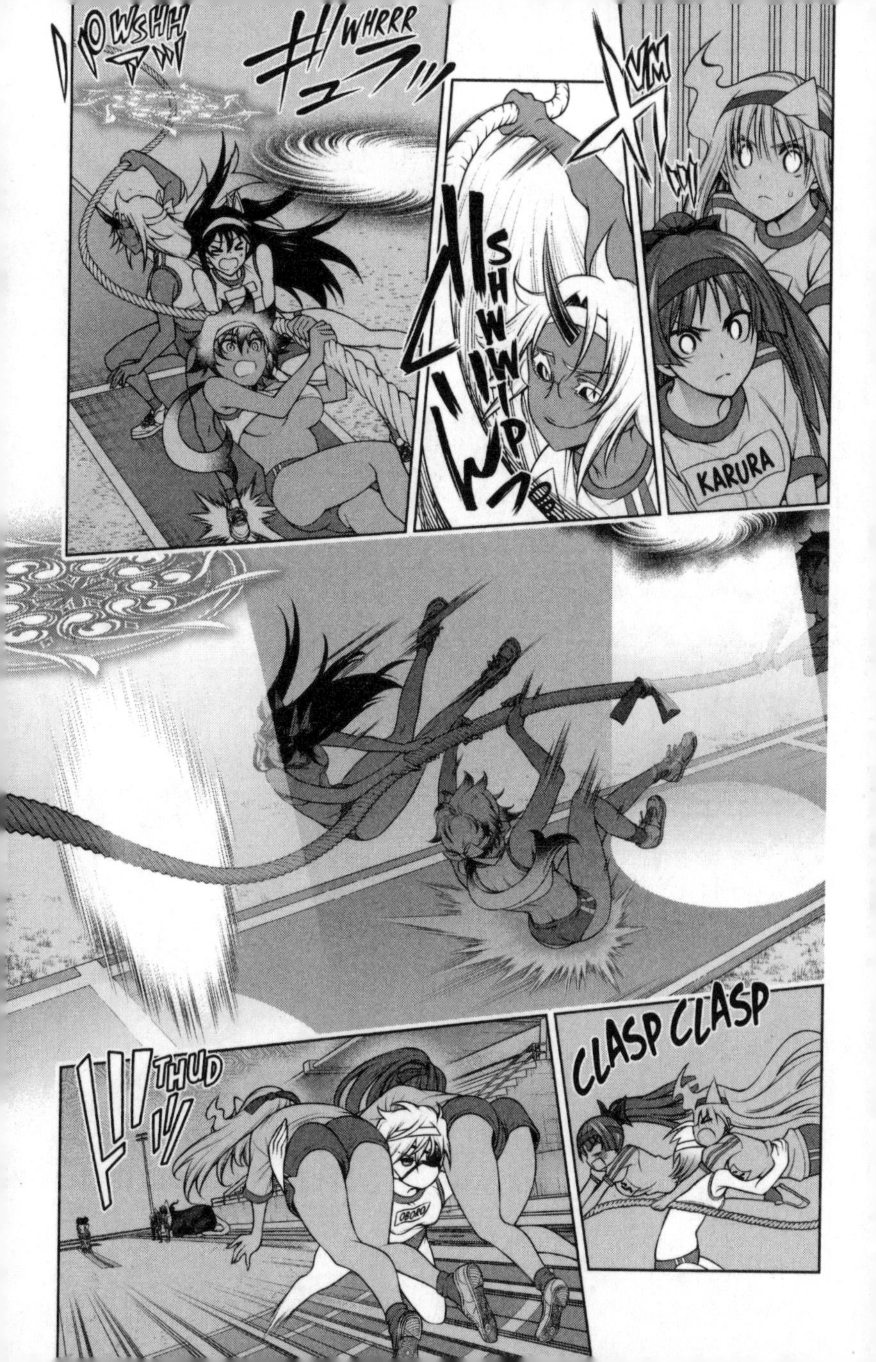
VM
KARURA
SHWIWIP
WSHH
WHRRR
CLASP CLASP
THUD
OBORO

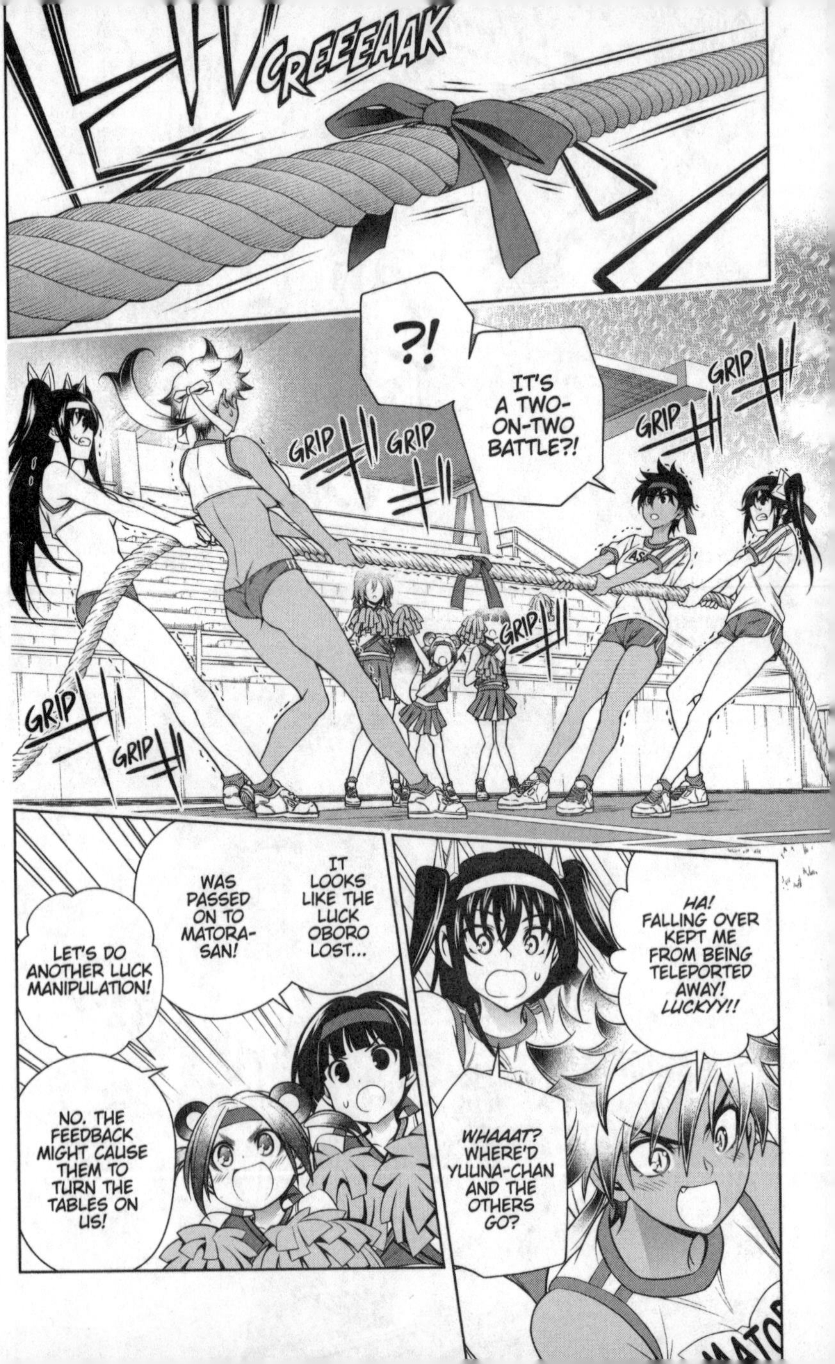
CREEEAAK
?!
IT'S A TWO-ON-TWO BATTLE?!
GRIP GRIP
GRIP GRIP
GRIP
GRIP
GRIP GRIP
HA! FALLING OVER KEPT ME FROM BEING TELEPORTED AWAY! LUCKYY!!
WHAAAT? WHERE'D YUUNA-CHAN AND THE OTHERS GO?
IT LOOKS LIKE THE LUCK OBORO LOST...
WAS PASSED ON TO MATORA-SAN!
LET'S DO ANOTHER LUCK MANIPULATION!
NO. THE FEEDBACK MIGHT CAUSE THEM TO TURN THE TABLES ON US!

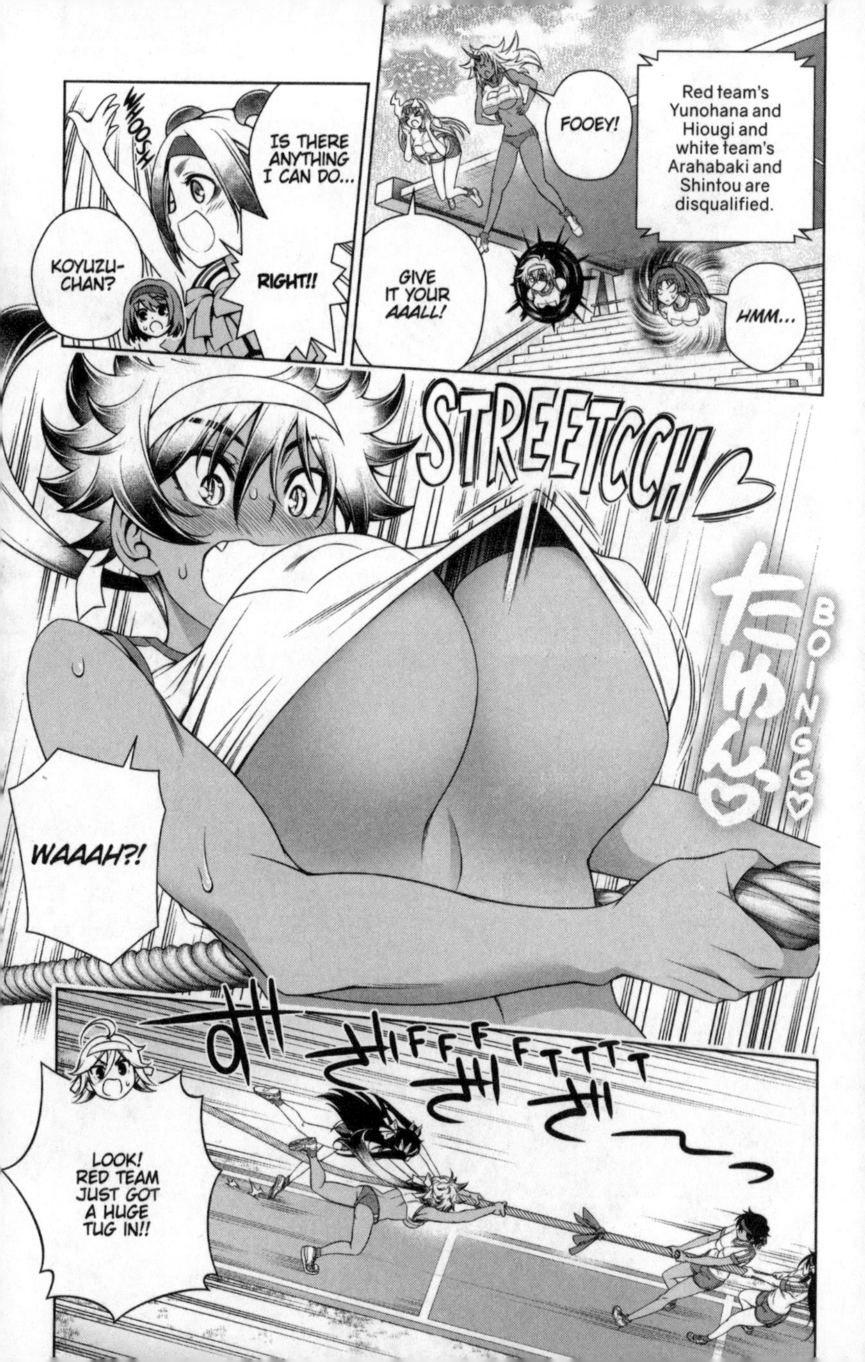

Red team's Yunohana and Hiougi and white team's Arahabaki and Shintou are disqualified.
FOOEY!
HMM...
GIVE IT YOUR AAALL!
IS THERE ANYTHING I CAN DO...
WHOOSH
RIGHT!!
KOYUZU-CHAN?
STREETCCH
たゆん♡
BOINGG♡
WAAAH?!
ずざざ〜っ
SHIFFFFFTTTTT
LOOK! RED TEAM JUST GOT A HUGE TUG IN!!

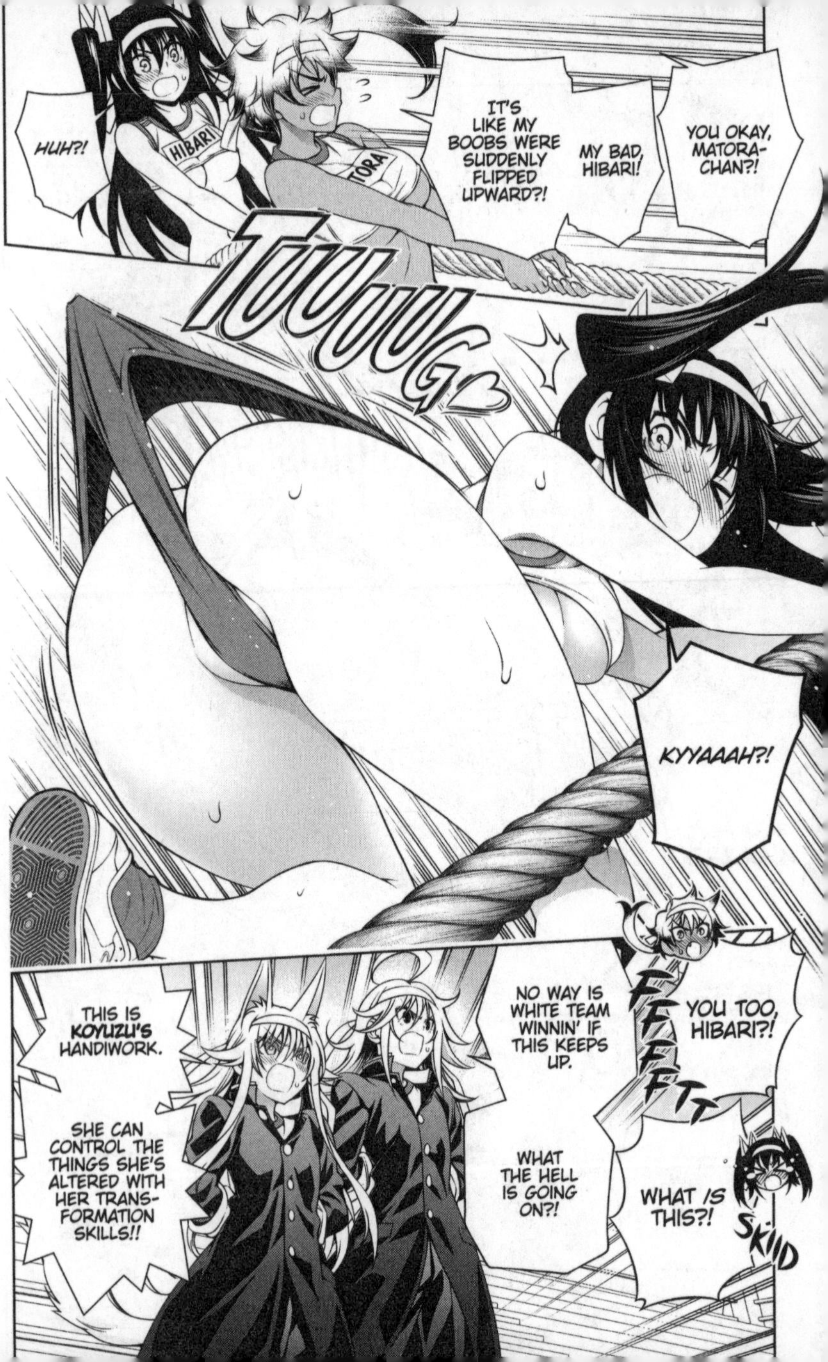
YOU OKAY, MATORA-CHAN?!
MY BAD, HIBARI!
IT'S LIKE MY BOOBS WERE SUDDENLY FLIPPED UPWARD?!
HUH?!
HIBARI
TORA
TUUUUG
KYYAAAH?!
YOU TOO, HIBARI?!
FFFFFTT
NO WAY IS WHITE TEAM WINNIN' IF THIS KEEPS UP.
WHAT IS THIS?!
SKIID
WHAT THE HELL IS GOING ON?!
THIS IS KOYUZU'S HANDIWORK.
SHE CAN CONTROL THE THINGS SHE'S ALTERED WITH HER TRANS-FORMATION SKILLS!!

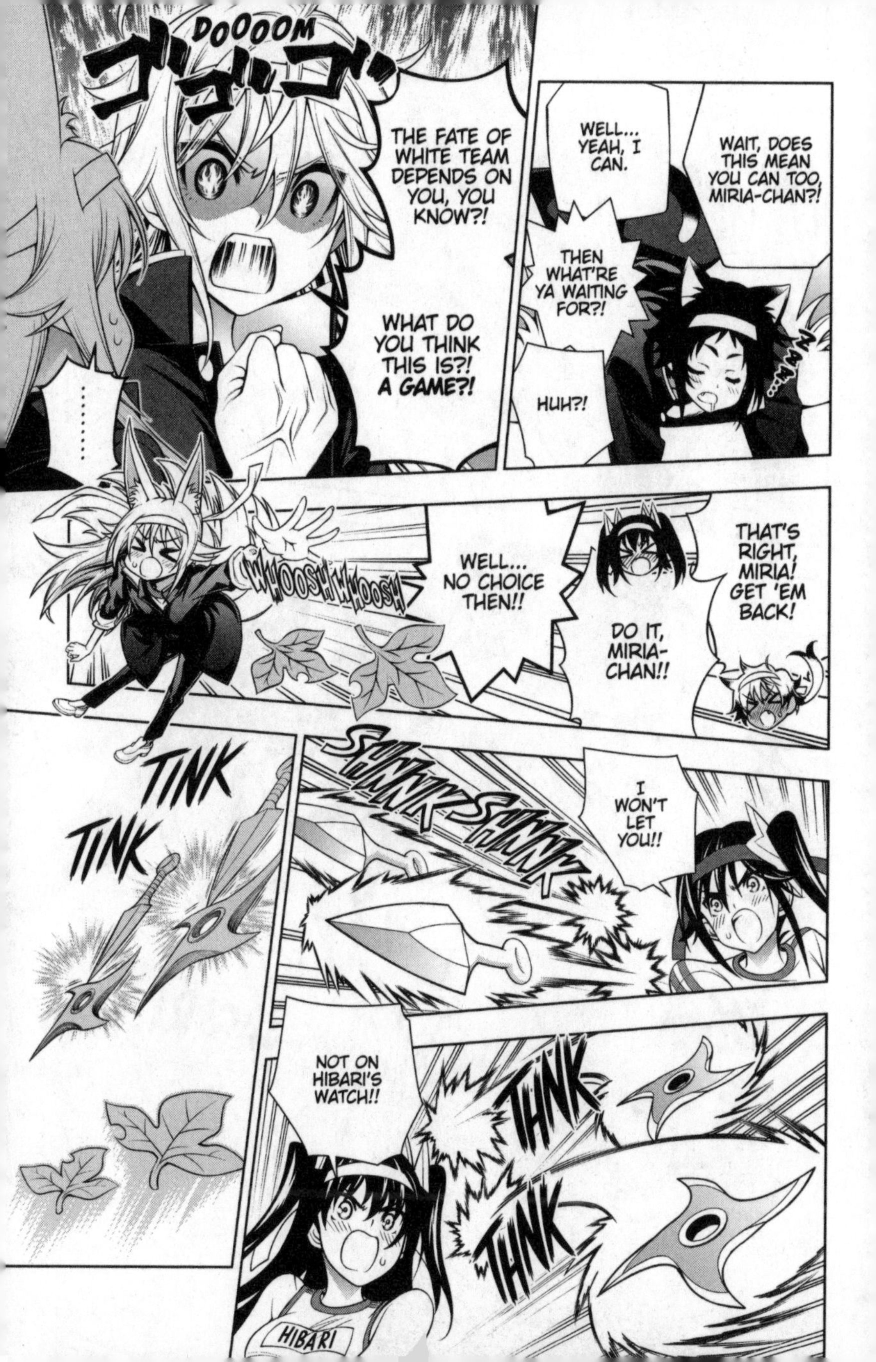
WAIT, DOES THIS MEAN YOU CAN TOO, MIRIA-CHAN?!
WELL... YEAH, I CAN.
THEN WHAT'RE YA WAITING FOR?!
HUH?!
DOOOOM
THE FATE OF WHITE TEAM DEPENDS ON YOU, YOU KNOW?!
WHAT DO YOU THINK THIS IS?! A GAME?!
......
THAT'S RIGHT, MIRIA! GET 'EM BACK!
DO IT, MIRIA-CHAN!!
WELL... NO CHOICE THEN!!
WHOOSH WHOOSH
I WON'T LET YOU!!
SHUNK SHUNK
TINK
TINK
THNK
NOT ON HIBARI'S WATCH!!
THNK
HIBARI

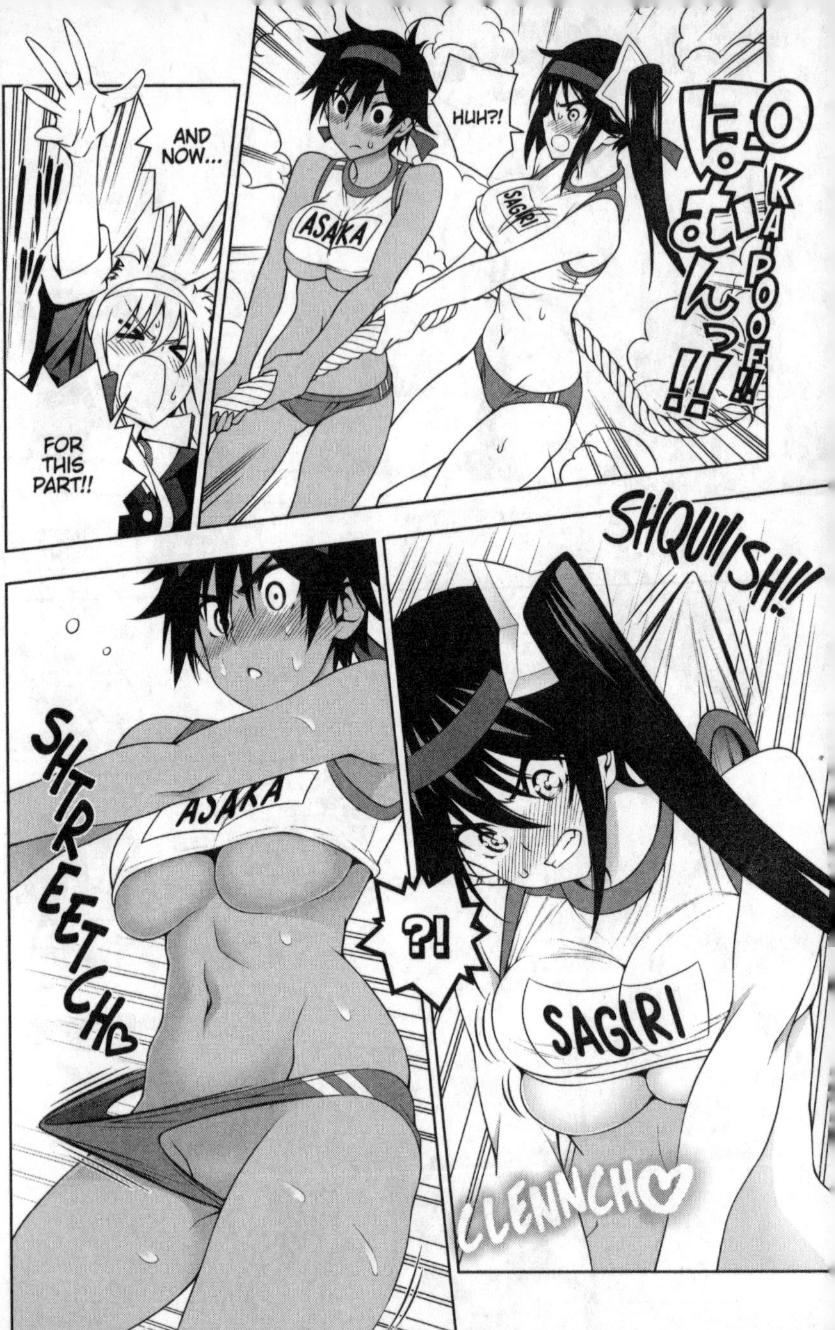
HUH?!
ASAKA
SAGIRI
ぼむんっ!!
KAPOOF!!
AND NOW...
FOR THIS PART!!
SHQUIIISH!!
SAGIRI
CLENNCH♡
ASAKA
?!
SHTREEETCH♡

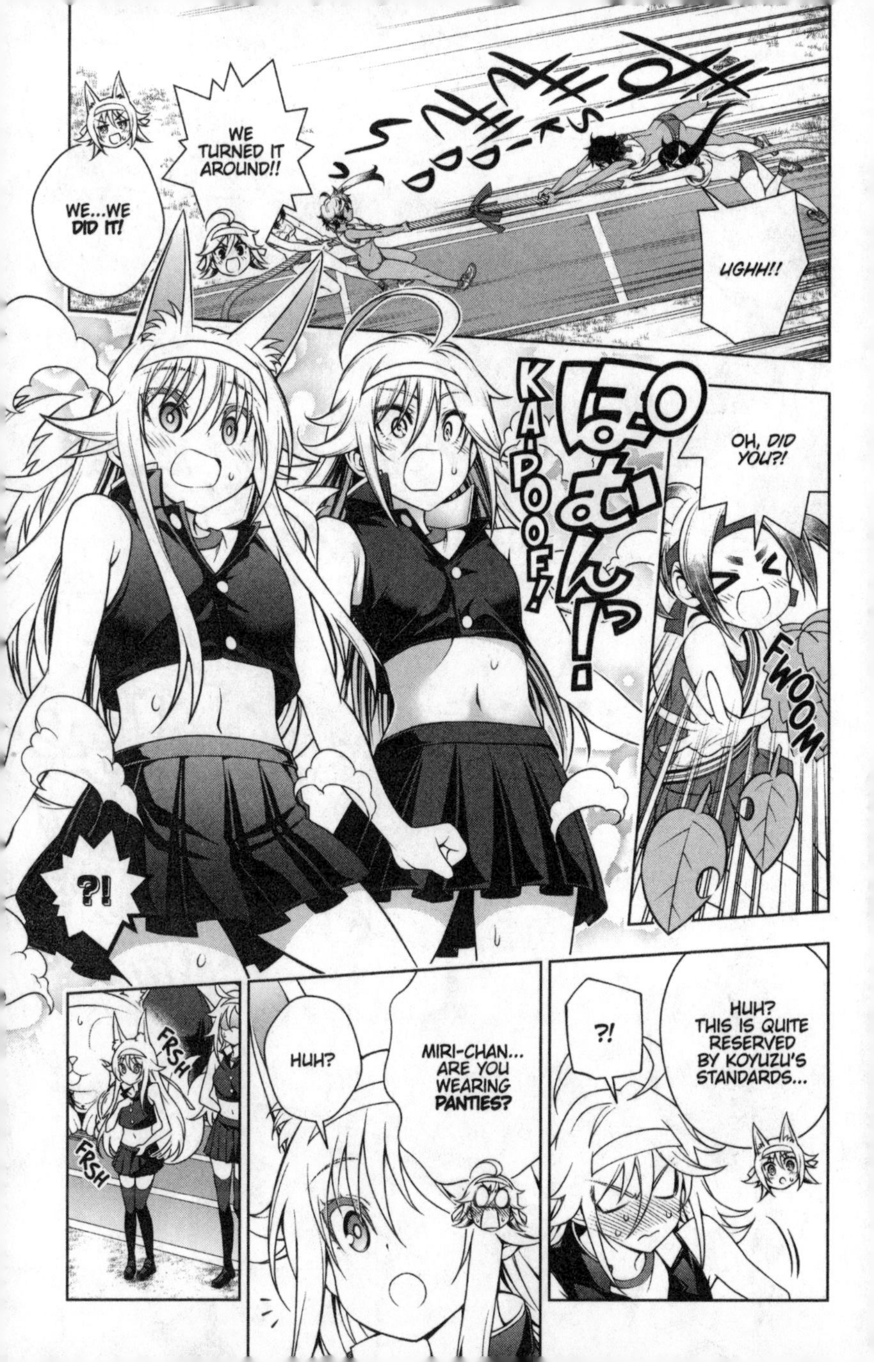
UGHH!!
WE TURNED IT AROUND!!
WE...WE DID IT!
OH, DID YOU?!
FWOOM
KAPOOF!
?!
HUH? THIS IS QUITE RESERVED BY KOYUZU'S STANDARDS...
?!
MIRI-CHAN... ARE YOU WEARING PANTIES?
HUH?
FRSH
FRSH

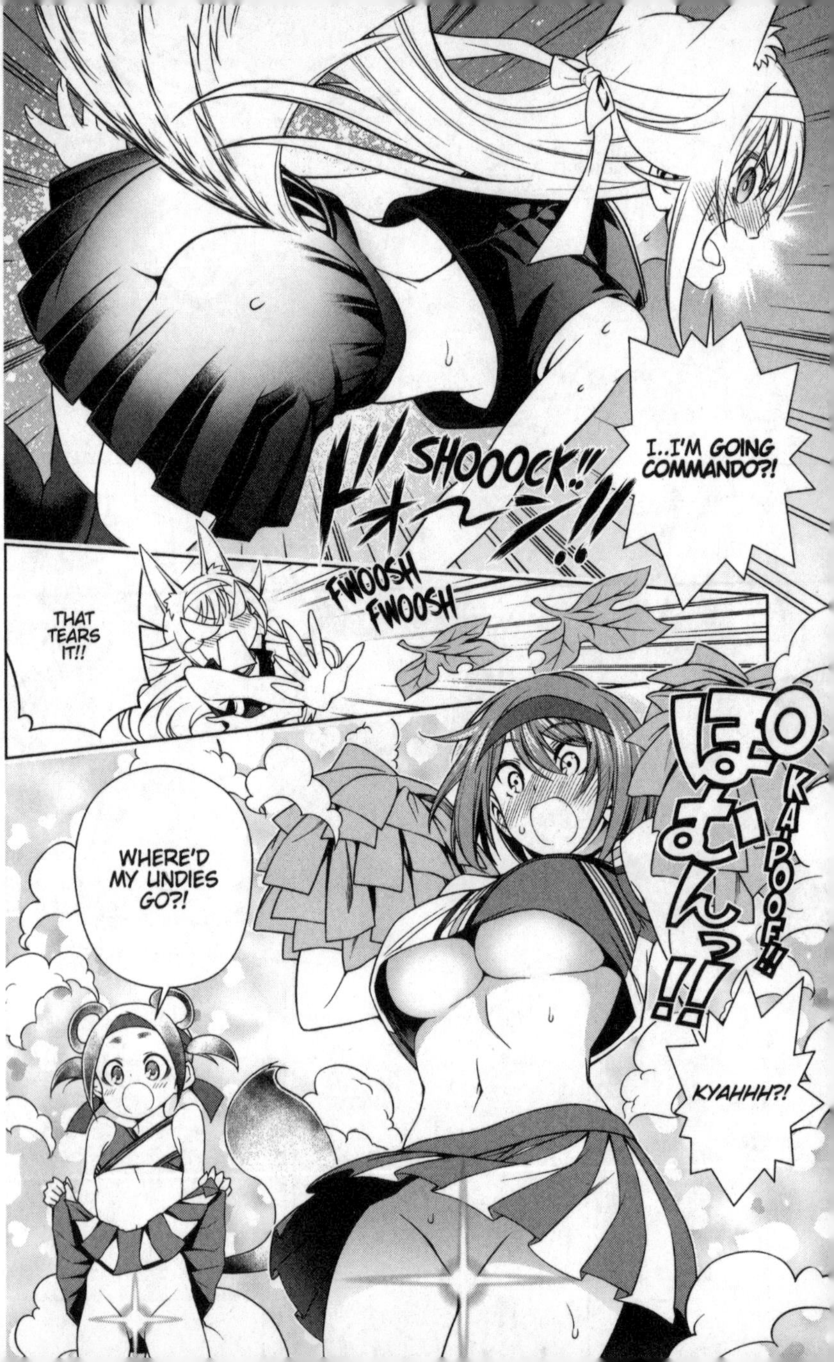
I..I'M GOING COMMANDO?!
SHOOOCK!!
ドォ～ン!!
FWOOSH FWOOSH
THAT TEARS IT!!
ぽむんっ!!
KAPOOF!!
KYAHHH?!
WHERE'D MY UNDIES GO?!

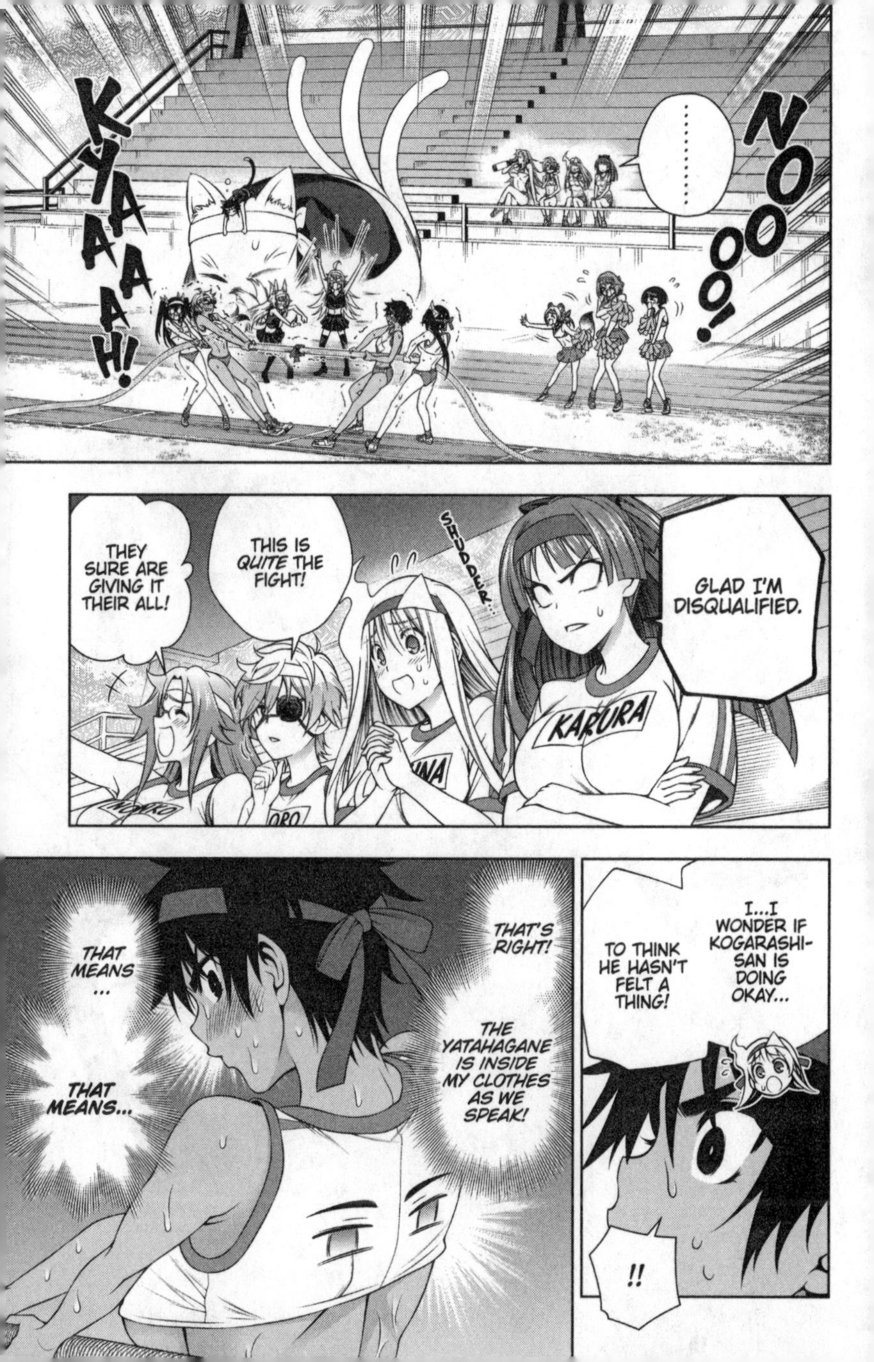
NOOOOO!
......
KYAAAAH!
GLAD I'M DISQUALIFIED.
KARURA
SHUDDER...
THIS IS *QUITE* THE FIGHT!
THEY SURE ARE GIVING IT THEIR ALL!
I...I WONDER IF KOGARASHI-SAN IS DOING OKAY...
TO THINK HE HASN'T FELT A THING!
!!
THAT'S RIGHT!
THE YATAHAGANE IS INSIDE MY CLOTHES AS WE SPEAK!
THAT MEANS...
THAT MEANS...

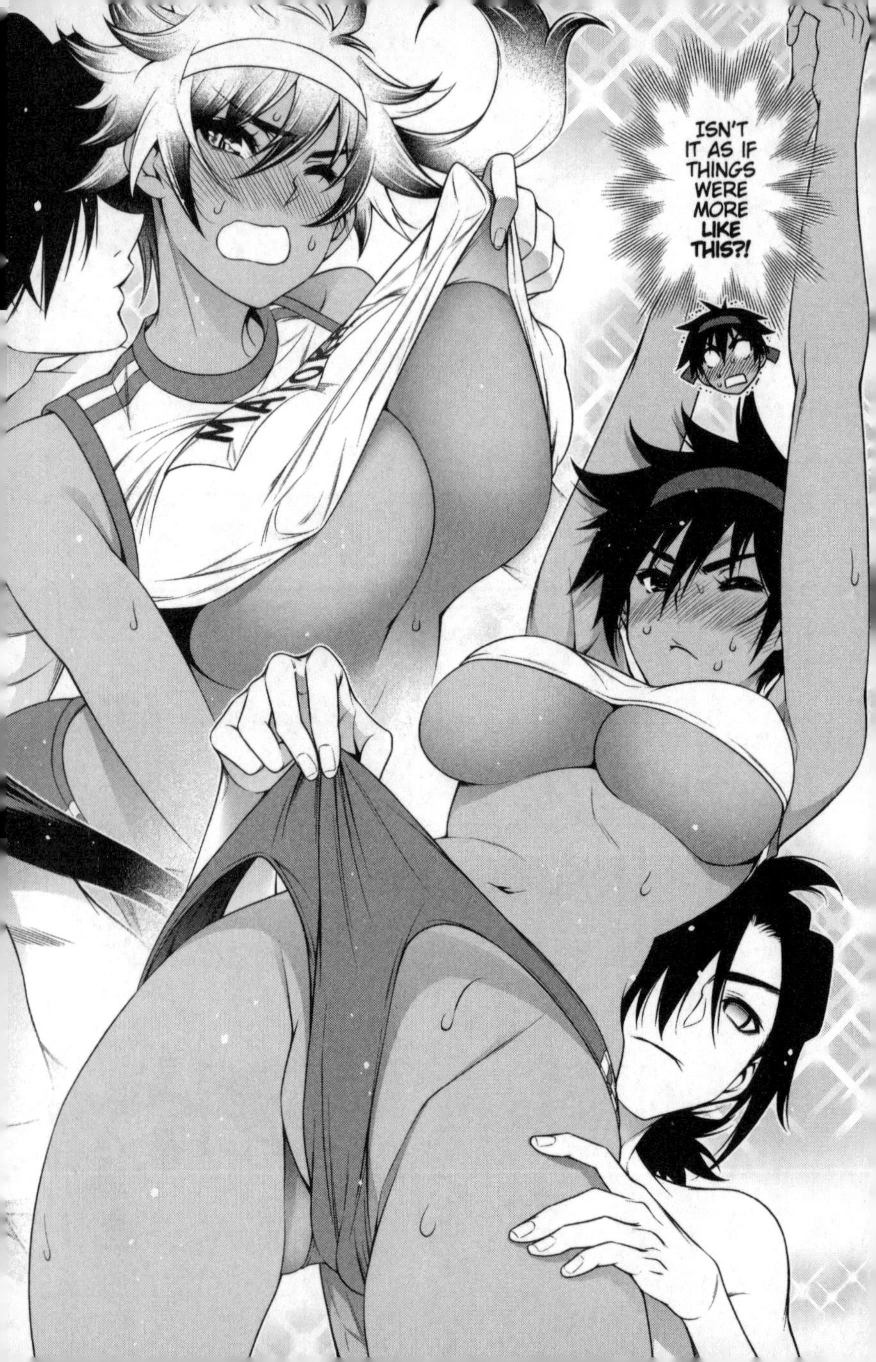
ISN'T IT AS IF THINGS WERE MORE LIKE THIS?!

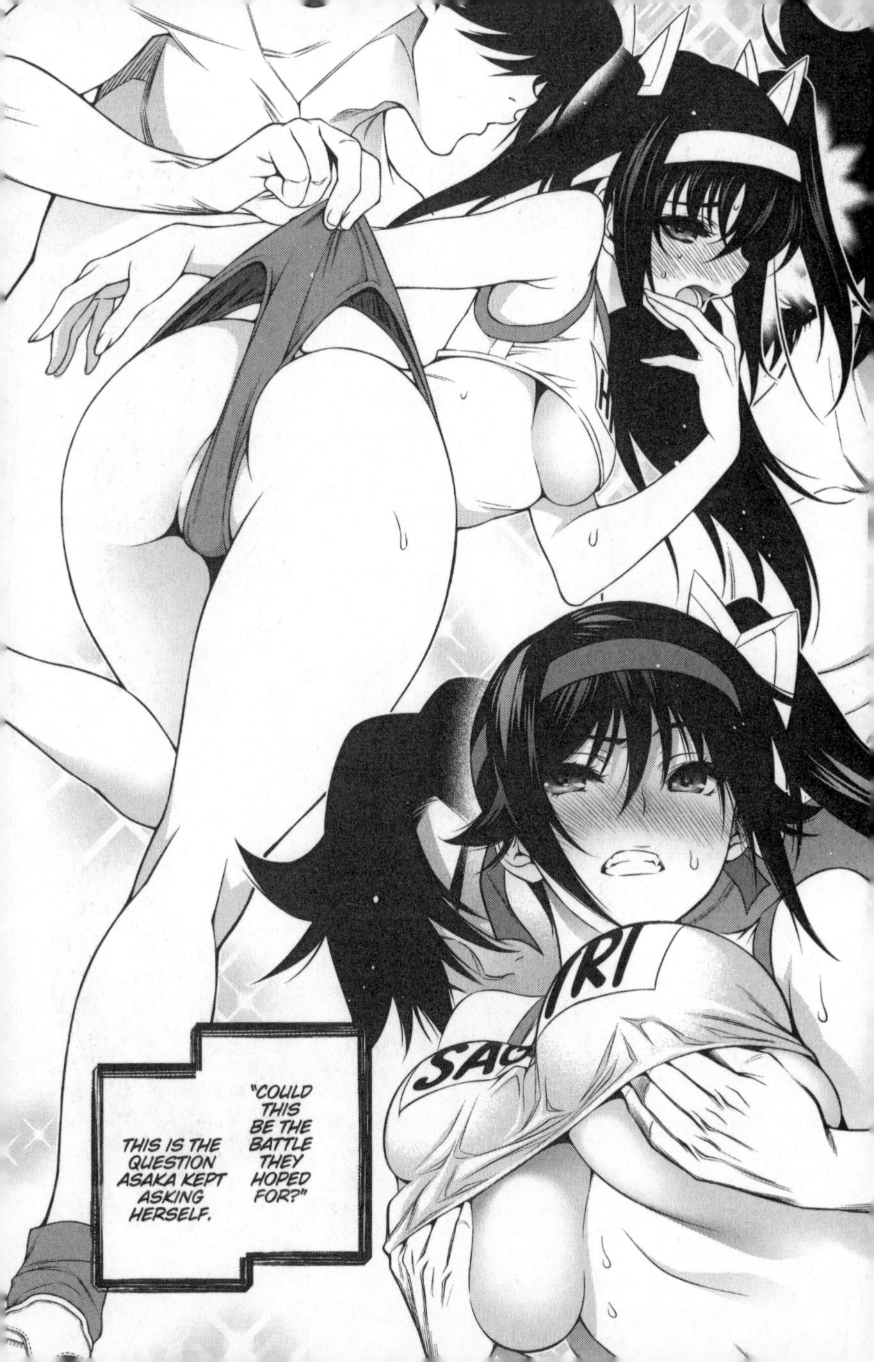
"COULD THIS BE THE BATTLE THEY HOPED FOR?"
THIS IS THE QUESTION ASAKA KEPT ASKING HERSELF.

175 Yuragi-sou's Ultimate Autumn Sports Festival Ends!

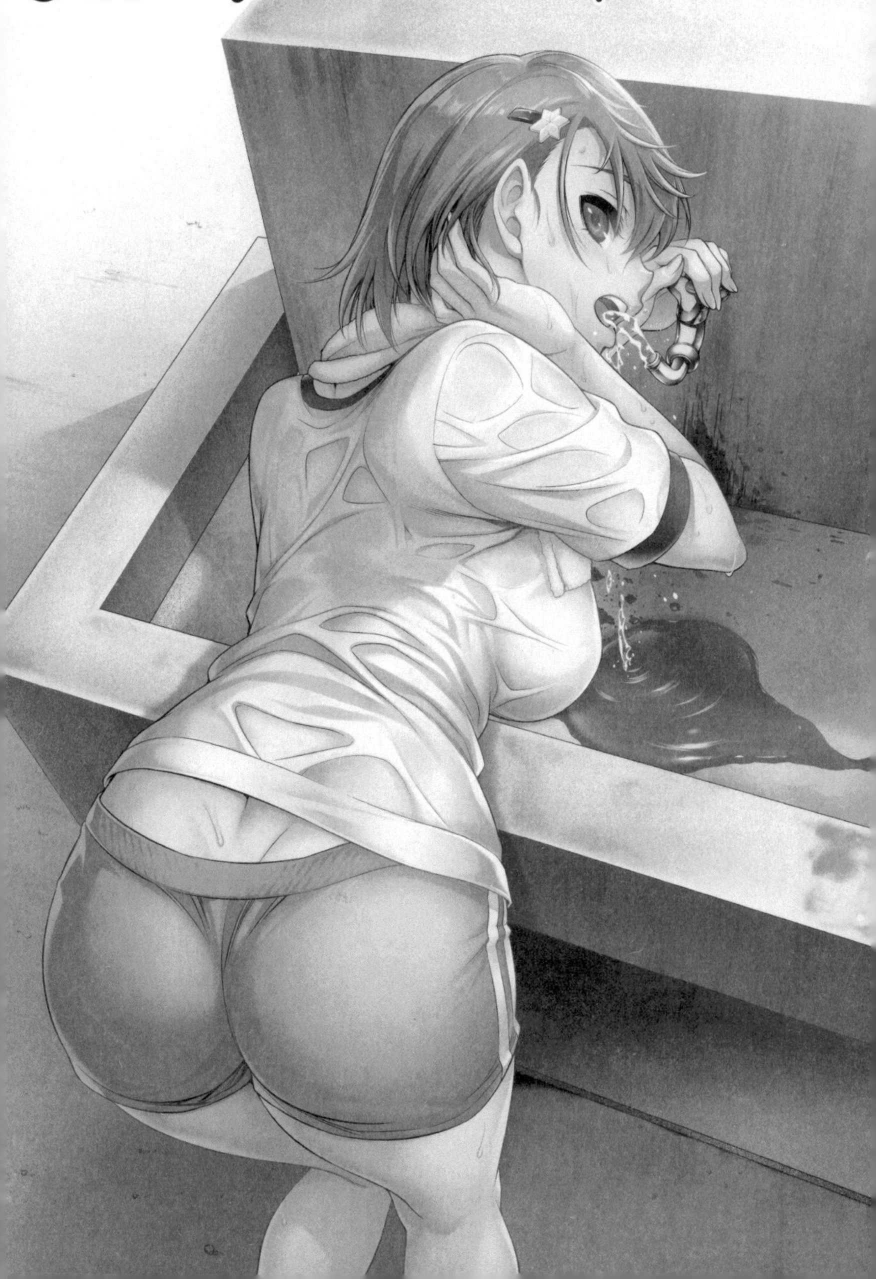

Yuuna and the Haunted Hot Springs

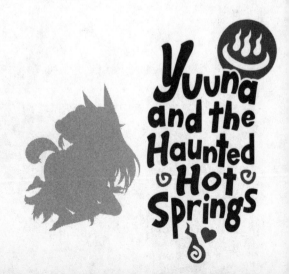

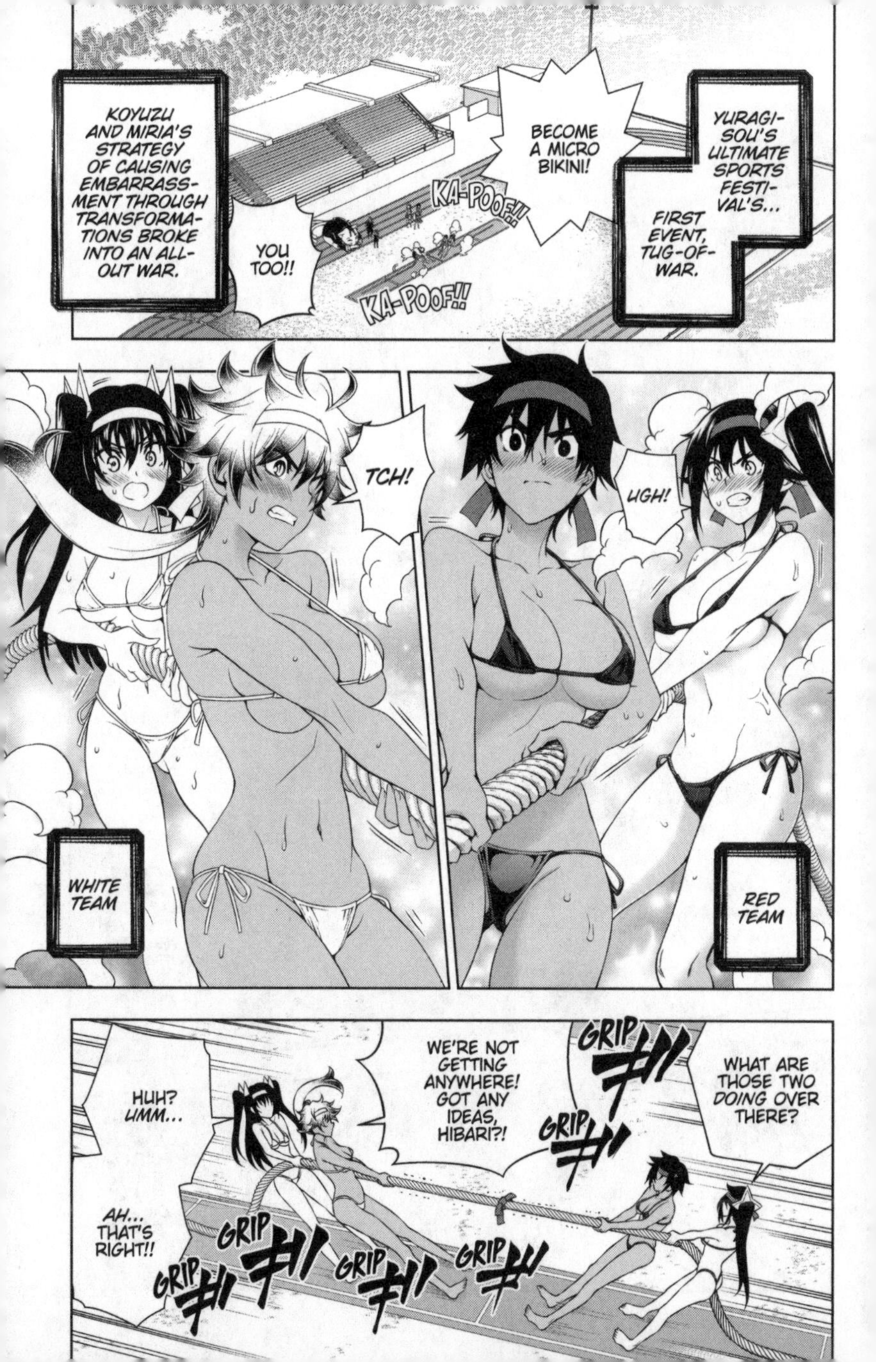
YURAGI-SOU'S ULTIMATE SPORTS FESTIVAL'S...
FIRST EVENT, TUG-OF-WAR.
BECOME A MICRO BIKINI!
KA-POOF!!
KOYUZU AND MIRIA'S STRATEGY OF CAUSING EMBARRASS-MENT THROUGH TRANSFORMA-TIONS BROKE INTO AN ALL-OUT WAR.
YOU TOO!!
KA-POOF!!
UGH!
RED TEAM
TCH!
WHITE TEAM
WHAT ARE THOSE TWO DOING OVER THERE?
GRIP
GRIP
WE'RE NOT GETTING ANYWHERE! GOT ANY IDEAS, HIBARI?!
HUH? UMM...
GRIP
GRIP
GRIP
GRIP
AH... THAT'S RIGHT!!

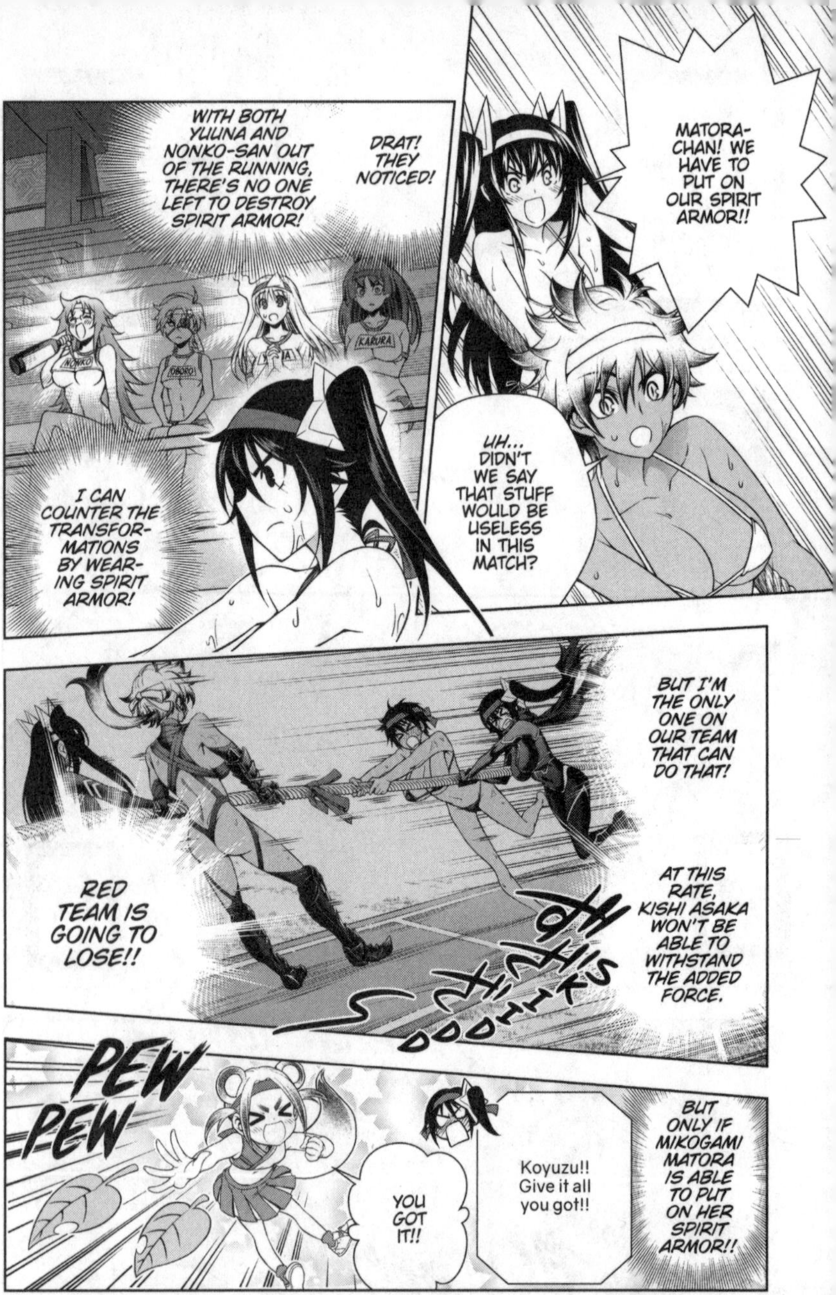
MATORA-CHAN! WE HAVE TO PUT ON OUR SPIRIT ARMOR!!
UH... DIDN'T WE SAY THAT STUFF WOULD BE USELESS IN THIS MATCH?
DRAT! THEY NOTICED!
WITH BOTH YUUNA AND NONKO-SAN OUT OF THE RUNNING, THERE'S NO ONE LEFT TO DESTROY SPIRIT ARMOR!
I CAN COUNTER THE TRANSFORMATIONS BY WEARING SPIRIT ARMOR!
BUT I'M THE ONLY ONE ON OUR TEAM THAT CAN DO THAT!
AT THIS RATE, KISHI ASAKA WON'T BE ABLE TO WITHSTAND THE ADDED FORCE.
RED TEAM IS GOING TO LOSE!!
BUT ONLY IF MIKOGAMI MATORA IS ABLE TO PUT ON HER SPIRIT ARMOR!!
Koyuzu!! Give it all you got!!
YOU GOT IT!!
PEW PEW

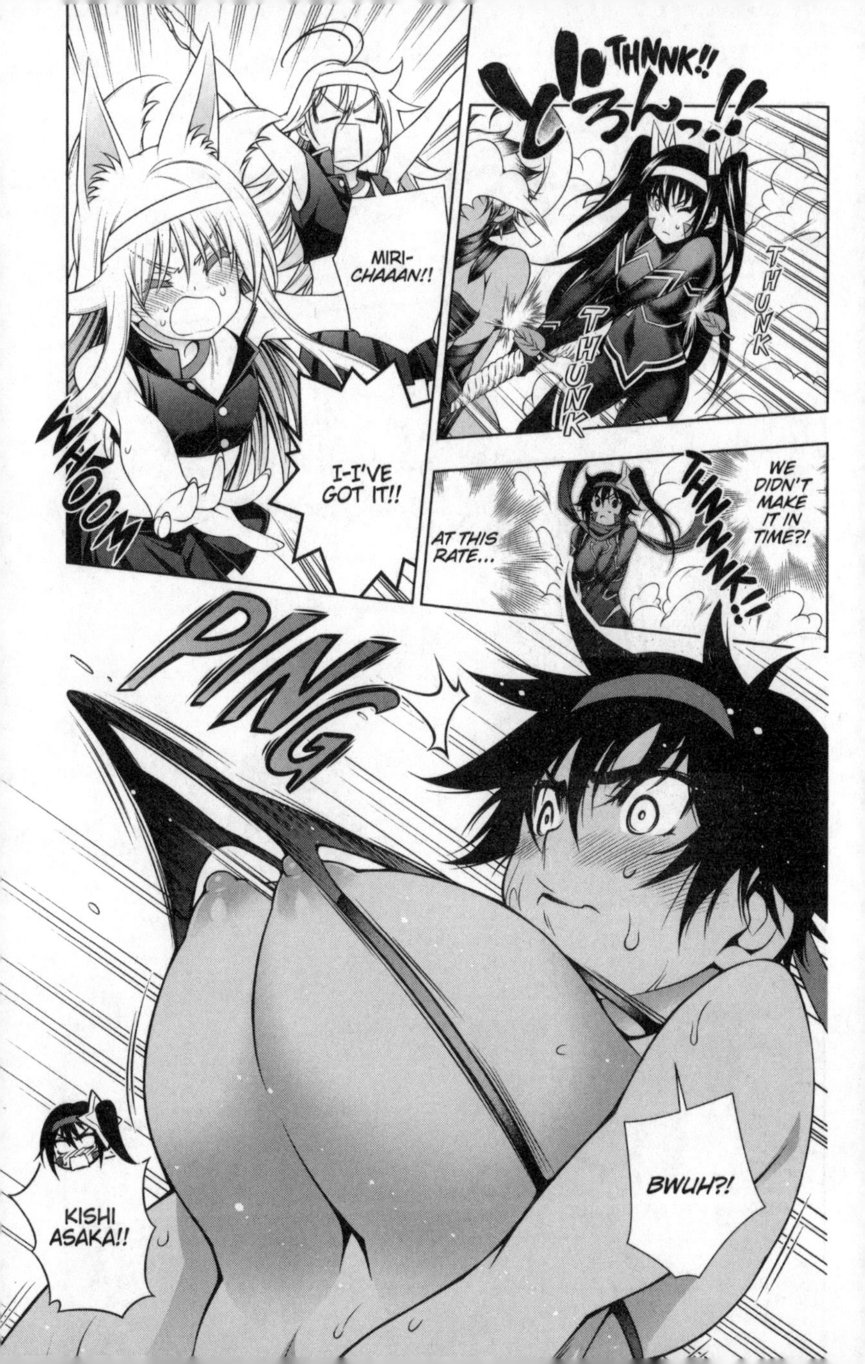
THNNK!!
とろんっ!!
THUNK
THUNK
WE DIDN'T MAKE IT IN TIME?!
THNNNNK!!!
AT THIS RATE...
MIRI-CHAAAN!!
I-I'VE GOT IT!!
WHOOM
PING
BWUH?!
KISHI ASAKA!!

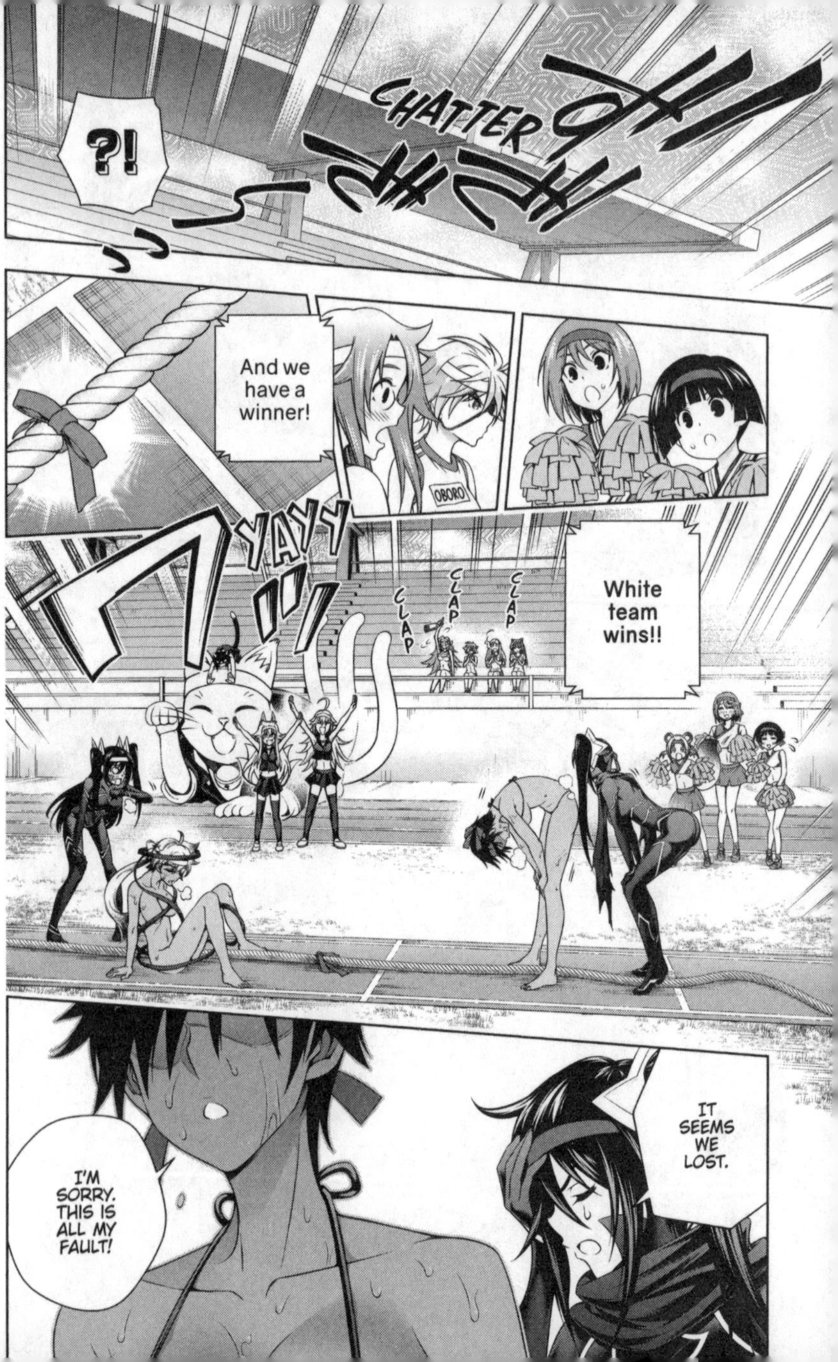
CHATTER
?!
And we have a winner!
White team wins!!
YAYY
CLAP CLAP CLAP
IT SEEMS WE LOST.
I'M SORRY. THIS IS ALL MY FAULT!

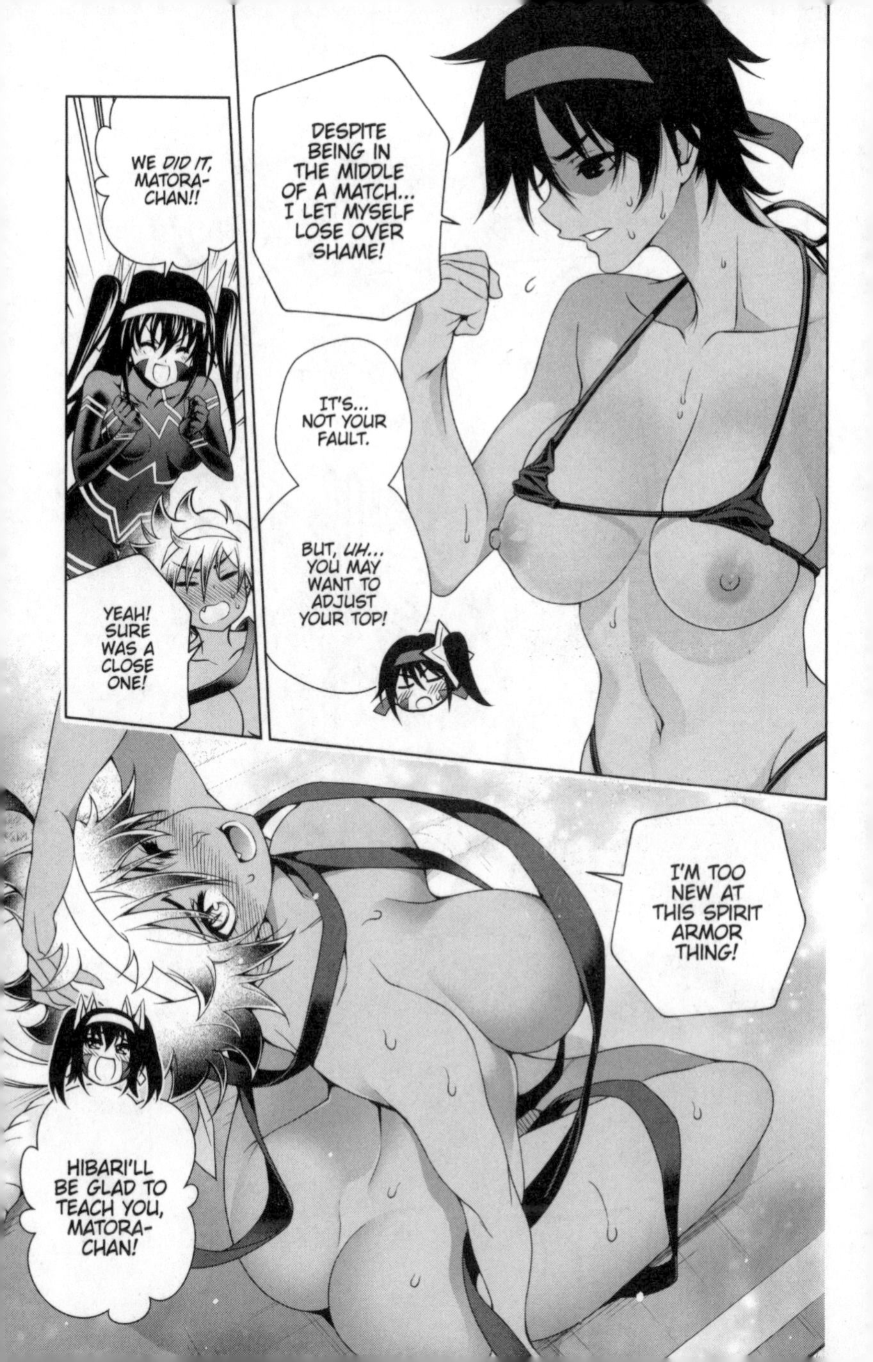
DESPITE BEING IN THE MIDDLE OF A MATCH... I LET MYSELF LOSE OVER SHAME!
IT'S... NOT YOUR FAULT.
BUT, *UH*... YOU MAY WANT TO ADJUST YOUR TOP!
WE *DID IT*, MATORA-CHAN!!
YEAH! SURE WAS A CLOSE ONE!
I'M TOO NEW AT THIS SPIRIT ARMOR THING!
HIBARI'LL BE GLAD TO TEACH YOU, MATORA-CHAN!

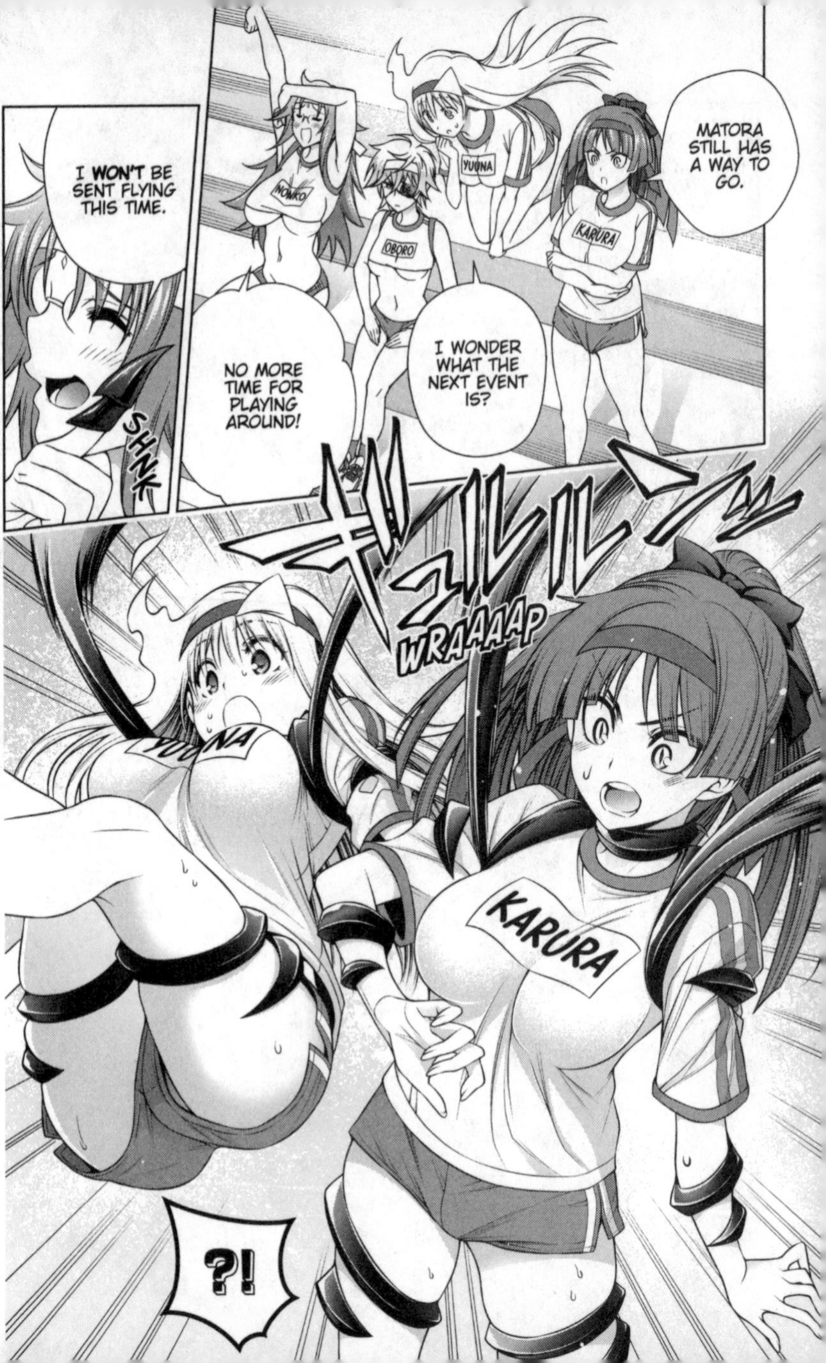
MATORA STILL HAS A WAY TO GO.
KARURA
YUUNA
OBORO
I WONDER WHAT THE NEXT EVENT IS?
NO MORE TIME FOR PLAYING AROUND!
I WON'T BE SENT FLYING THIS TIME.
SHNK
ギュルルンッ
WRAAAAP
YUUNA
KARURA
?!

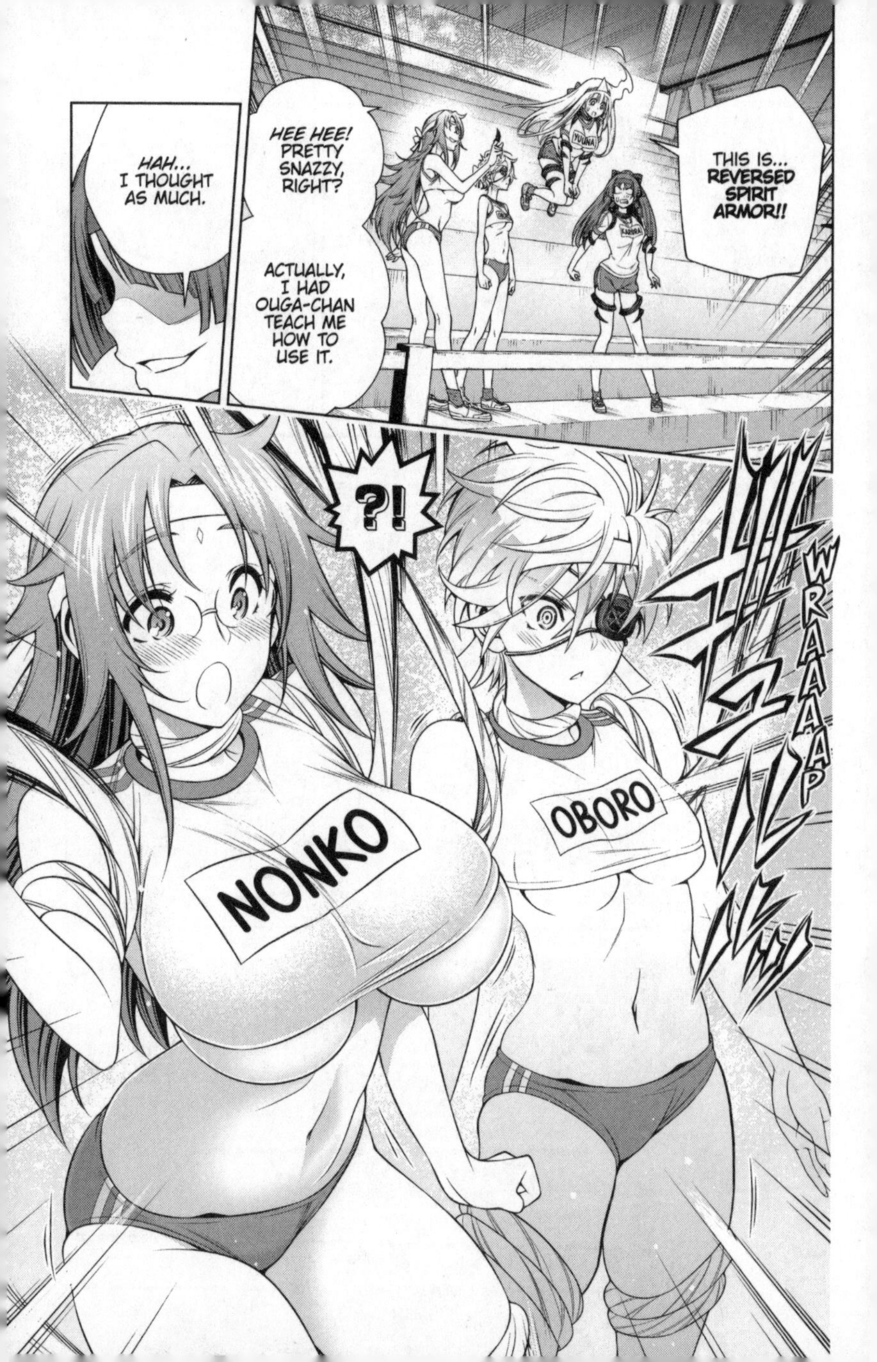
THIS IS... REVERSED SPIRIT ARMOR!!
HEE HEE! PRETTY SNAZZY, RIGHT?
ACTUALLY, I HAD OUGA-CHAN TEACH ME HOW TO USE IT.
HAH... I THOUGHT AS MUCH.
WRAAAAP
?!
OBORO
NONKO

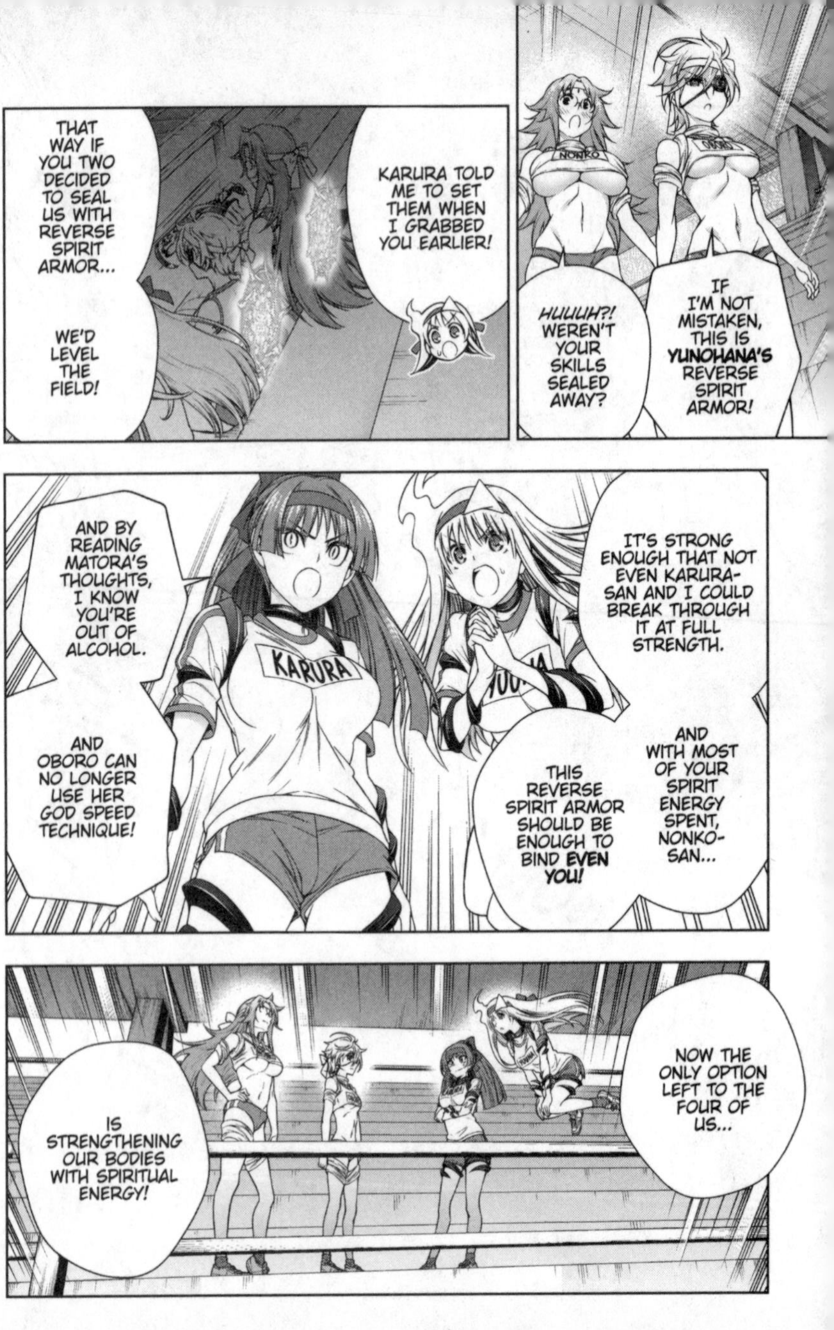

IF I'M NOT MISTAKEN, THIS IS **YUNOHANA'S** REVERSE SPIRIT ARMOR!
HUUUH?! WEREN'T YOUR SKILLS SEALED AWAY?
KARURA TOLD ME TO SET THEM WHEN I GRABBED YOU EARLIER!
THAT WAY IF YOU TWO DECIDED TO SEAL US WITH REVERSE SPIRIT ARMOR...
WE'D LEVEL THE FIELD!
IT'S STRONG ENOUGH THAT NOT EVEN KARURA-SAN AND I COULD BREAK THROUGH IT AT FULL STRENGTH.
AND WITH MOST OF YOUR SPIRIT ENERGY SPENT, NONKO-SAN...
THIS REVERSE SPIRIT ARMOR SHOULD BE ENOUGH TO BIND **EVEN YOU!**
AND BY READING MATORA'S THOUGHTS, I KNOW YOU'RE OUT OF ALCOHOL.
AND OBORO CAN NO LONGER USE HER GOD SPEED TECHNIQUE!
NOW THE ONLY OPTION LEFT TO THE FOUR OF US...
IS STRENGTHENING OUR BODIES WITH SPIRITUAL ENERGY!

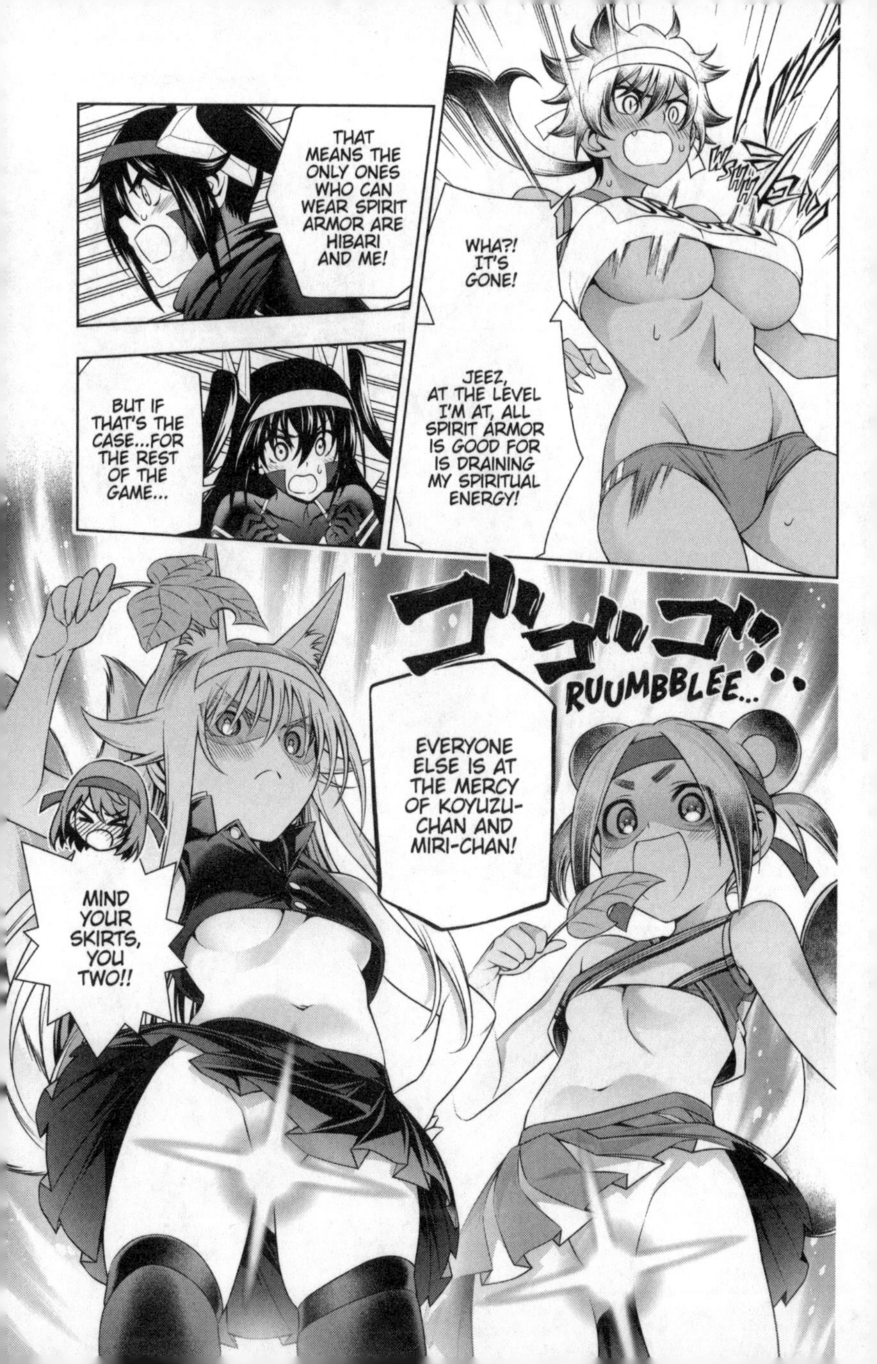
WHA?! IT'S GONE!
JEEZ, AT THE LEVEL I'M AT, ALL SPIRIT ARMOR IS GOOD FOR IS DRAINING MY SPIRITUAL ENERGY!
THAT MEANS THE ONLY ONES WHO CAN WEAR SPIRIT ARMOR ARE HIBARI AND ME!
BUT IF THAT'S THE CASE...FOR THE REST OF THE GAME...
RUUMBBLEE...
EVERYONE ELSE IS AT THE MERCY OF KOYUZU-CHAN AND MIRI-CHAN!
MIND YOUR SKIRTS, YOU TWO!!

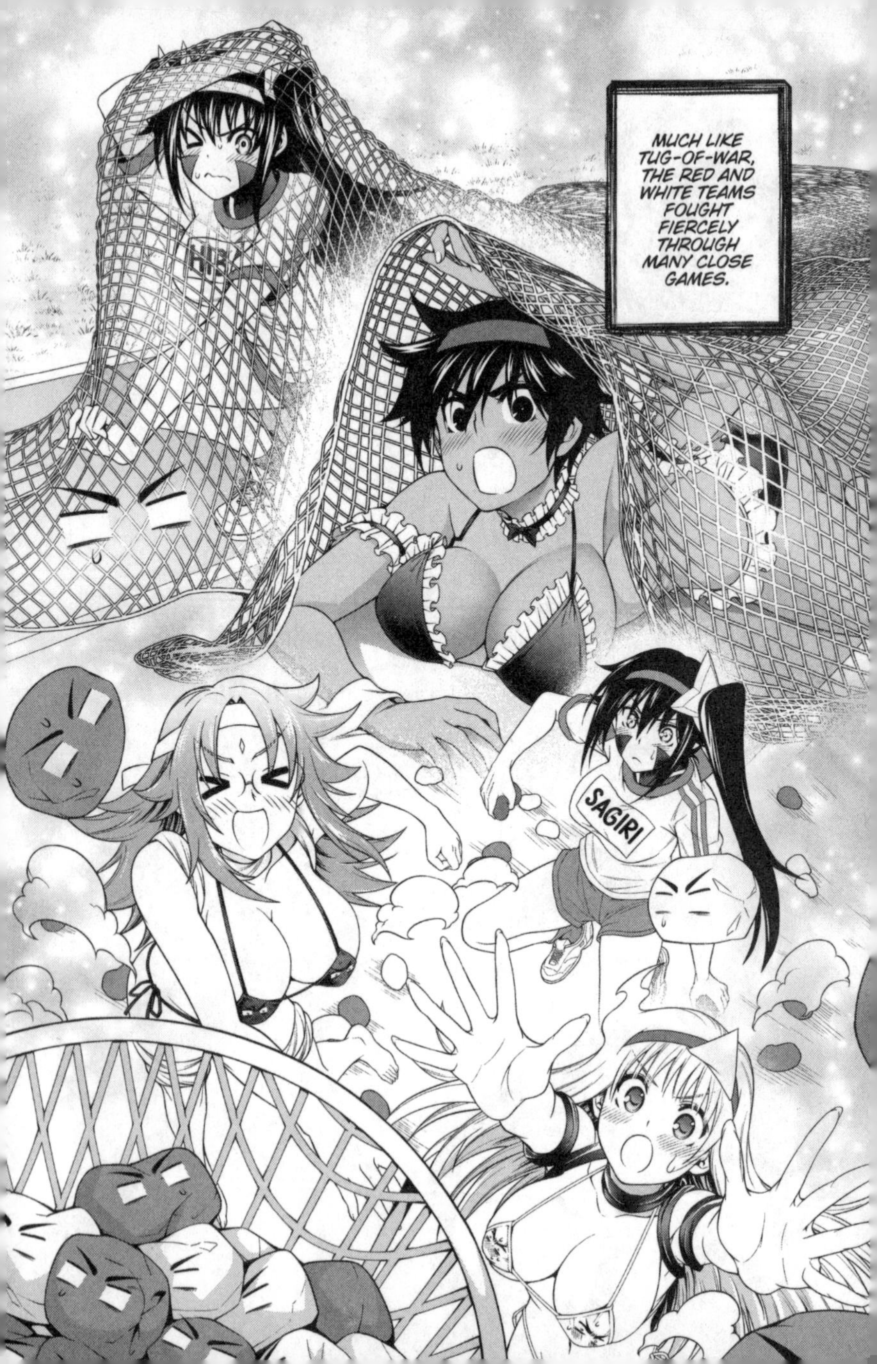
MUCH LIKE TUG-OF-WAR, THE RED AND WHITE TEAMS FOUGHT FIERCELY THROUGH MANY CLOSE GAMES.
SAGIRI

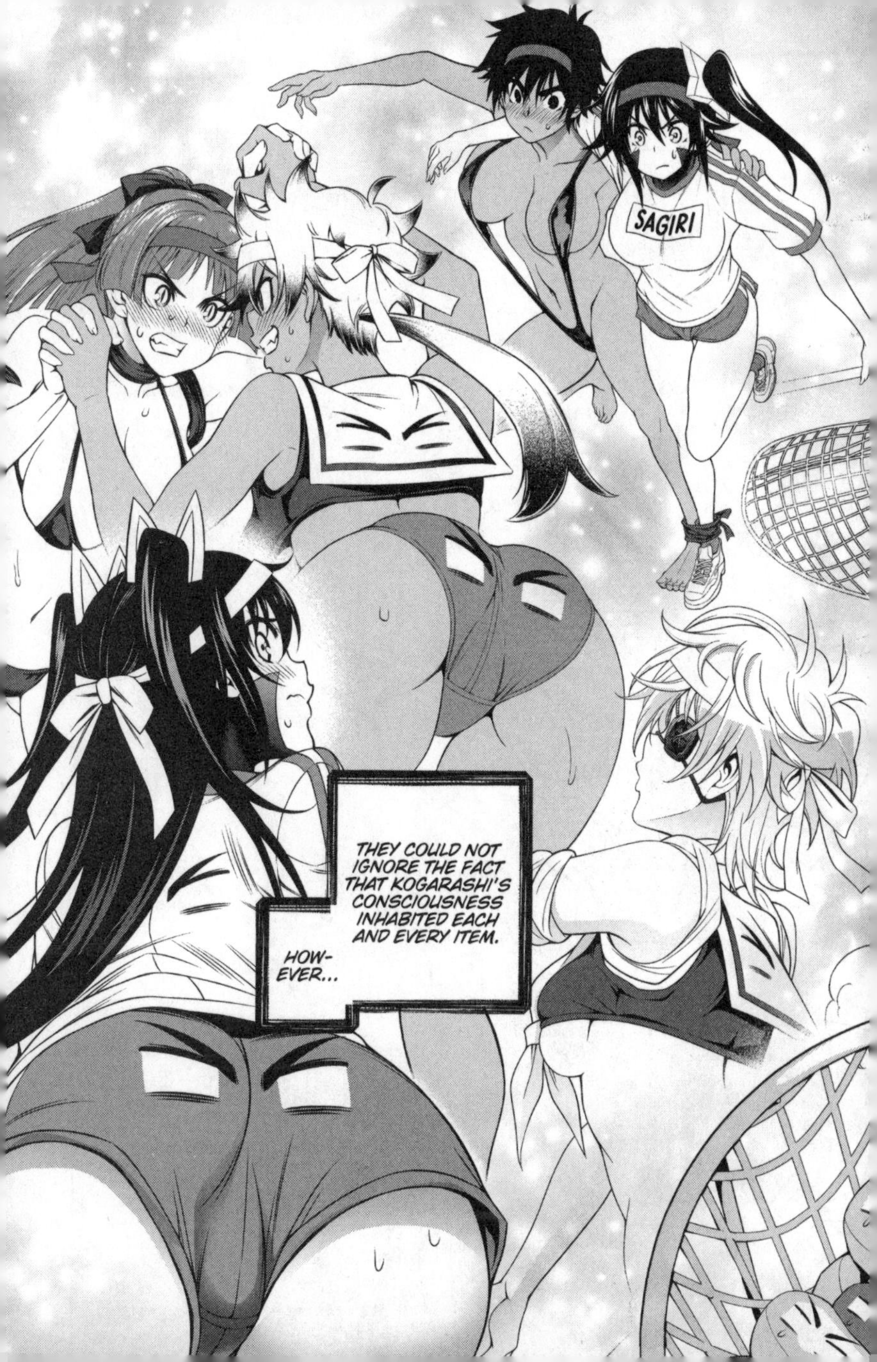
SAGIRI
THEY COULD NOT IGNORE THE FACT THAT KOGARASHI'S CONSCIOUSNESS INHABITED EACH AND EVERY ITEM.
HOW-EVER...

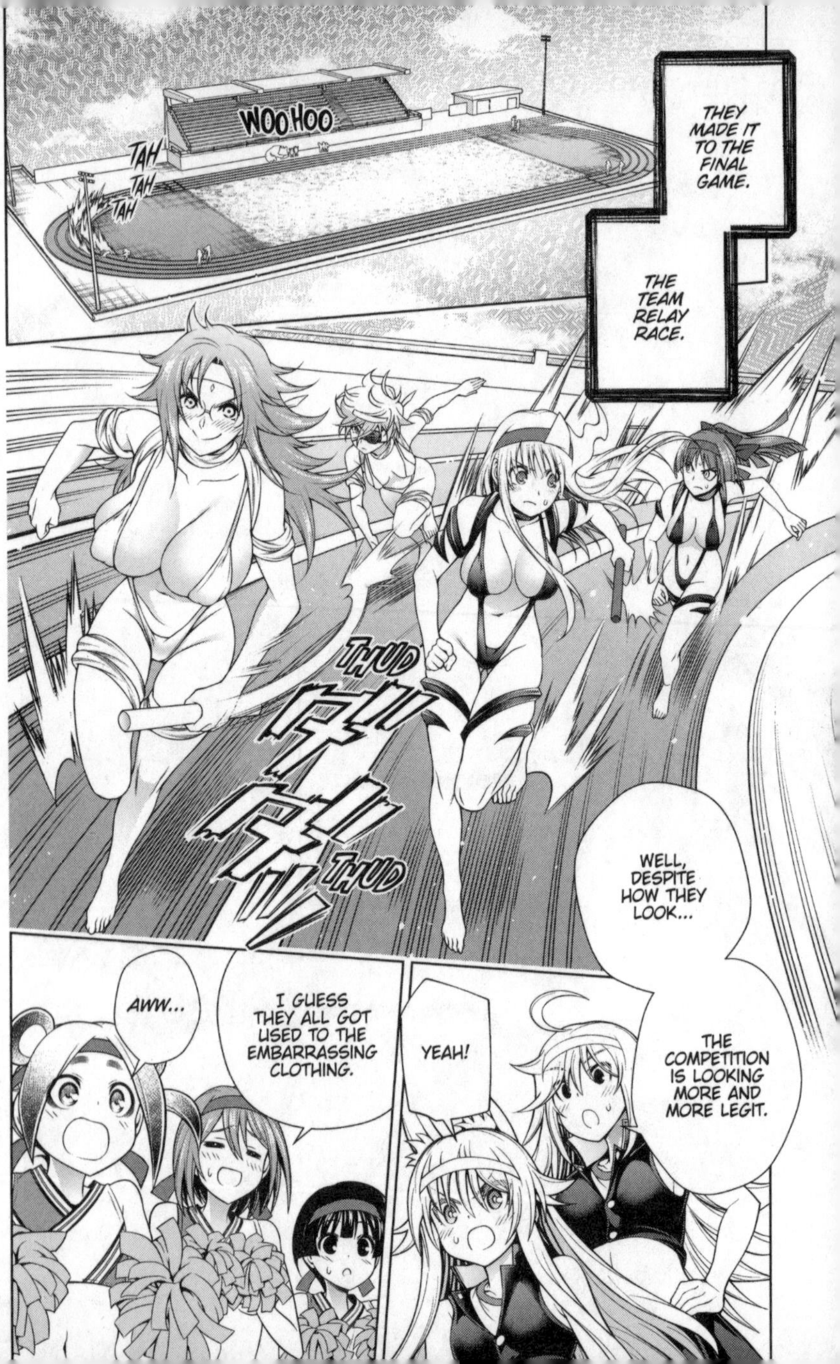
THEY MADE IT TO THE FINAL GAME.
THE TEAM RELAY RACE.
WOOHOO
TAH
TAH
TAH
THUD
THUD
WELL, DESPITE HOW THEY LOOK...
THE COMPETITION IS LOOKING MORE AND MORE LEGIT.
YEAH!
I GUESS THEY ALL GOT USED TO THE EMBARRASSING CLOTHING.
AWW...

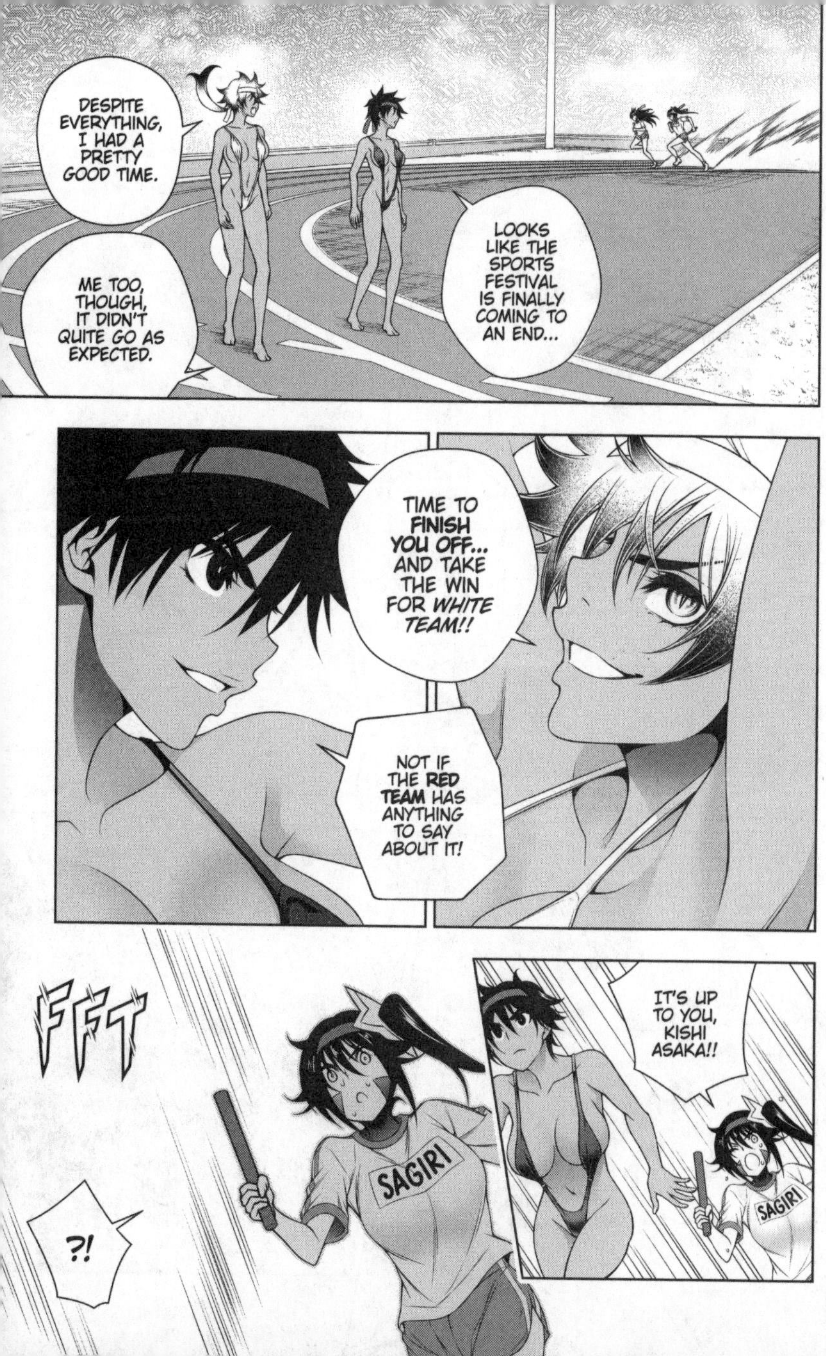
LOOKS LIKE THE SPORTS FESTIVAL IS FINALLY COMING TO AN END...
DESPITE EVERYTHING, I HAD A PRETTY GOOD TIME.
ME TOO, THOUGH, IT DIDN'T QUITE GO AS EXPECTED.
TIME TO **FINISH YOU OFF...** AND TAKE THE WIN FOR *WHITE TEAM!!*
NOT IF THE **RED TEAM** HAS ANYTHING TO SAY ABOUT IT!
IT'S UP TO YOU, KISHI ASAKA!!
SAGIRI
SAGIRI
FFFT
?!

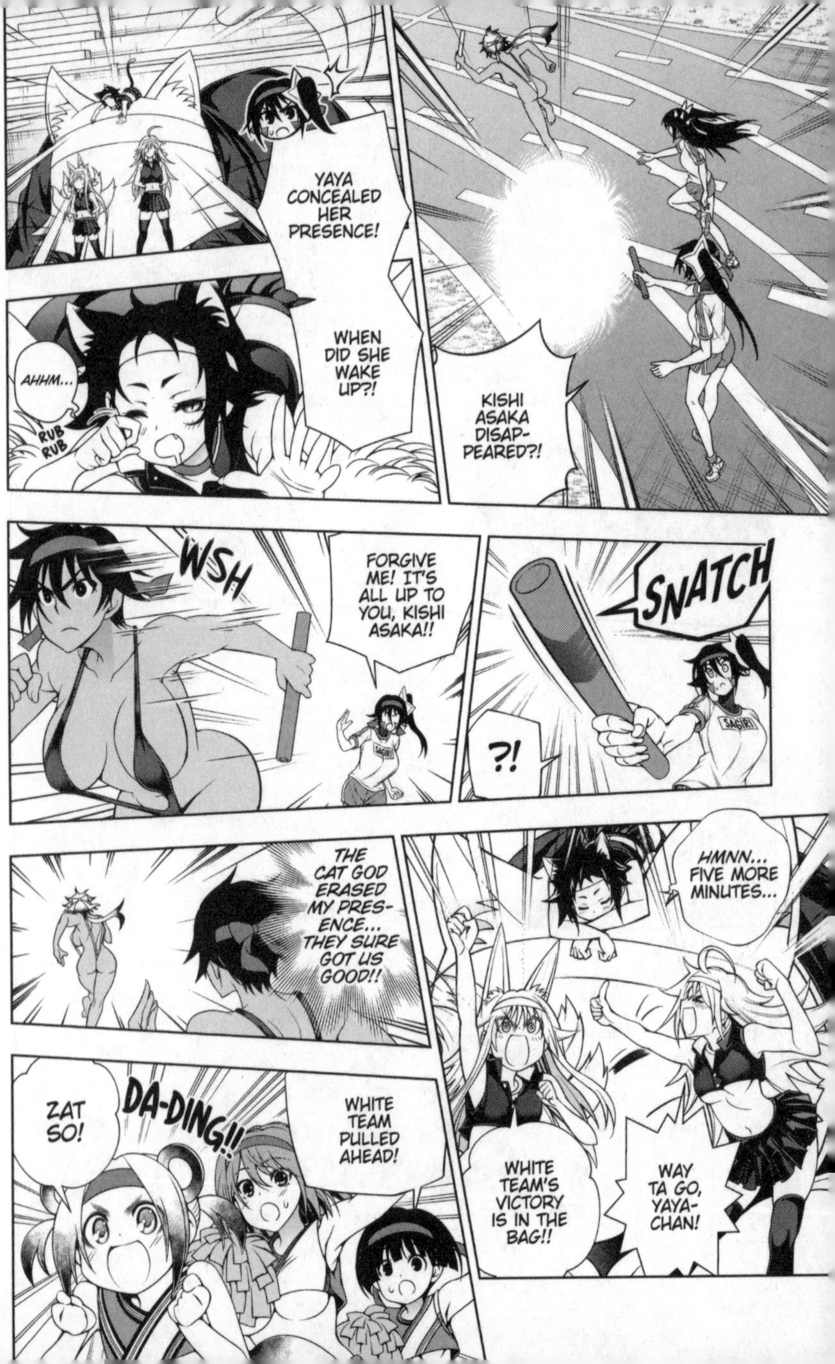

KISHI ASAKA DISAP-PEARED?!
YAYA CONCEALED HER PRESENCE!
WHEN DID SHE WAKE UP?!
AHHM...
RUB RUB
SNATCH
?!
FORGIVE ME! IT'S ALL UP TO YOU, KISHI ASAKA!!
WSH
HMNN... FIVE MORE MINUTES...
WAY TA GO, YAYA-CHAN!
WHITE TEAM'S VICTORY IS IN THE BAG!!
THE CAT GOD ERASED MY PRES-ENCE... THEY SURE GOT US GOOD!!
WHITE TEAM PULLED AHEAD!
DA-DING!!
ZAT SO!

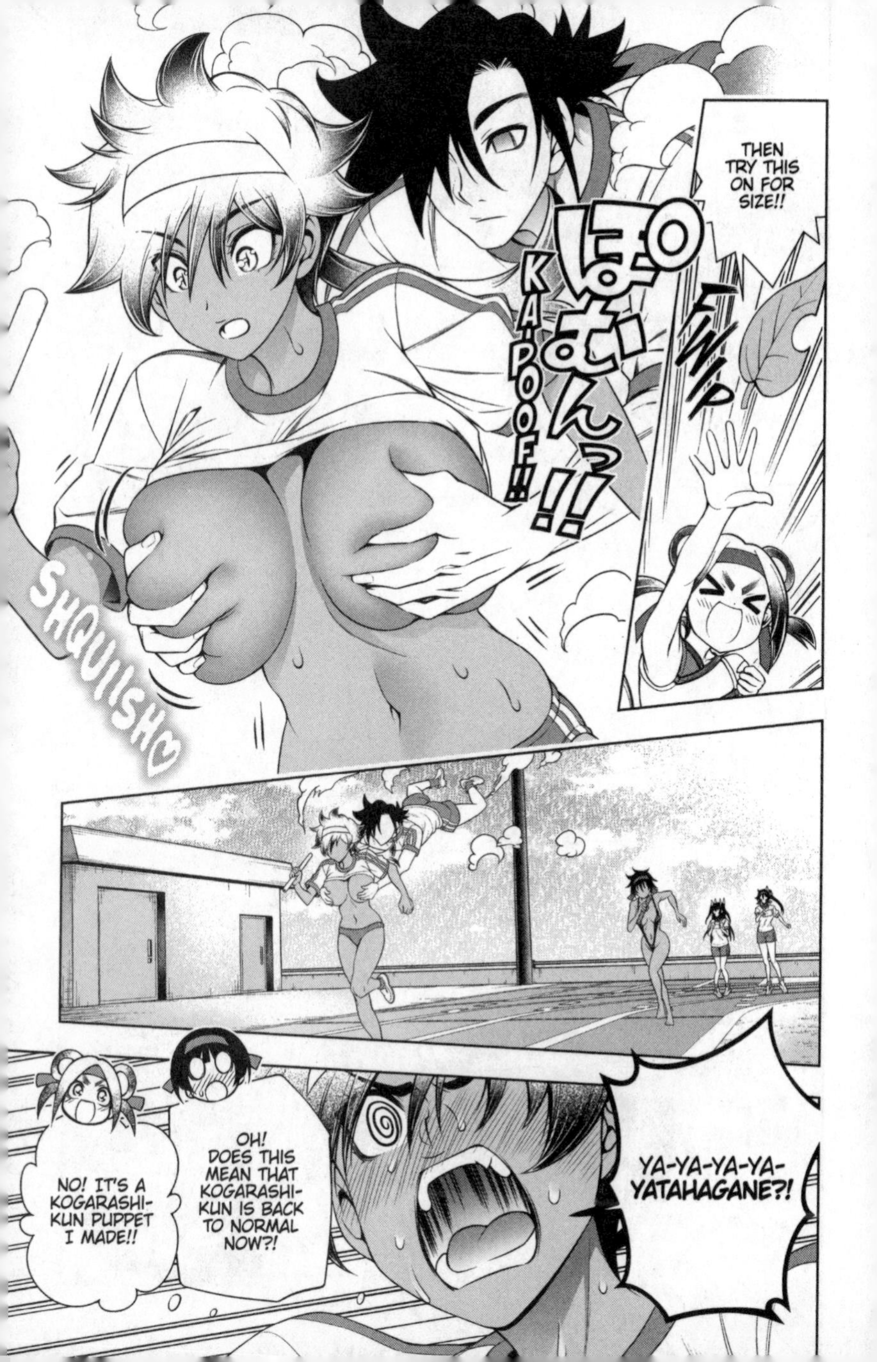
THEN TRY THIS ON FOR SIZE!!
FWIP
ぽむんっ!!
KAPOOF!!
SHQUIISH♡
YA-YA-YA-YA-YATAHAGANE?!
OH! DOES THIS MEAN THAT KOGARASHI-KUN IS BACK TO NORMAL NOW?!
NO! IT'S A KOGARASHI-KUN PUPPET I MADE!!

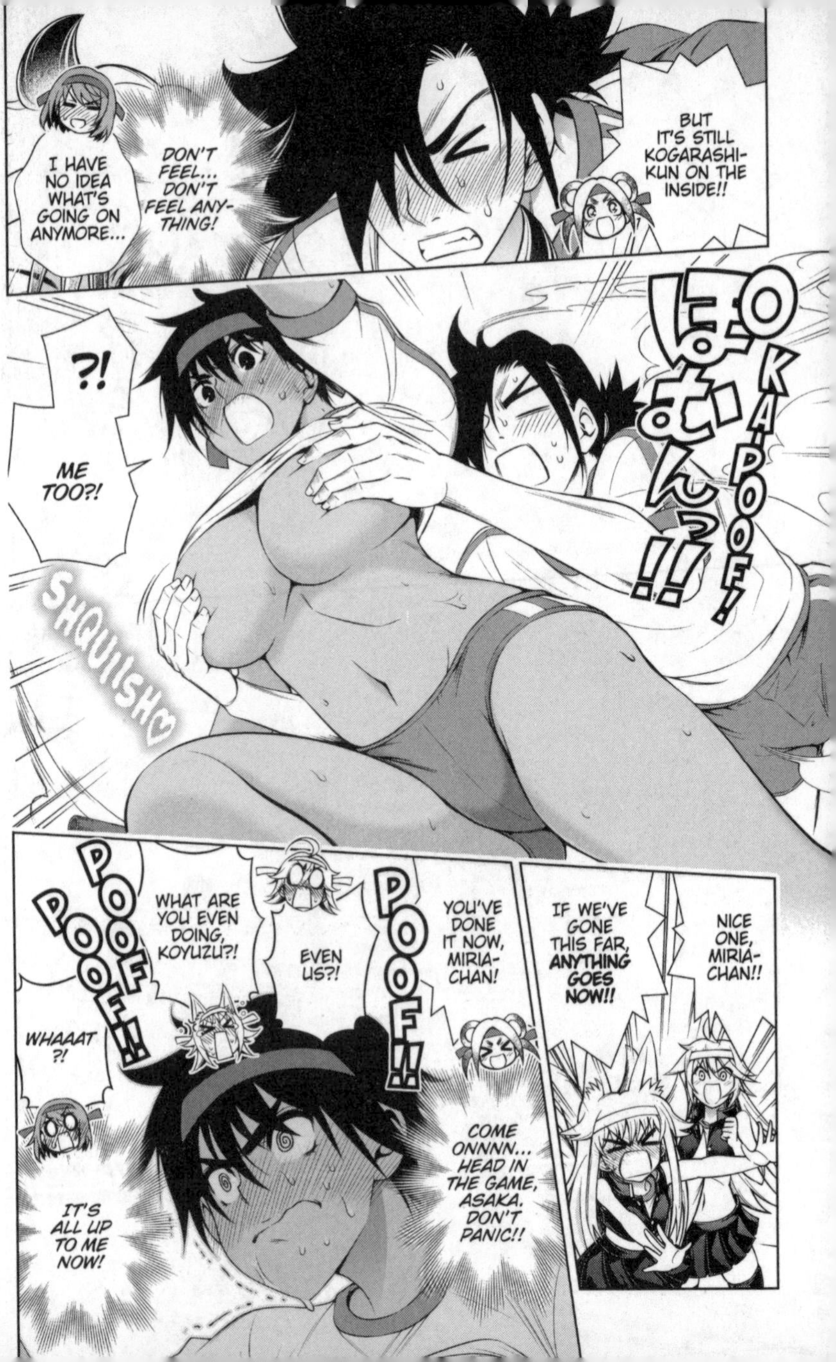
BUT IT'S STILL KOGARASHI-KUN ON THE INSIDE!!
DON'T FEEL... DON'T FEEL ANY-THING!
I HAVE NO IDEA WHAT'S GOING ON ANYMORE...
ぽむんっ!!
KAPOOF!
?!
ME TOO?!
SHQUIISH♥
NICE ONE, MIRIA-CHAN!!
IF WE'VE GONE THIS FAR, **ANYTHING GOES** NOW!!
YOU'VE DONE IT NOW, MIRIA-CHAN!
POOF!!
EVEN US?!
WHAT ARE YOU EVEN DOING, KOYUZU?!
POOF POOF!!
WHAAAT?!
COME ONNNN... HEAD IN THE GAME, ASAKA. DON'T PANIC!!
IT'S ALL UP TO ME NOW!

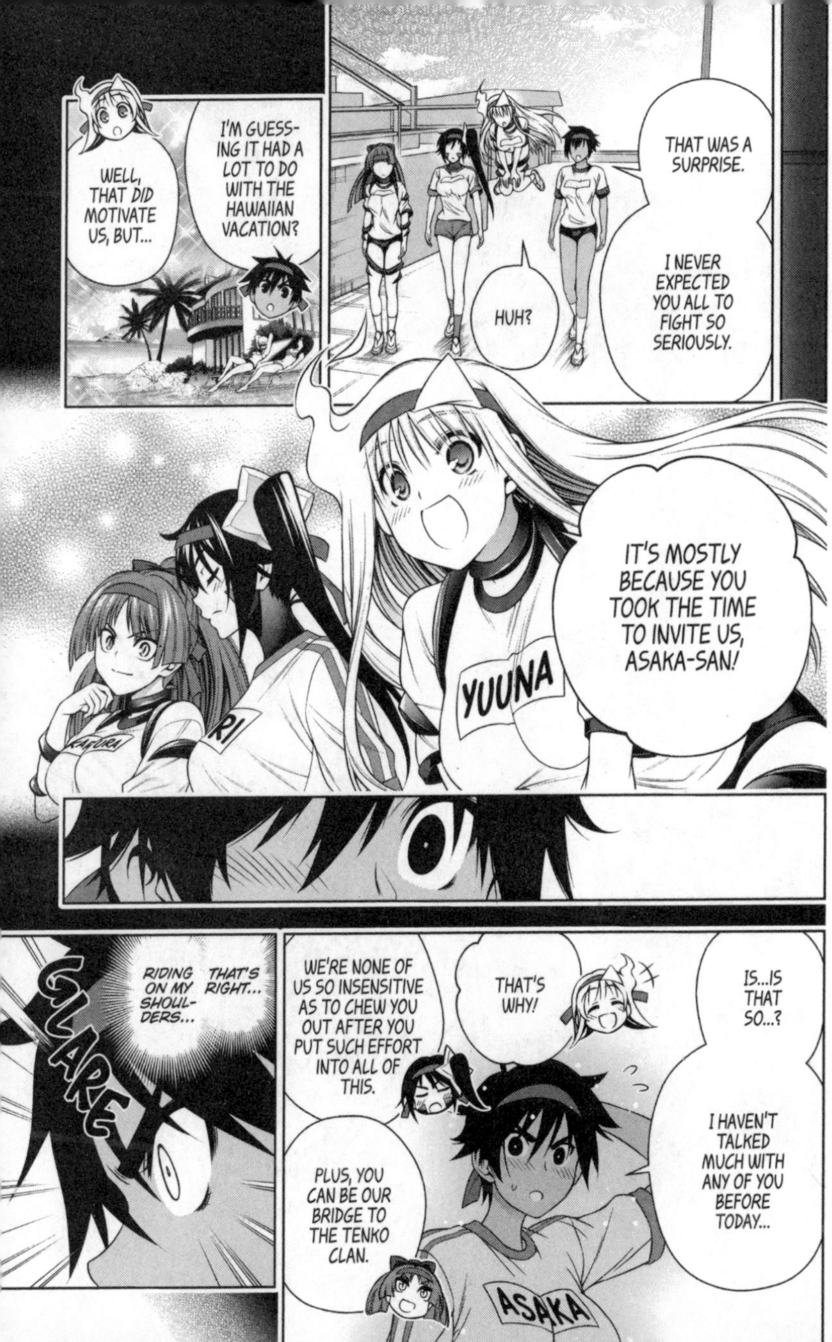
THAT WAS A SURPRISE.
I NEVER EXPECTED YOU ALL TO FIGHT SO SERIOUSLY.
HUH?
I'M GUESSING IT HAD A LOT TO DO WITH THE HAWAIIAN VACATION?
WELL, THAT DID MOTIVATE US, BUT...
IT'S MOSTLY BECAUSE YOU TOOK THE TIME TO INVITE US, ASAKA-SAN!
YUUNA
IS...IS THAT SO...?
I HAVEN'T TALKED MUCH WITH ANY OF YOU BEFORE TODAY...
THAT'S WHY!
WE'RE NONE OF US SO INSENSITIVE AS TO CHEW YOU OUT AFTER YOU PUT SUCH EFFORT INTO ALL OF THIS.
PLUS, YOU CAN BE OUR BRIDGE TO THE TENKO CLAN.
ASAKA
THAT'S RIGHT...
RIDING ON MY SHOULDERS...
GLARE

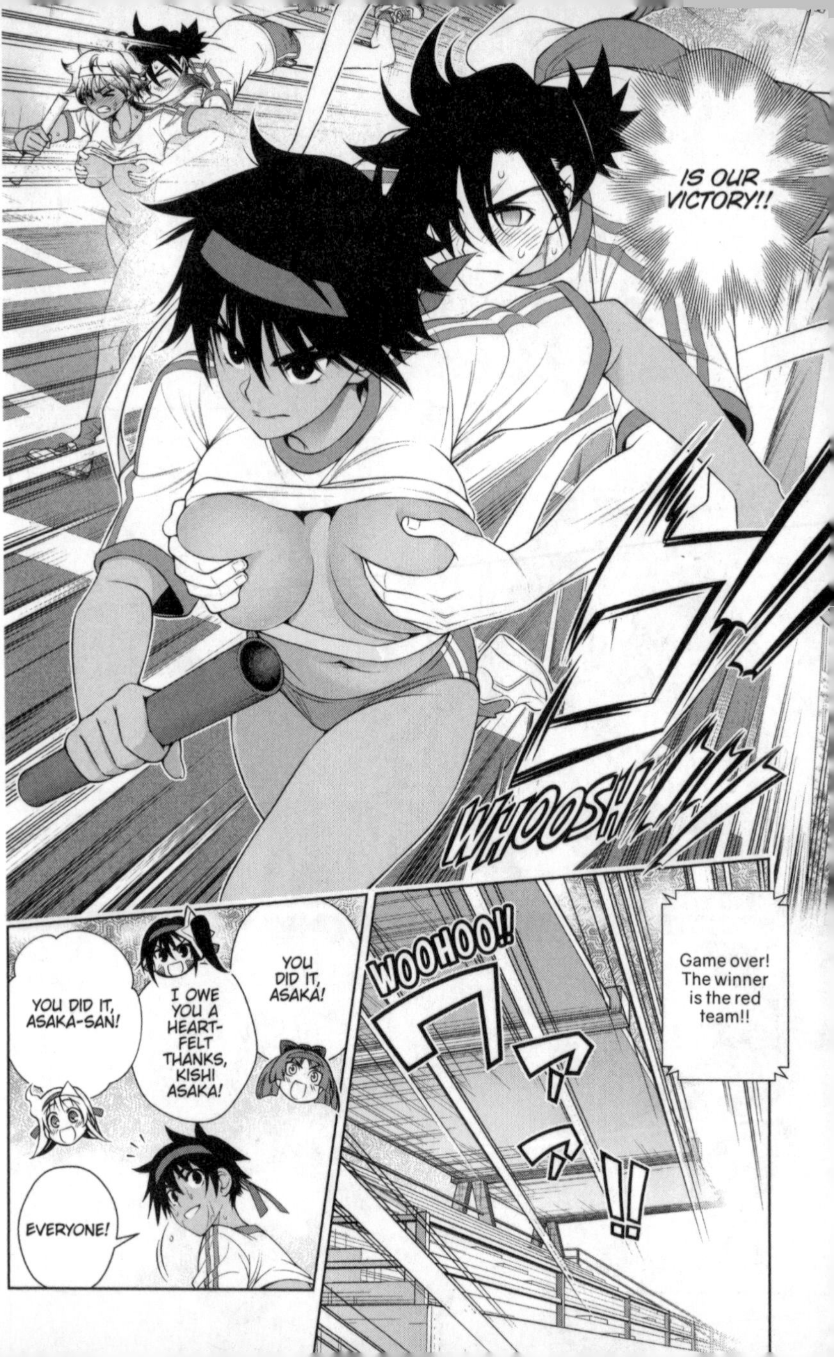
IS OUR VICTORY!!
WHOOSH
Game over! The winner is the red team!!
WOOHOO!!
YOU DID IT, ASAKA!
I OWE YOU A HEART-FELT THANKS, KISHI ASAKA!
YOU DID IT, ASAKA-SAN!
EVERYONE!

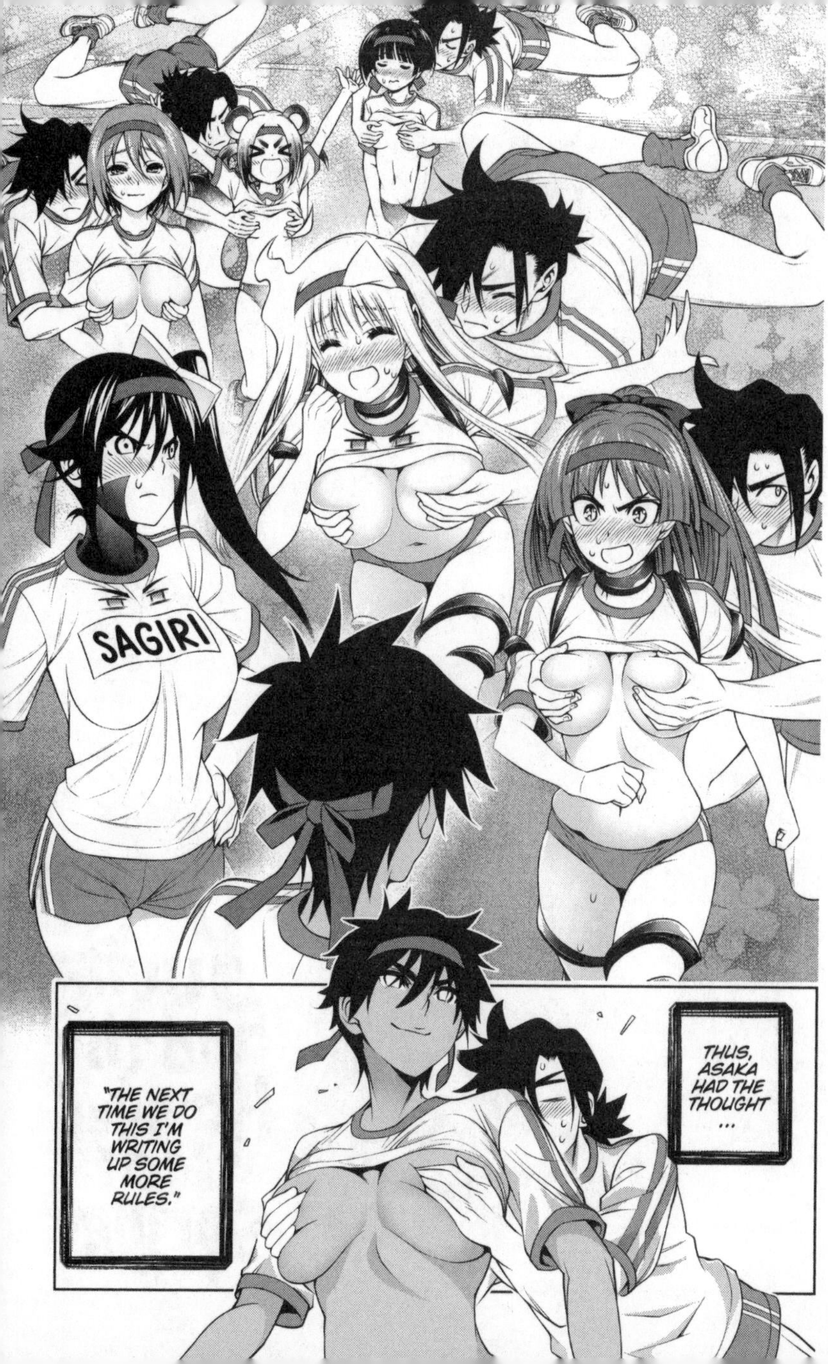
SAGIRI
THUS, ASAKA HAD THE THOUGHT ...
"THE NEXT TIME WE DO THIS I'M WRITING UP SOME MORE RULES."

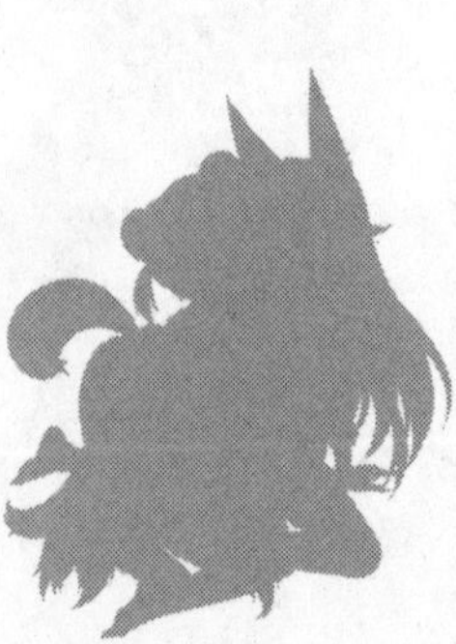

Yuuna and the Haunted Hot Springs

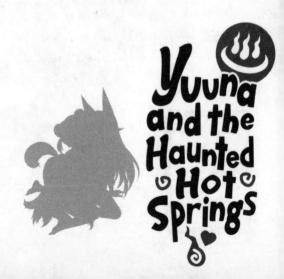

176 Off-Duty Sagiri

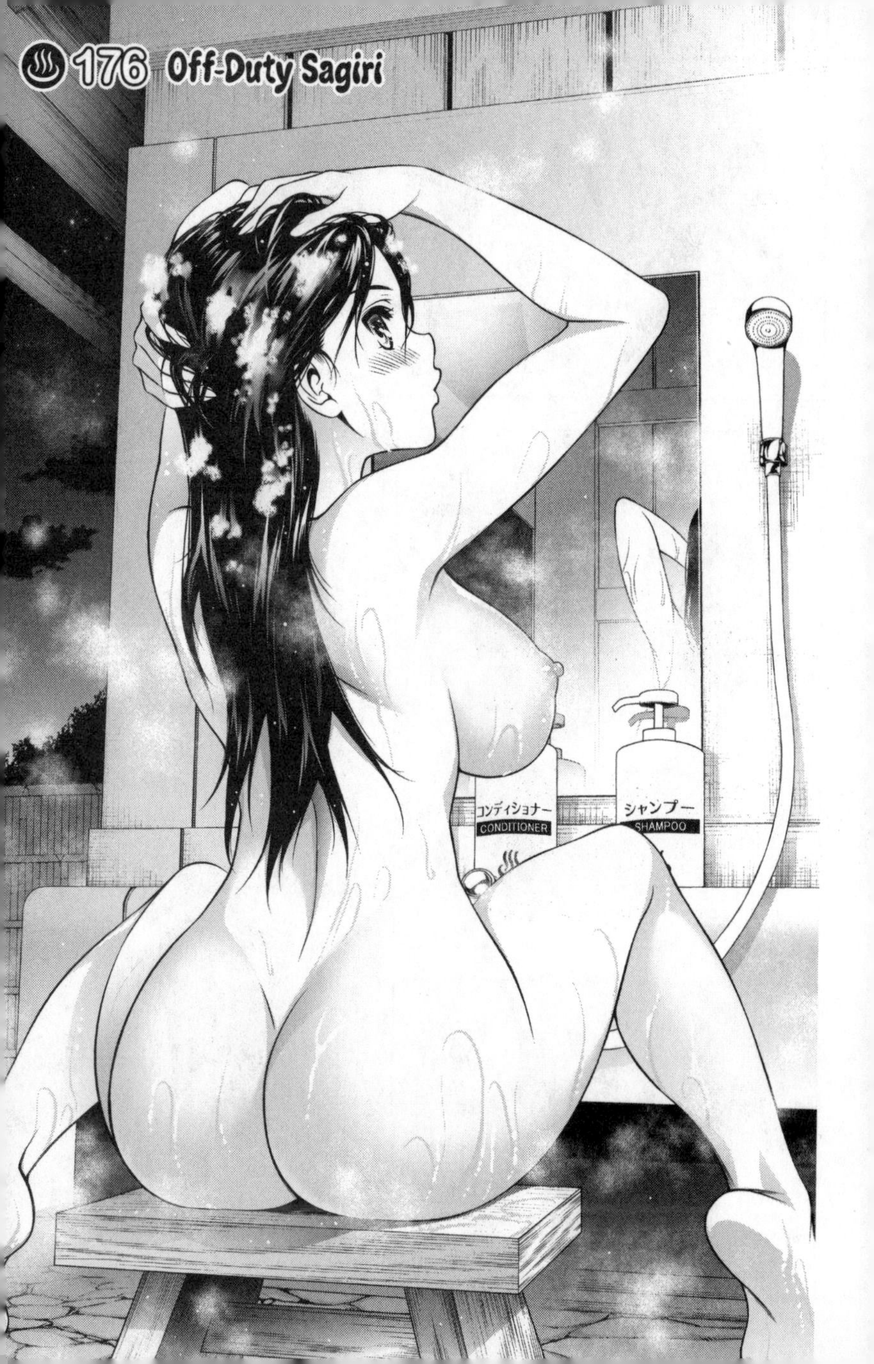
シャンプー
SHAMPOO
コンディショナー
CONDITIONER

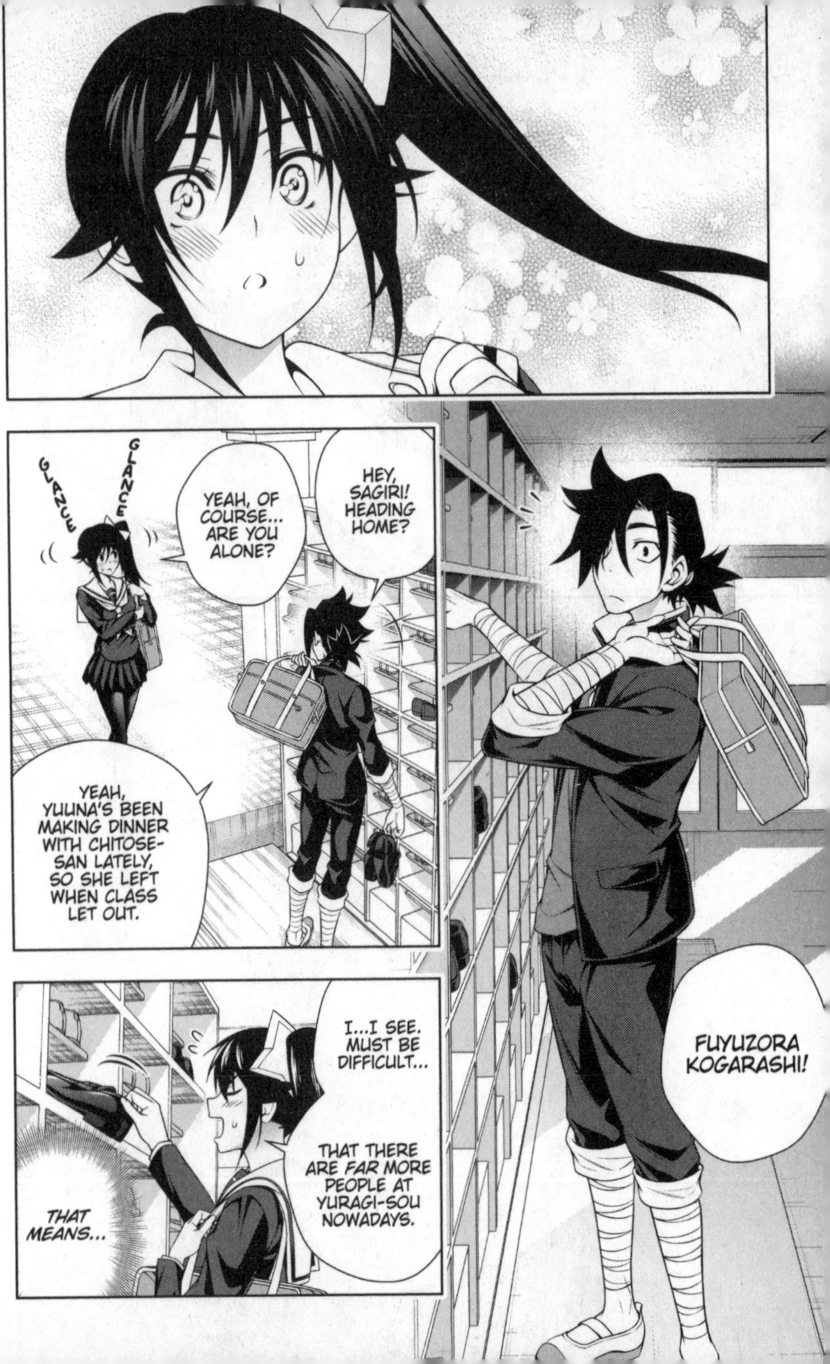
FUYUZORA KOGARASHI!
HEY, SAGIRI! HEADING HOME?
YEAH, OF COURSE... ARE YOU ALONE?
GLANCE
GLANCE
YEAH, YUUNA'S BEEN MAKING DINNER WITH CHITOSE-SAN LATELY, SO SHE LEFT WHEN CLASS LET OUT.
I...I SEE. MUST BE DIFFICULT...
THAT THERE ARE *FAR* MORE PEOPLE AT YURAGI-SOU NOWADAYS.
THAT MEANS...

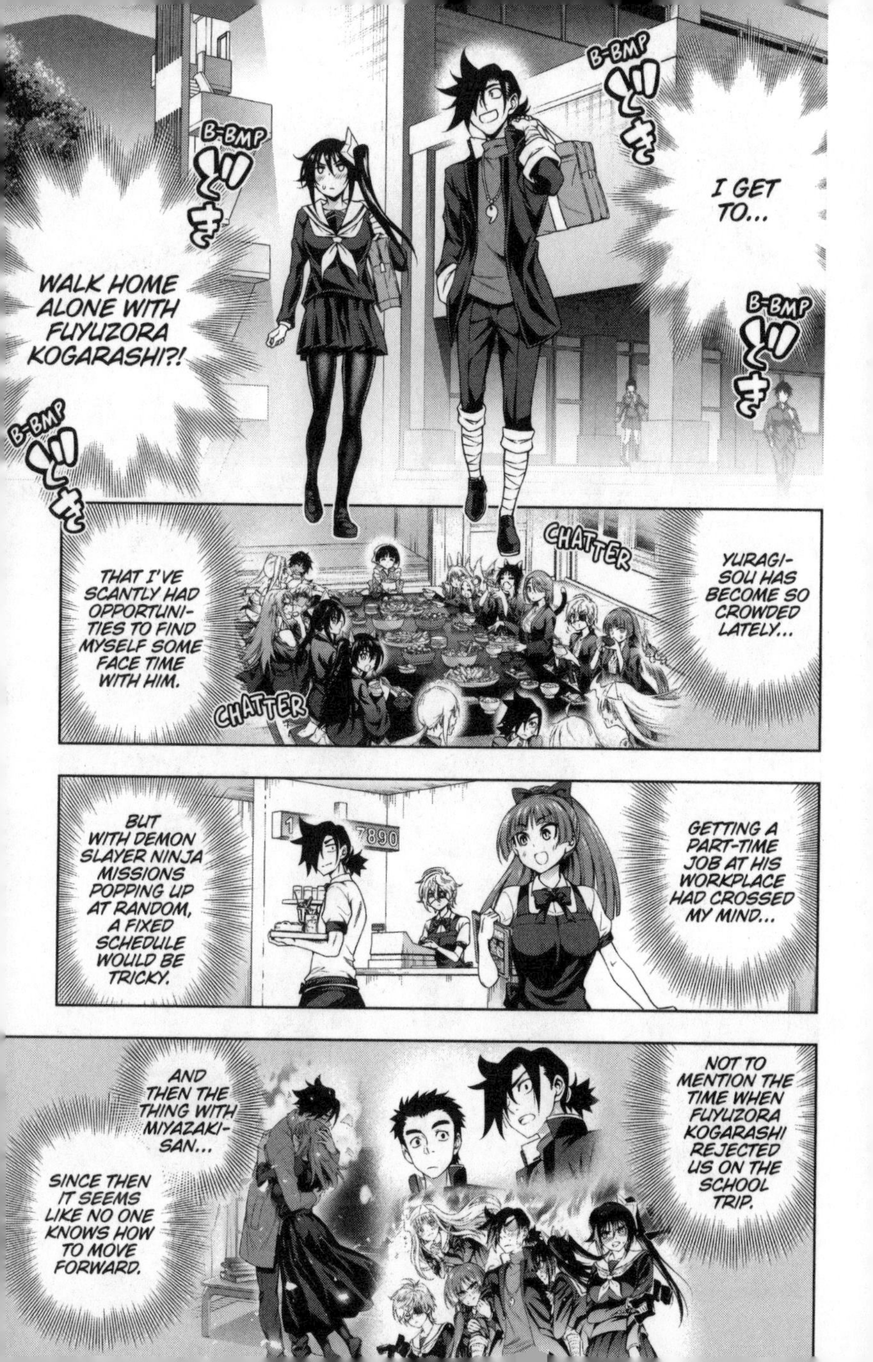
B-BMP
どき
I GET TO...
B-BMP
どき
B-BMP
どき
WALK HOME ALONE WITH FUYUZORA KOGARASHI?!
B-BMP
どき
YURAGI-SOU HAS BECOME SO CROWDED LATELY...
CHATTER
THAT I'VE SCANTLY HAD OPPORTUNI-TIES TO FIND MYSELF SOME FACE TIME WITH HIM.
CHATTER
GETTING A PART-TIME JOB AT HIS WORKPLACE HAD CROSSED MY MIND...
BUT WITH DEMON SLAYER NINJA MISSIONS POPPING UP AT RANDOM, A FIXED SCHEDULE WOULD BE TRICKY.
NOT TO MENTION THE TIME WHEN FUYUZORA KOGARASHI REJECTED US ON THE SCHOOL TRIP.
AND THEN THE THING WITH MIYAZAKI-SAN...
SINCE THEN IT SEEMS LIKE NO ONE KNOWS HOW TO MOVE FORWARD.

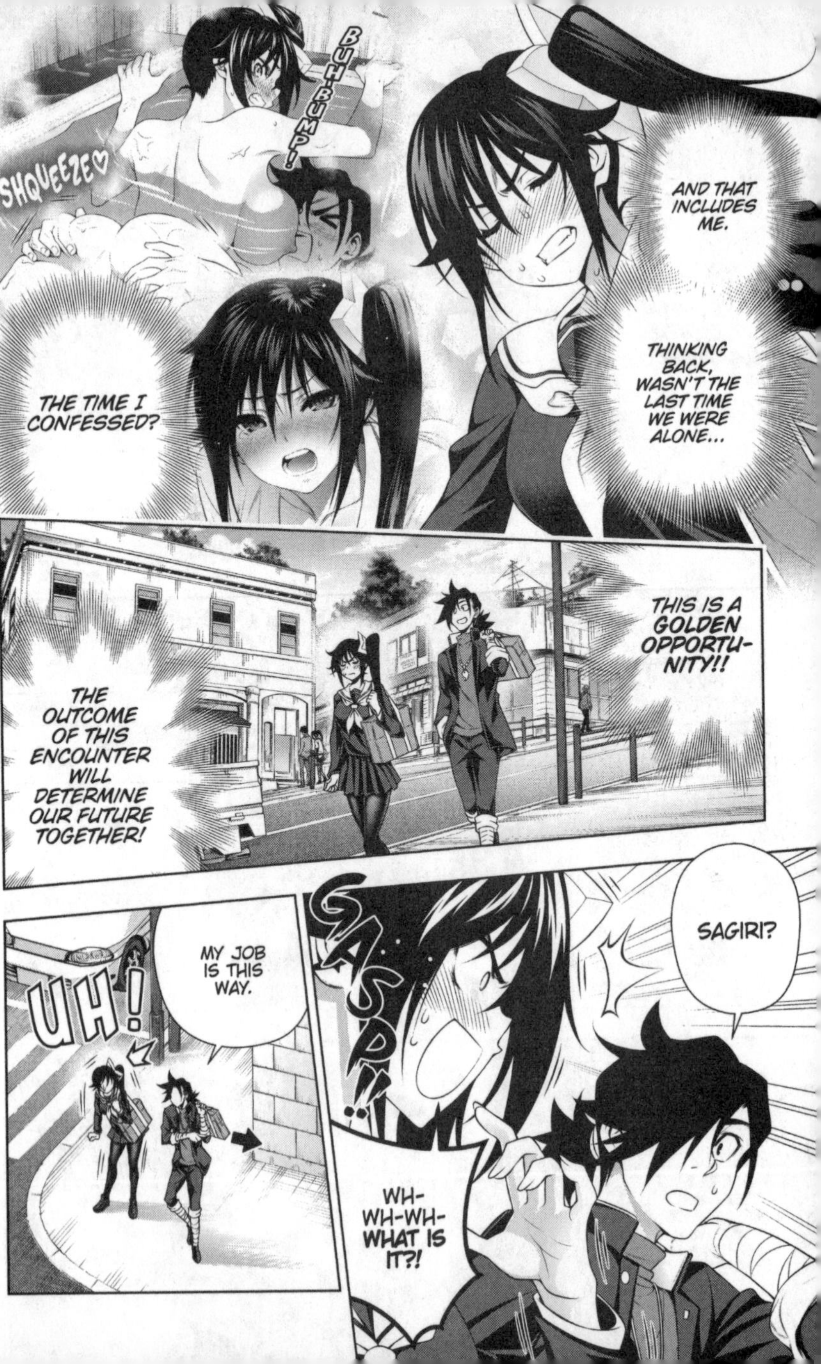
AND THAT INCLUDES ME.
THINKING BACK, WASN'T THE LAST TIME WE WERE ALONE...
BUH-BUMP!
SHQUEEZE♡
THE TIME I CONFESSED?
THIS IS A GOLDEN OPPORTU-NITY!!
THE OUTCOME OF THIS ENCOUNTER WILL DETERMINE OUR FUTURE TOGETHER!
SAGIRI?
GASP!!
WH-WH-WH-WHAT IS IT?!
MY JOB IS THIS WAY.
UH!

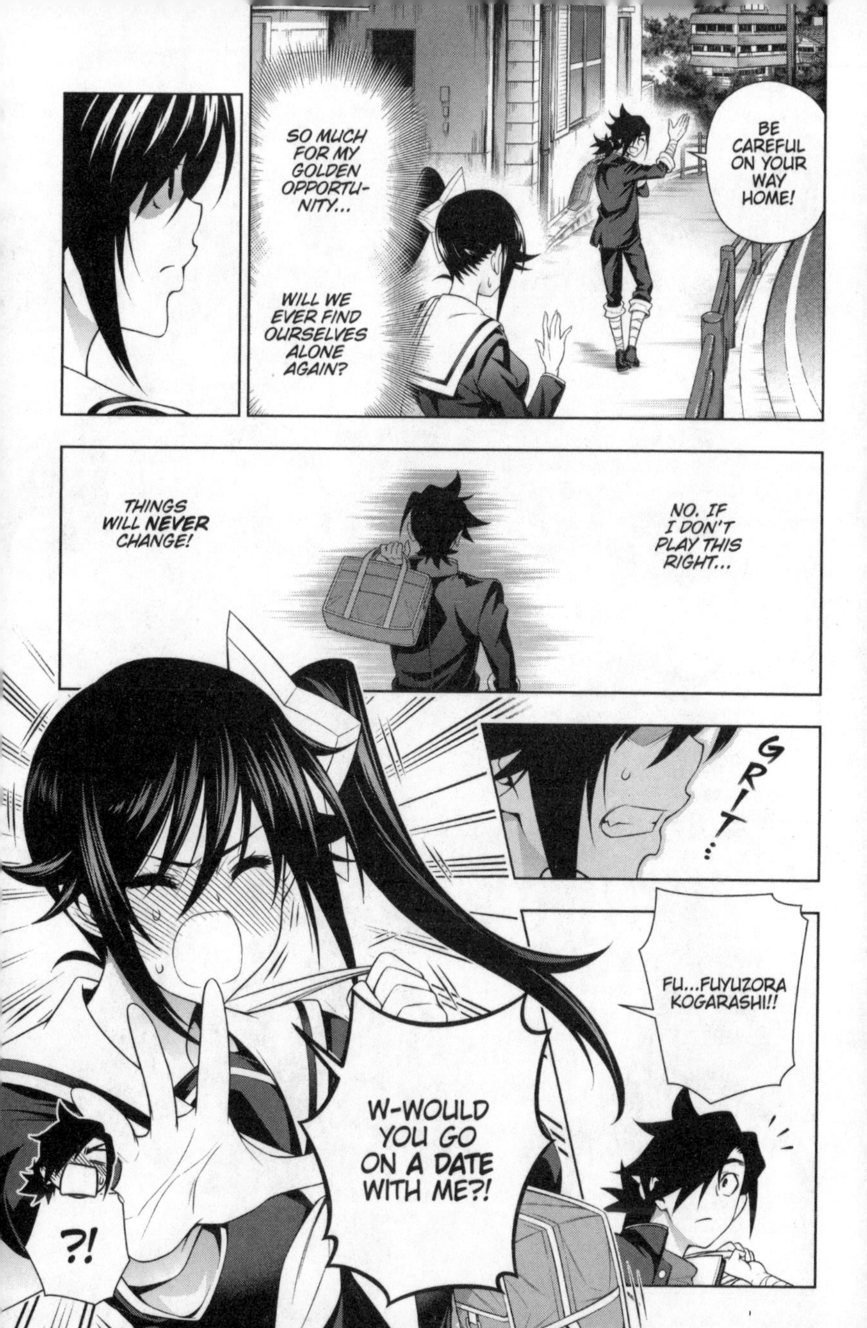
BE CAREFUL ON YOUR WAY HOME!
SO MUCH FOR MY GOLDEN OPPORTUNITY...
WILL WE EVER FIND OURSELVES ALONE AGAIN?
NO. IF I DON'T PLAY THIS RIGHT...
THINGS WILL **NEVER** CHANGE!
GRIT...
FU...FUYUZORA KOGARASHI!!
W-WOULD YOU GO ON A DATE WITH ME?!
?!

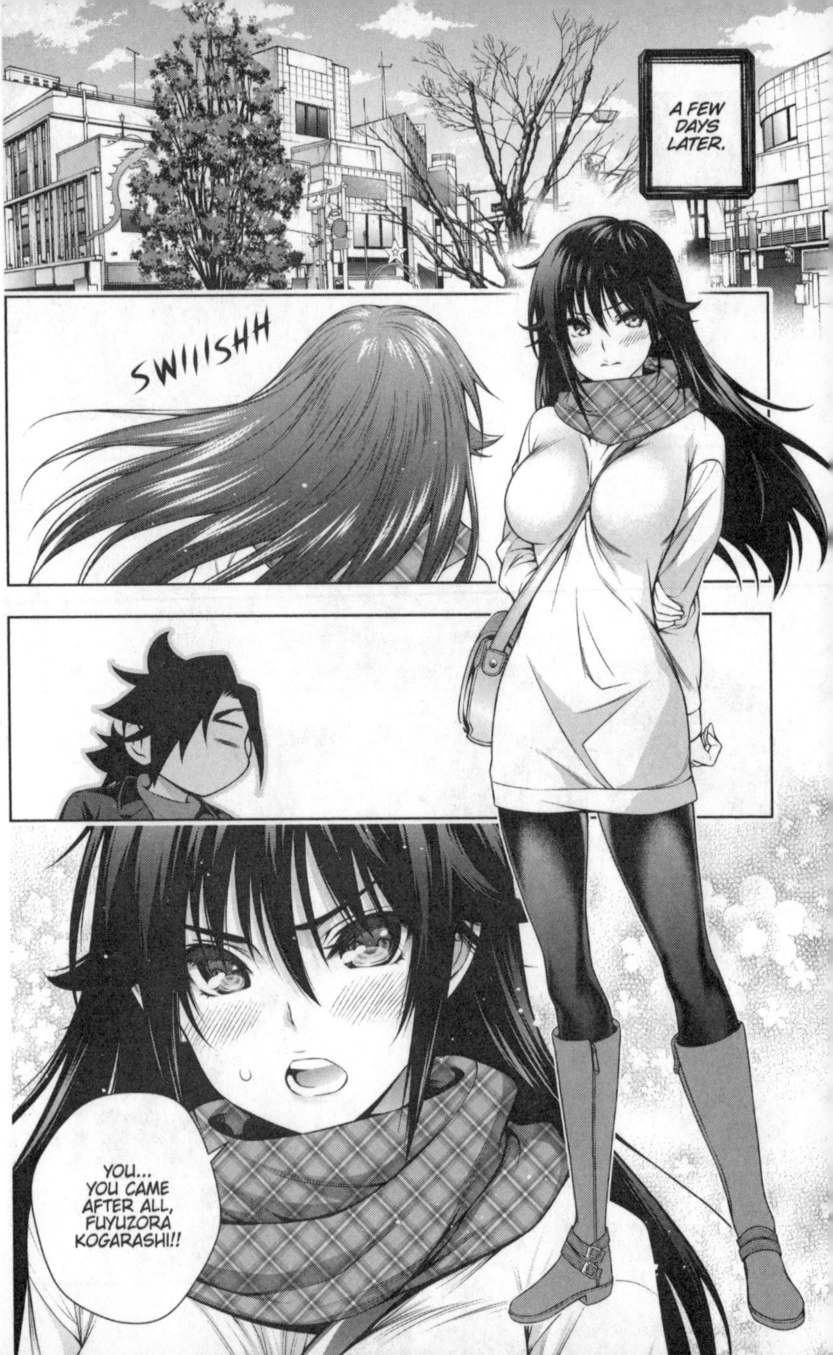
A FEW DAYS LATER.
SWIIISHH
YOU... YOU CAME AFTER ALL, FUYUZORA KOGARASHI!!

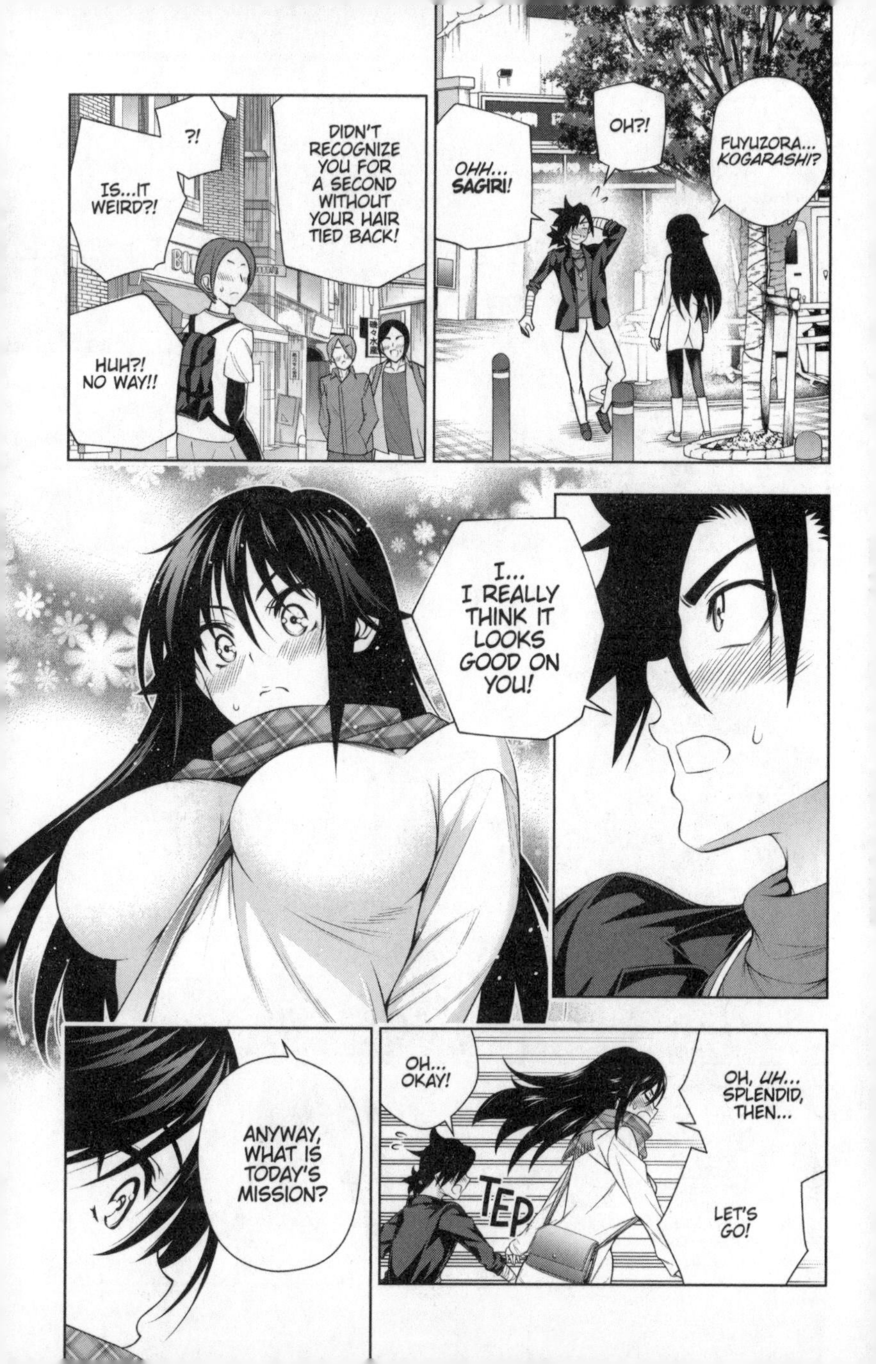
FUYUZORA... KOGARASHI?
OH?!
OHH... SAGIRI!
DIDN'T RECOGNIZE YOU FOR A SECOND WITHOUT YOUR HAIR TIED BACK!
?!
IS...IT WEIRD?!
HUH?! NO WAY!!
I... I REALLY THINK IT LOOKS GOOD ON YOU!
OH, UH... SPLENDID, THEN...
OH... OKAY!
TEP
LET'S GO!
ANYWAY, WHAT IS TODAY'S MISSION?

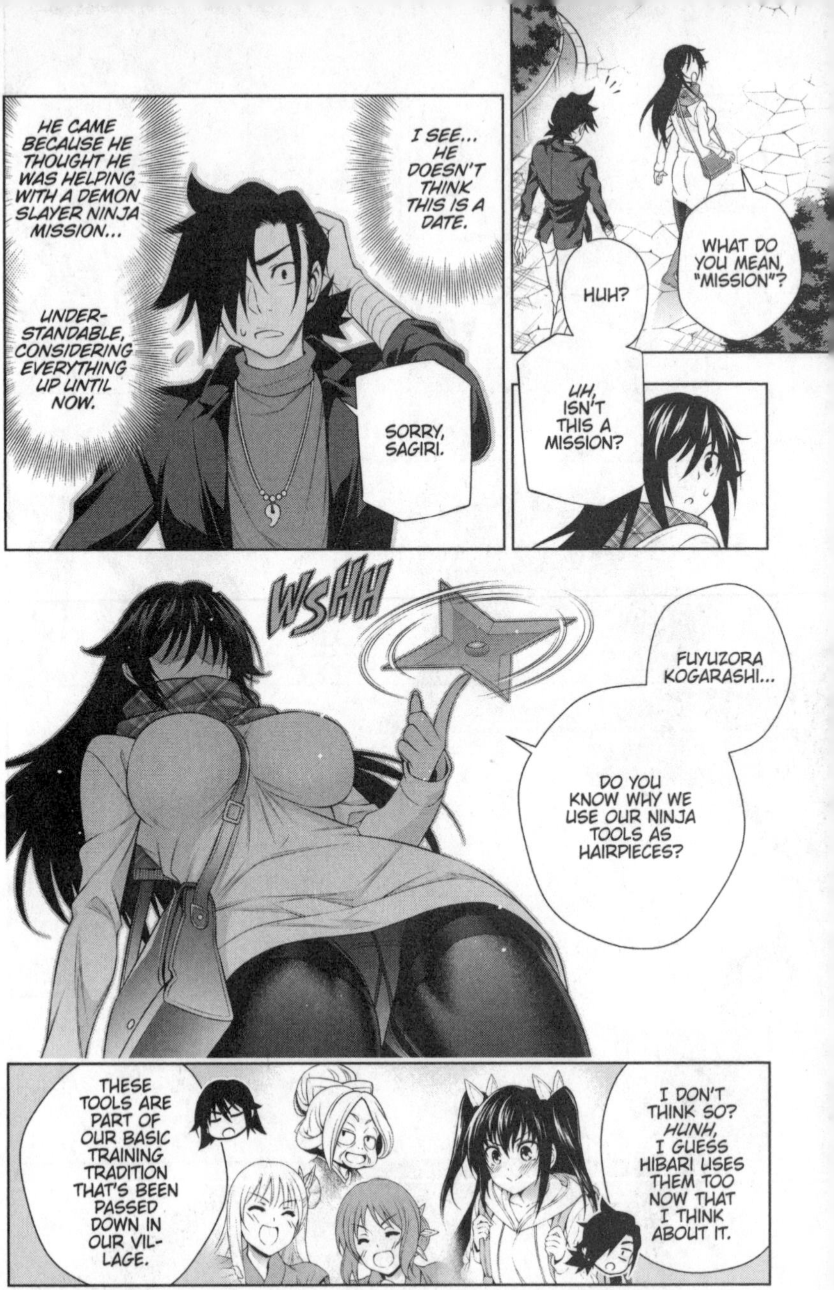
WHAT DO YOU MEAN, "MISSION"?
HUH?
UH, ISN'T THIS A MISSION?
I SEE... HE DOESN'T THINK THIS IS A DATE.
HE CAME BECAUSE HE THOUGHT HE WAS HELPING WITH A DEMON SLAYER NINJA MISSION...
SORRY, SAGIRI.
UNDER-STANDABLE, CONSIDERING EVERYTHING UP UNTIL NOW.
WSHH
FUYUZORA KOGARASHI...
DO YOU KNOW WHY WE USE OUR NINJA TOOLS AS HAIRPIECES?
I DON'T THINK SO? HUNH, I GUESS HIBARI USES THEM TOO NOW THAT I THINK ABOUT IT.
THESE TOOLS ARE PART OF OUR BASIC TRAINING TRADITION THAT'S BEEN PASSED DOWN IN OUR VIL-LAGE.

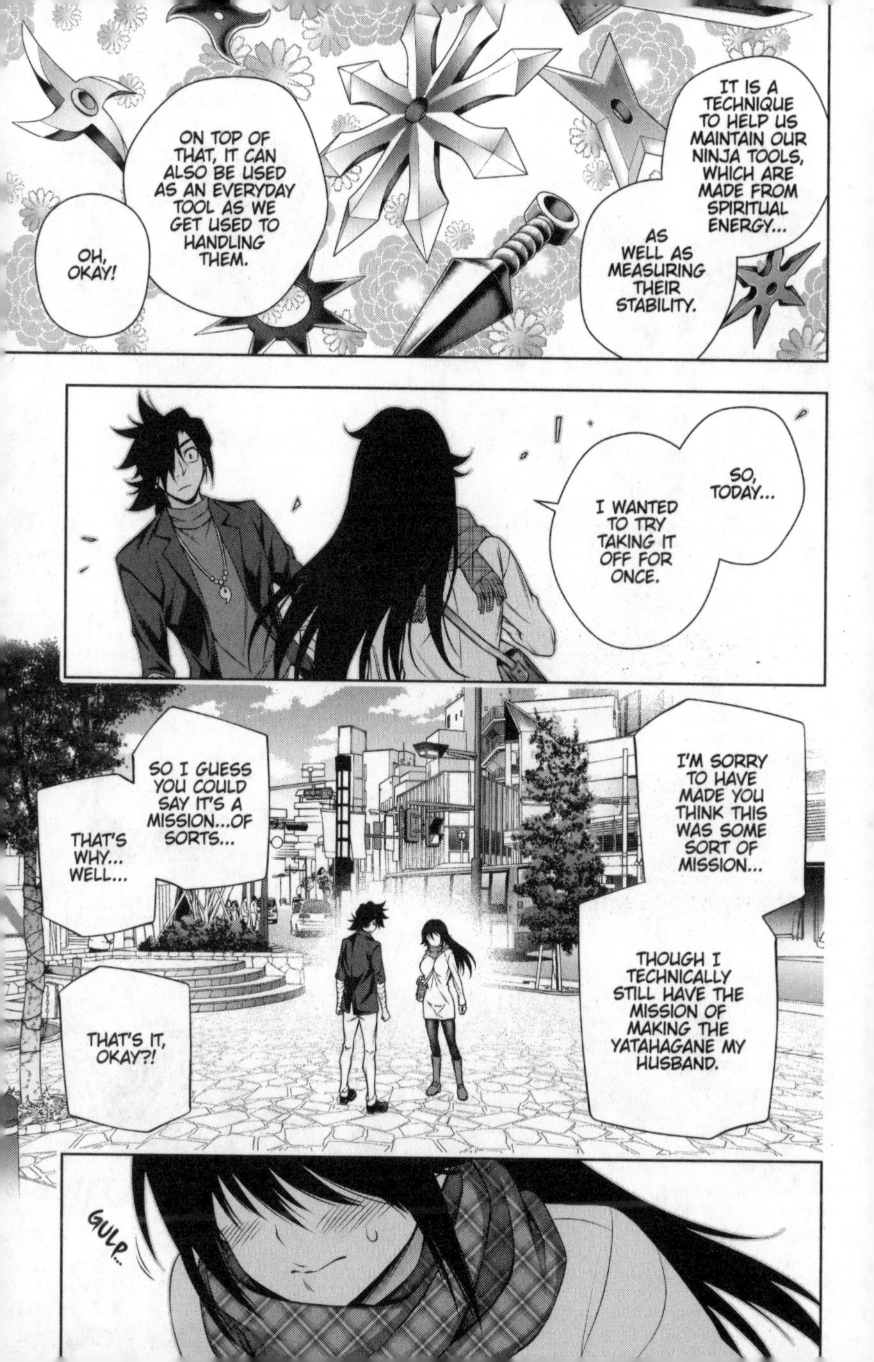
IT IS A TECHNIQUE TO HELP US MAINTAIN OUR NINJA TOOLS, WHICH ARE MADE FROM SPIRITUAL ENERGY...
AS WELL AS MEASURING THEIR STABILITY.
ON TOP OF THAT, IT CAN ALSO BE USED AS AN EVERYDAY TOOL AS WE GET USED TO HANDLING THEM.
OH, OKAY!
SO, TODAY...
I WANTED TO TRY TAKING IT OFF FOR ONCE.
I'M SORRY TO HAVE MADE YOU THINK THIS WAS SOME SORT OF MISSION...
THOUGH I TECHNICALLY STILL HAVE THE MISSION OF MAKING THE YATAHAGANE MY HUSBAND.
SO I GUESS YOU COULD SAY IT'S A MISSION...OF SORTS...
THAT'S WHY... WELL...
THAT'S IT, OKAY?!
GULP...

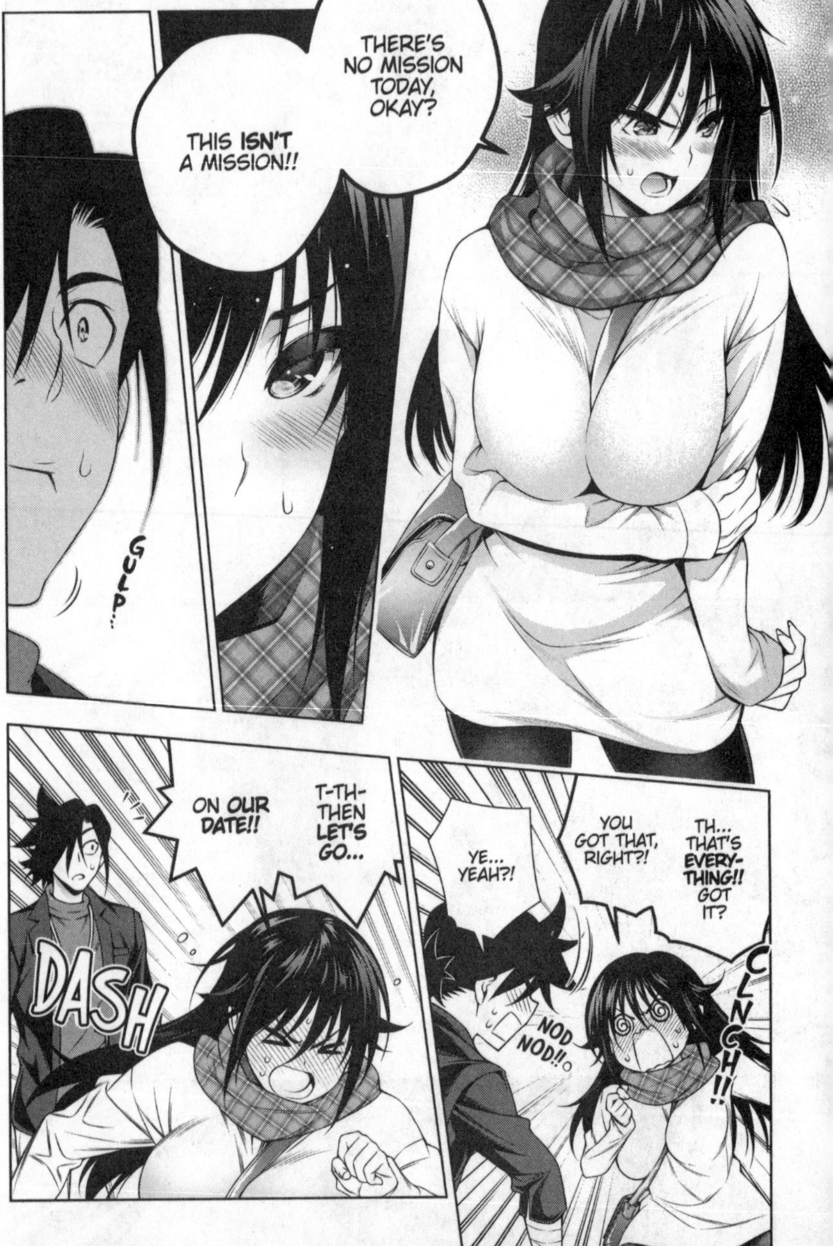
THERE'S NO MISSION TODAY, OKAY?
THIS ISN'T A MISSION!!
GULP...
TH... THAT'S EVERY-THING!! GOT IT?
YOU GOT THAT, RIGHT?!
CLNCH!!
YE... YEAH?!
NOD NOD!!
T-TH-THEN LET'S GO...
ON OUR DATE!!
DASH

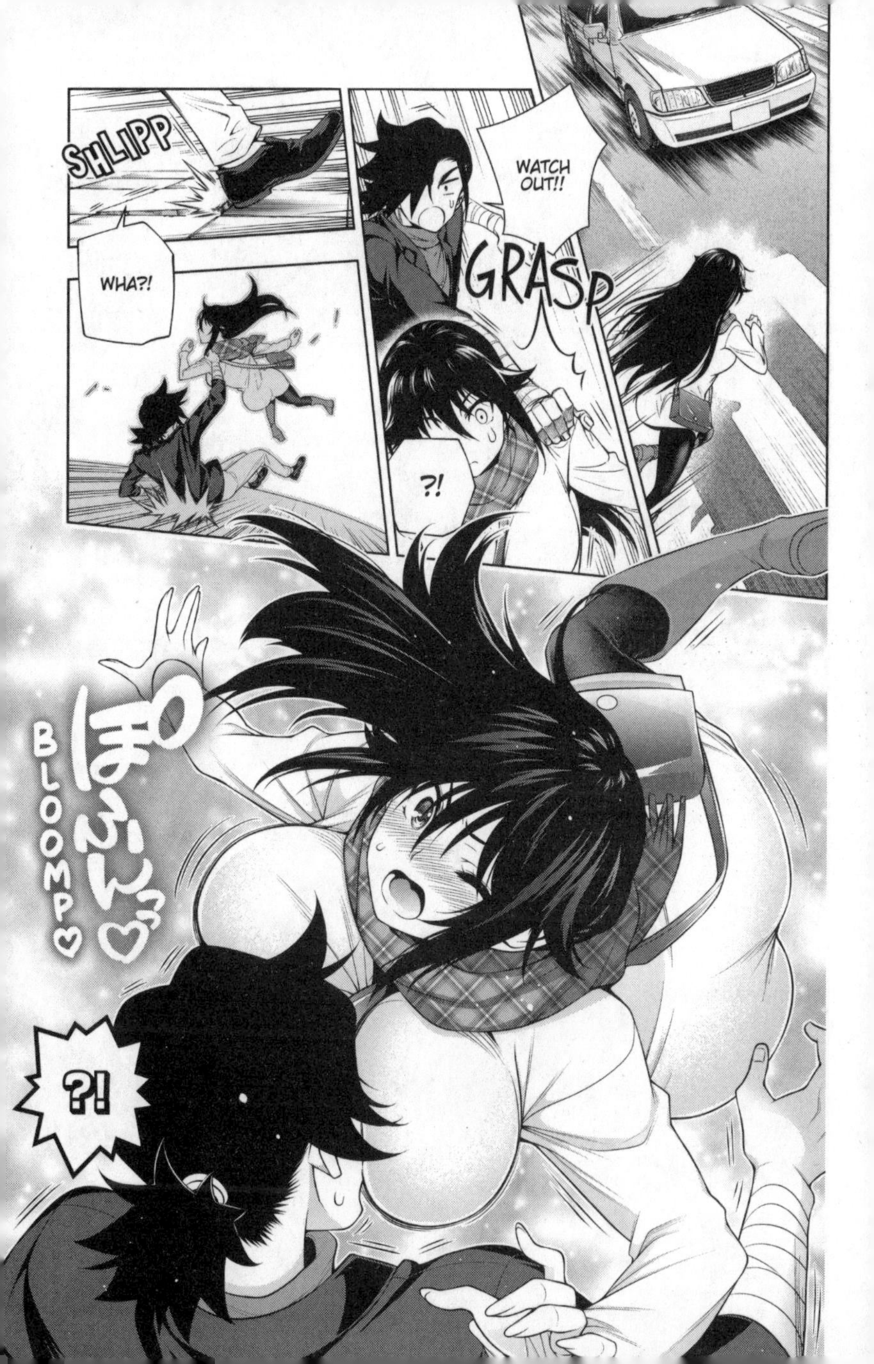
WATCH OUT!!
GRASP
?!
SHLIPP
WHA?!
ぽふんっ♡
BLOOMP♡
?!

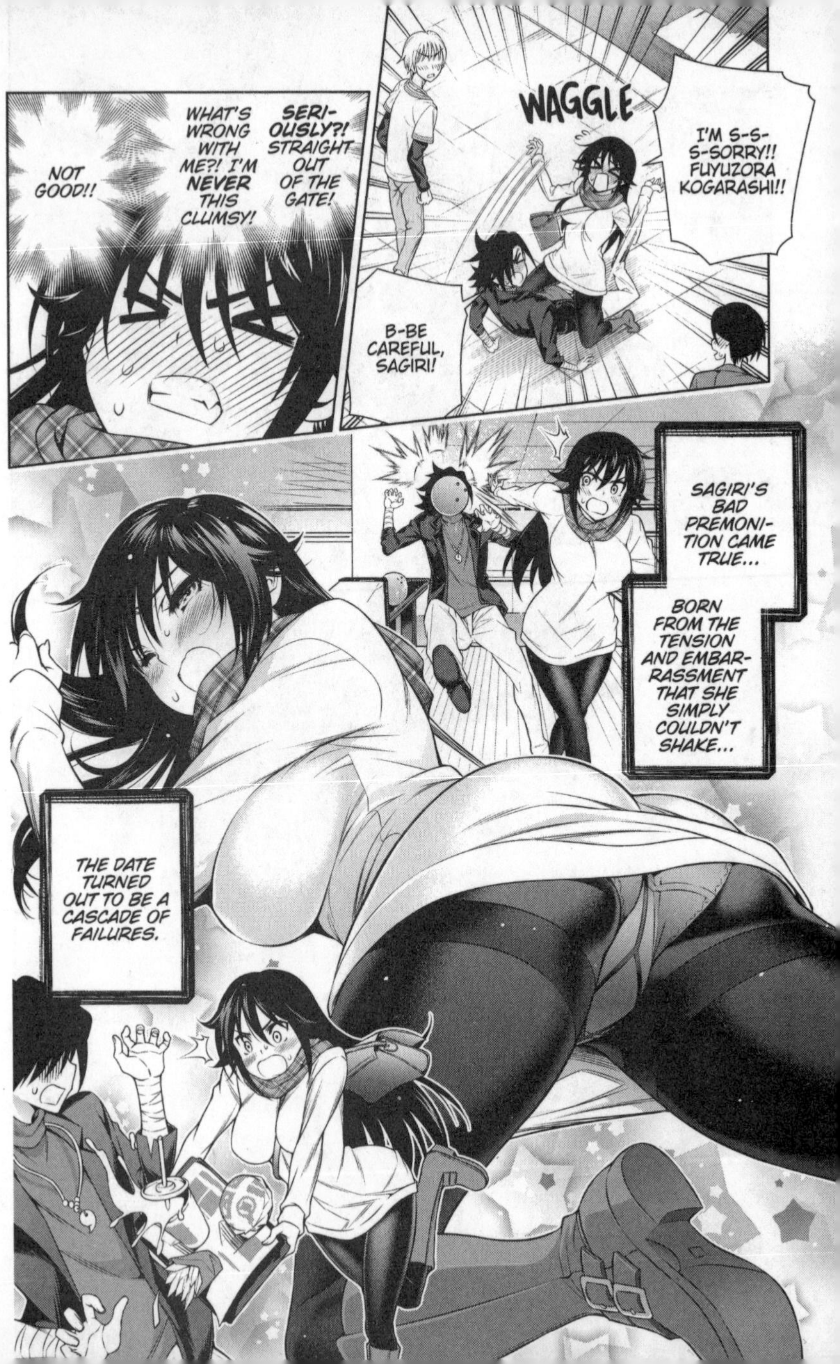
I'M S-S-S-SORRY!! FUYUZORA KOGARASHI!!
WAGGLE
B-BE CAREFUL, SAGIRI!
SERI-OUSLY?! STRAIGHT OUT OF THE GATE!
WHAT'S WRONG WITH ME?! I'M NEVER THIS CLUMSY!
NOT GOOD!!
SAGIRI'S BAD PREMONI-TION CAME TRUE...
BORN FROM THE TENSION AND EMBAR-RASSMENT THAT SHE SIMPLY COULDN'T SHAKE...
THE DATE TURNED OUT TO BE A CASCADE OF FAILURES.

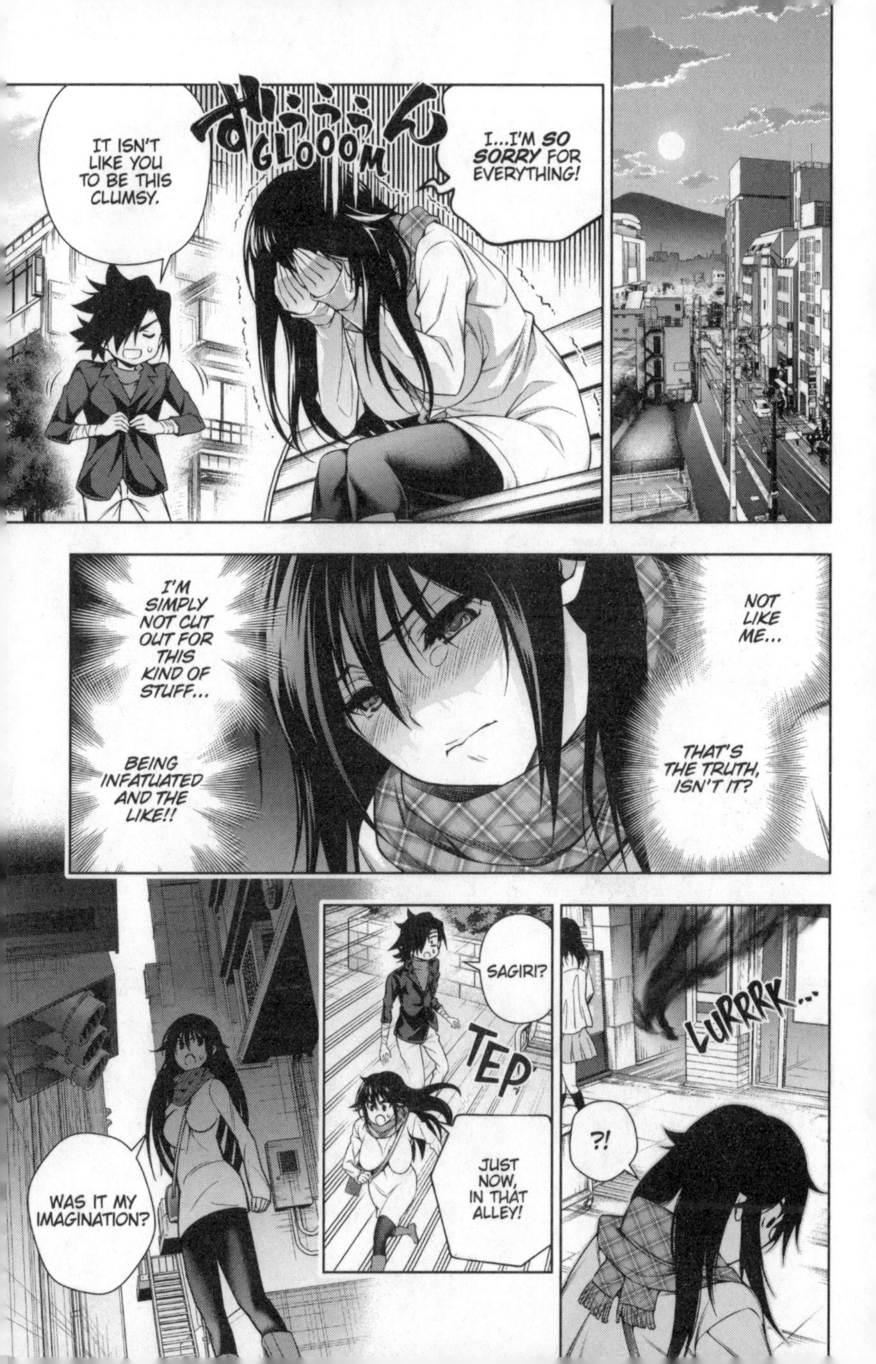
I...I'M SO SORRY FOR EVERYTHING!
GLOOOM
IT ISN'T LIKE YOU TO BE THIS CLUMSY.
NOT LIKE ME...
THAT'S THE TRUTH, ISN'T IT?
I'M SIMPLY NOT CUT OUT FOR THIS KIND OF STUFF...
BEING INFATUATED AND THE LIKE!!
LURRRK...
?!
SAGIRI?
TEP
JUST NOW, IN THAT ALLEY!
WAS IT MY IMAGINATION?

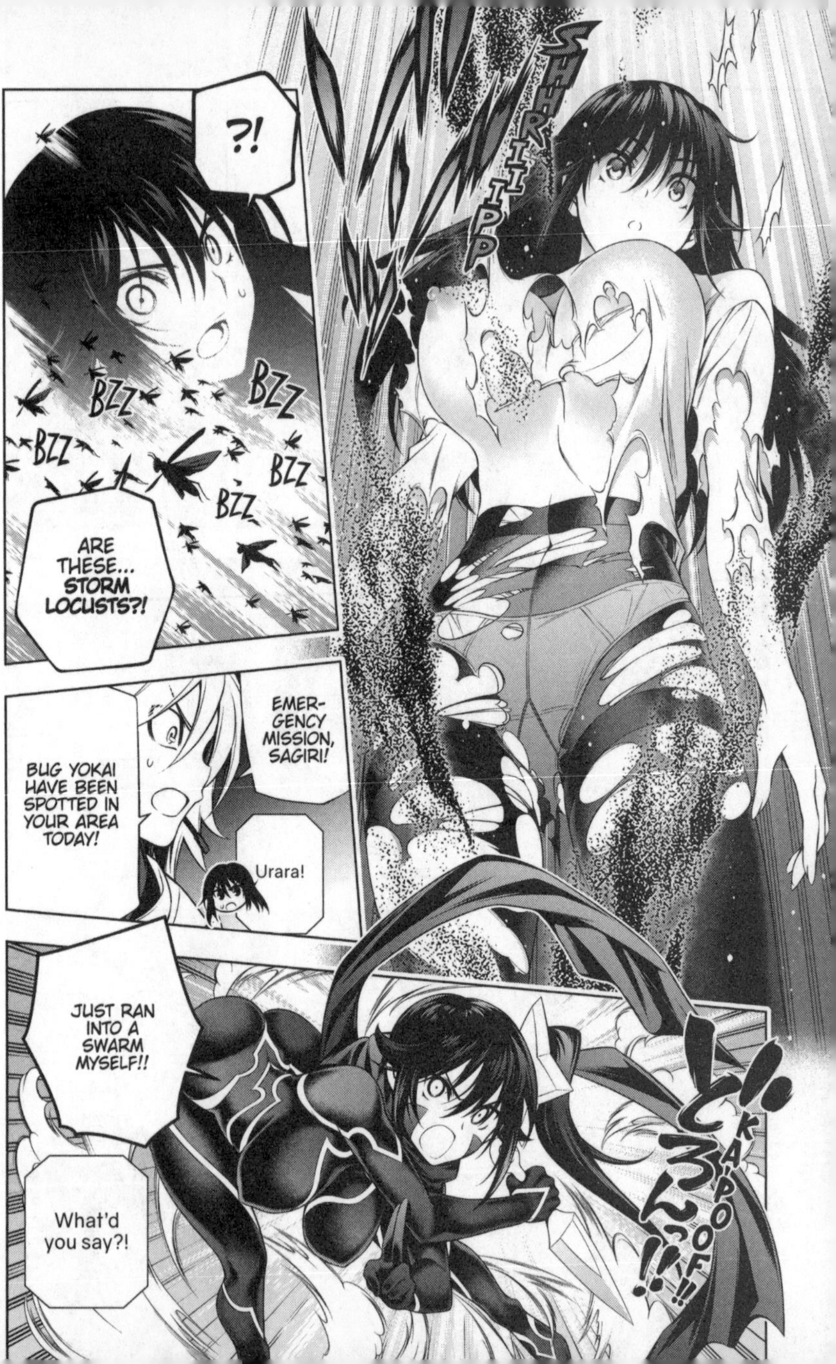
SHHRIIPP
?!
BZZ
BZZ
BZZ
BZZ
BZZ
ARE THESE... STORM LOCUSTS?!
EMERGENCY MISSION, SAGIRI!
BUG YOKAI HAVE BEEN SPOTTED IN YOUR AREA TODAY!
Urara!
JUST RAN INTO A SWARM MYSELF!!
どろんっ!!
KAPOOF!!
What'd you say?!

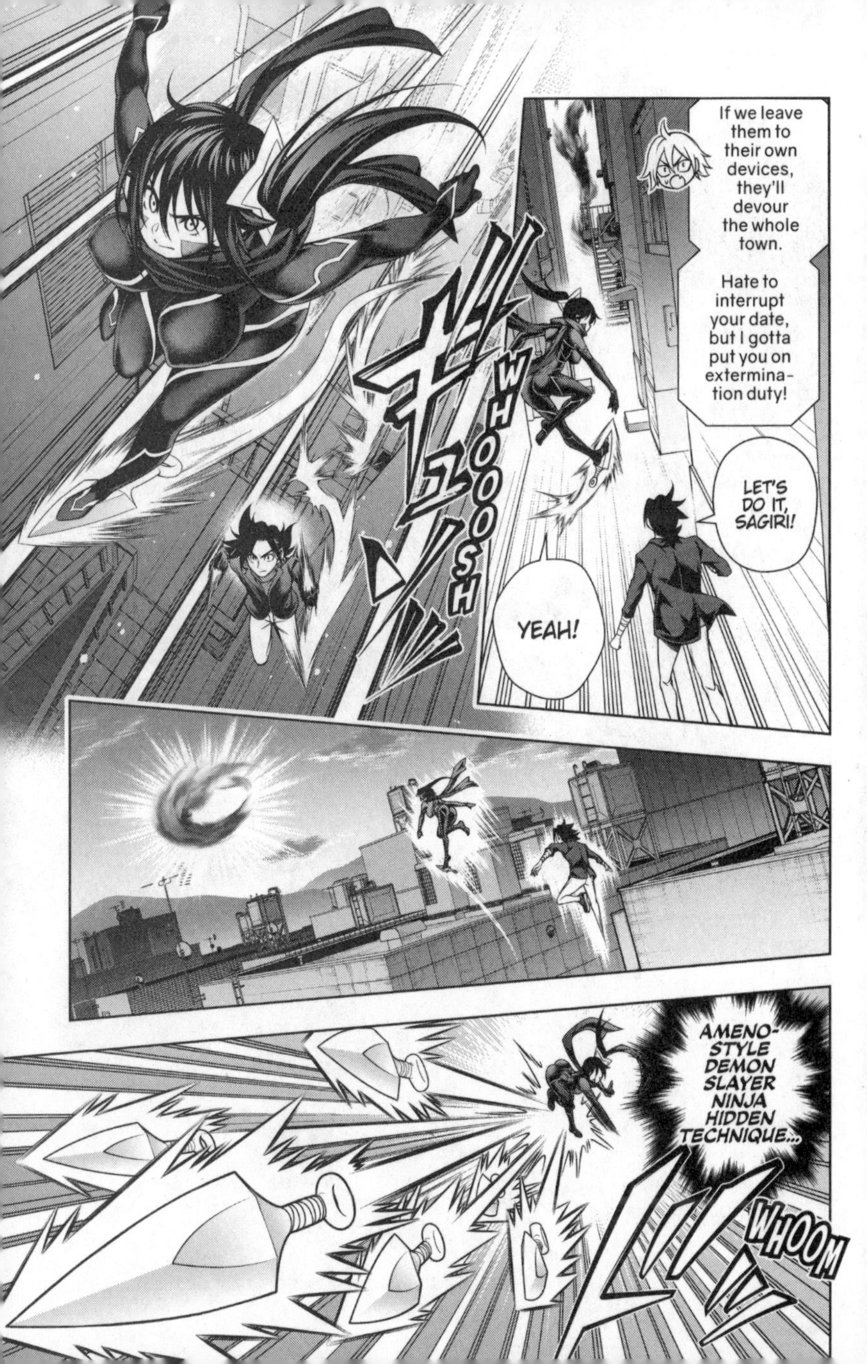
If we leave them to their own devices, they'll devour the whole town.
Hate to interrupt your date, but I gotta put you on extermination duty!
LET'S DO IT, SAGIRI!
YEAH!
WHOOOOOSH
AMENO-STYLE DEMON SLAYER NINJA HIDDEN TECHNIQUE...
WHOOM

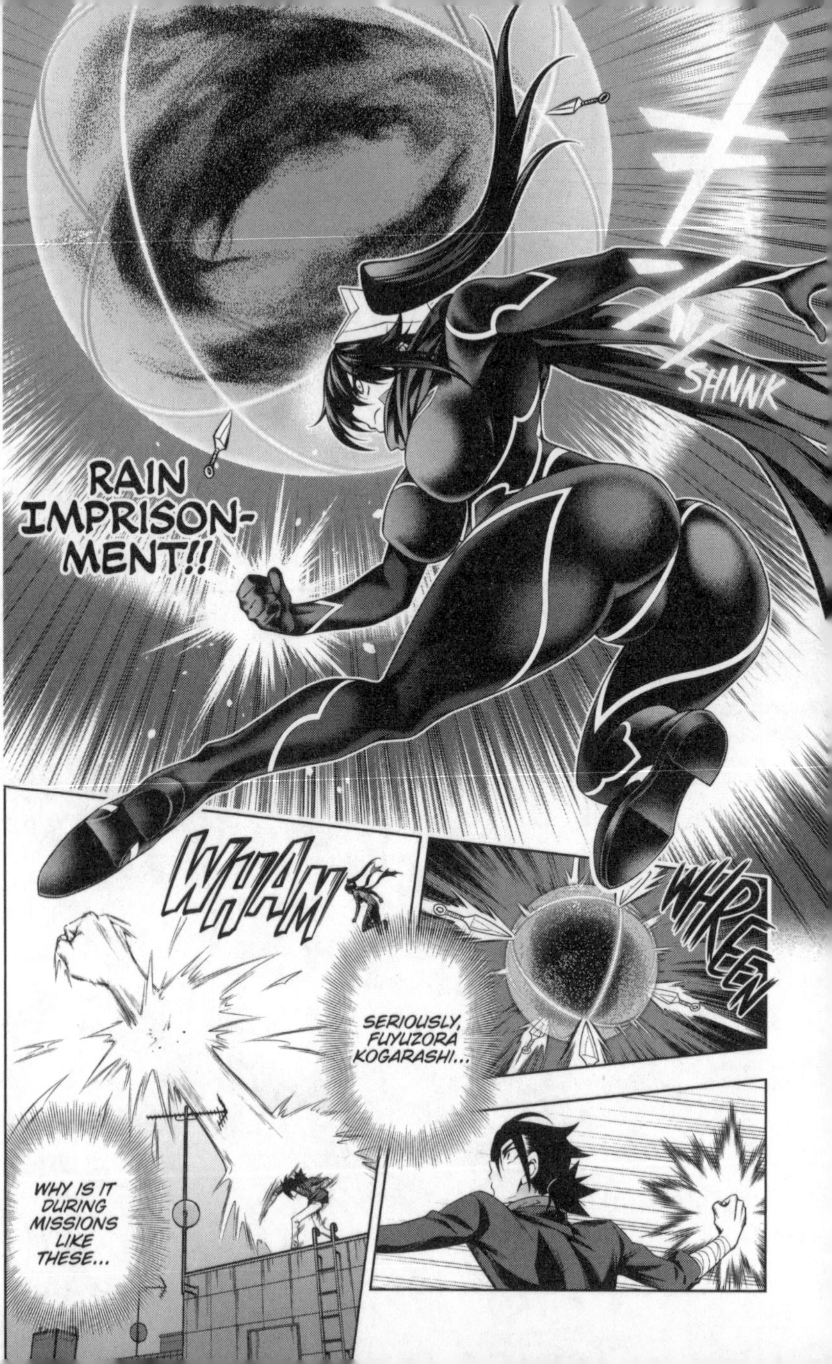
SHNNK
RAIN IMPRISON-MENT!!
WHREEN
WHAM
SERIOUSLY, FUYUZORA KOGARASHI...
WHY IS IT DURING MISSIONS LIKE THESE...

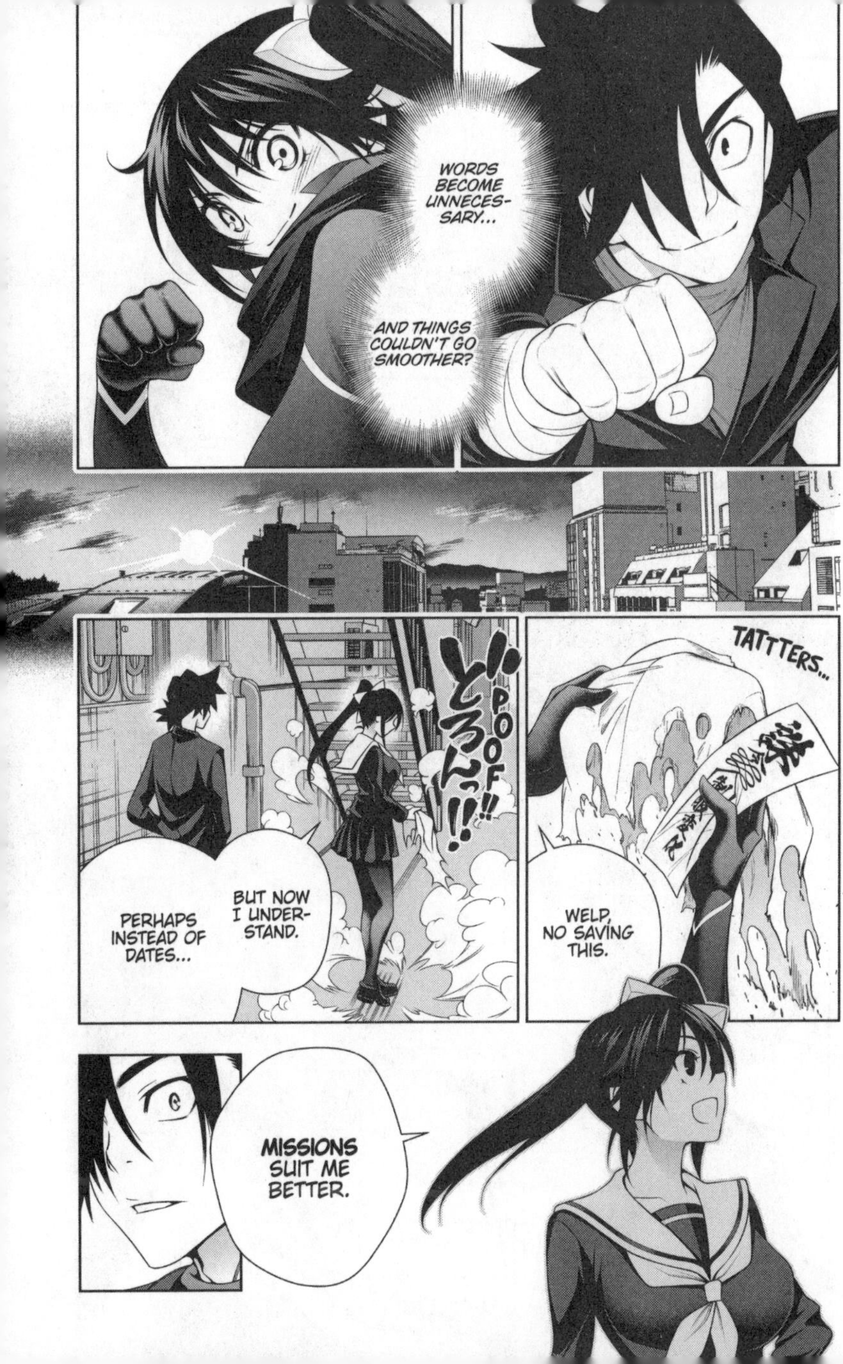
WORDS BECOME UNNECES-SARY...
AND THINGS COULDN'T GO SMOOTHER?
TATTTERS...
WELP, NO SAVING THIS.
POOF!!
どろんっ!!
BUT NOW I UNDER-STAND.
PERHAPS INSTEAD OF DATES...
MISSIONS SUIT ME BETTER.

Text: School Uniform Transformation

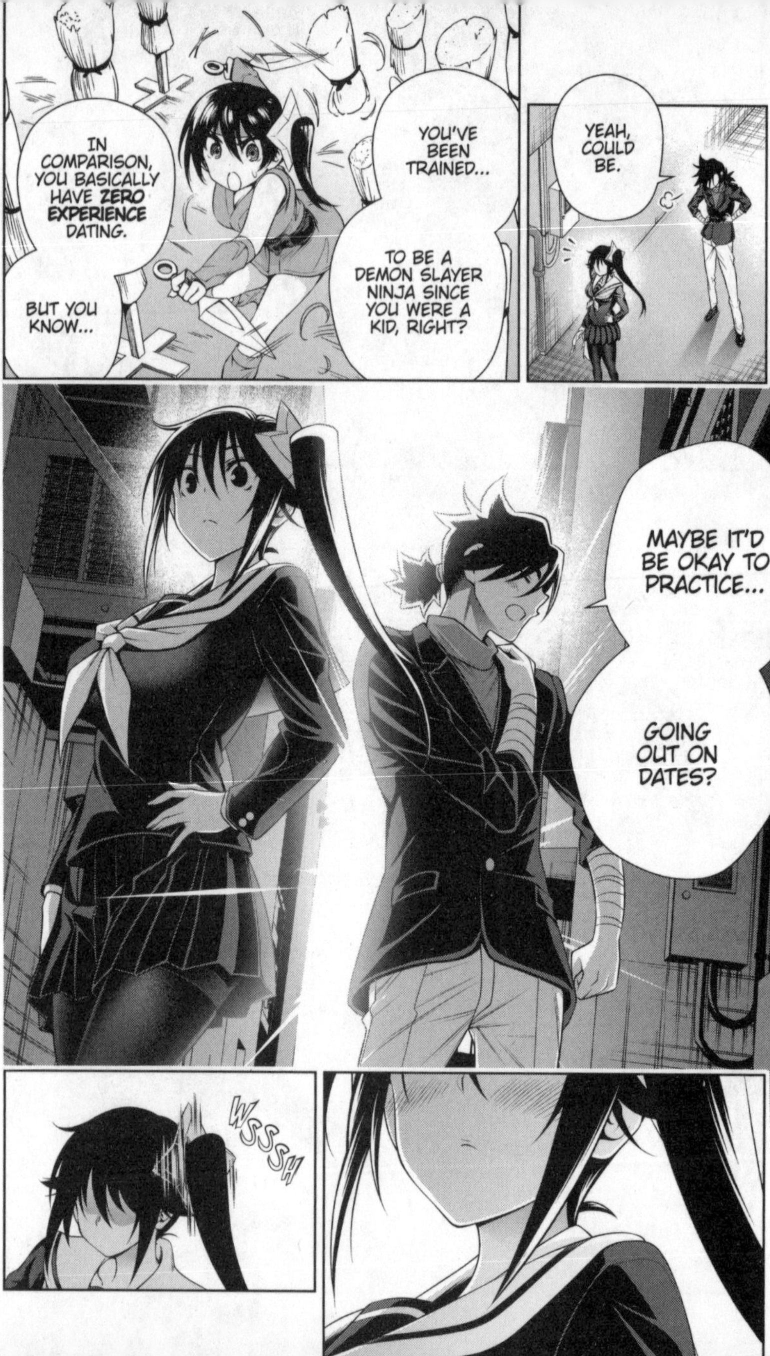
YEAH, COULD BE.
YOU'VE BEEN TRAINED...
TO BE A DEMON SLAYER NINJA SINCE YOU WERE A KID, RIGHT?
IN COMPARISON, YOU BASICALLY HAVE **ZERO EXPERIENCE** DATING.
BUT YOU KNOW...
MAYBE IT'D BE OKAY TO PRACTICE...
GOING OUT ON DATES?
WSSSH

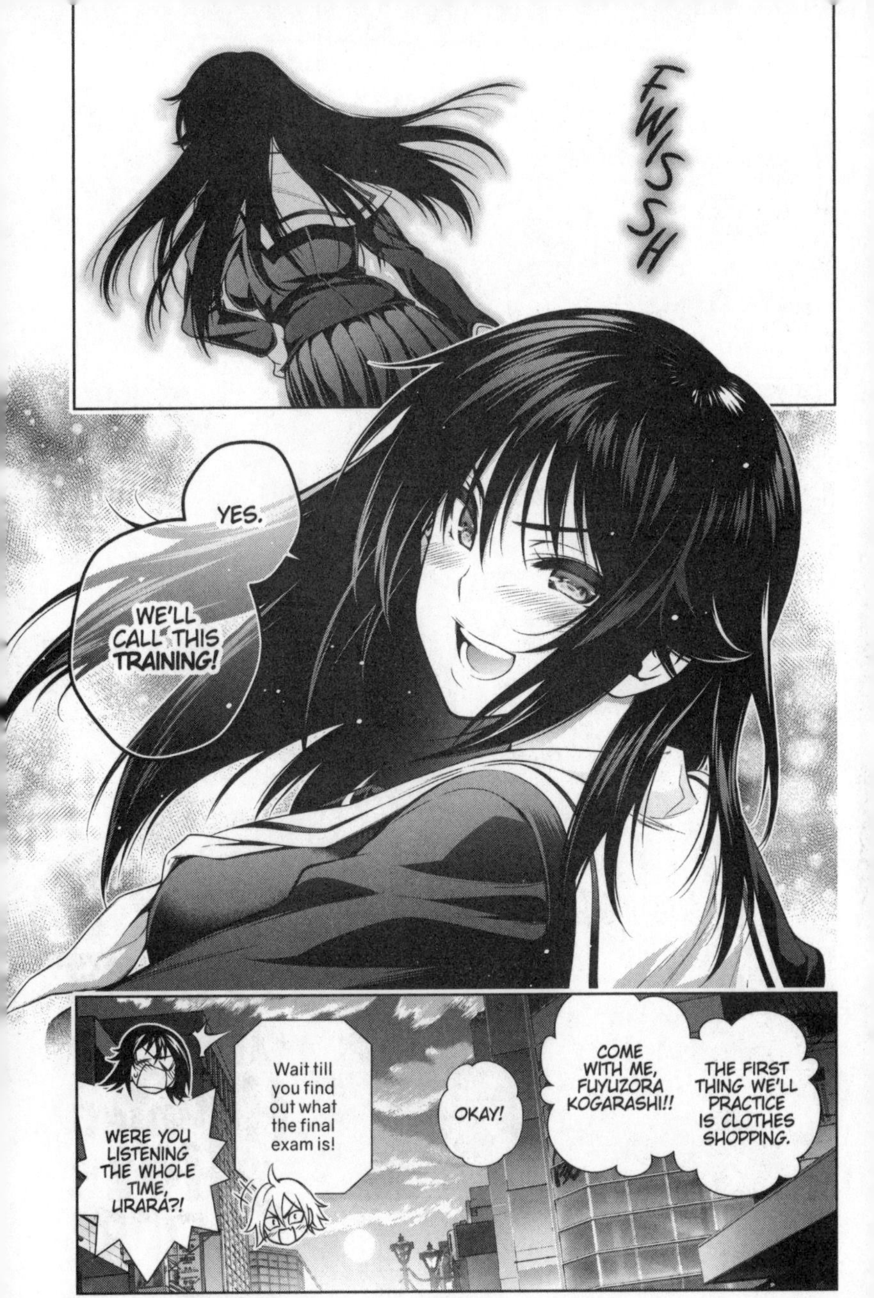
FWISSH
YES.
WE'LL CALL THIS TRAINING!
THE FIRST THING WE'LL PRACTICE IS CLOTHES SHOPPING.
COME WITH ME, FUYUZORA KOGARASHI!!
OKAY!
Wait till you find out what the final exam is!
WERE YOU LISTENING THE WHOLE TIME, URARA?!

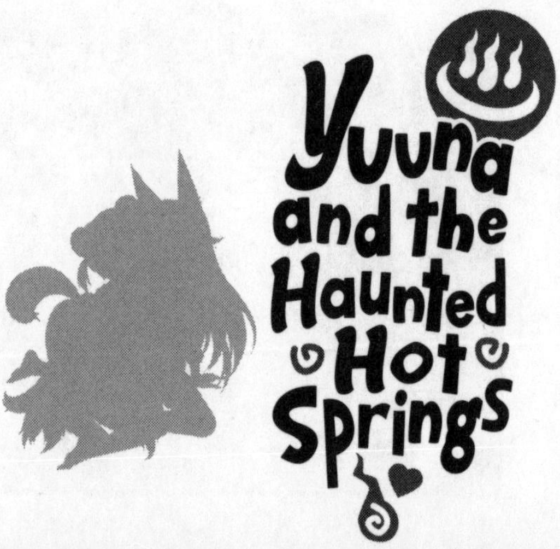

Yuuna and the Haunted Hot Springs

177 Silent Yuragi-sou

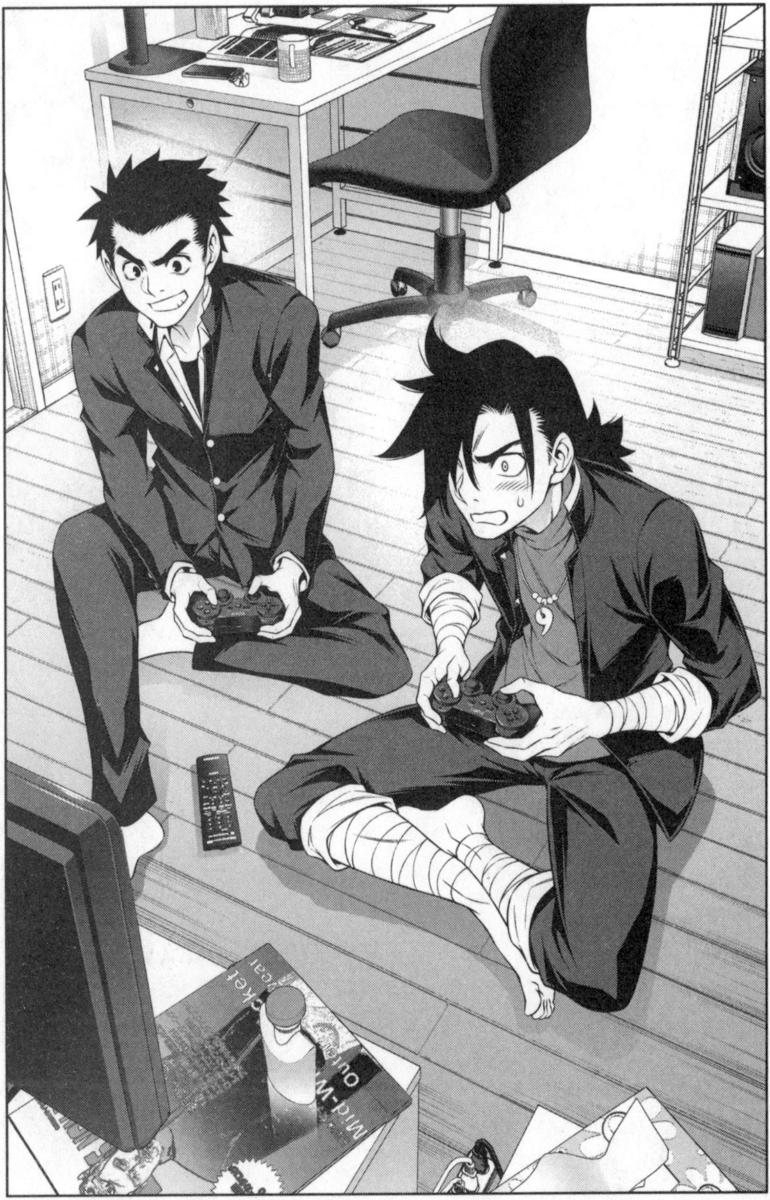

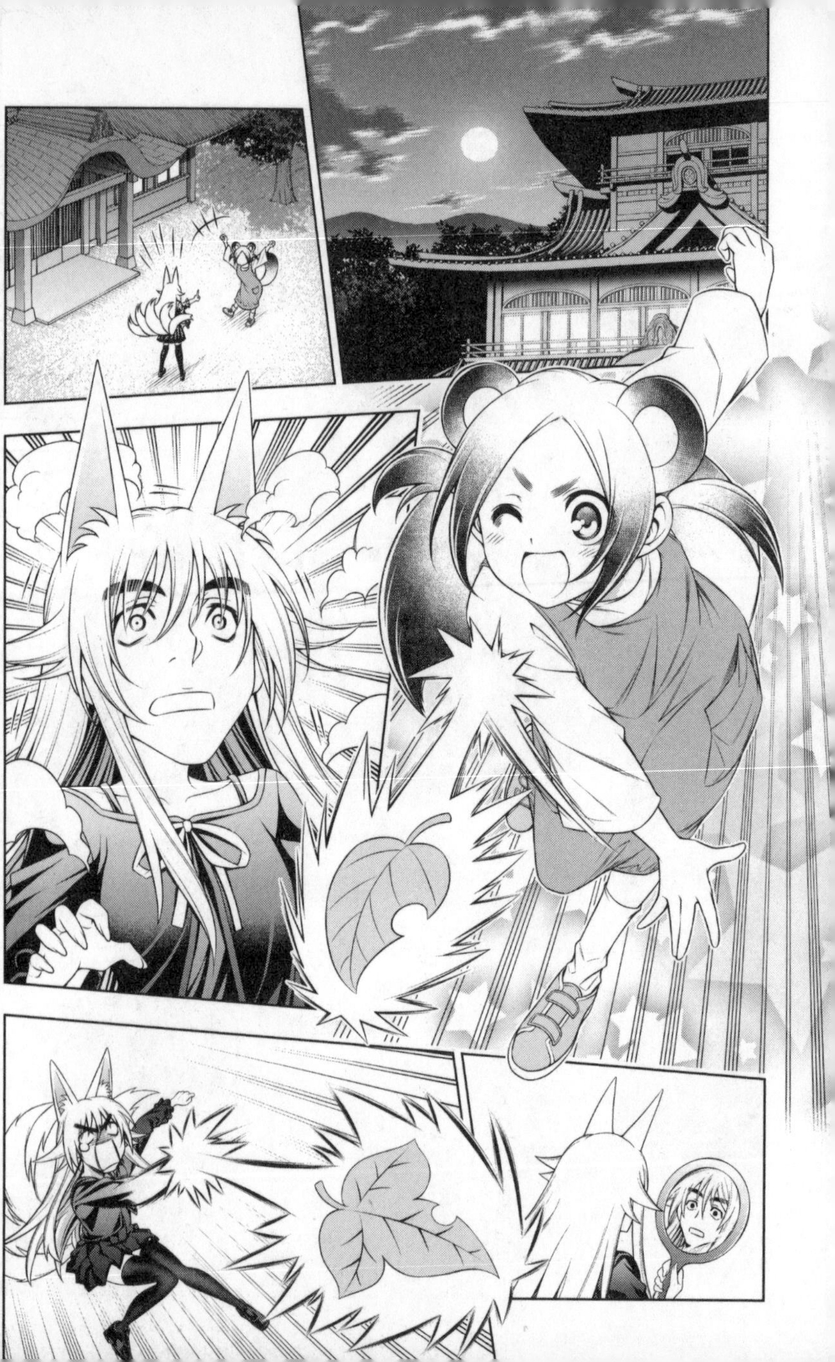

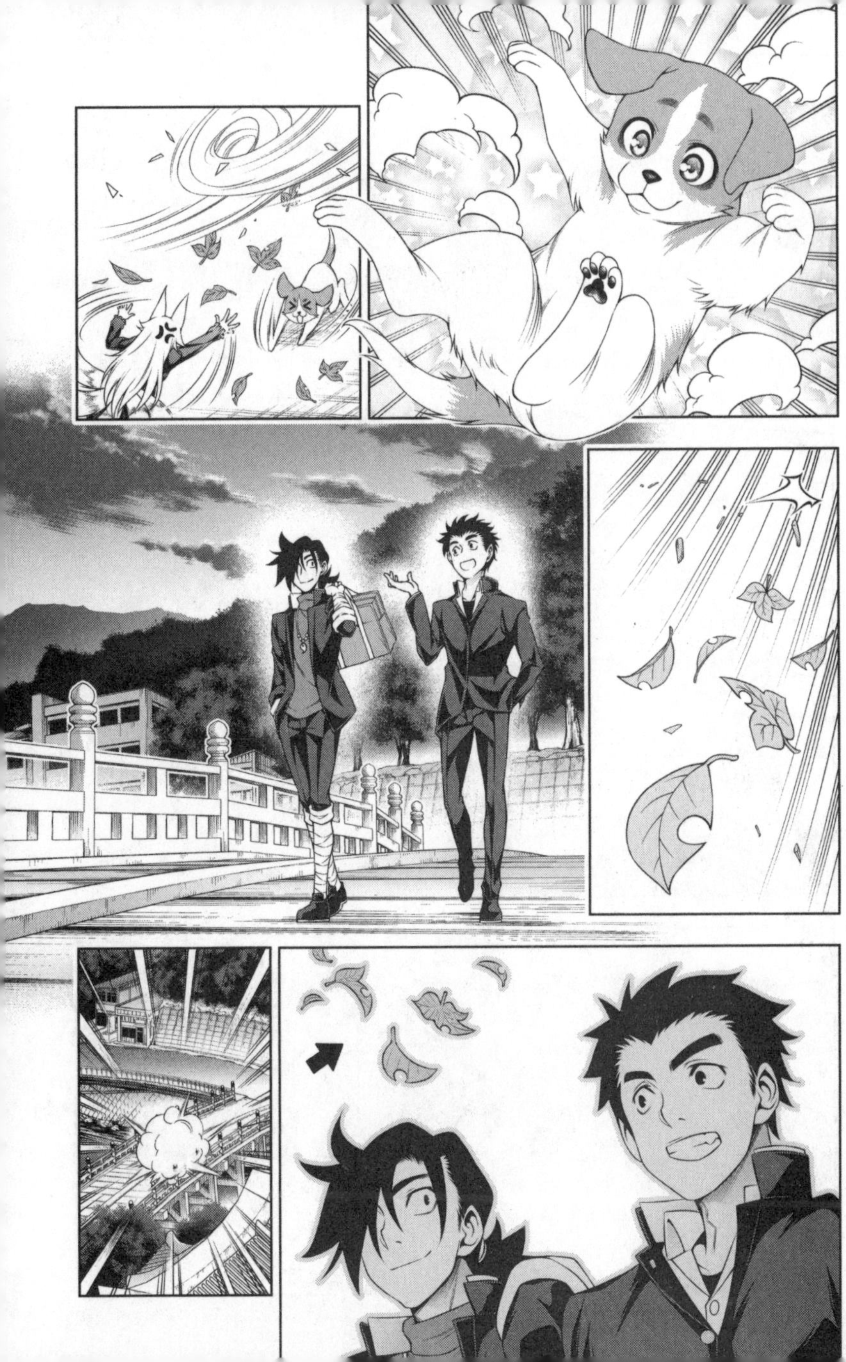

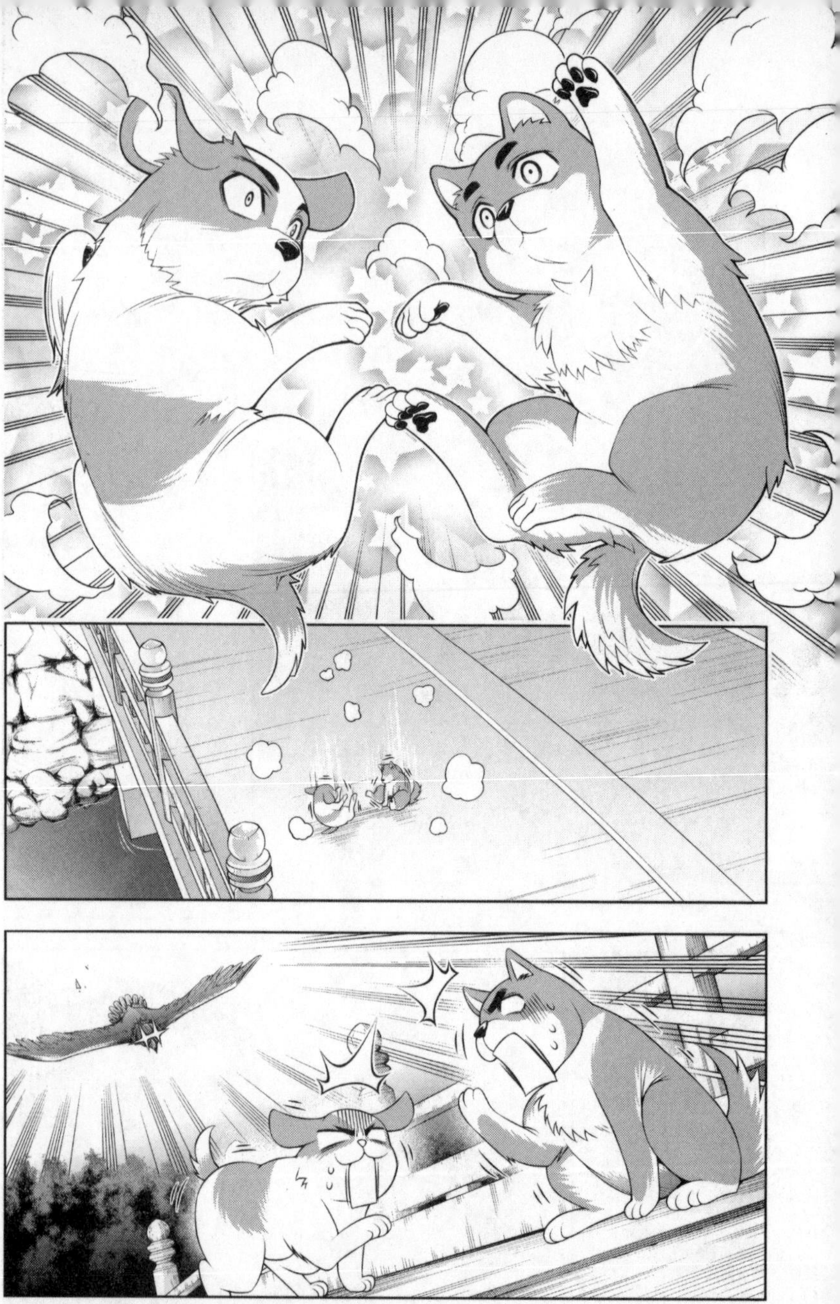

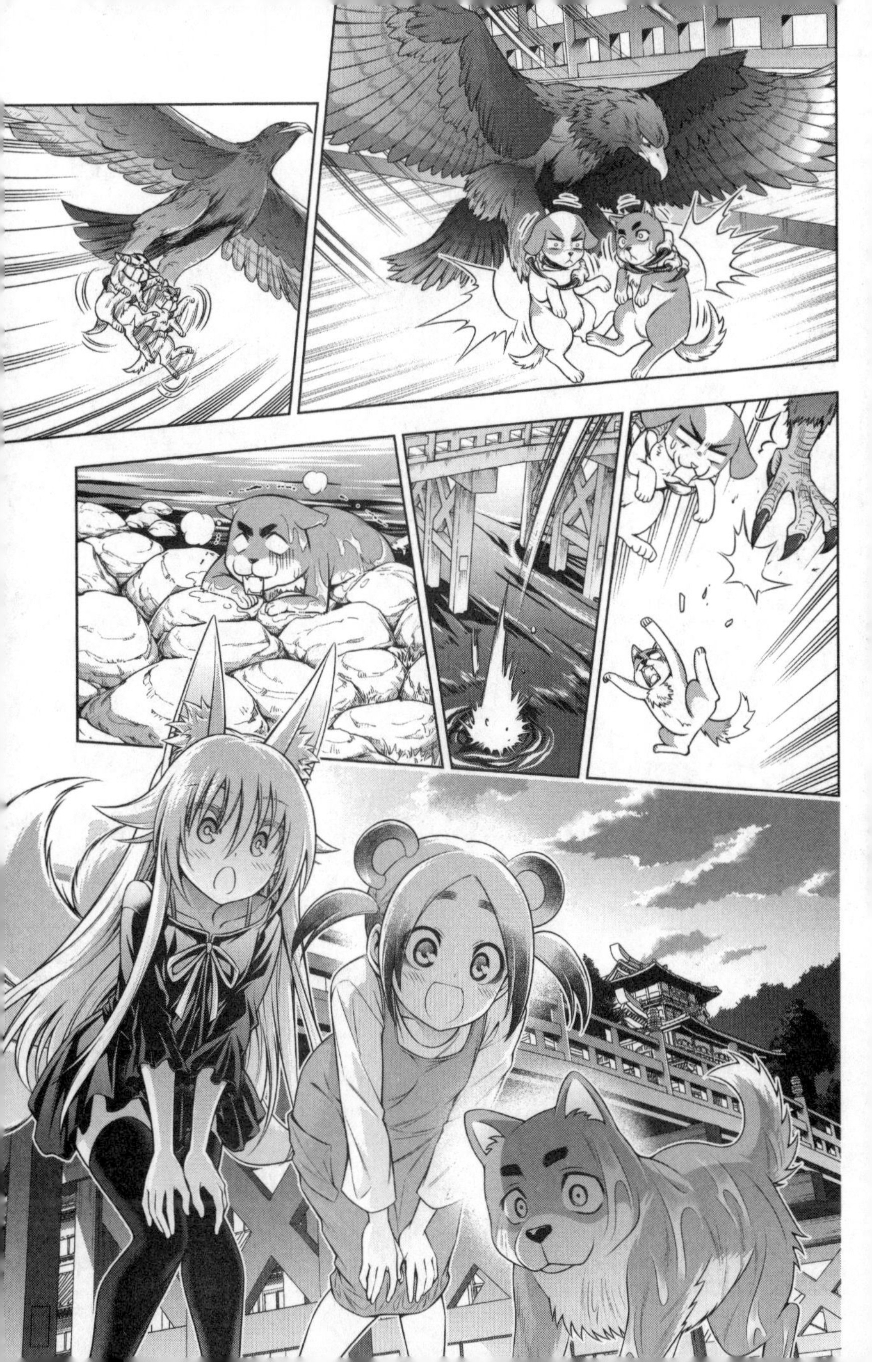

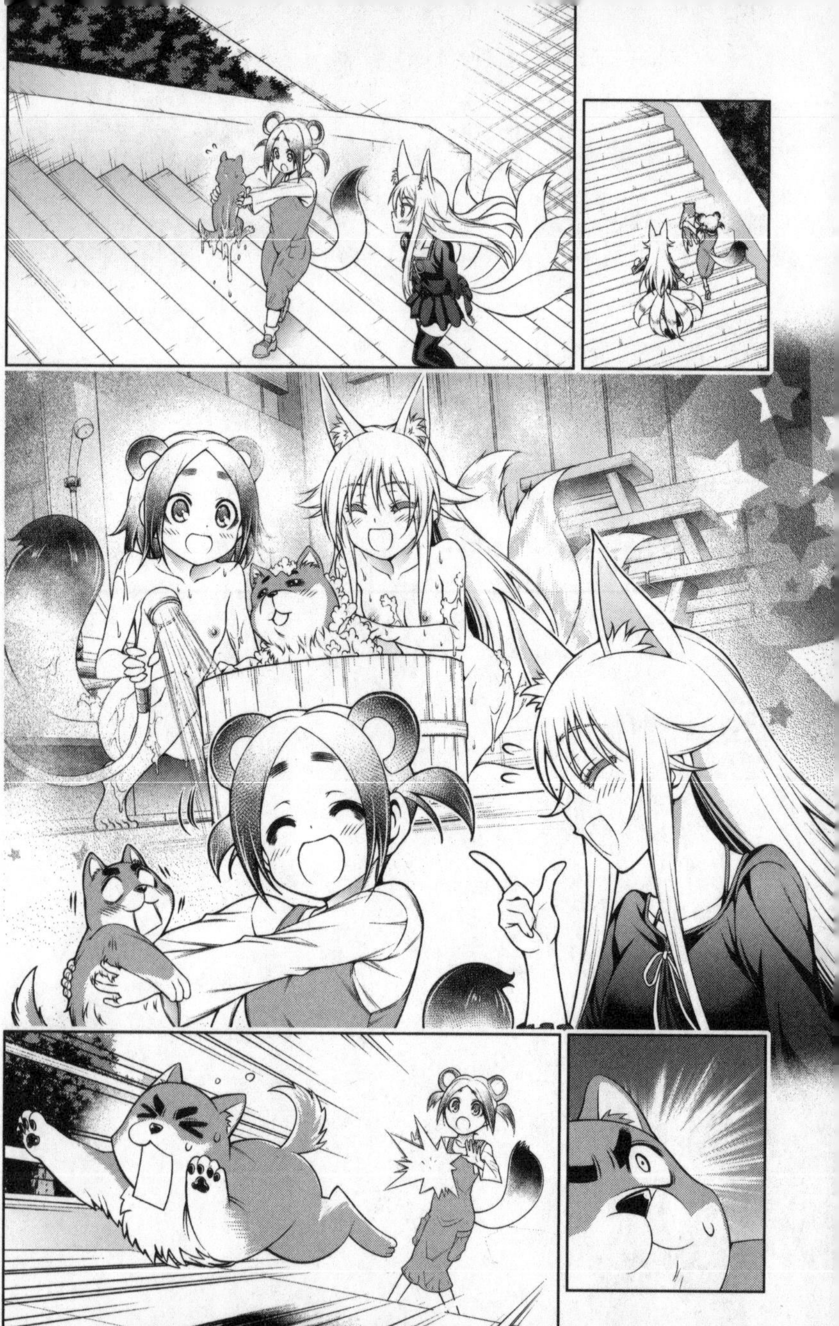

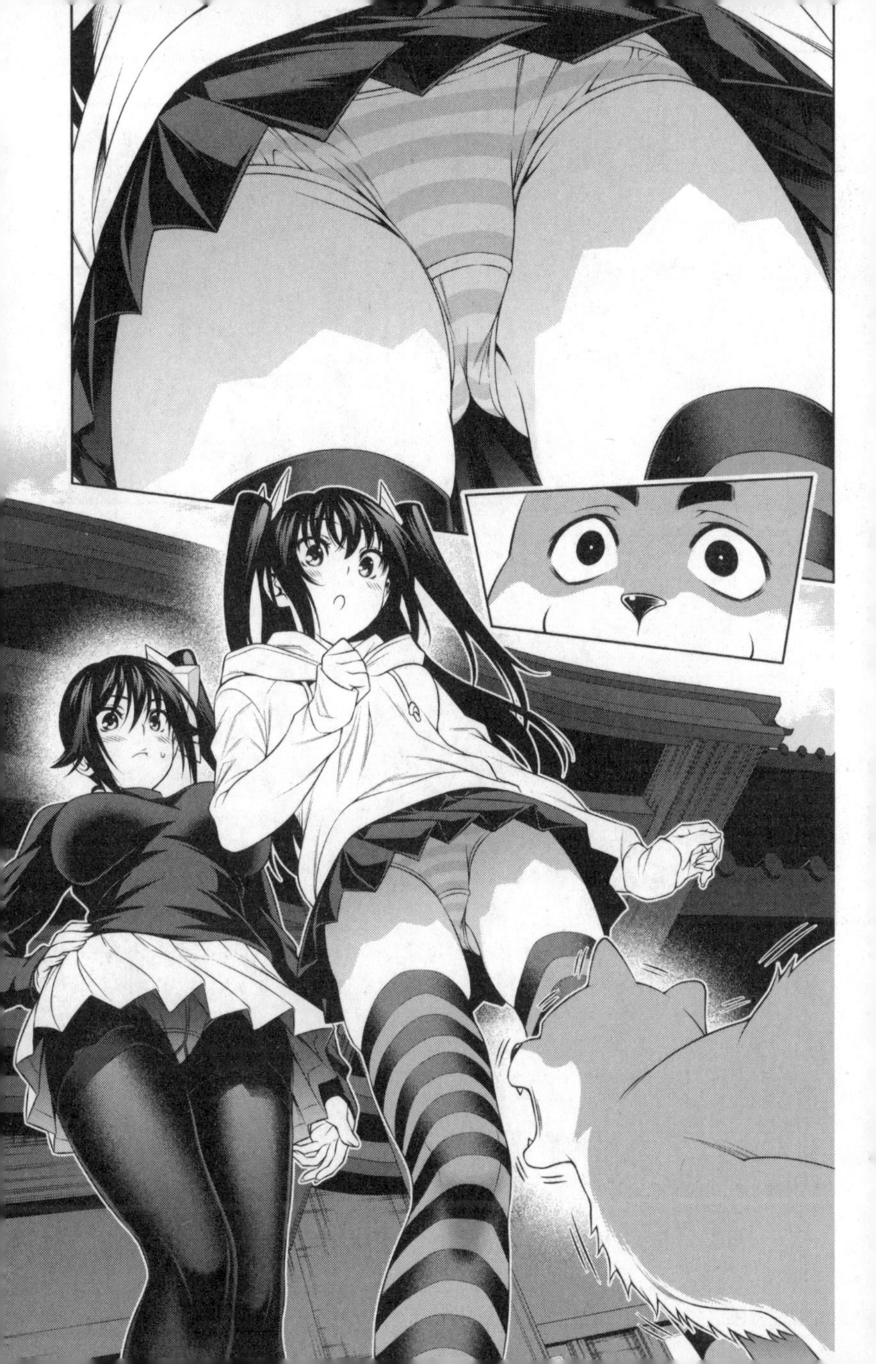

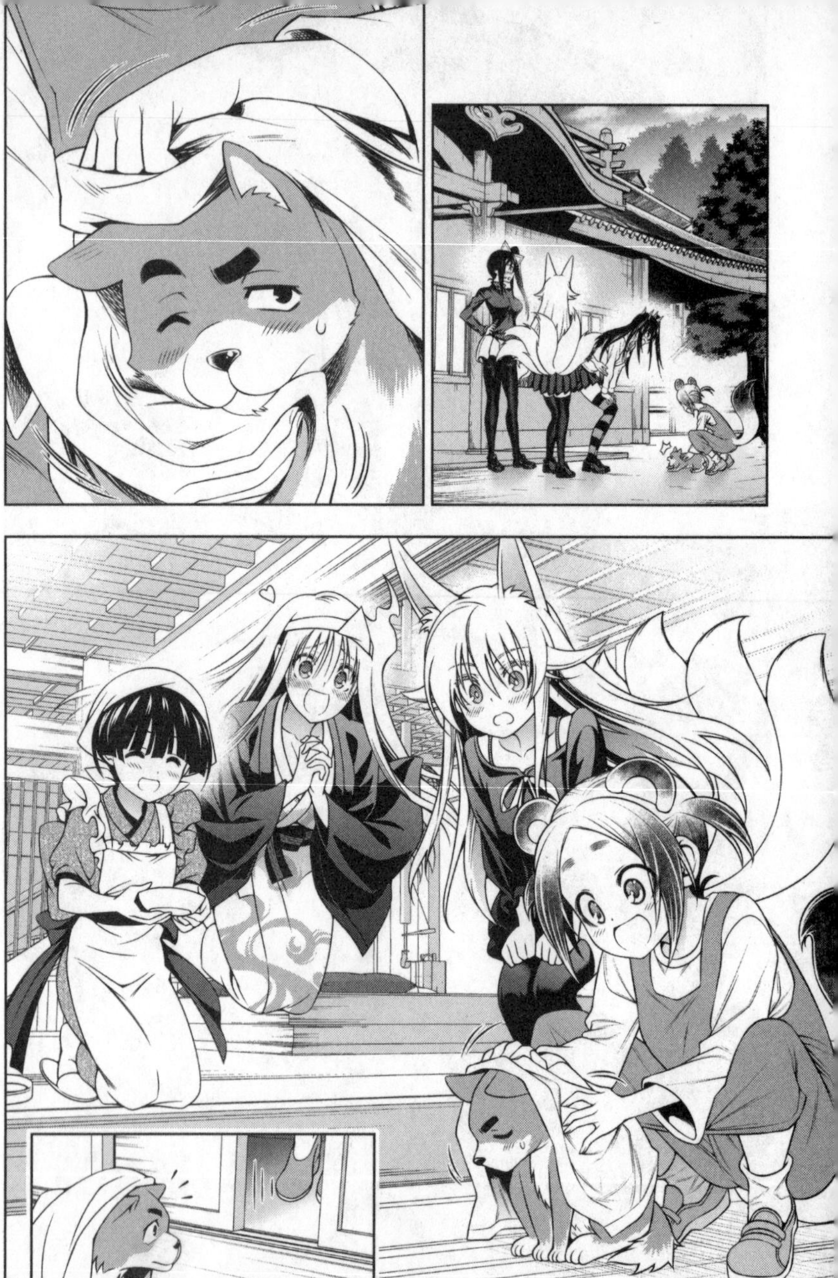

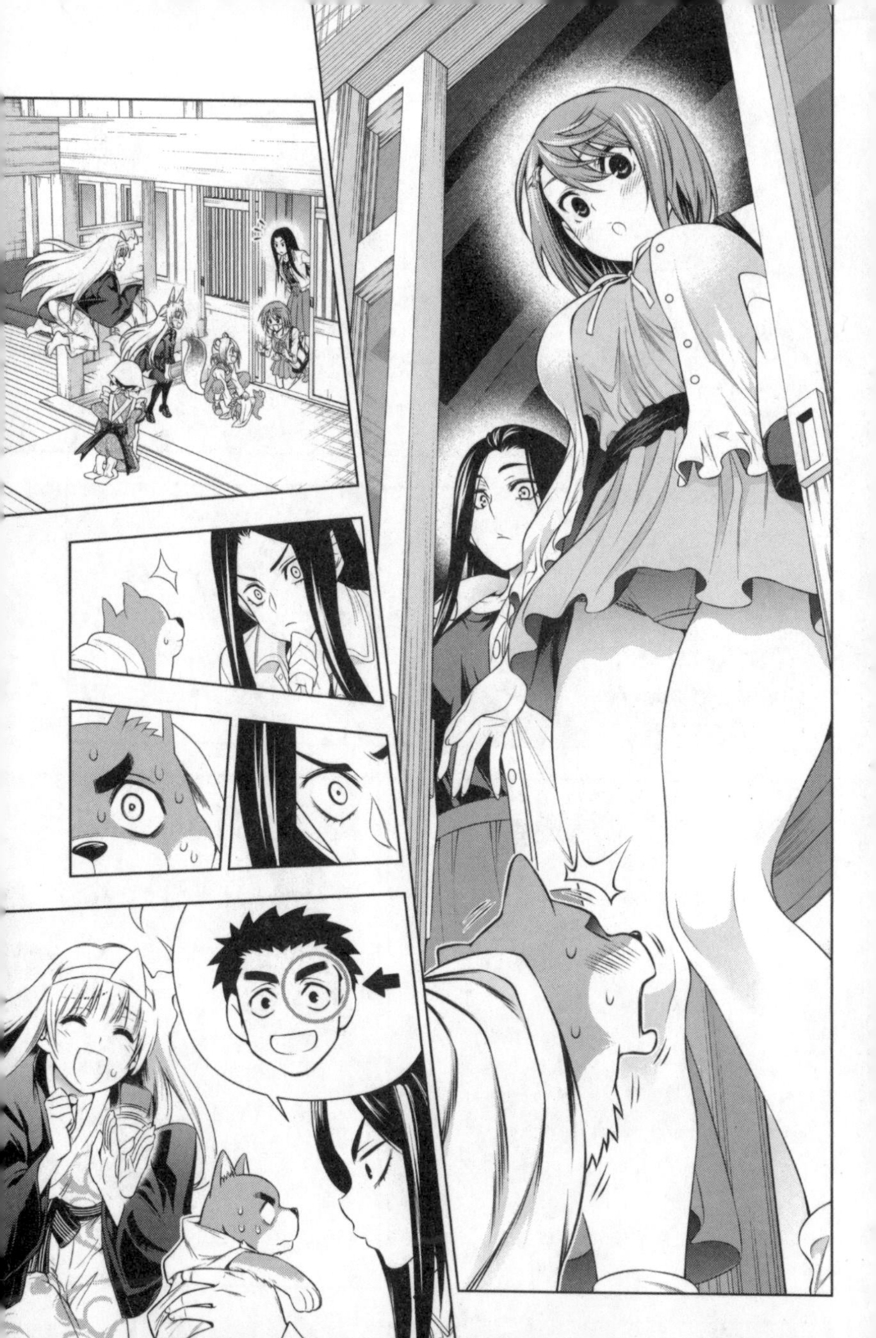

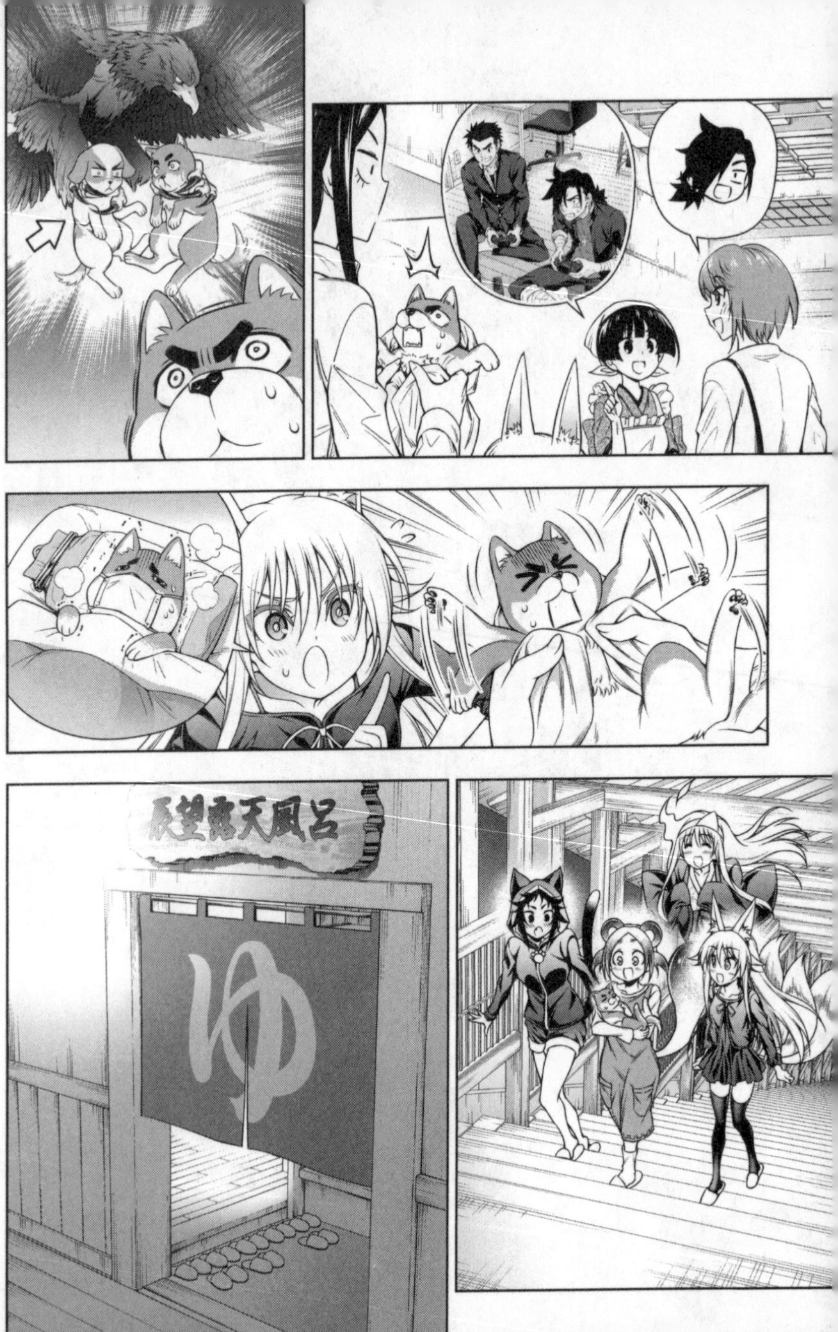
展望露天風呂
ゆ

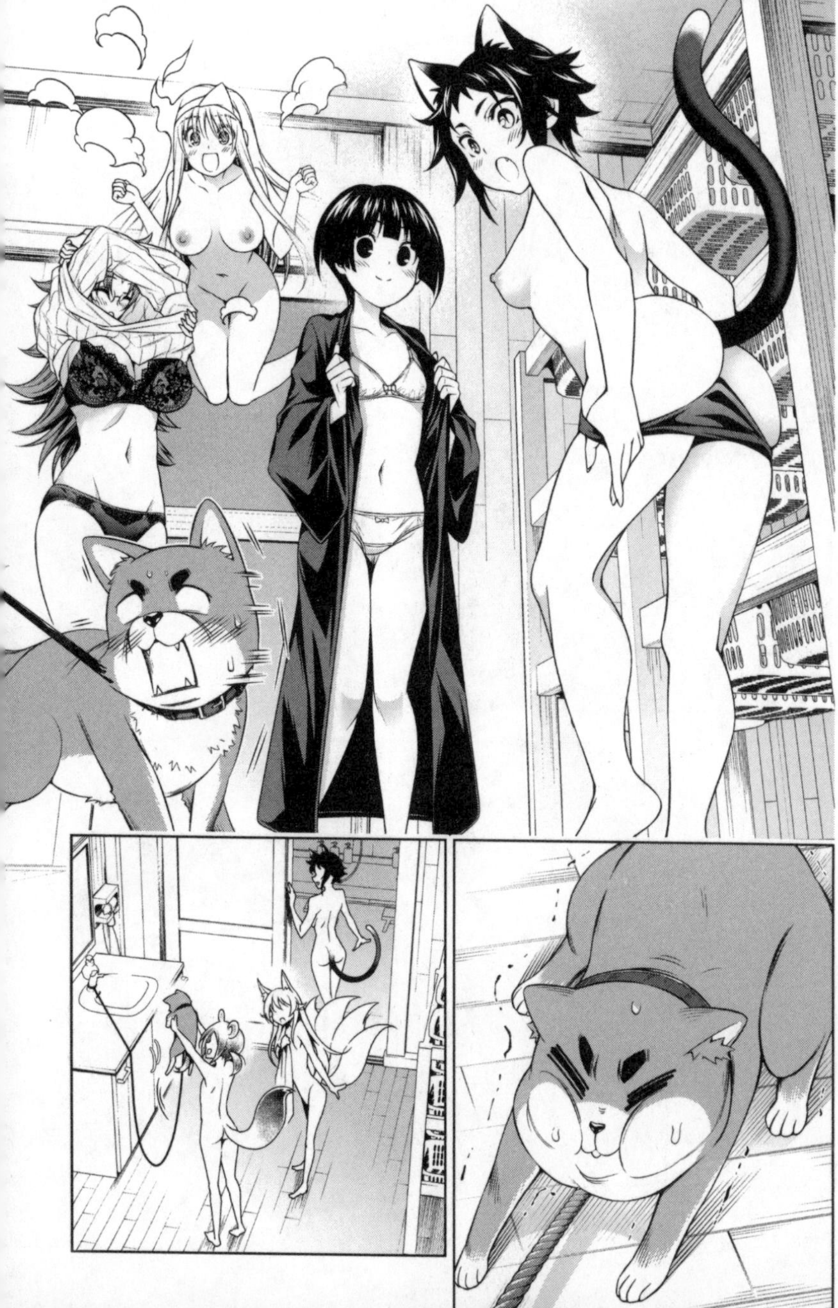

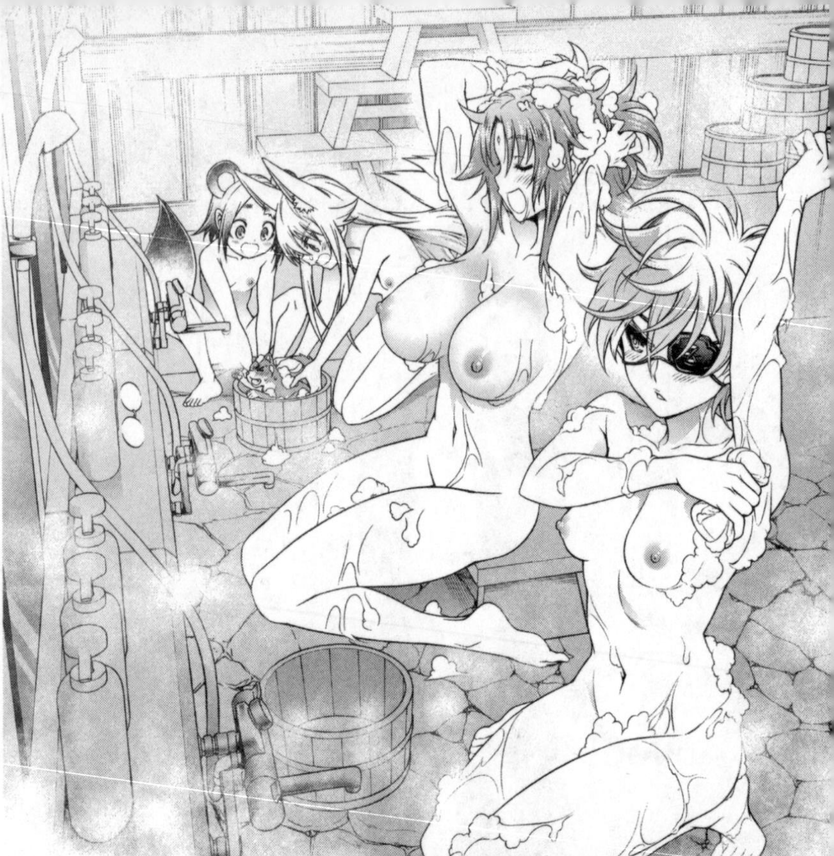
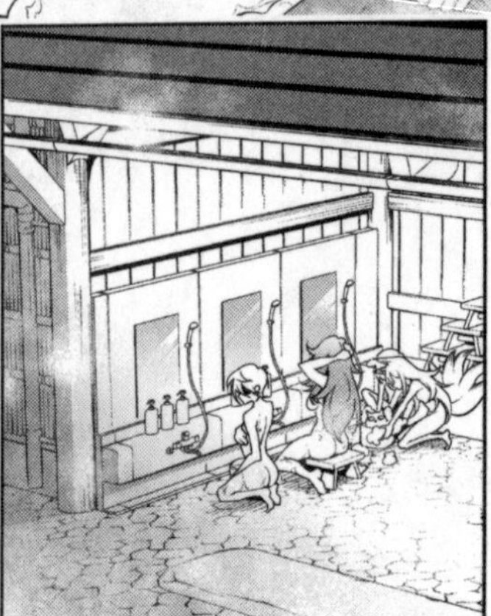
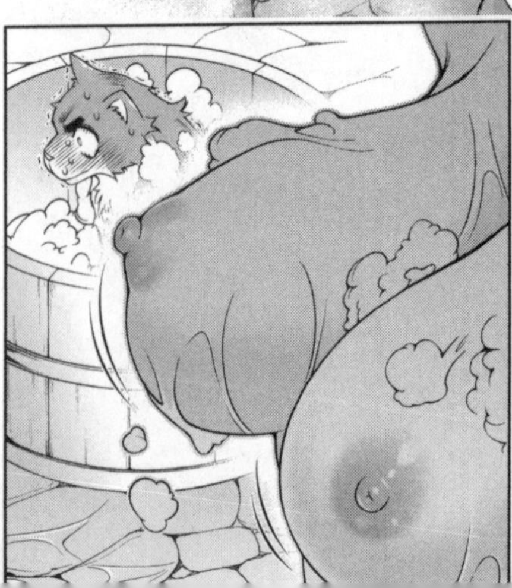

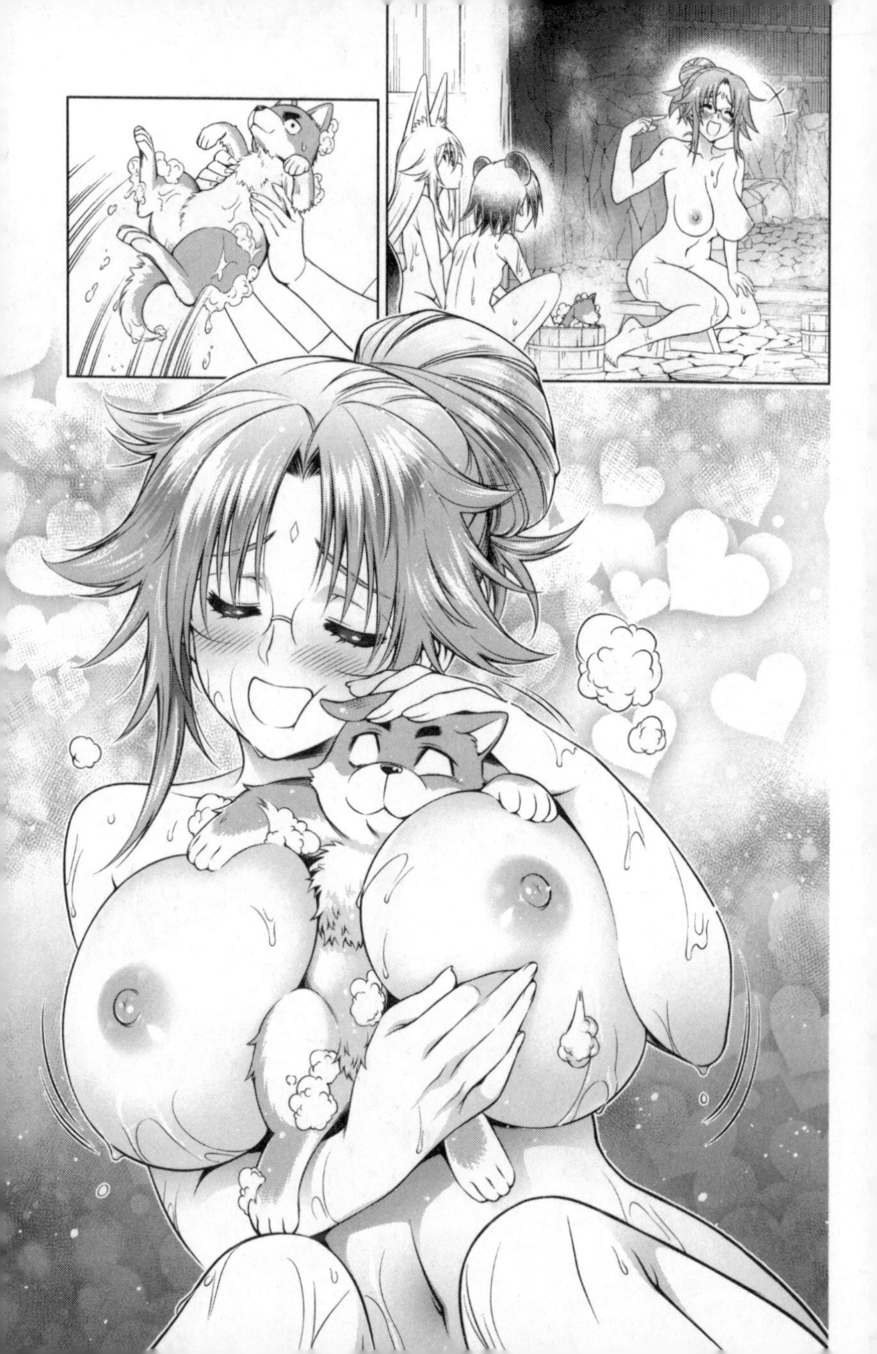

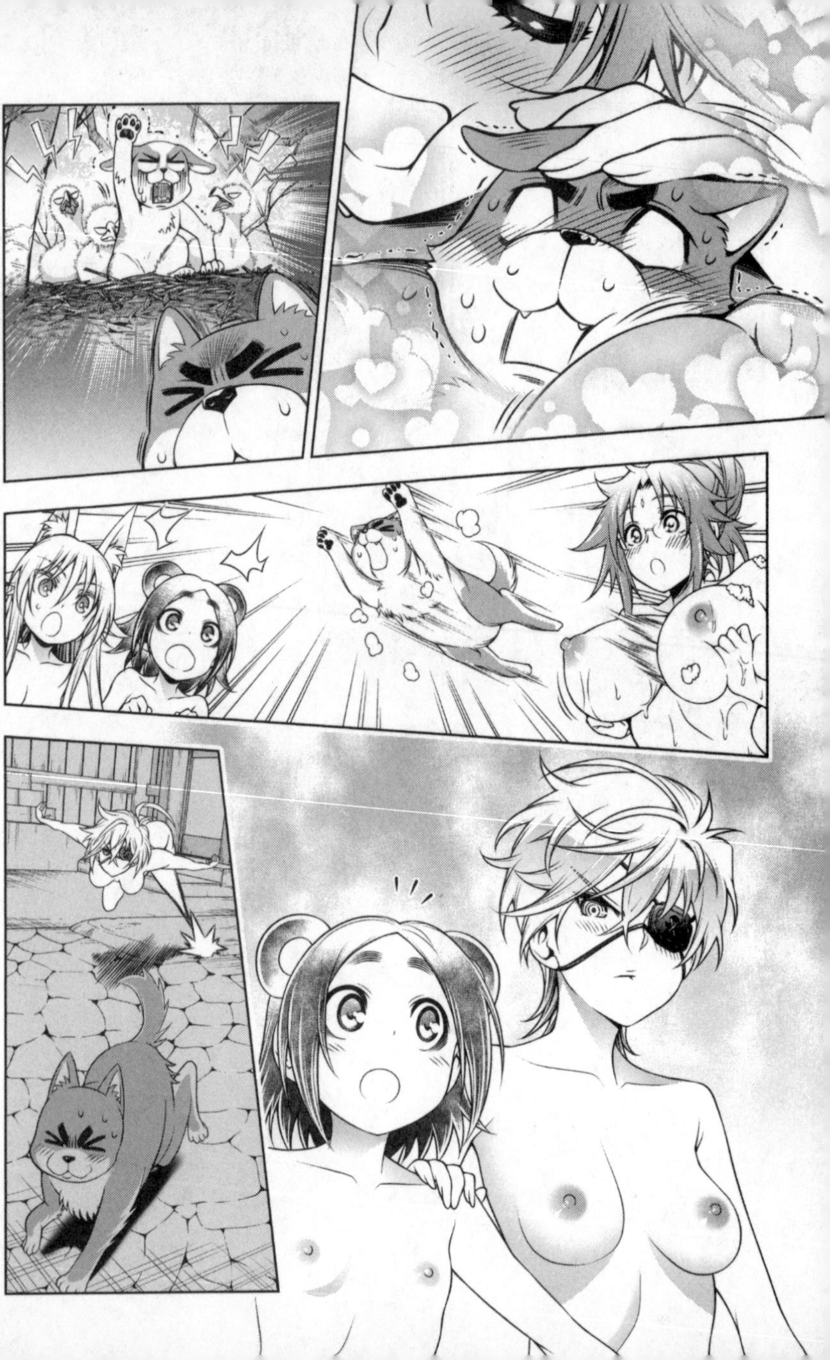

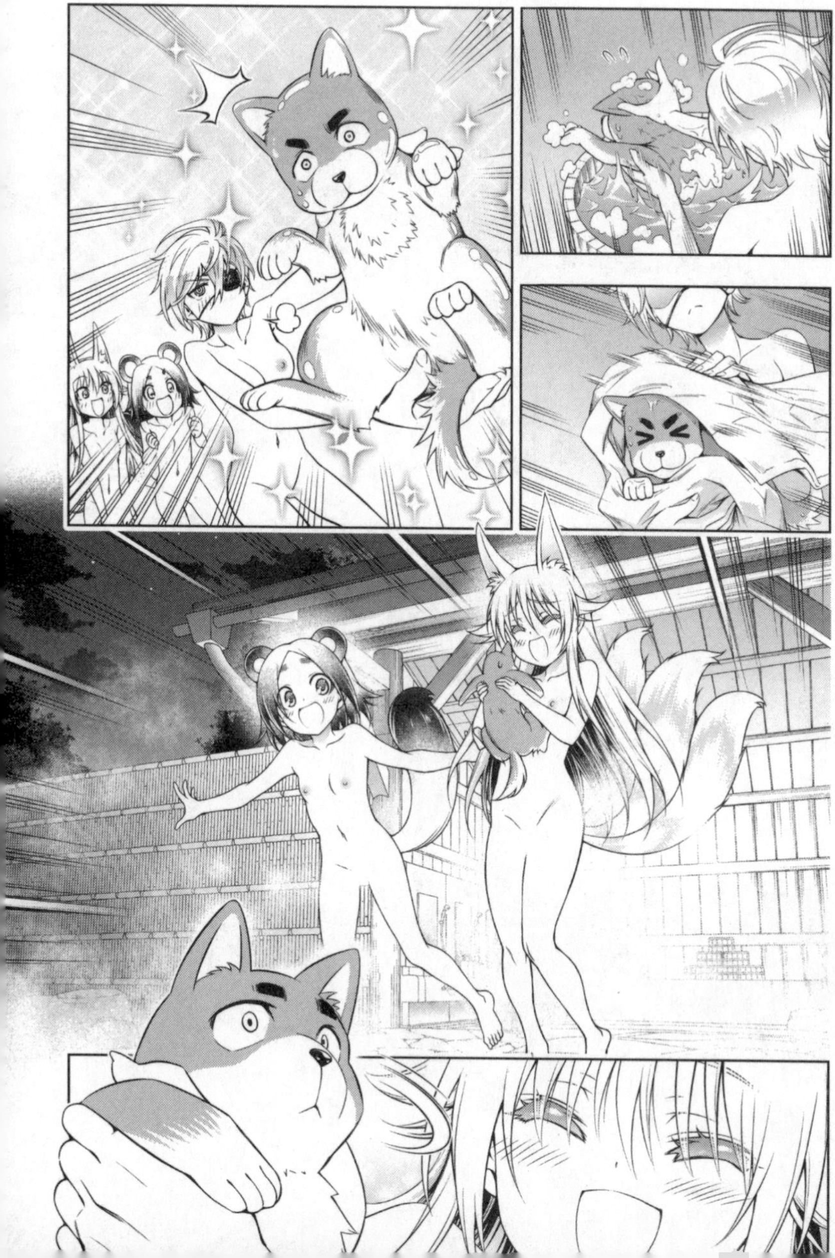

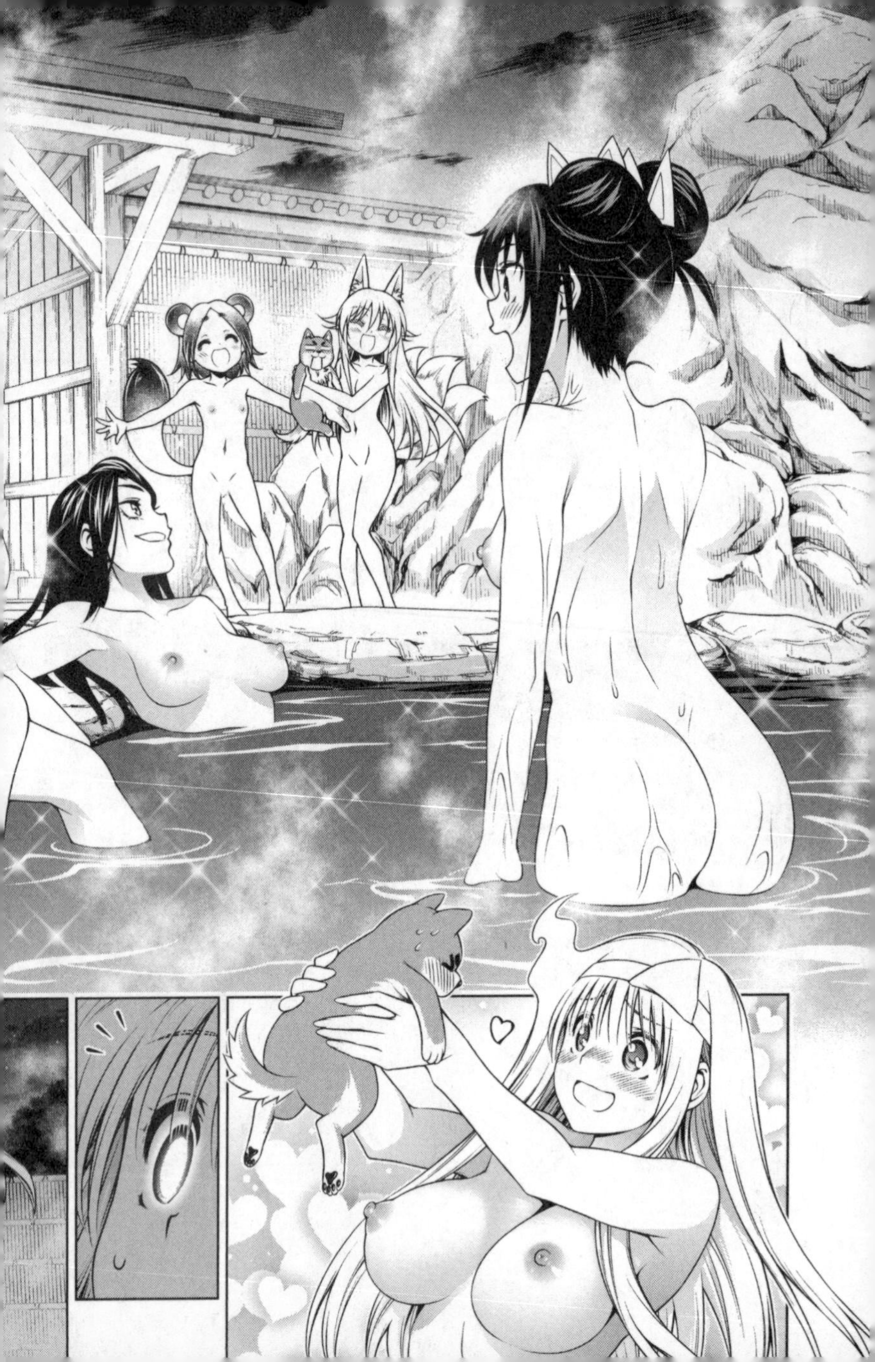

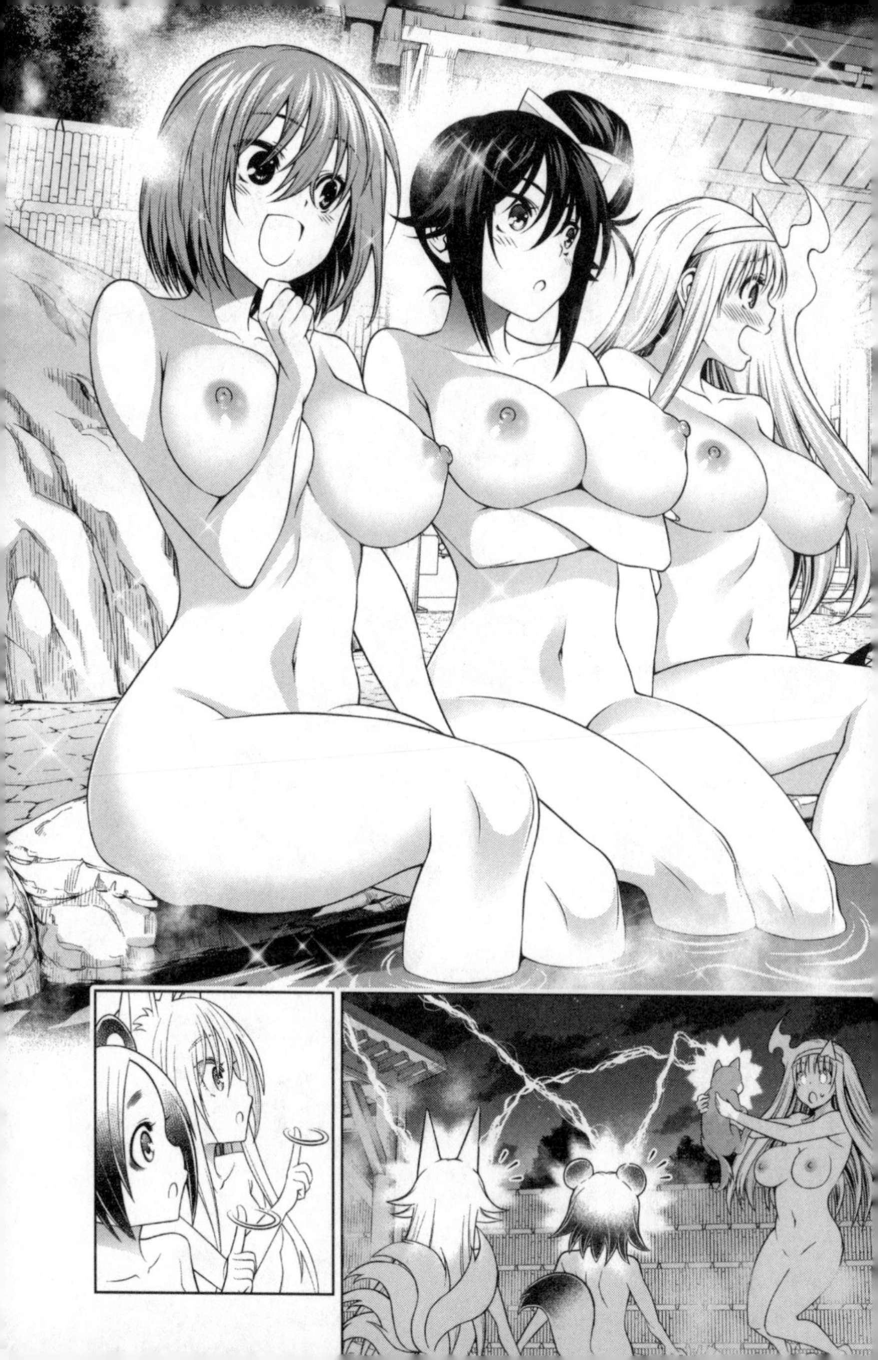

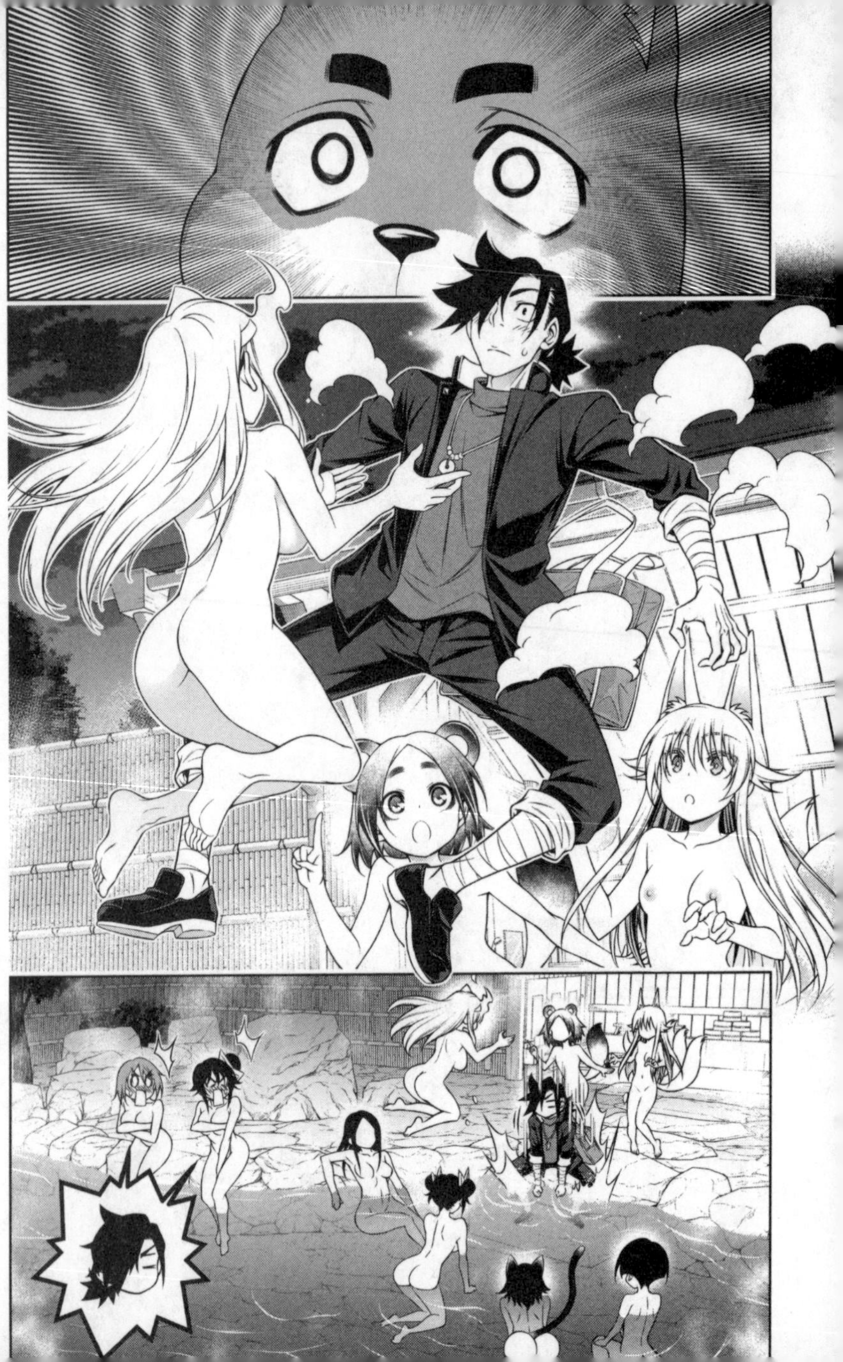

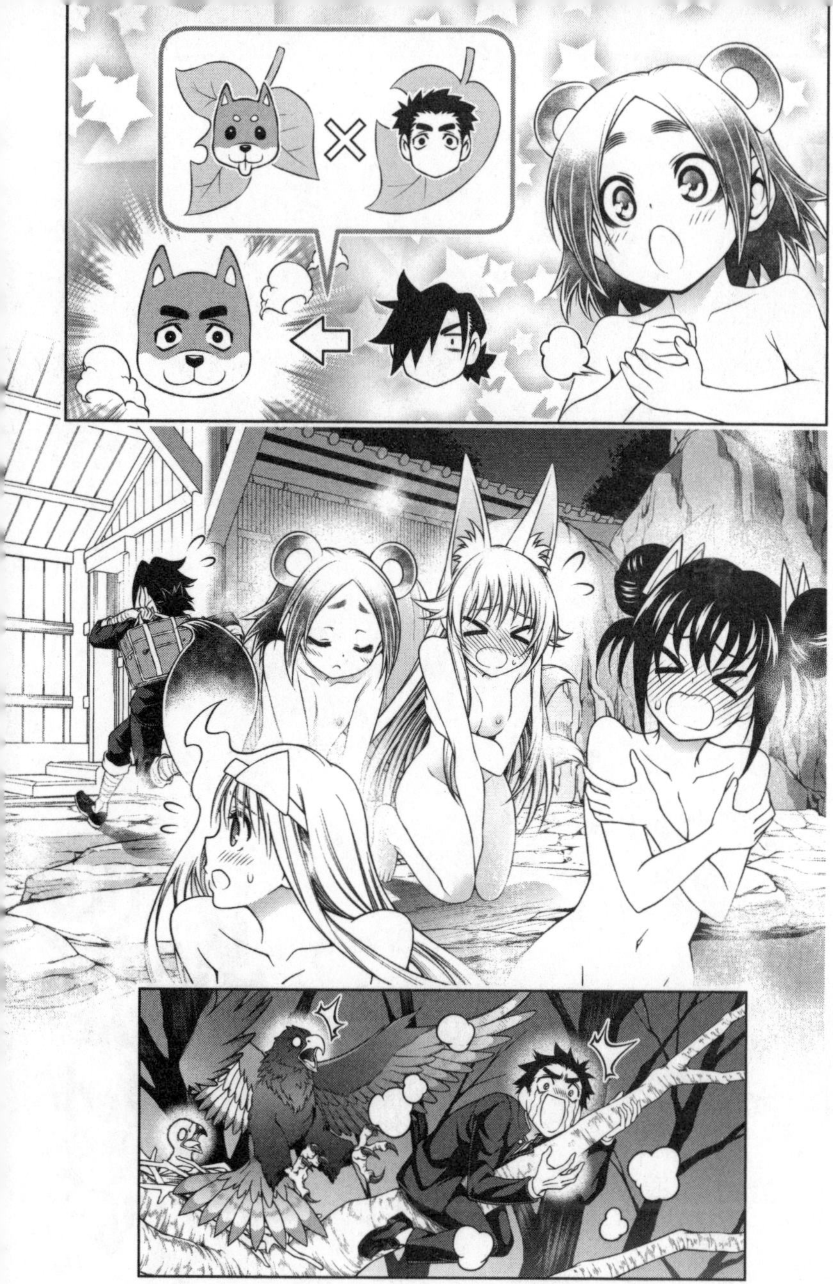

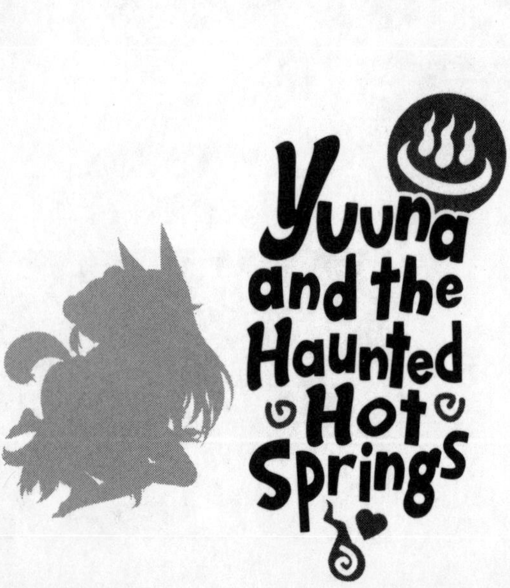

Yuuna and the Haunted Hot Springs

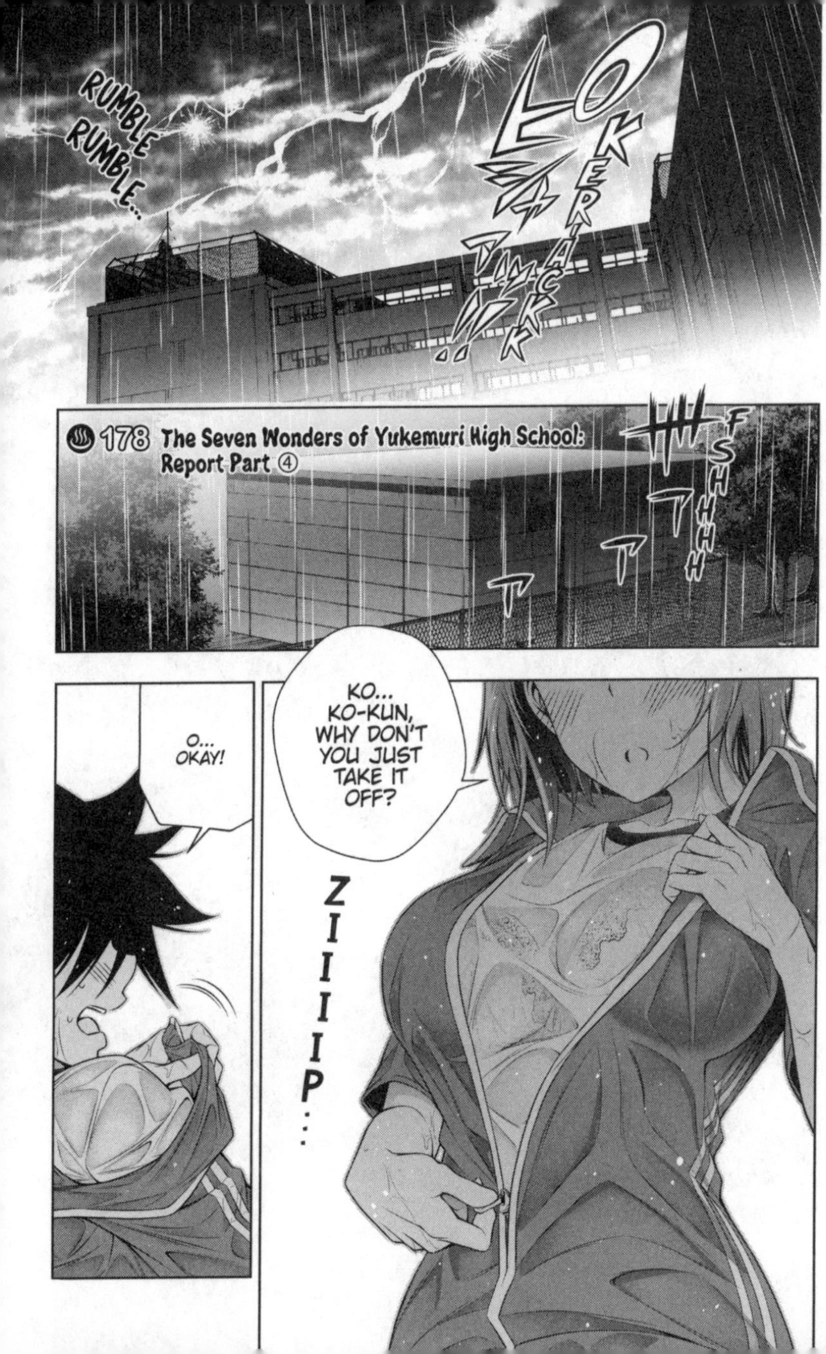
KERRACKK
RUMBLE RUMBLE...
178 The Seven Wonders of Yukemuri High School: Report Part ④
FSHHHHH
KO... KO-KUN, WHY DON'T YOU JUST TAKE IT OFF?
ZIIIIIP...
O... OKAY!

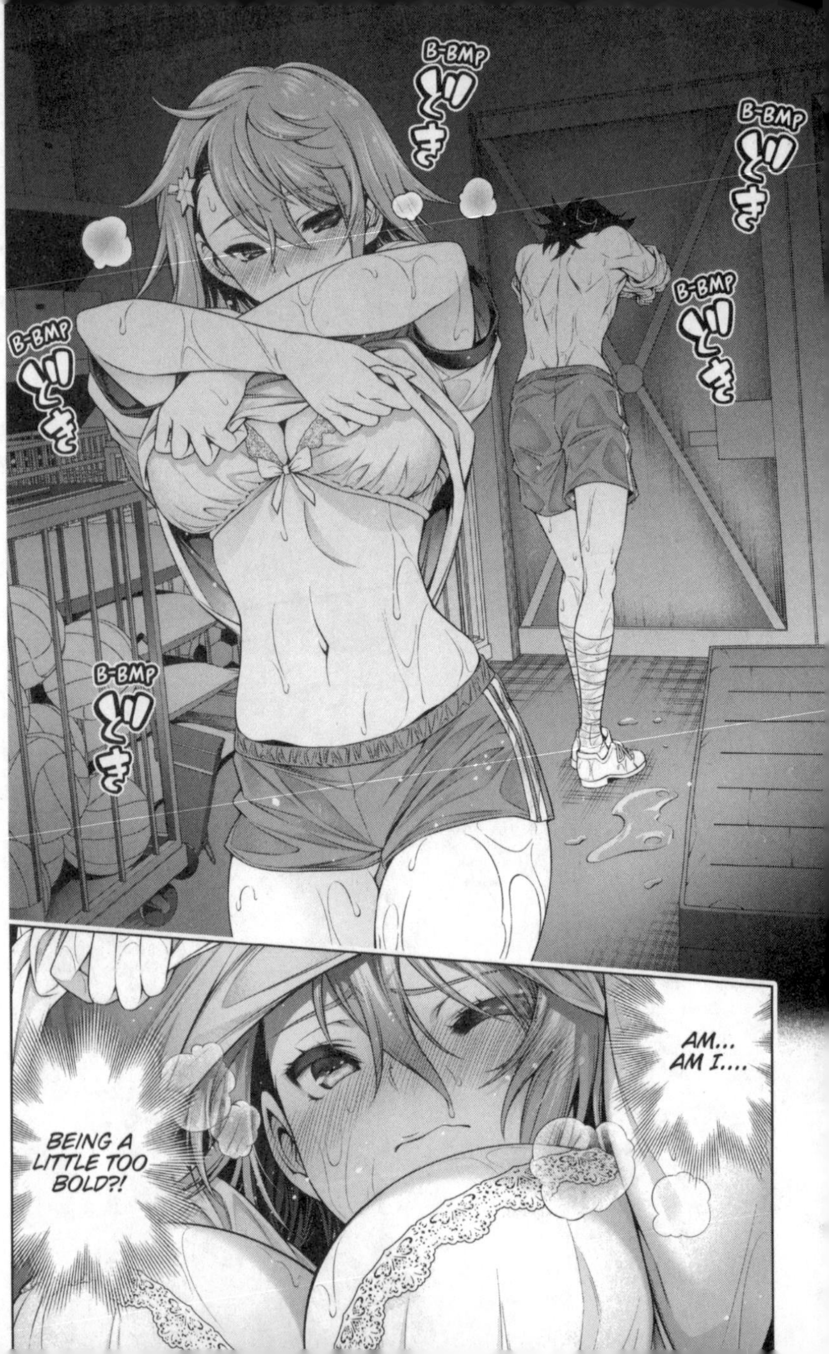
B-BMP
どき
B-BMP
どき
B-BMP
どき
B-BMP
どき
B-BMP
どき
AM... AM I....
BEING A LITTLE TOO BOLD?!

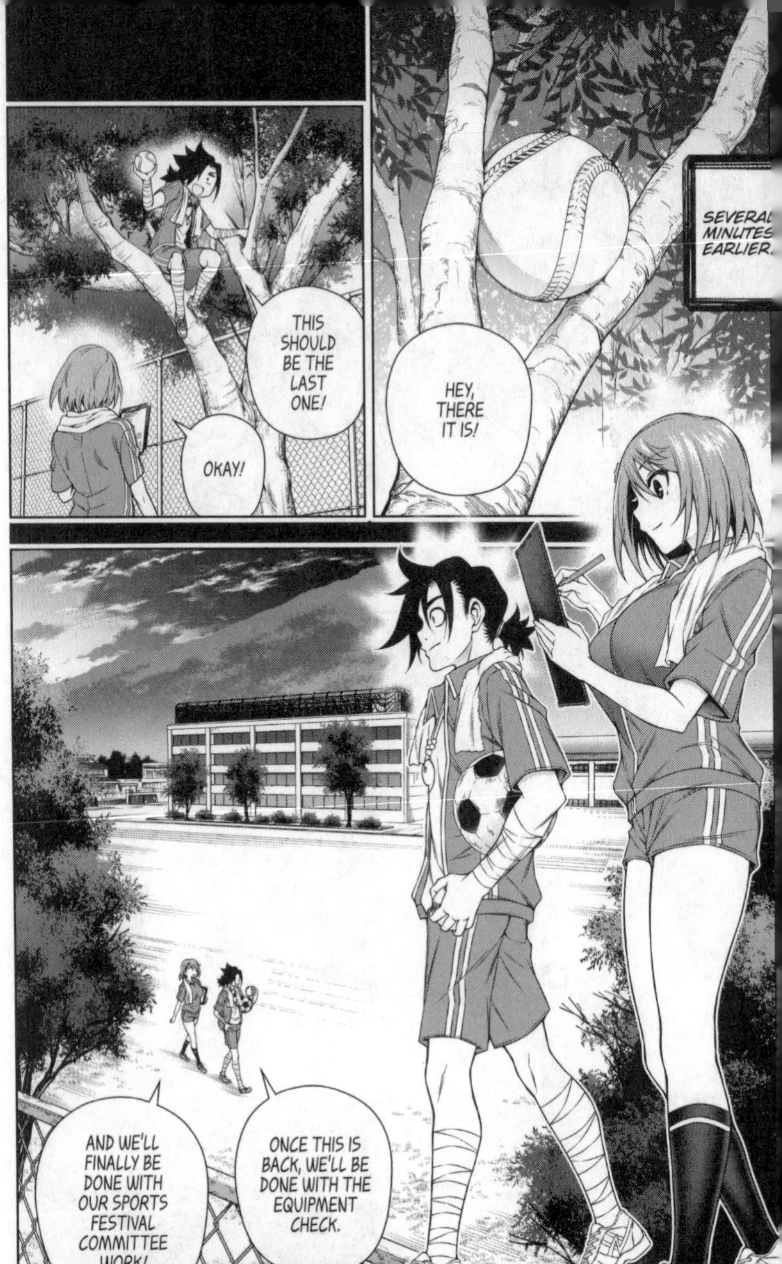
SEVERAL MINUTES EARLIER...
HEY, THERE IT IS!
THIS SHOULD BE THE LAST ONE!
OKAY!
ONCE THIS IS BACK, WE'LL BE DONE WITH THE EQUIPMENT CHECK.
AND WE'LL FINALLY BE DONE WITH OUR SPORTS FESTIVAL COMMITTEE WORK!

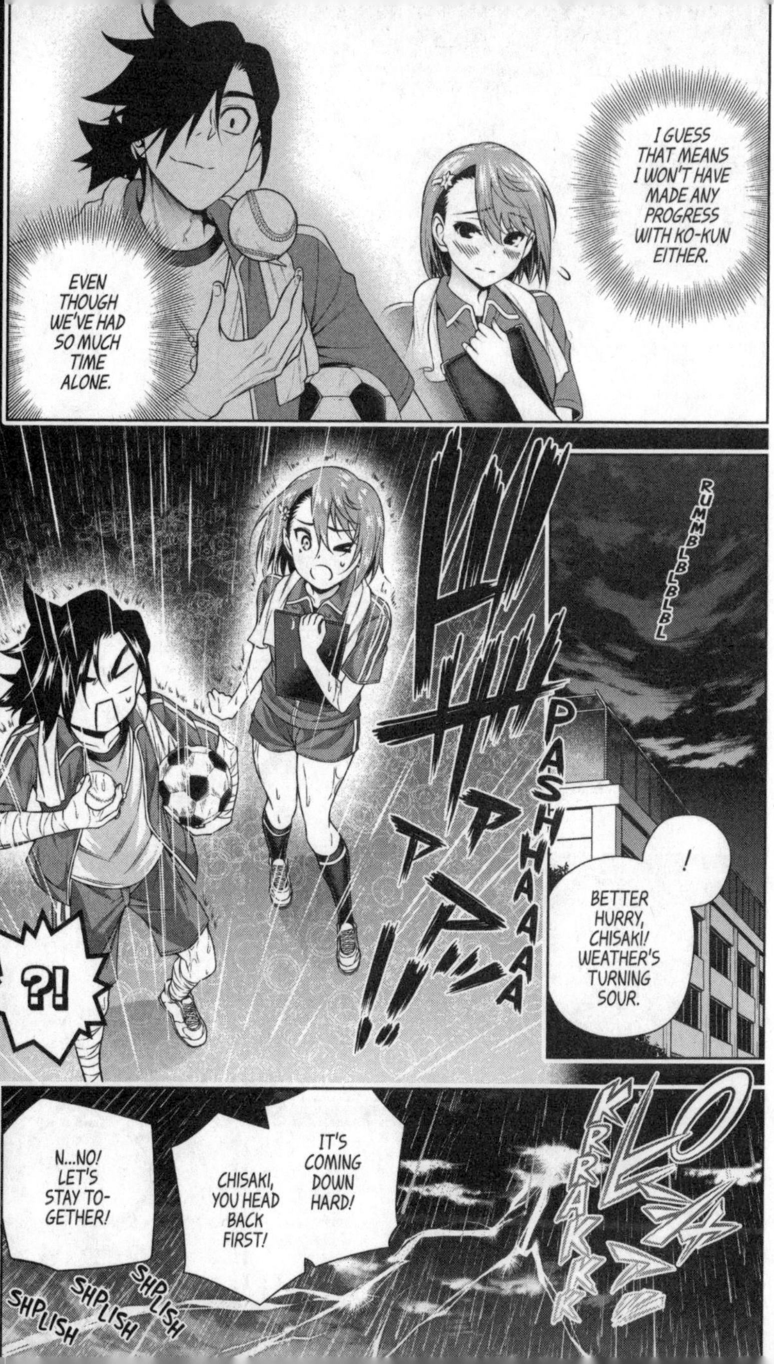
I GUESS THAT MEANS I WON'T HAVE MADE ANY PROGRESS WITH KO-KUN EITHER.
EVEN THOUGH WE'VE HAD SO MUCH TIME ALONE.
RUMMBLBLBLBL
!
BETTER HURRY, CHISAKI! WEATHER'S TURNING SOUR.
PASHHAAAAA
?!
KRRAKKK
IT'S COMING DOWN HARD!
CHISAKI, YOU HEAD BACK FIRST!
N...NO! LET'S STAY TO-GETHER!
SHPLISH
SHPLISH
SHPLISH

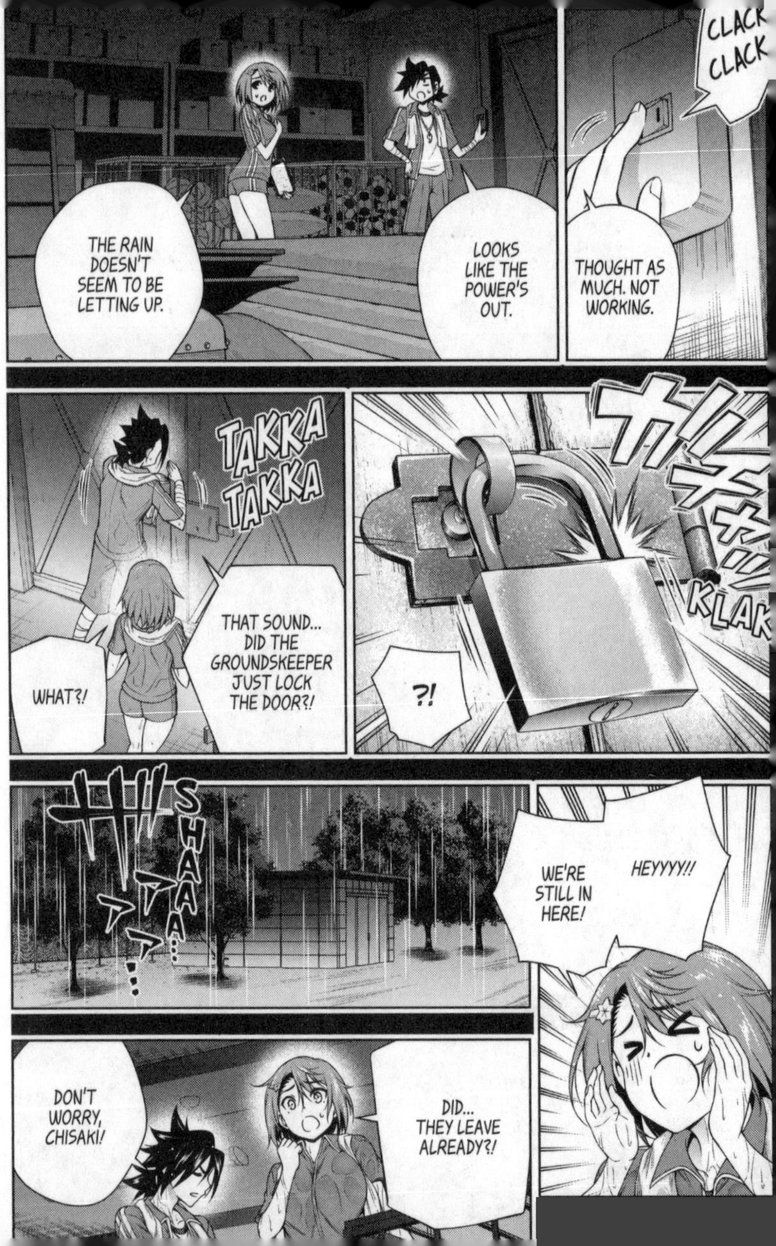
CLACK CLACK
THOUGHT AS MUCH. NOT WORKING.
LOOKS LIKE THE POWER'S OUT.
THE RAIN DOESN'T SEEM TO BE LETTING UP.
KLAK
?!
TAKKA TAKKA
THAT SOUND... DID THE GROUNDSKEEPER JUST LOCK THE DOOR?!
WHAT?!
HEYYYY!!
WE'RE STILL IN HERE!
SHAAAA...
DID... THEY LEAVE ALREADY?!
DON'T WORRY, CHISAKI!

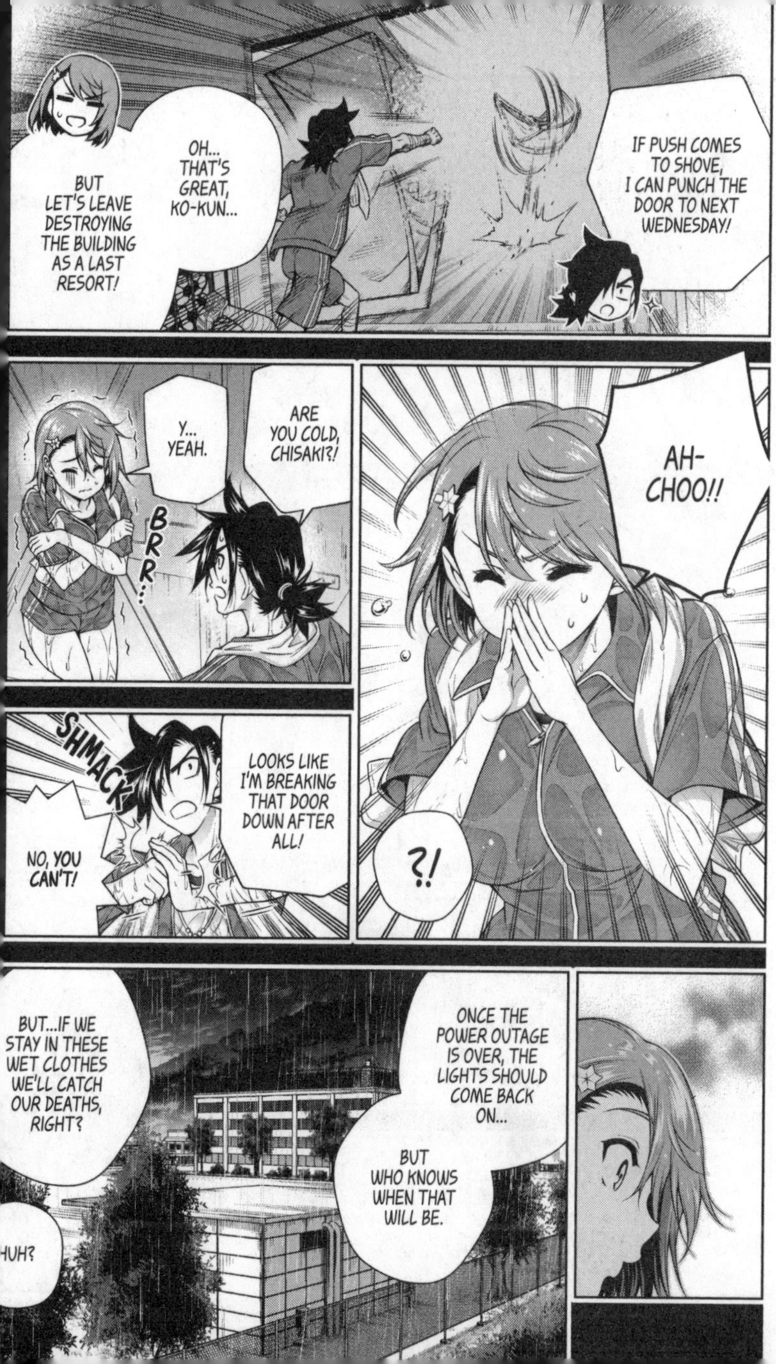
IF PUSH COMES TO SHOVE, I CAN PUNCH THE DOOR TO NEXT WEDNESDAY!
OH... THAT'S GREAT, KO-KUN...
BUT LET'S LEAVE DESTROYING THE BUILDING AS A LAST RESORT!
AH-CHOO!!
?!
ARE YOU COLD, CHISAKI?!
Y... YEAH.
BRR...
LOOKS LIKE I'M BREAKING THAT DOOR DOWN AFTER ALL!
SHMACK
NO, YOU CAN'T!
ONCE THE POWER OUTAGE IS OVER, THE LIGHTS SHOULD COME BACK ON...
BUT WHO KNOWS WHEN THAT WILL BE.
BUT...IF WE STAY IN THESE WET CLOTHES WE'LL CATCH OUR DEATHS, RIGHT?
HUH?

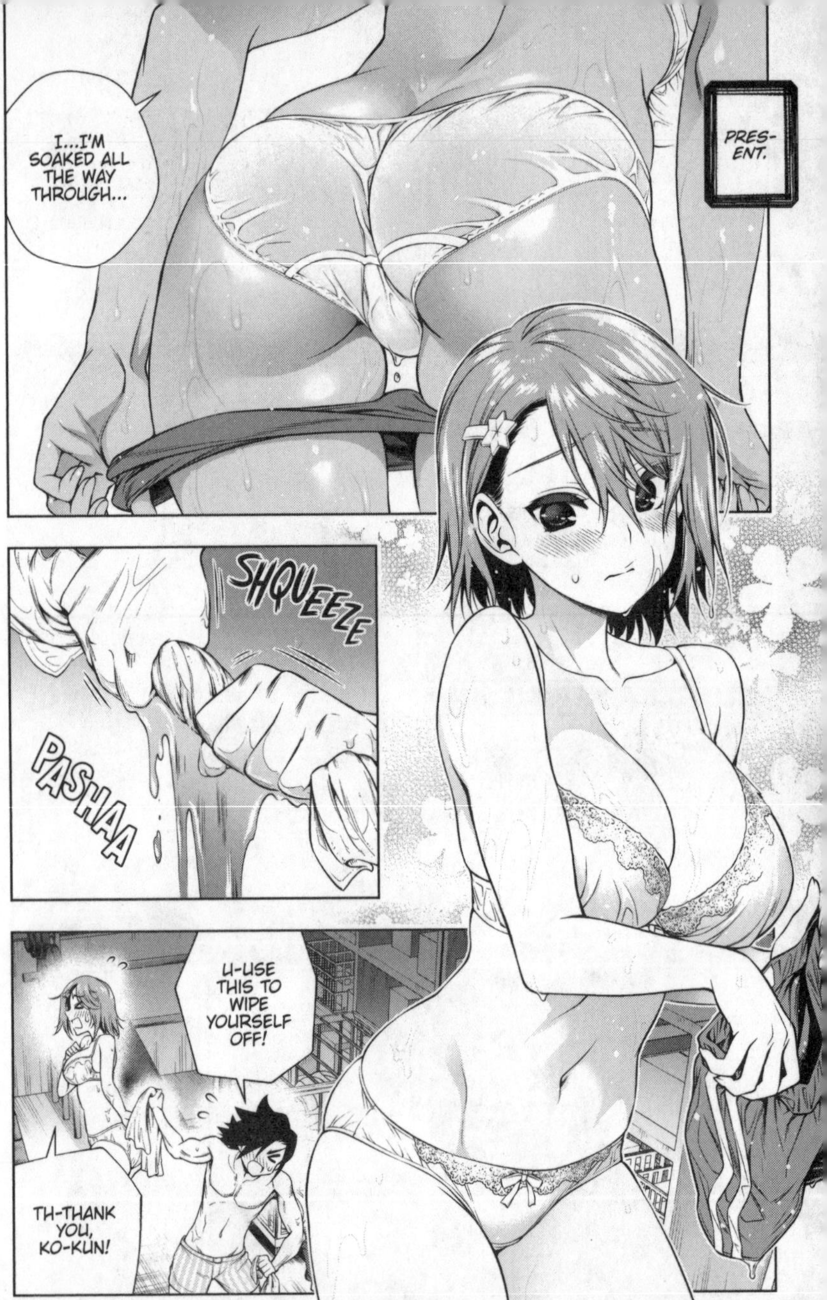
PRES-
ENT.
I...I'M SOAKED ALL THE WAY THROUGH...
SHQUEEZE
PASHAA
U-USE THIS TO WIPE YOURSELF OFF!
TH-THANK YOU, KO-KUN!

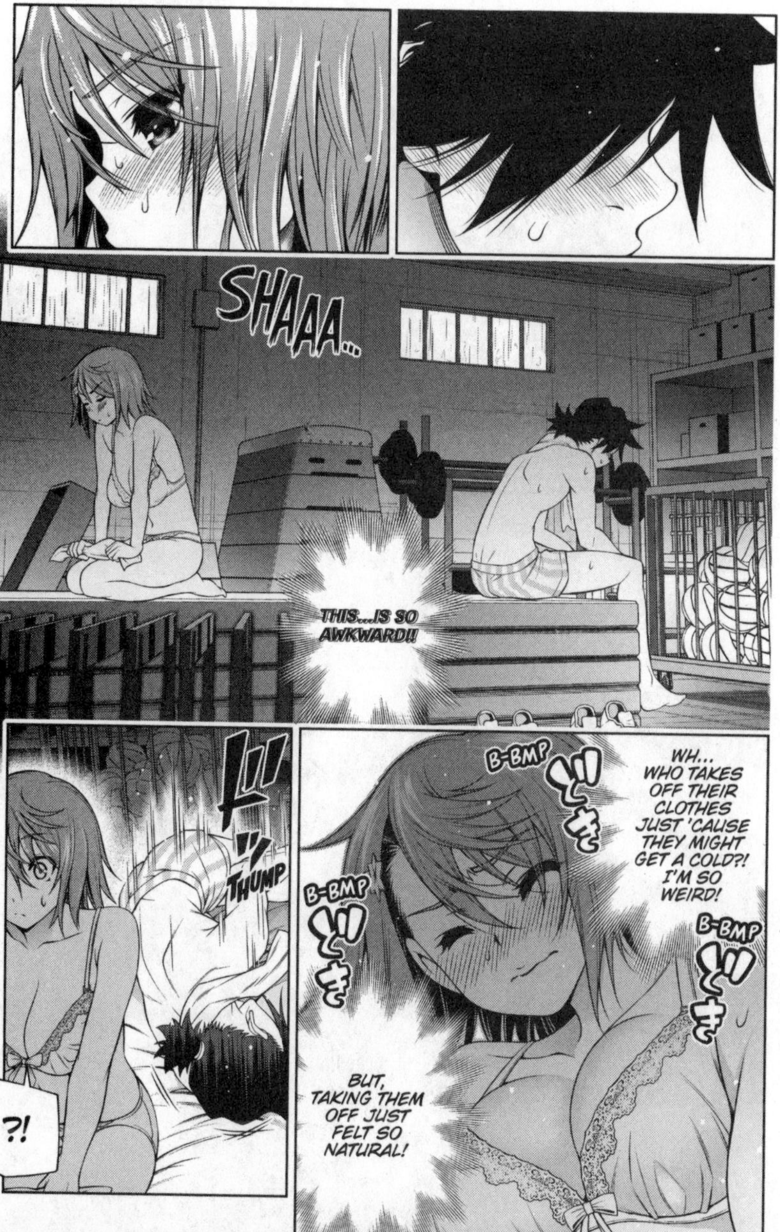
SHAAA...
THIS...IS SO AWKWARD!!
B-BMP
どき
WH... WHO TAKES OFF THEIR CLOTHES JUST 'CAUSE THEY MIGHT GET A COLD?! I'M SO WEIRD!
B-BMP
どき
B-BMP
どき
BUT, TAKING THEM OFF JUST FELT SO NATURAL!
THUMP
?!

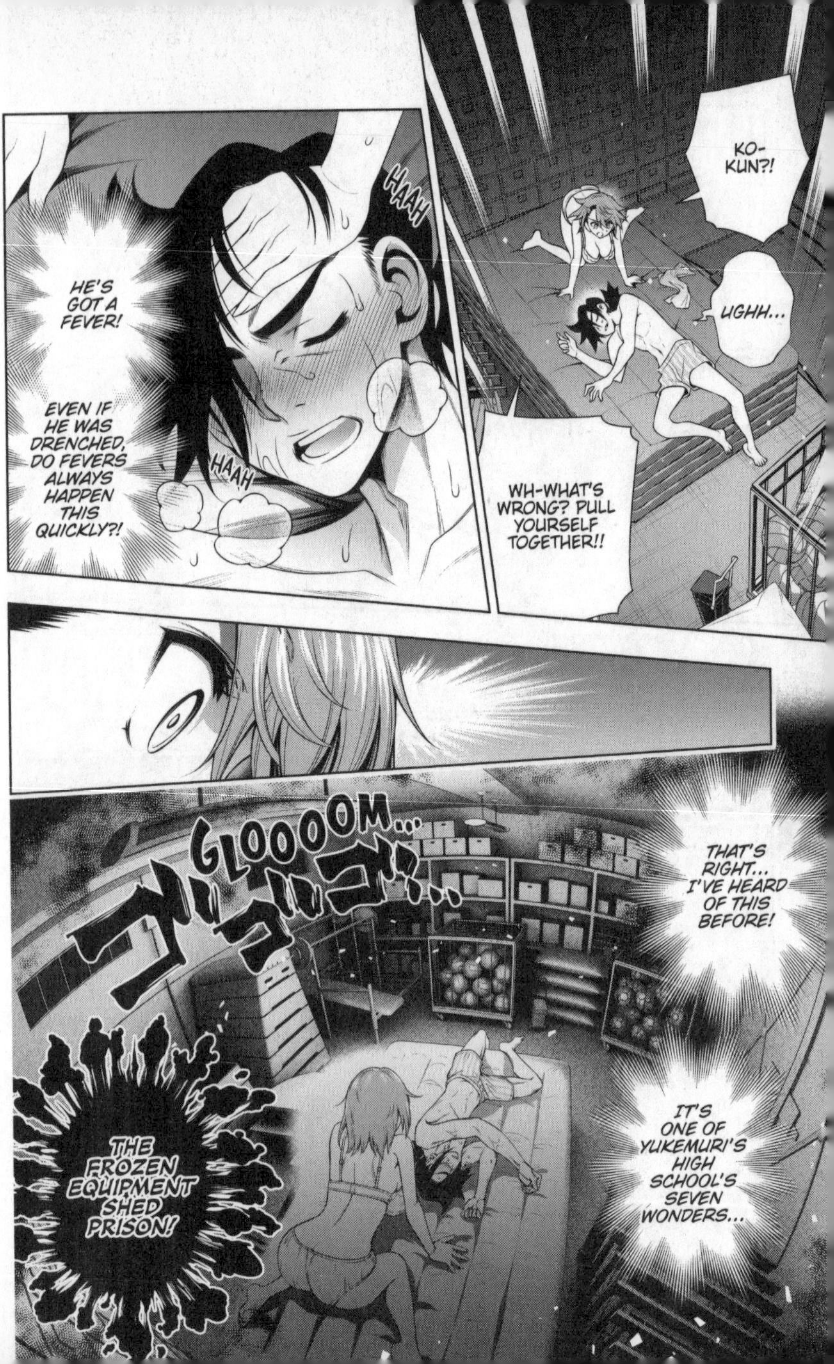
KO-KUN?!
UGHH...
WH-WHAT'S WRONG? PULL YOURSELF TOGETHER!!
HAAH
HE'S GOT A FEVER!
EVEN IF HE WAS DRENCHED, DO FEVERS ALWAYS HAPPEN THIS QUICKLY?!
HAAH
THAT'S RIGHT... I'VE HEARD OF THIS BEFORE!
GLOOOOM...
IT'S ONE OF YUKEMURI'S HIGH SCHOOL'S SEVEN WONDERS...
THE FROZEN EQUIPMENT SHED PRISON!

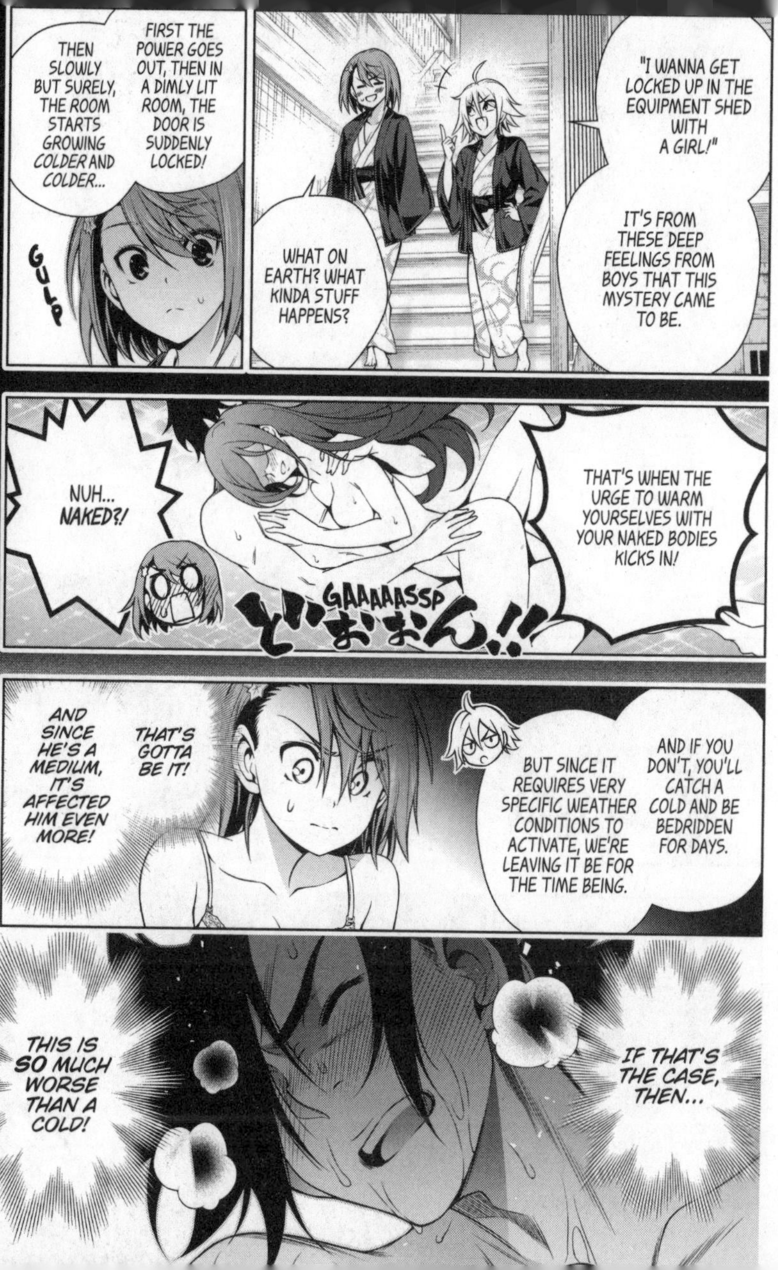
"I WANNA GET LOCKED UP IN THE EQUIPMENT SHED WITH A GIRL!"
IT'S FROM THESE DEEP FEELINGS FROM BOYS THAT THIS MYSTERY CAME TO BE.
WHAT ON EARTH? WHAT KINDA STUFF HAPPENS?
FIRST THE POWER GOES OUT, THEN IN A DIMLY LIT ROOM, THE DOOR IS SUDDENLY LOCKED!
THEN SLOWLY BUT SURELY, THE ROOM STARTS GROWING COLDER AND COLDER...
GULP
THAT'S WHEN THE URGE TO WARM YOURSELVES WITH YOUR NAKED BODIES KICKS IN!
GAAAAASSP
NUH... NAKED?!
AND IF YOU DON'T, YOU'LL CATCH A COLD AND BE BEDRIDDEN FOR DAYS.
BUT SINCE IT REQUIRES VERY SPECIFIC WEATHER CONDITIONS TO ACTIVATE, WE'RE LEAVING IT BE FOR THE TIME BEING.
THAT'S GOTTA BE IT!
AND SINCE HE'S A MEDIUM, IT'S AFFECTED HIM EVEN MORE!
IF THAT'S THE CASE, THEN...
THIS IS SO MUCH WORSE THAN A COLD!

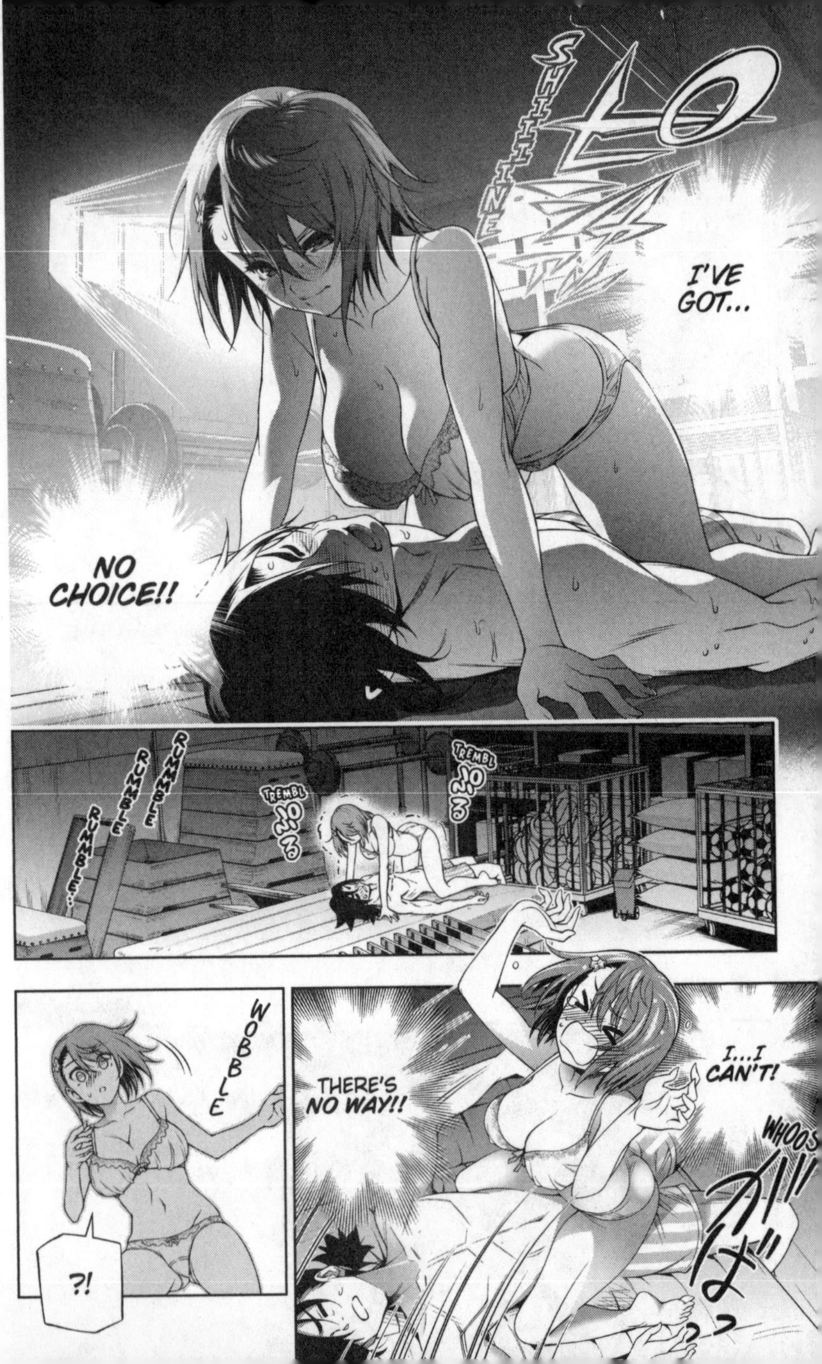
SHIIINE
I'VE GOT...
NO CHOICE!!
TREMBL
TREMBL
RUMMBLE
RUMMBLE
RUMMBLE...
I...I CAN'T!
THERE'S NO WAY!!
WHOOS
WOBBLE
?!

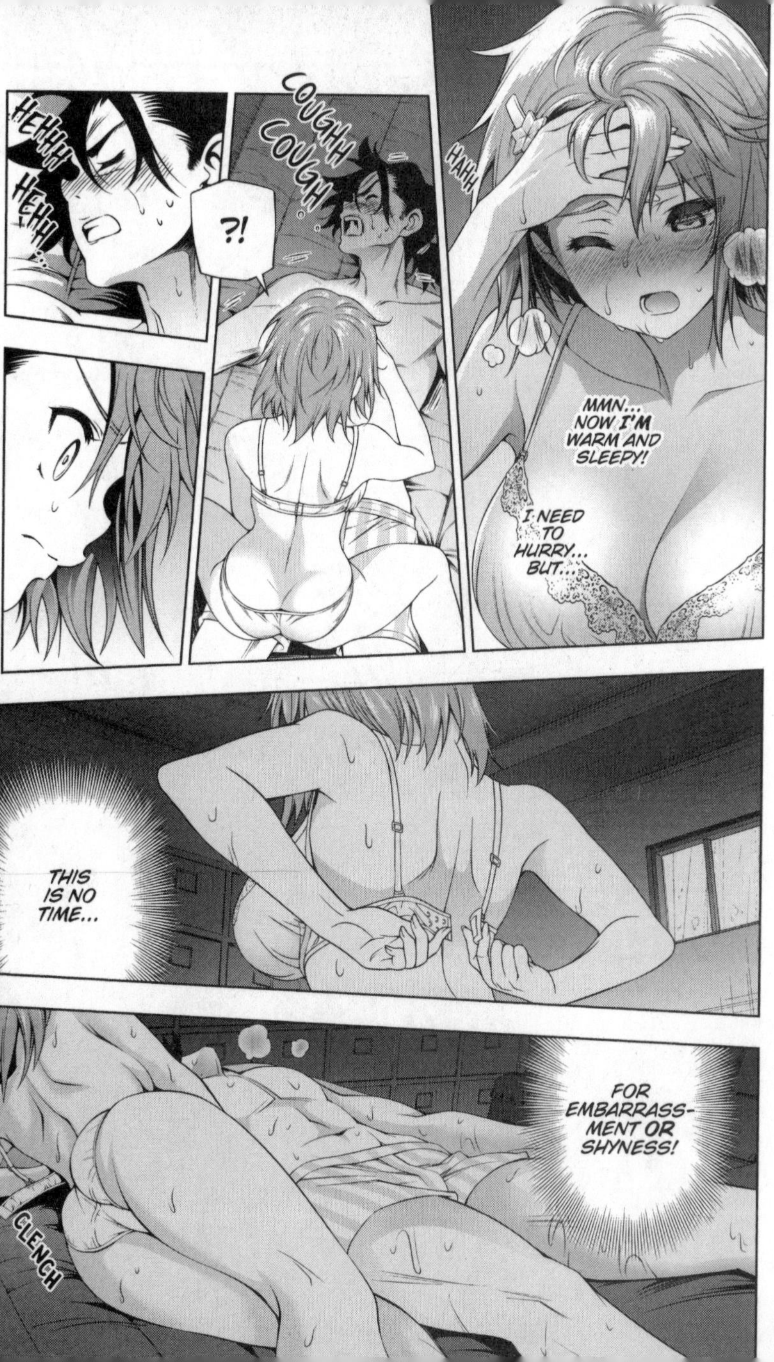
HAHH
MMN... NOW I'M WARM AND SLEEPY!
I NEED TO HURRY... BUT...
COUGHH COUGH
HEHHH HEHH
?!
THIS IS NO TIME...
FOR EMBARRASS-MENT OR SHYNESS!
CLENCH

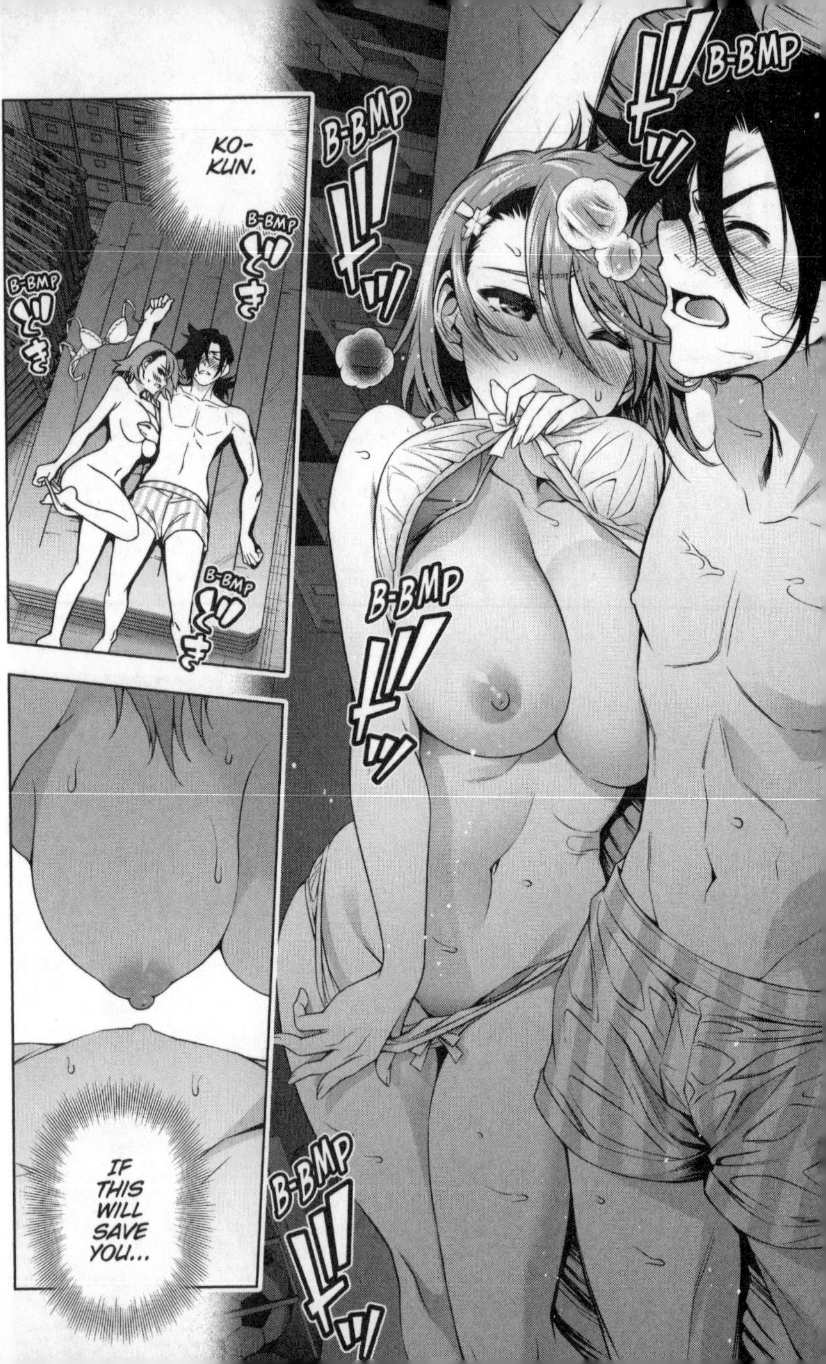
B-BMP
ドッ
B-BMP
ドッ
B-BMP
ドッ
B-BMP
ドッ
KO-KUN.
B-BMP
どき
B-BMP
どき
B-BMP
どき
IF THIS WILL SAVE YOU...

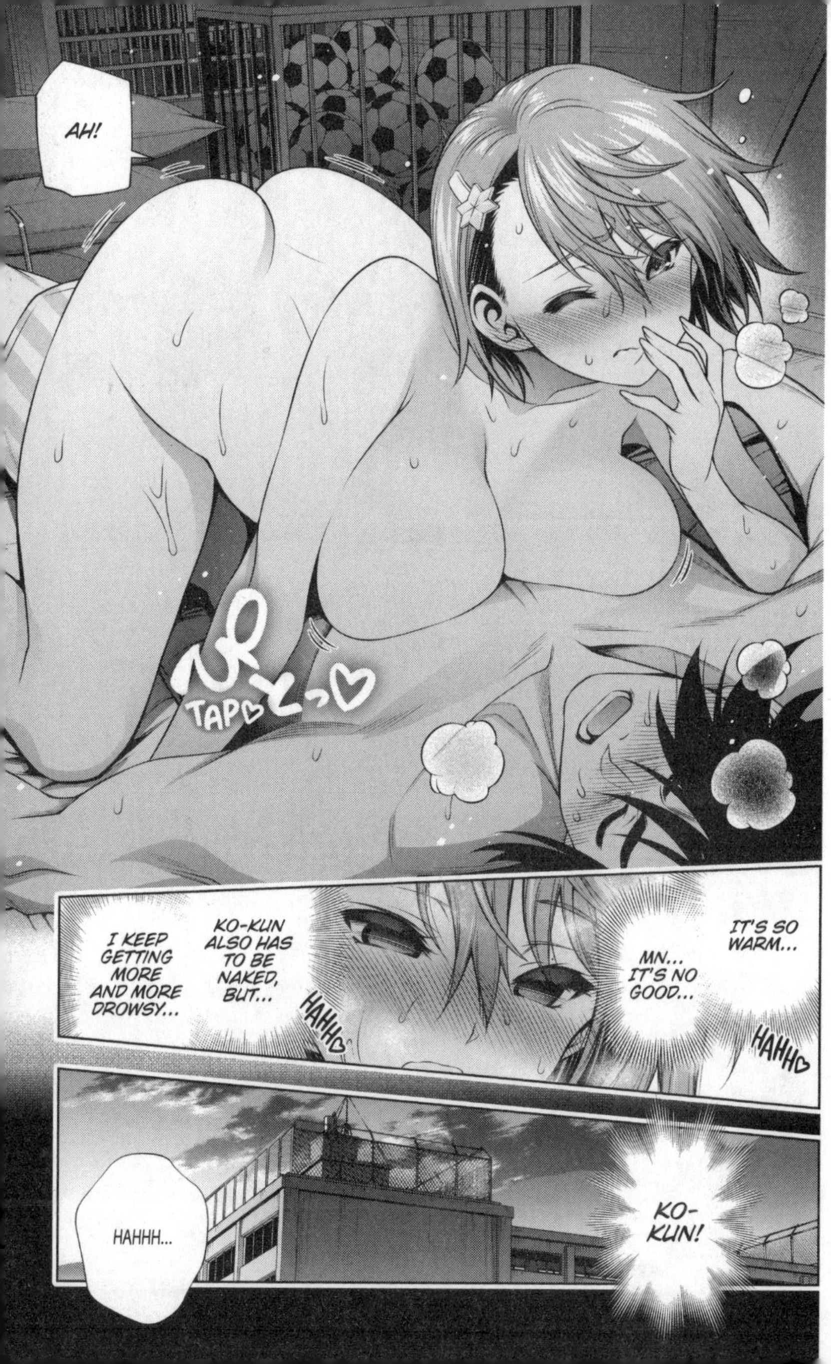
AH!
ぴとっ♡
TAP♡
IT'S SO WARM...
MN... IT'S NO GOOD...
HAHH♡
KO-KUN ALSO HAS TO BE NAKED, BUT...
I KEEP GETTING MORE AND MORE DROWSY...
HAHH♡
KO-KUN!
HAHHH...

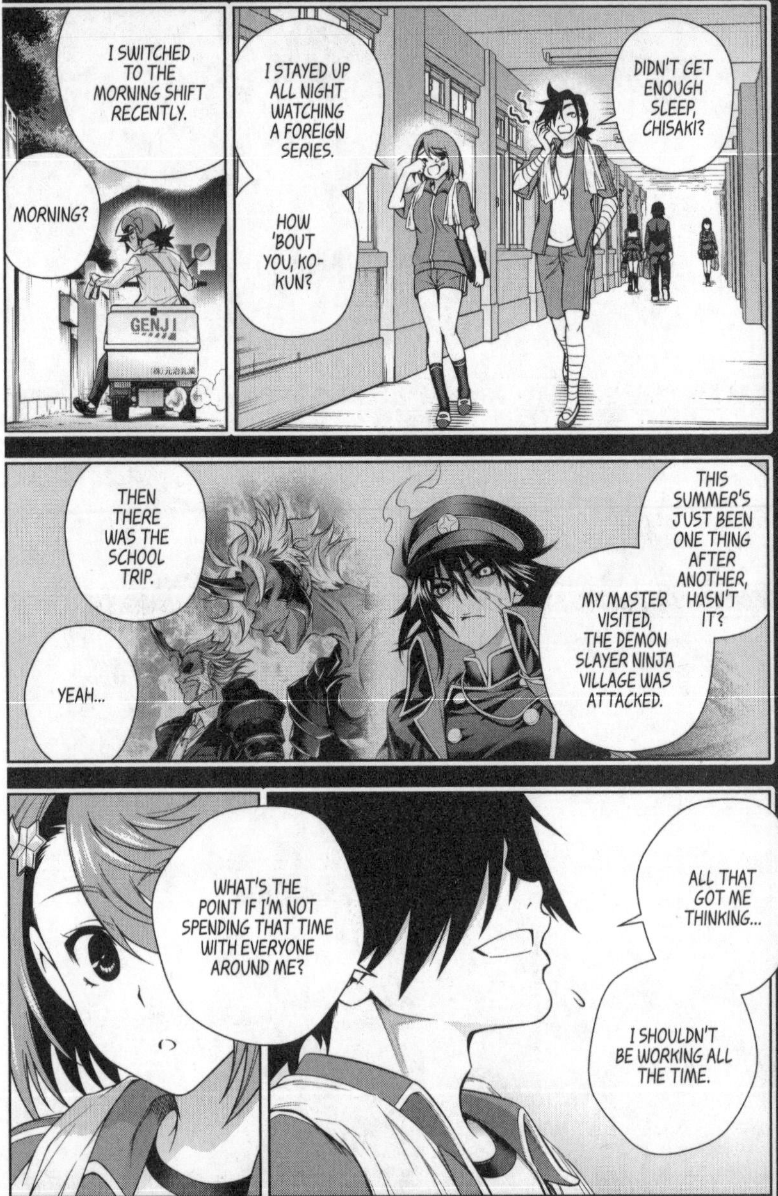
DIDN'T GET ENOUGH SLEEP, CHISAKI?
I STAYED UP ALL NIGHT WATCHING A FOREIGN SERIES.
HOW 'BOUT YOU, KO-KUN?
I SWITCHED TO THE MORNING SHIFT RECENTLY.
MORNING?
GENJI
THIS SUMMER'S JUST BEEN ONE THING AFTER ANOTHER, HASN'T IT?
MY MASTER VISITED, THE DEMON SLAYER NINJA VILLAGE WAS ATTACKED.
THEN THERE WAS THE SCHOOL TRIP.
YEAH...
ALL THAT GOT ME THINKING...
I SHOULDN'T BE WORKING ALL THE TIME.
WHAT'S THE POINT IF I'M NOT SPENDING THAT TIME WITH EVERYONE AROUND ME?

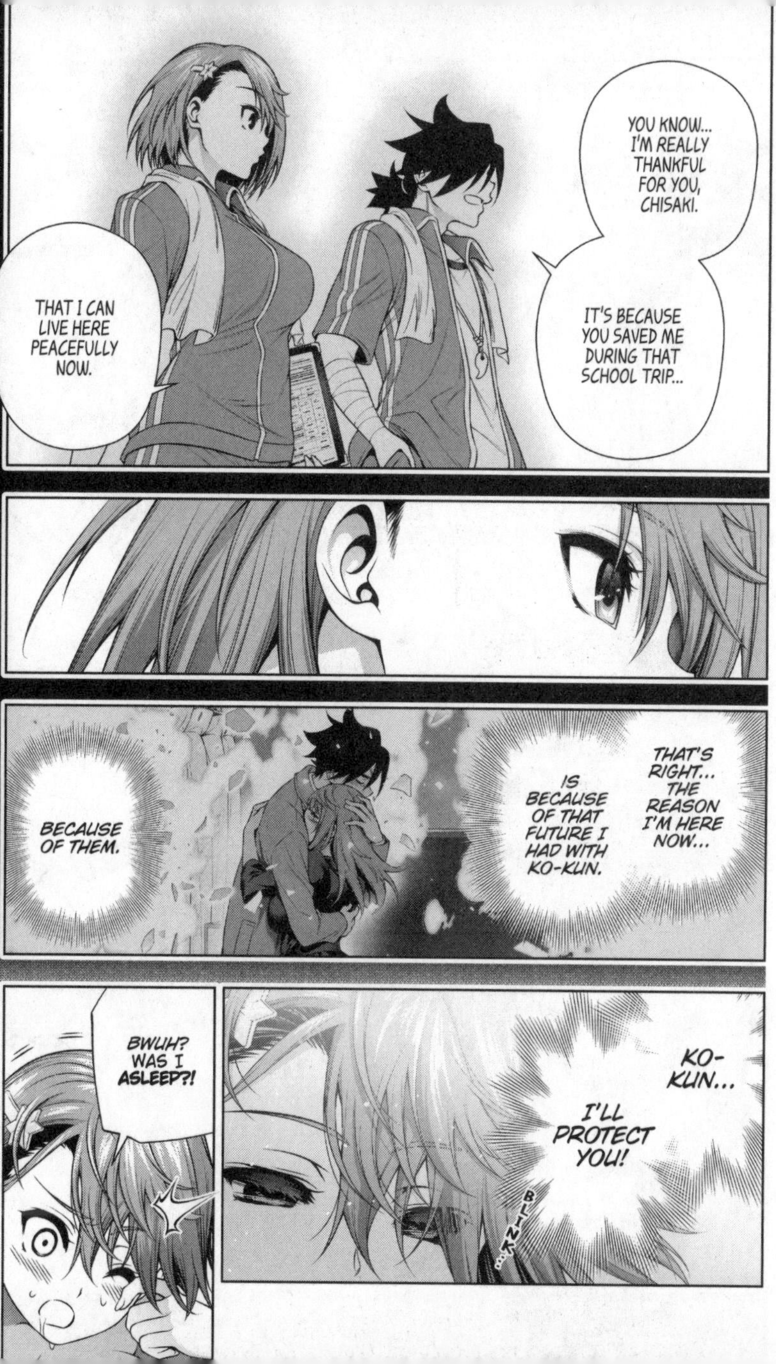
YOU KNOW... I'M REALLY THANKFUL FOR YOU, CHISAKI.
IT'S BECAUSE YOU SAVED ME DURING THAT SCHOOL TRIP...
THAT I CAN LIVE HERE PEACEFULLY NOW.
THAT'S RIGHT... THE REASON I'M HERE NOW...
IS BECAUSE OF THAT FUTURE I HAD WITH KO-KUN.
BECAUSE OF THEM.
KO-KUN...
I'LL PROTECT YOU!
BLINK...
BWUH? WAS I ASLEEP?!

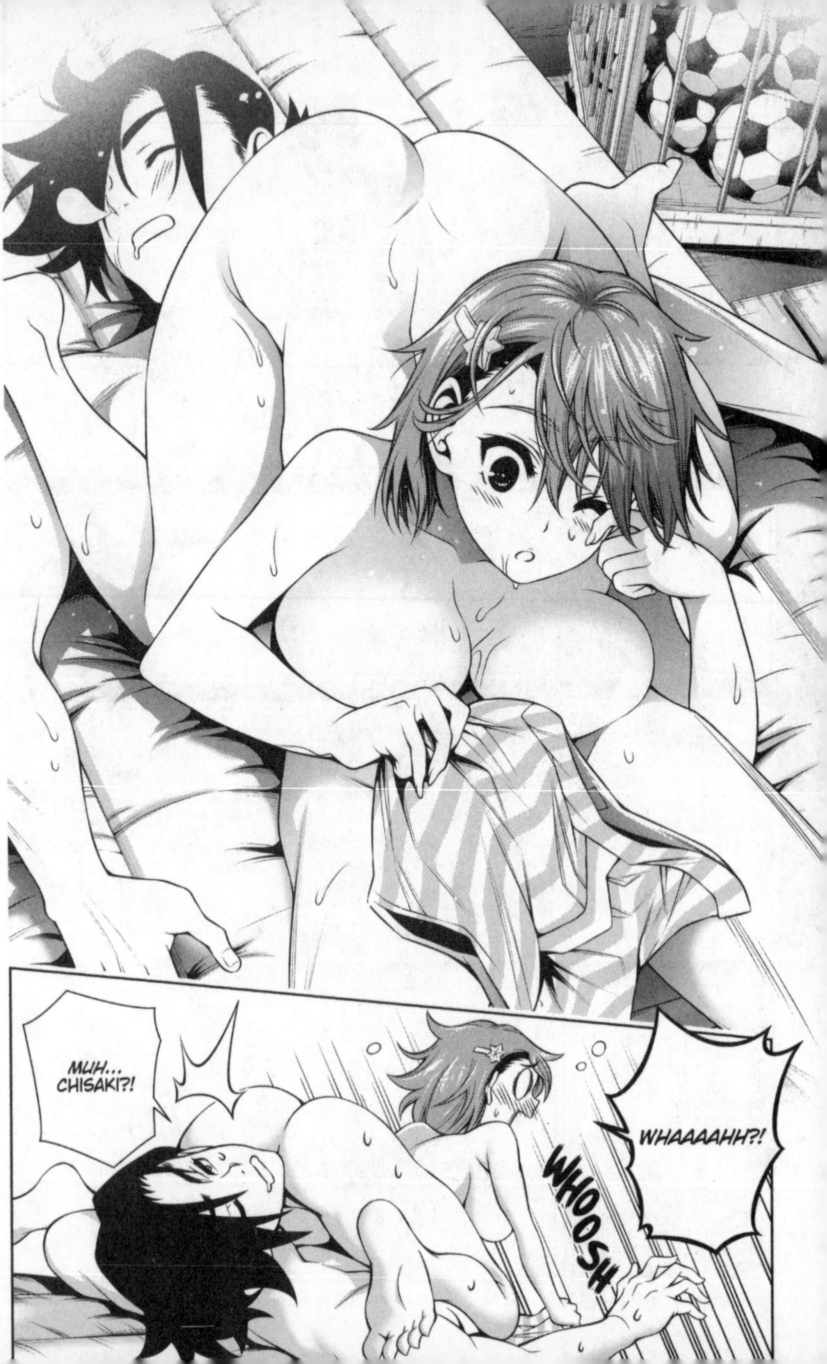
WHAAAAHH?!
WHOOSH
MUH... CHISAKI?!

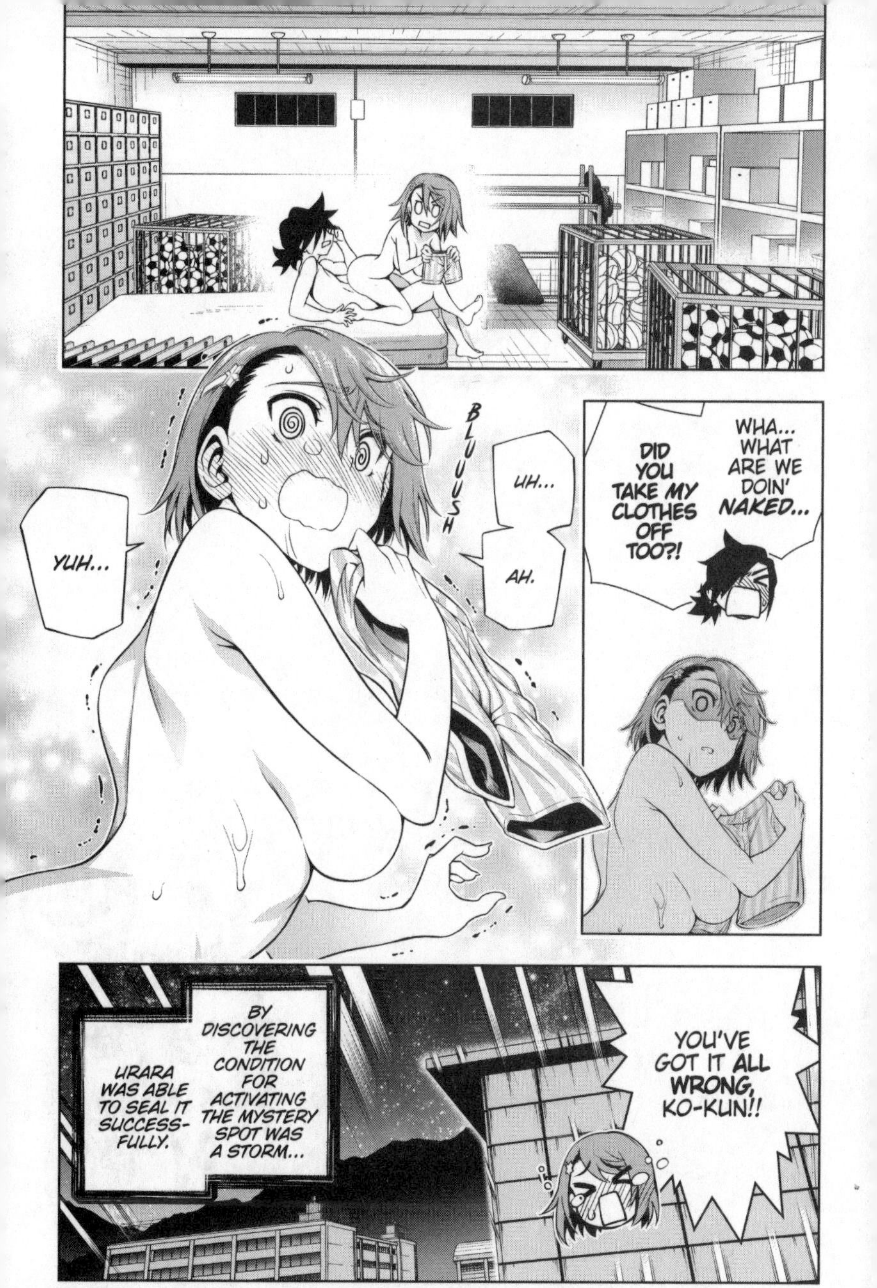
WHA... WHAT ARE WE DOIN' NAKED...
DID YOU TAKE MY CLOTHES OFF TOO?!
UH...
AH.
BLUUUSH
YUH...
YOU'VE GOT IT ALL WRONG, KO-KUN!!
BY DISCOVERING THE CONDITION FOR ACTIVATING THE MYSTERY SPOT WAS A STORM...
URARA WAS ABLE TO SEAL IT SUCCESS-FULLY.

20 Yuragi-sou's Ultimate Autumn Sports Festival Begins! (End)

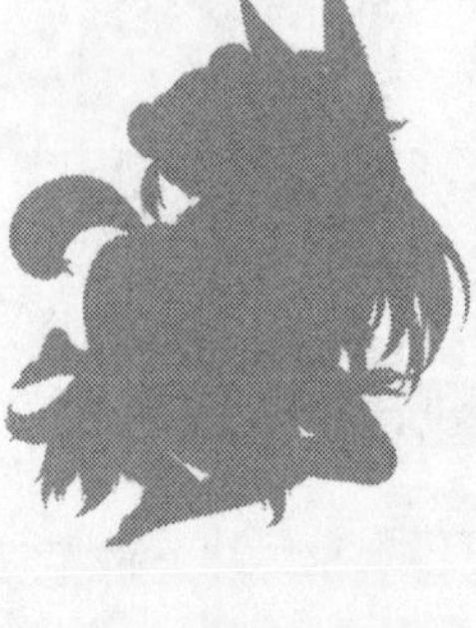

Yuuna and the Haunted Hot Springs

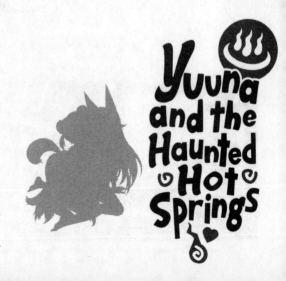

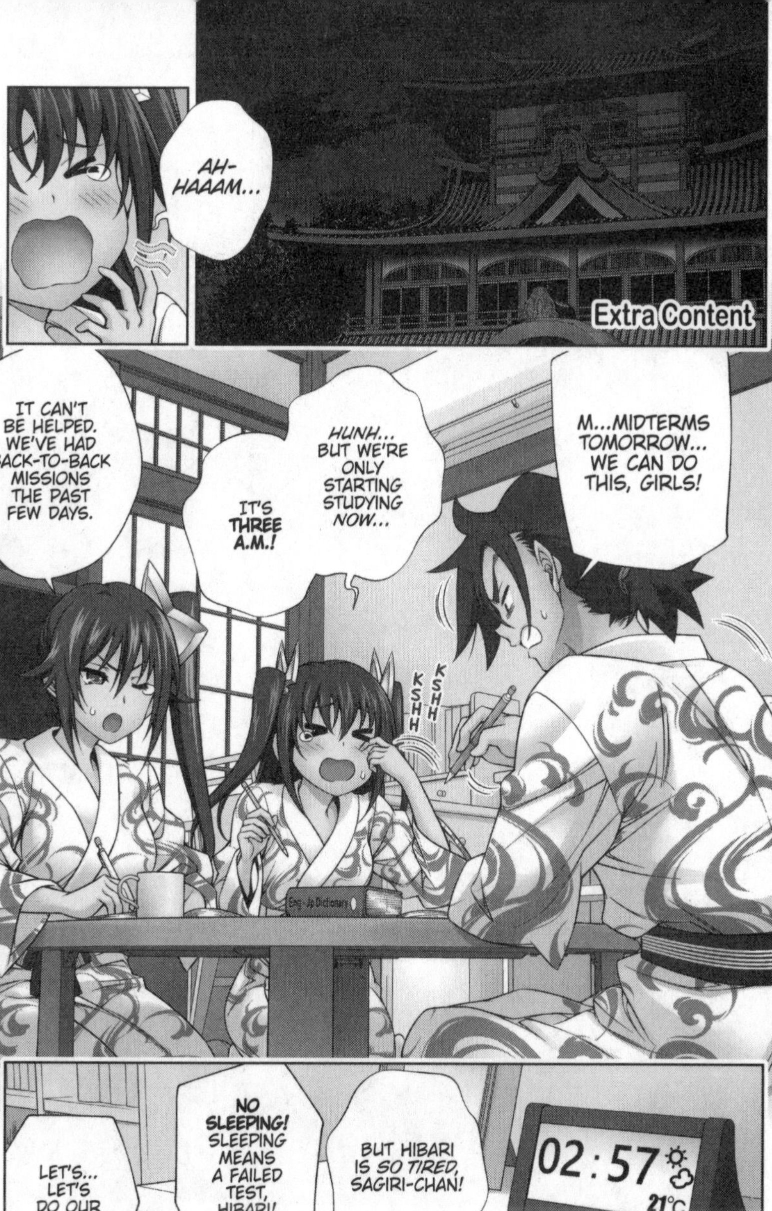
Extra Content
AH-HAAAM...
M...MIDTERMS TOMORROW... WE CAN DO THIS, GIRLS!
HUNH... BUT WE'RE ONLY STARTING STUDYING NOW...
IT'S THREE A.M.!
IT CAN'T BE HELPED. WE'VE HAD BACK-TO-BACK MISSIONS THE PAST FEW DAYS.
KSHH KSHH
Eng.-Jp Dictionary
02:57
21°C
BUT HIBARI IS SO TIRED, SAGIRI-CHAN!
NO SLEEPING! SLEEPING MEANS A FAILED TEST, HIBARI!
LET'S... LET'S DO OUR BEST!

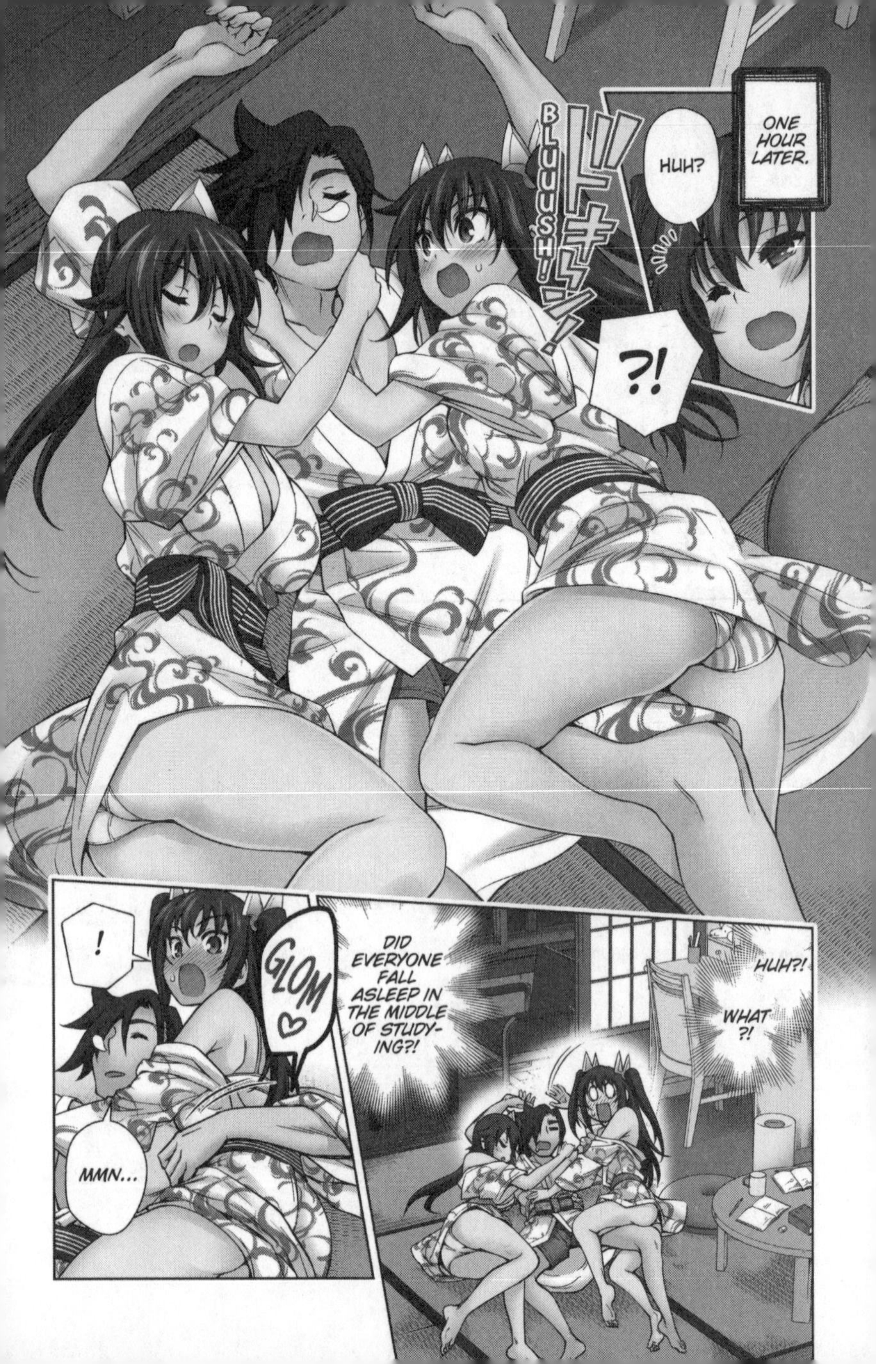
ONE HOUR LATER.
HUH?
BLUUUSH!
?!
HUH?!
WHAT?!
DID EVERYONE FALL ASLEEP IN THE MIDDLE OF STUDY-ING?!
GLOM
!
MMN...

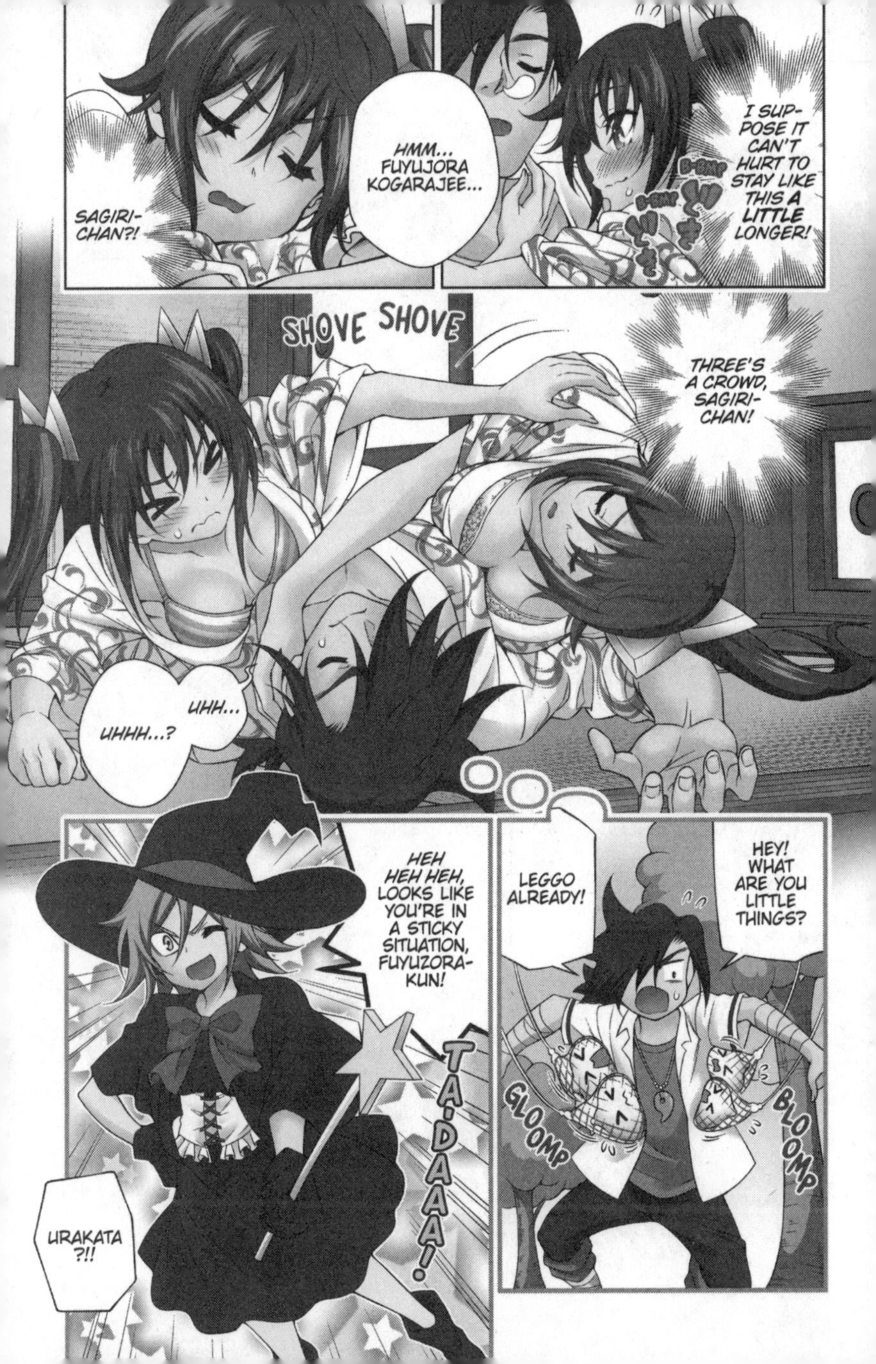
I SUPPOSE IT CAN'T HURT TO STAY LIKE THIS A LITTLE LONGER!
HMM... FUYUJORA KOGARAJEE...
SAGIRI-CHAN?!
THREE'S A CROWD, SAGIRI-CHAN!
SHOVE SHOVE
UHH... UHHH...?
HEY! WHAT ARE YOU LITTLE THINGS?
LEGGO ALREADY!
BLOOMP
GLOOMP
HEH HEH HEH, LOOKS LIKE YOU'RE IN A STICKY SITUATION, FUYUZORA-KUN!
TA-DAAAA!
URAKATA?!!

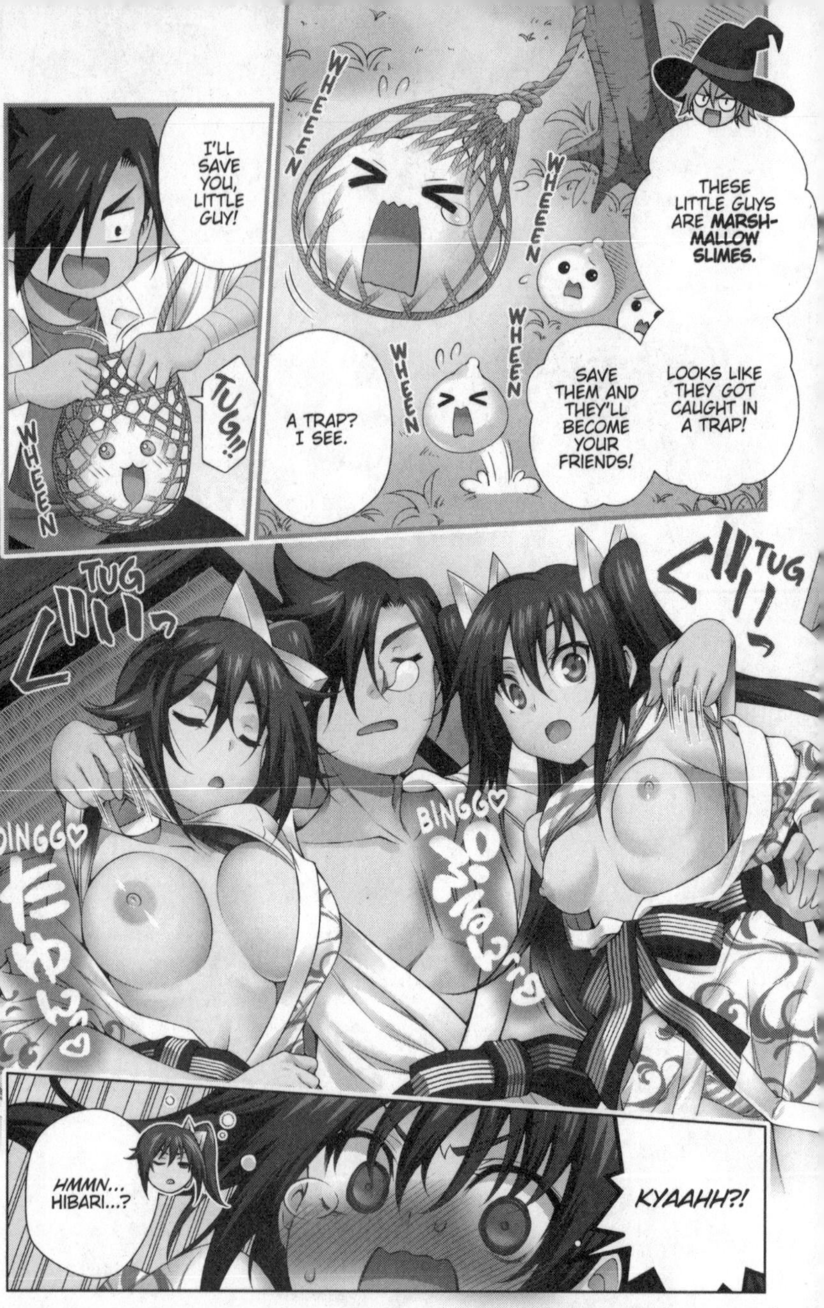
THESE LITTLE GUYS ARE MARSHMALLOW SLIMES.
LOOKS LIKE THEY GOT CAUGHT IN A TRAP!
SAVE THEM AND THEY'LL BECOME YOUR FRIENDS!
WHEEEEN
WHEEEEN
WHEEN
WHEEN
A TRAP? I SEE.
I'LL SAVE YOU, LITTLE GUY!
TUG!!
WHEEEN
TUG
TUG
BINGG♡
BOINGG♡
たゆんっ♡
KYAAHH?!
HMMN... HIBARI...?

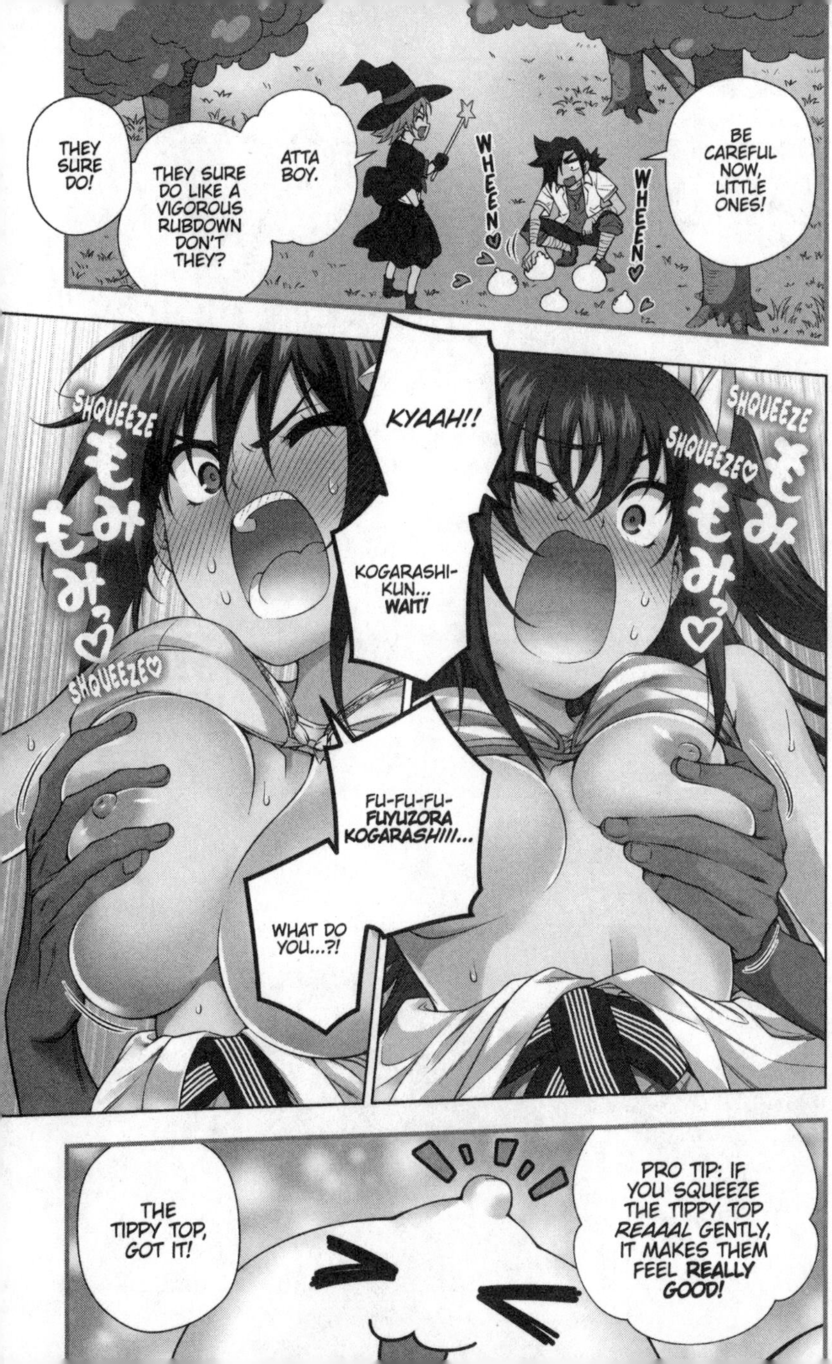
BE CAREFUL NOW, LITTLE ONES!
WHEEN♡
WHEEN♡
ATTA BOY.
THEY SURE DO LIKE A VIGOROUS RUBDOWN DON'T THEY?
THEY SURE DO!
SHQUEEZE SHQUEEZE♡
もみもみっ♡
KYAAH!!
KOGARASHI-KUN... **WAIT!**
SHQUEEZE SHQUEEZE♡
もみもみっ♡
FU-FU-FU-**FUYUZORA KOGARASHI!!!...**
WHAT DO YOU...?!
PRO TIP: IF YOU SQUEEZE THE TIPPY TOP *REAAAL* GENTLY, IT MAKES THEM FEEL **REALLY GOOD!**
THE TIPPY TOP, GOT IT!

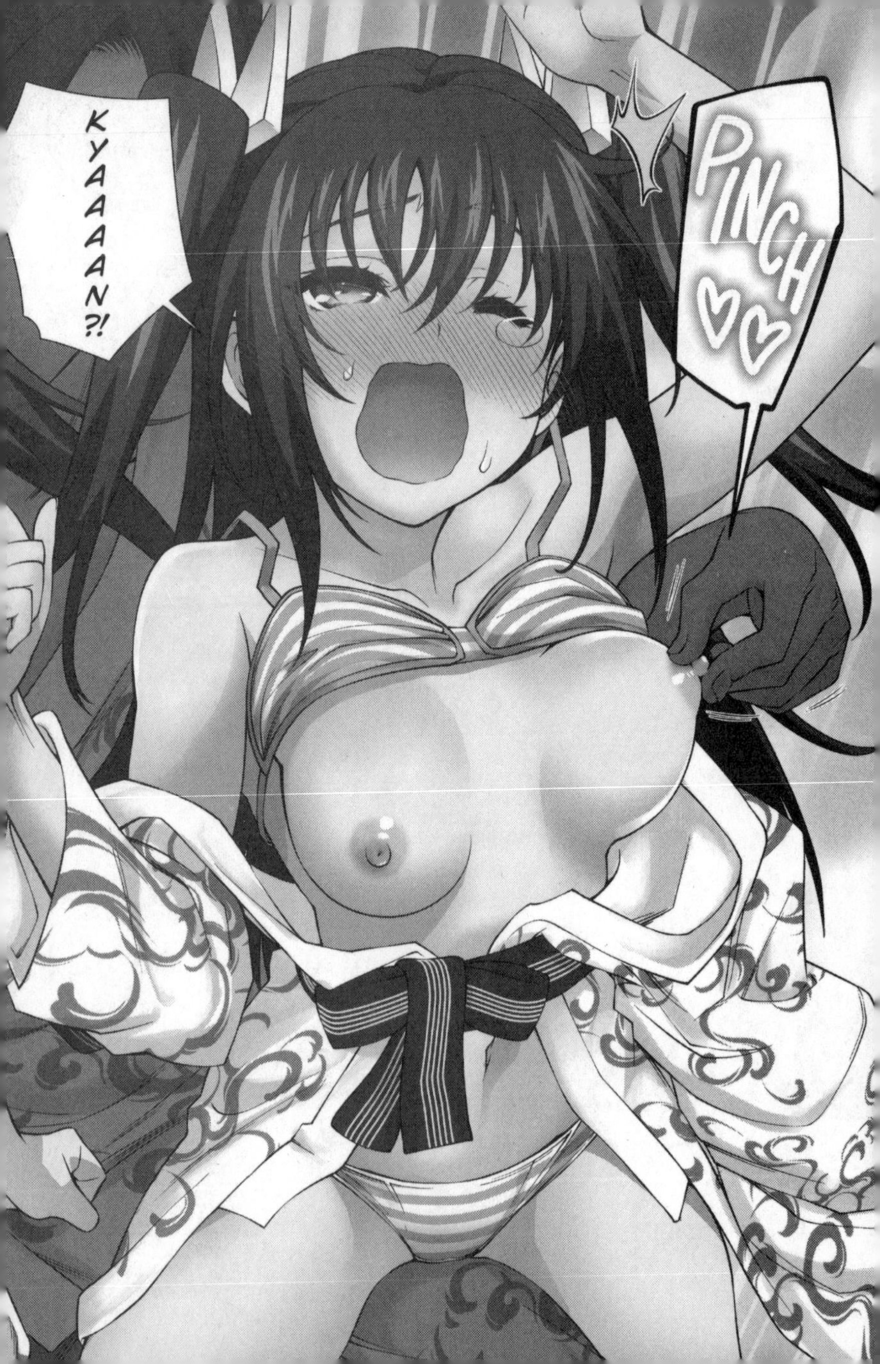
PINCH ♥♥
KYAAAAAN?!

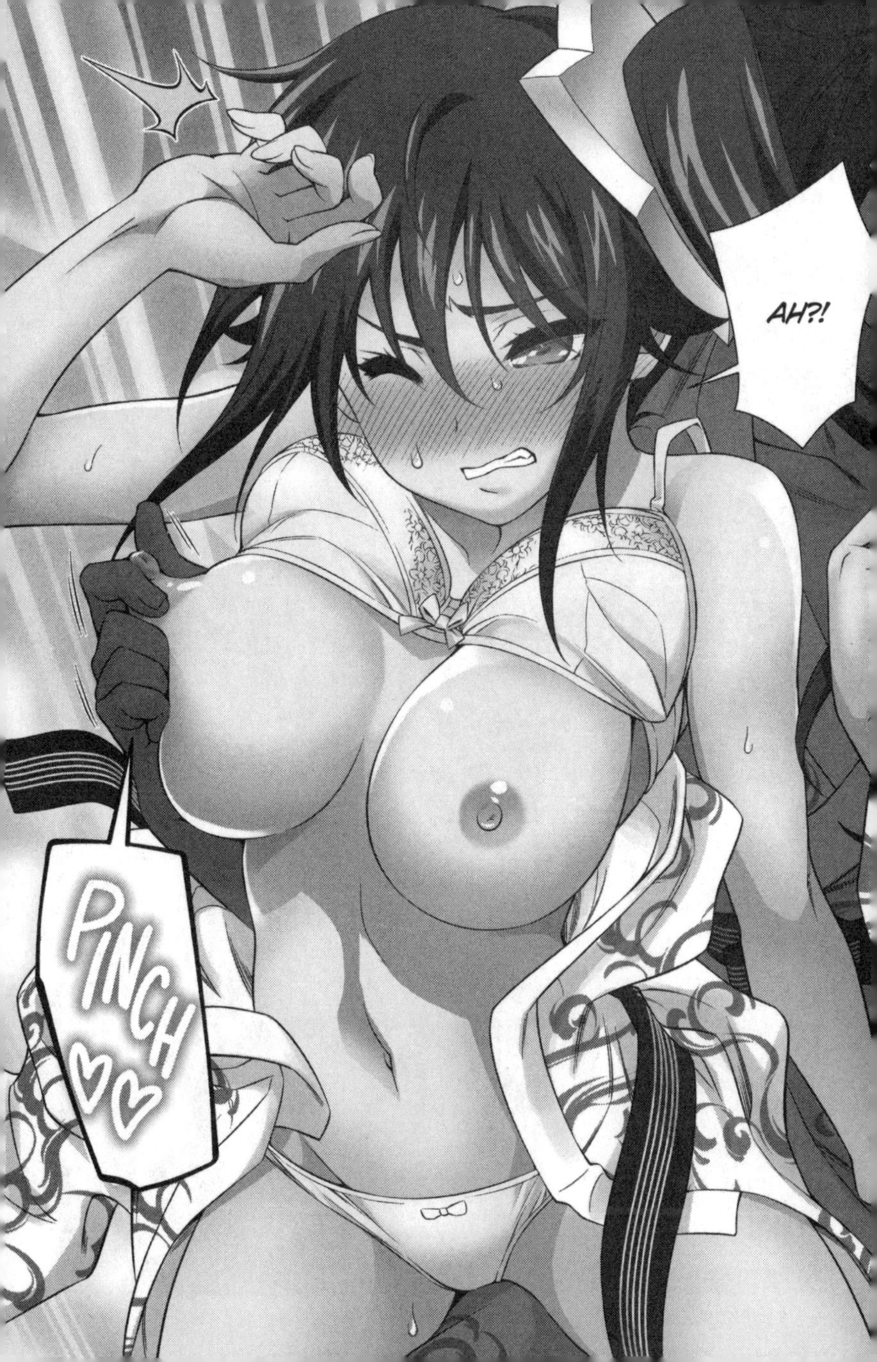
AH?!
PINCH ♥♥

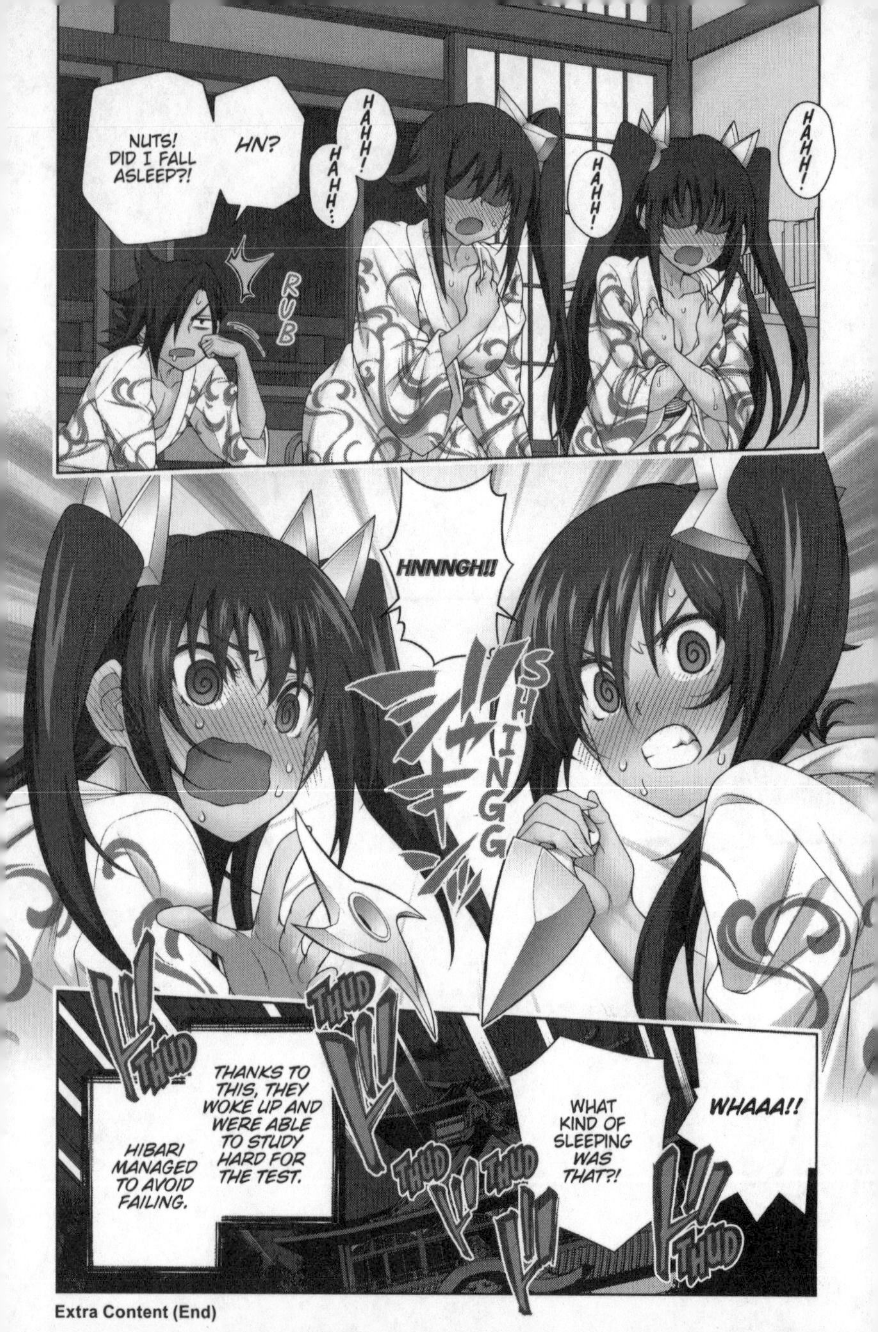
HAHH!
HAHH!
HAHH! HAHH...
HN?
NUTS! DID I FALL ASLEEP?!
RUB
HNNNGH!!
SHINGG
WHAAA!!
WHAT KIND OF SLEEPING WAS THAT?!
THUD
THUD
THUD
THANKS TO THIS, THEY WOKE UP AND WERE ABLE TO STUDY HARD FOR THE TEST.
HIBARI MANAGED TO AVOID FAILING.
THUD
THUD

Extra Content (End)

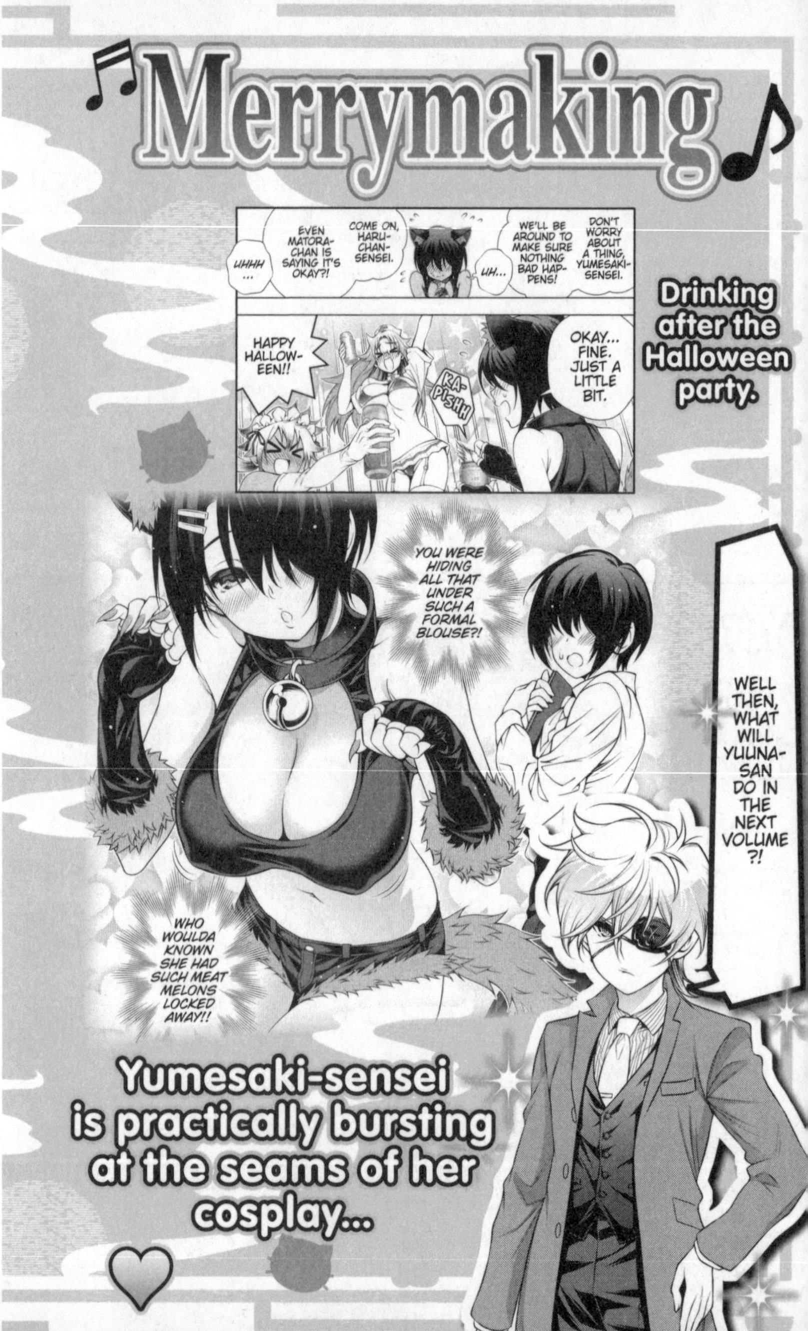
Merrymaking
Drinking after the Halloween party.
DON'T WORRY ABOUT A THING, YUMESAKI-SENSEI.
WE'LL BE AROUND TO MAKE SURE NOTHING BAD HAPPENS!
UH...
COME ON, HARU-CHAN-SENSEI.
EVEN MATORA-CHAN IS SAYING IT'S OKAY?!
UHHH...
OKAY... FINE. JUST A LITTLE BIT.
KA-PISHH
HAPPY HALLOWEEN!!
WELL THEN, WHAT WILL YUUNA-SAN DO IN THE NEXT VOLUME?!
YOU WERE HIDING ALL THAT UNDER SUCH A FORMAL BLOUSE?!
WHO WOULDA KNOWN SHE HAD SUCH MEAT MELONS LOCKED AWAY!!
Yumesaki-sensei is practically bursting at the seams of her cosplay...

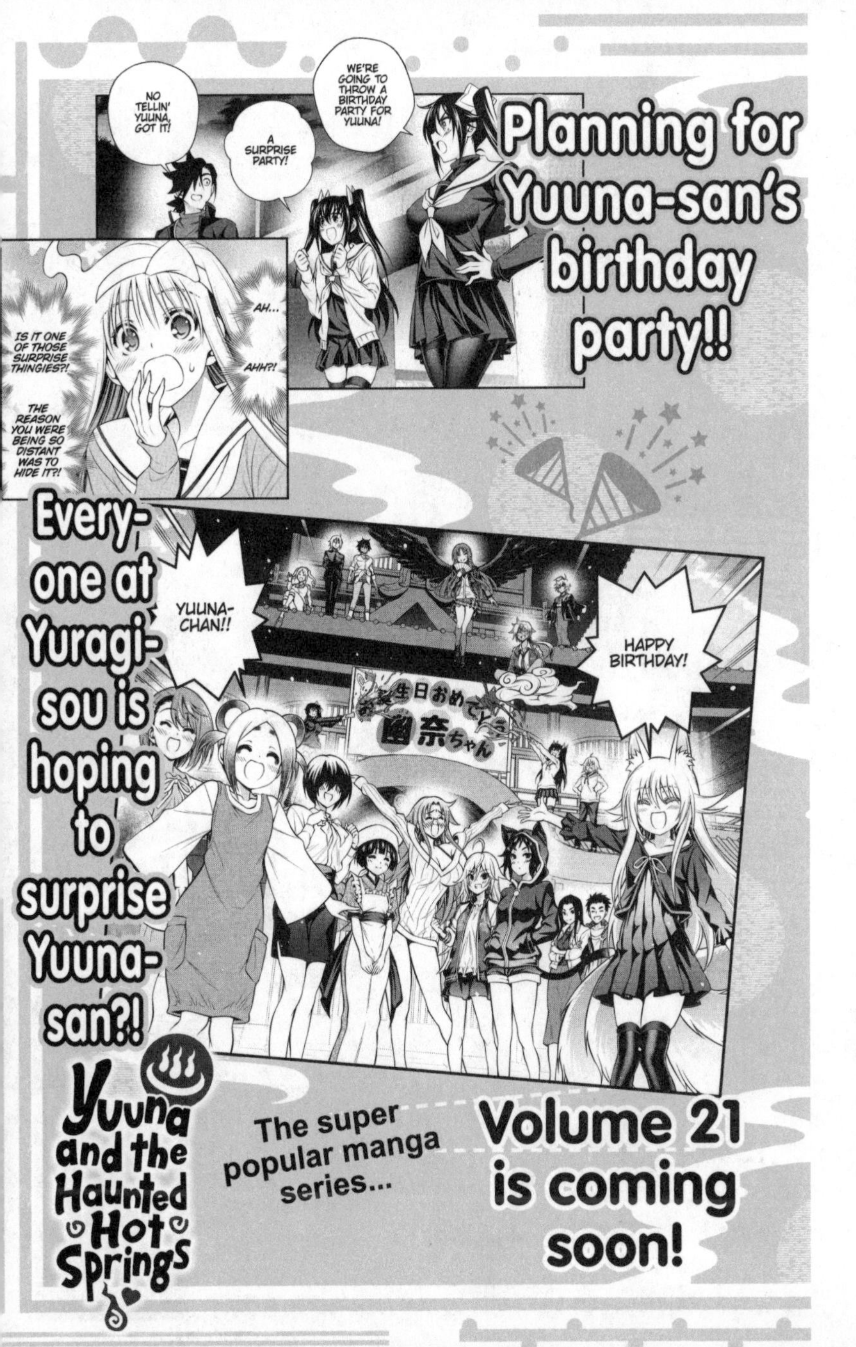
Planning for Yuuna-san's birthday party!!
WE'RE GOING TO THROW A BIRTHDAY PARTY FOR YUUNA!
A SURPRISE PARTY!
NO TELLIN' YUUNA, GOT IT!
AH...
AHH?!
IS IT ONE OF THOSE SURPRISE THINGIES?!
THE REASON YOU WERE BEING SO DISTANT WAS TO HIDE IT?!
Everyone at Yuragi-sou is hoping to surprise Yuuna-san?!
HAPPY BIRTHDAY!
幽奈ちゃん
YUUNA-CHAN!!
Yuuna and the Haunted Hot Springs
The super popular manga series...
Volume 21 is coming soon!

1

Desire Pandora

story & art by
Akira Hizuki

story and art by
MEGURU
UENO

1

Does a
Hot Elf
Live NEXT
DOOR to You

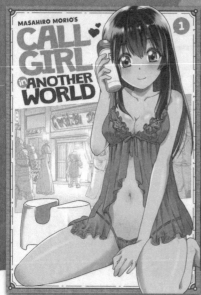

MASAHIRO MORIO'S

1

CALL GIRL in **ANOTHER WORLD**

WARNING
PARENTAL ADVISORY
EXPLICIT CONTENT

Ghost Ship

Find us online at: GhostShipManga.com

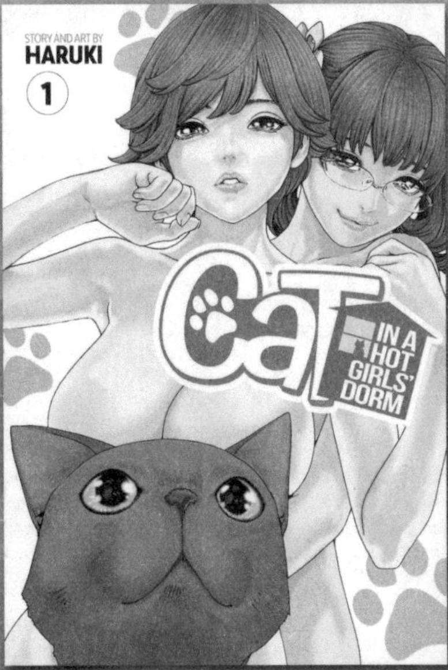
STORY AND ART BY
HARUKI
1
Cat
IN A HOT GIRLS' DORM

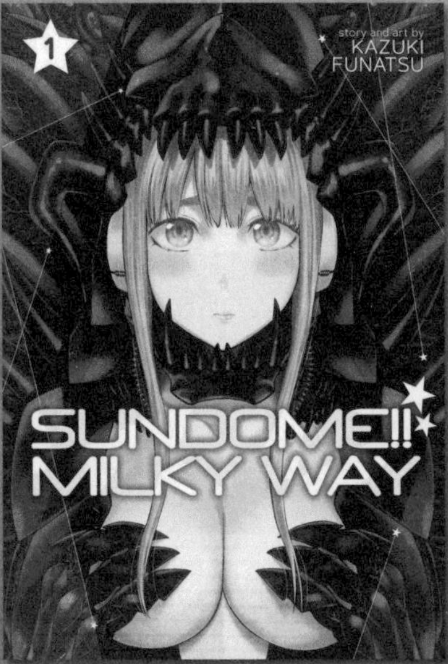
1
story and art by
KAZUKI FUNATSU
SUNDOME!! MILKY WAY

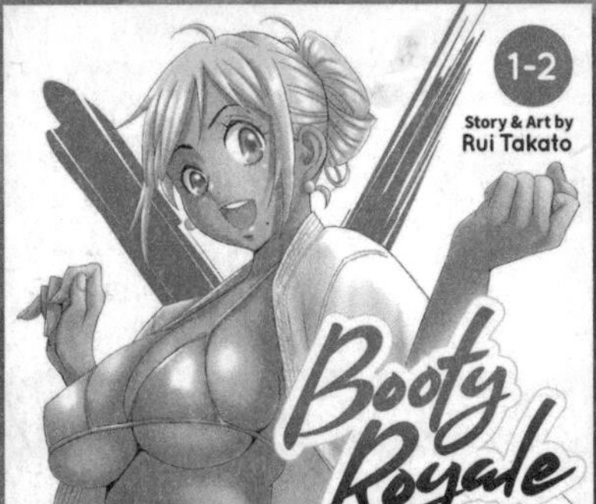
1-2
Story & Art by
Rui Takato
Booty Royale
Never Go Down Without a Fight!

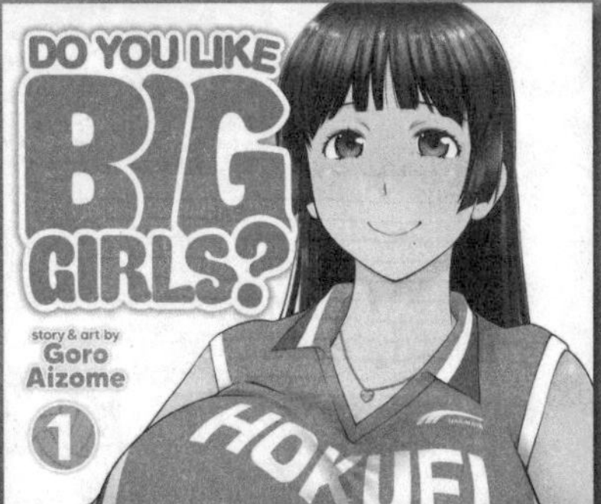
DO YOU LIKE
BIG GIRLS?
story & art by
Goro Aizome
1
HOKUEI

Dedicated to SEXY manga for MATURE readers!

SEVEN SEAS' GHOST SHIP PRESENTS

Yuuna and the Haunted Hot Springs VOL.20

story and art by TADAHIRO MIURA

TRANSLATION
Thomas Zimmerman

ADAPTATION
David Lumsdon

LETTERING AND RETOUCH
Phil Christie

COVER DESIGN
Nicky Lim
(LOGO) **H. Qi**

PROOFREADER
Kurestin Armada

EDITOR
Abby Lehrke

PRINT MANAGER
Rhiannon Rasmussen-Silverstein

PRODUCTION DESIGNER
George Panella

EDITOR-IN-CHIEF
Julie Davis

ASSOCIATE PUBLISHER
Adam Arnold

PUBLISHER
Jason DeAngelis

Seven Seas press and purchase enquiries can be sent to Marketing Manager
Lianne Sentar at press@gomanga.com. Information regarding the distribution
and purchase of digital editions is available from Digital Manager CK Russell
at digital@gomanga.com.

Seven Seas, Ghost Ship, and their accompanying logos are trademarks of
Seven Seas Entertainment. All rights reserved.

ISBN: 978-1-63858-207-6

Printed in Canada

First Printing: July 2022

10 9 8 7 6 5 4 3 2 1

FOLLOW US ONLINE: *www.ghostshipmanga.com*

READING DIRECTIONS

This book reads from *right to left*, Japanese style. If this is your first time reading manga, you start reading from the top right panel on each page and take it from there. If you get lost, just follow the numbered diagram here. It may seem backwards at first, but you'll get the hang of it! Have fun!!

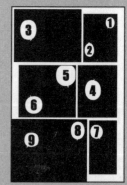